Guantánamo Frames

Rebecca Boguska is a film and media studies scholar whose research focuses on military, infrastructural, and filmic forms of knowledge.

Guantánamo Frames

Rebecca Boguska

 meson press

Bibliographical Information of the German National Library
The German National Library lists this publication in the Deutsche
Nationalbibliografie (German National Bibliography); detailed bibliographic
information is available online at http://dnb.d-nb.de.

Published in 2022 by meson press, Lüneburg, Germany
www.meson.press

Design concept: Torsten Köchlin, Silke Krieg
Cover image: Patrycja Okuljar
Copy editing: Dan J. Ruppel

The print edition of this book is printed by Lightning Source,
Milton Keynes, United Kingdom.

ISBN (Print): 978-3-95796-206-5
ISBN (PDF):   978-3-95796-207-2
DOI: 10.14619/2065

The digital editions of this publication can be downloaded freely at:
www.meson.press

D.30

Contents

And if there is a critical role for visual culture during times of war it is precisely to thematize the forcible frame, the one that conducts the dehumanizing norm, that restricts what is perceivable and, indeed, what can be. Although restriction is necessary for focus, and there is no seeing without selection, this restriction we have been asked to live with imposes constraints on what can be heard, read, seen, felt, and known, and so works to undermine both a sensate understanding of war, and the conditions for a sensate opposition to war.

– Judith Butler, *Frames of War: When Is Life Grievable?*, 100.

Introduction: Reframing Guantánamo Frames

On June 12, 2022, more than 20 years after the first detainees were deported to the Guantánamo detention camp, *The New York Times* published a series of images it had received from the US National Archives as a result of their *Freedom of Information Act* (FOIA) request. Carol Rosenberg writes in the accompanying article that "[f]or 20 years, the US military has tightly controlled what the world could see of the detainees at Guantánamo Bay. No images of prisoners struggling with guards. No hunger strikers being tackled, put into restraints, and force-fed" (Lieberman, Rosenberg, and Taylor 2022). One of the very first images published in this article, shot by Staff Sergeant Jeremy Lock, shows shackled, blindfolded, and duct-taped detainees on an US Air Force cargo plane while they were being transported to Guantánamo in January 2002. The caption tells us that the detainees were "restrained and deprived of their sensory information" (Lieberman, Rosenberg, and Taylor 2022). Another photograph shows David Hicks, an Australian citizen who was captured while fighting for the Taliban, as he descends the airplane ramp wearing the distinctive orange clothing that has become a symbol of Guantánamo. The caption describes the goggles covered by duct tape and earmuffs the detainees were forced to wear during transport, framing the photograph according to the narrative put forth by the US military, which labels these restraints an appropriate "alternative to black hoods" (Lieberman, Rosenberg, and Taylor 2022), while also pointing to the medical mask used to prevent the spread of tuberculosis presumed to be rampant amongst the detainees, and to the tattoo on Hicks' forearm. "Hicks, who pleaded guilty to war crimes ... [,] was repatriated in 2007" (Lieberman, Rosenberg, and Taylor 2022), reads the final part of the caption. Other images show detainees receiving medical attention during the so-called "in-processing procedure"; others show them while praying or being given food.

The publication of these images stands out from the way the US Department of Defense (DoD) and Joint Task Force-Guantánamo (JTF-Guantánamo) have restricted our access to images from Guantánamo up to this point. Rosenberg offers the following comments on this situation:

> *The practice of managing the visual narrative started the very first day detainees arrived at the base, Jan. 11, 2002.* The military forbade two news photographers, from CNN and The Miami Herald, from capturing history as it unfolded: They could watch the first prisoners arrive but had to leave their cameras behind. Instead, about a week later, the Defense Department handed out a picture of the first 20 prisoners on their knees at Camp X-Ray, the makeshift prison camp where captives were kept in the earliest months of the operation. It was taken by a Navy photographer

[Shane T. McCoy] and initially intended for the eyes of only the Pentagon's leaders. (Lieberman, Rosenberg, and Taylor 2022; italics added)

Thus, something appears to be changing in the US government's "practice of managing the visual narrative" (Lieberman, Rosenberg, and Taylor 2022). Maybe, from the perspective of the current government, the 20 years that have elapsed since the camp's opening create enough distance for the public not to be enraged by what has been happening to the men detained at Guantánamo. Maybe the current administration of President Joseph R. Biden Jr. will keep its promise of closing Guantánamo, and in the meantime, has adopted a different policy on censoring photographs showing the real circumstances at the camp. Or maybe, this is just a "freak" image event that will be perceived as a minor mistake in the US government's long history of managing the Guantánamo detention camp's visual culture.

What is about to come remains yet to be seen.

This book, however, is about what preceded this image event. It is precisely about how the US government has managed – and controlled – the visual narrative of the Guantánamo detention camp over the past 20 years. On January 11, 2022, only 5 months prior to the publication of the new set of images, the international press marked the 20th anniversary of the detention camp's opening by reminding us of Shane T. McCoy's iconic images [fig. 1 and 3], one of which Rosenberg also reproduced in her article for *The New York Times* from June 2022. These images are still present today, even if the people and the circumstances we now perceive in them are supposedly absent, or will become absent in the moment when the last detainees are released from, convicted at, or die in Guantánamo. The visual and institutional framing of these images, however, along with the history of the camp, show that counteracting the ongoing violent detention practices instituted by the US government after 9/11 is just as important now as it was in 2002, when the first detainees were brought to Guantánamo. This book is a manifestation of the urgency with which I believe the Guantánamo detention camp and its images should continue to be discussed by scholars and the public. By reconsidering photographs, videos, and documents from the camp, and the way they were institutionally framed, this book sheds light on a future that is still uncertain. Nothing is settled yet – including our understanding of what Guantánamo is, and how we have come to perceive it. Even after Guantánamo is shut down, it will no doubt remain an open and unsettled case for scholarship – a case which we must continue to debate, and which must be reframed over and over again.

Writing about what media objects – such as photographs, videos, and documents – allow us to perceive of the Guantánamo detention camp must begin with two fundamental premises. Firstly, we must recognize that the answer to the question of what Guantánamo is, and how the public has come to perceive it, is far less self-evident than these objects make it appear. Secondly, we have to acknowledge that what the public has been permitted to see so far of this facility is not only highly restricted, but also that these restrictions were and continue to be intentionally designed. Crucially, the DoD is deeply involved in "industrial sense making and trade theorizing" (Caldwell 2008, 346) and systematically engages with questions concerning what (audio)visual productions are, and how they are supposed to operate and be perceived by the broader public. Building on these foundations, this book investigates how photographs, virtual tours to the camp posted as online videos, and other media objects related to the camp, produced and distributed by the DoD and the JTF-Guantánamo, have never simply been a given. Despite their "documentary" appearance, these objects do not merely depict circumstances at the camp as they are, simply showing us what can be seen at and known about the facility. Quite the opposite, in fact: throughout the four chapters of this book, I demonstrate how these media objects are the result of intense planning, production, distribution, and framing efforts undertaken by the US government. Thus, a critical engagement with the question of how the US government tries to control our perception of Guantánamo requires an in-depth analysis of the various institutional framing devices it has deployed to circumscribe what we can perceive – and ultimately know – about the camp and the situation of the detainees.[1]

Following Judith Butler's observation about our understanding of war, as cited in my epigraph, these "Guantánamo frames" – be they visual, technological, or institutional frames related to the detention camp – have consistently imposed "constraints on what can be heard, read, seen, felt, and known" (Butler 2009, 100) about the detention camp. Although these constraints may at first be imperceptible, they can be rendered visible, and then subverted, by undertaking an analysis of the Guantánamo frames, and particularly, by exploring how these frames often fail in their "ideological projects" (Kellner 1995, 5). By creating the awareness that seeing in an opaque and fragmented way is the "visual norm" (Butler 2009, 100) for Guantánamo, this book reflects on the question of what, exactly, we see if we acknowledge and analyze the nonvisible operations of power effected by these frames. Guantánamo frames are by no means neutral and never solely restrict the visual field; instead, "forms of social and state power are 'embedded' in [them] ... , including state and military regulatory regimes" (Butler 2009, 72). These frames define the

---

1   In this book, I am referring to the men detained at Guantánamo in the course of the US "Global War on Terror" as "detainees" or "detained men" in order to emphasize the legal status assigned to them by the US government, which I will discuss in detail in the next subsection. While I am aware that, to a certain degree, this terminology reproduces the rhetoric of the state, this term has also been employed by the detained men themselves, as well as by their lawyers.

realm of representation and condition "the domain of representability itself" (Butler 2009, 74), without necessarily becoming visible themselves. The Guantánamo frames are thus a form of power that has no figurative form, or, in Butler words, is "non-figurable" (Butler 2009, 74), and cannot be translated into the visual (or written) domain. Hence, Butler is right to argue that "what is shown when it [the non-figurable power] comes into view is the staging apparatus itself, the maps that exclude certain regions, the directives of the army, the positioning of the cameras, the punishments that lie in wait if reporting protocols are breached" (Butler 2009, 74). The frames of Guantánamo are thus mostly invisible, even as they shape and structure what we can apprehend via photographs, online videos, or military documents. Rendering them visible requires us to turn our attention to the violent staging apparatus of the US military, which mediates how these objects appear and what they show.

Most scholars engaging with the legal, administrative, and visual dimensions of Guantánamo are invested in creating a macro-image of the camp and its histories (Greenberg 2009; Khalili 2013; Pugliese 2013). In this book, however, I am adopting a different approach, and look at what I call minor media objects. Beginning with an analysis of these marginal or smaller objects, each of my chapters seeks to trace broader tendencies in the ways the DoD deploys visibility and non-visibility in relation to the camp, thus extending the violence inflicted upon the detainees into the visual domain. The initial impulse for each chapter was an encounter with a particular media object whose status appeared ambiguous to me, insofar as I could perceive its visible surface and content, but could not fully see or comprehend the conditions of its production, its ideological premises, the reasons for its distribution, or the effects it might have on the viewer. Some of these media objects have already been prominently discussed by cultural, communication, and media studies scholars, while others figure as more marginal objects, and have so far received little to no attention in those fields. Confronting their ambiguity requires an elaboration of how their incomprehensibility results from the "forcible frame[s]" (Butler 2009, 100) that circumscribe Guantánamo's representation. By taking an in-depth look at the various frames associated with such minor media objects, this book seeks to determine how these frames regulate our perception of the circumstances in the camp, and how the media objects themselves are part of broader violent operations conducted by the DoD and the JTF-Guantánamo.

Despite being a powerful tool to limit what we can perceive, the Guantánamo frames are flawed in themselves. The small ruptures in these frames have come to figure as points of departure for interventions initiated in various fields – for example, by human rights lawyers, artists, journalists, and the detainees themselves – which reveal that the efforts made by the DoD and

JTF-Guantánamo to normatively regulate what we can perceive from the detention camp are often "shadowed by ... [their] own failure" (Butler 2009, 7). Hence, this book follows the ways in which institutional attempts to regulate the production, distribution, and perception of these objects have often failed, insofar as the US government could not control the way they were perceived and comprehended. By thinking about these objects and their operations in terms of such institutional failures, I emphasize the fact that "[f]ailure, by definition, takes us beyond assumptions and what we think we know" (Le Feuvre 2010, 12). By acknowledging the US government's repeated failure to control the ways in which Guantánamo's media objects are perceived, we can also move beyond the idea that there is a "*self-evidence*" (Berlant 2007, 669) to what Guantánamo is.

In this book, I reflect on media objects "against [their] ... ideological grain, to ferret out critical and subversive moments, and to analyze how the[ir] ideological projects ... often fail" (Kellner 1995, 5). More specifically, in each of the chapters, I describe how lawyers, artists, journalists, and detainees have intervened in the discourses around these media objects, their frames, operations, and effects, and show how the institutional framings of these objects were either porous from the start, or were made to fail by the subsequent interventions. I propose to understand these counter-discourses as *reframing* practices which demonstrate that the DoD's frames have neither been stable nor successful in their ideological agendas. Despite the fact that the DoD has continuously sought to regulate and control what we can see and perceive of the Guantánamo detention camp, the media objects they themselves have released into circulation are "ambiguous ... and [their] effects ... can be appropriated in various ways" (Kellner 1995, 6).

Legal and Geographic Frames

The US government's decision to build this detention camp at its naval base on the island of Cuba was grounded in the idea that the men who would be detained there would not have "access to legal representation and American courts" (Goldman 2014, 160). Moreover, because the US has no diplomatic agreements in place with Cuba, which considers the US Naval Base at Guantánamo Bay to be an illegitimate occupation of its territory, the detainees would also be denied access to the Cuban legal system (Kaplan 2005, 836). Immediately after the 9/11 attacks, the George W. Bush's administration began to develop legal strategies that were intended to enable the US government to exercise absolute control over the treatment of men suspected of terrorist activities, outside of the US legal and penal system. As the administration itself acknowledged, one of its biggest legal challenges at that time was finding strategies to avoid the constraints imposed upon it by national and international laws.

The US government, for instance, publicly negotiated ways to evade the limitations imposed by *Geneva Convention III*, and specifically, the limitations imposed by *Article 4*, which describes the treatment of "Prisoners of War" (POW):

> Prisoners of war must at all times be *humanely treated*. Any unlawful act or omission by the Detaining Power causing *death or seriously endangering the health of a prisoner of war in its custody is prohibited*, and will be regarded as a serious breach of the present Convention. In particular, no prisoner of war may be subjected to physical mutilation or to medical or scientific experiments of any kind which are not justified by the medical, dental or hospital treatment of the prisoner concerned and carried out in his interest. Likewise, prisoners of war *must at all times be protected, particularly against acts of violence or intimidation and against insults and public curiosity*. Measures of reprisal against prisoners of war are prohibited. (*Geneva Convention III* (August 12, 1949), 87; italics added)

As a result of the legal opinions issued by the US Department of Justice, Office of Legal Counsel with regard to the limitations imposed on countries subject to *Geneva Convention III*, the US government officially denied any of the men detained at Guantánamo the status of POW leaving them largely unprotected by the international law put in place after World War II. Instead, the DoD referred to most of the people captured in the course of the US "Global War on Terror" (GWoT) as "unlawful combatants,"[2] or "detainees." Although the Bush administration repeatedly stated that the detainees were to be treated "'to the extent appropriate' in a manner consistent with the Geneva Conventions of 1949" (Rumsfeld as cited in Greenberg and Dratel 2005, xxv), it was clear from the start, even before the camp officially opened, that the US government would not treat these men in accordance with international law. Instead, they were subjected to torture techniques including the use of "stress positions," the "[u]se of the isolation facility for up to 30 days," and "deprivation of light and auditory stimuli" (Phifer 2002, 1f.)[3] – treatment that led to the death of several detainees at the Guantánamo detention camp, at other military prisons abroad, and at Central Intelligence Agency (CIA) interrogation sites all over the world (Hickman 2015).

Since the end of 2001, the DoD's discourse has reinforced its claims that law, and the legal debates about the treatment of the detainees at Guantánamo,

---

2   The legal understanding of the term "unlawful combatant" in the US judiciary system goes back to 1942 and the case, *Ex Parte Quirin* (Davis 2008). In this ruling, the Supreme Court upheld the decision of the Military Courts which convicted eight German saboteurs, with the result that six of them faced execution (Davis 2008, 124). The men were charged with the "offense against the law of war" (*Ex Parte Quirin* 1942, 317 US 1), making them eligible to be tried by a military tribunal instead of a civilian court with a jury.

3   Some of the listed techniques were later approved by Donald Rumsfeld, at the time US Secretary of Defense (Haynes II 2002, 1).

were intended to limit violence on a global scale and prevent further terrorist attacks. The legal history of the Guantánamo detention camp thus supports Christoph Menke's critique of the assumption that, in places bound by law, there is no violence and, conversely, that in places where violence is enacted, there is no law (Menke 2020, 292). In Guantánamo, violence has continuously been given a legal and bureaucratic form, codified in government documents, and enacted in Standard Operating Procedures (SOPs) – testifying to the intimate entanglement of law and violence in the camp. The US government's negotiations concerning the extent and "legality" of the violence inflicted upon detainees at Guantánamo thus went hand-in-hand with negotiations about the universality of human rights. In their book, *Philosophie der Menschenrechte zur Einführung* (Eng. *Introduction into the Philosophy of Human Rights*), Menke and Arnd Pollmann argue that, following the attacks of 9/11, "religiously motivated terrorism turned out to be a specific *human rights* problem" (Menke and Pollmann 2007, 53; my translation). The question posed by the authors – whether "*in the name of* human rights, the state is allowed to *violate* human rights?" (Menke and Pollmann 2007, 53; my translation) – encapsulates the wider discursive efforts undertaken by the US government to circumvent those sections of *Geneva Convention III* regulating the treatment of POWs.

With regard to the issues of terrorism and torture in the 21st century, Menke and Pollmann identify three discursive strategies which governments employ to exempt themselves from their obligation to protect human rights. Firstly, they can assign different priorities to different types of human rights. Secondly, they can redefine certain terms, reframing them with such an exemption in mind – for instance, by using euphemistic vocabulary like "enhanced interrogation techniques" to describe torture practices. Thirdly, they can argue that if people fail to follow their basic constitutional obligations, they will no longer be protected by human rights law (Menke and Pollmann 2007, 54). In order to enable the violent treatment of the detainees at the Guantánamo detention camp, a treatment which was fueled by the fantasy of torture as an efficient means of information acquisition, the US government publicly deployed all three strategies described by Menke and Pollmann.

This rhetoric of exemption and the hunt for loopholes to evade the "human rights problem" (Menke and Pollmann 2007, 53; my translation) – by, for instance, determining the status of the men detained at Guantánamo as "unlawful combatants" – was openly discussed by then Vice President, Richard B. "Dick" Cheney, in an interview on *Fox News Sunday* on January 27, 2002, after the first detainees had already arrived at Guantánamo:

> We're all in agreement – Colin [Powell], me, Don Rumsfeld – that these are not lawful combatants, they're not prisoners of law [*sic*]. There is a legal issue involved as to whether they should be treated within the confines

of the Geneva Convention, which does have a section that deals with
unlawful combatants, or whether they should be dealt with outside the
Geneva Convention. (Cheney 2002)

The denial of the legal status of POW to Taliban and al Qaeda detainees within
the context of the US GWoT was subsequently confirmed by Bush in a legal
memorandum published on February 7, 2002 (Bush 2002a). Disguised as a
memo about "Humane Treatment of Taliban and al Qaeda Detainees," the
text functioned as an official announcement of the planned violation of what
Geneva Convention III defines as humane treatment of POWs (Bush 2002a).
The memo was based on a legal opinion formulated by Attorney General
John Ashcroft in his letter to Bush dated February 1, 2002, where he stated
that "Afghanistan was a failed state," and hence not qualified to be "party to
the treaty" of *Geneva Convention III*, and that the Taliban were "not entitled to
Geneva III prisoner of war status," since they "acted as unlawful combatants"
(Ashcroft 2002, 1). On February 7, 2002, Bush declared the following: "I determine that the Taliban detainees are unlawful combatants and, therefore, do
not qualify as prisoners of war under Article 4 of Geneva. I note that, because
Geneva does not apply to our conflict with al Qaeda, al Qaeda detainees also
do not qualify as prisoners of war" (Bush 2002a, 2).[4]

Analyzing a wide range of texts dealing with the issue of torture after
the attacks of 9/11 reveals that military personnel have not been alone in
deploying "enhanced interrogation techniques." A statement made by Bush on
national television on September 6, 2006, as well as the US Senate's *The Official
Senate Report on CIA Torture: Committee Study of the Central Intelligence Agency's
Detention and Interrogation Program*, make it clear that the CIA established a
large network of so-called "black sites" in which their agents interrogated and
tortured POWs and detainees (Denbeaux and Hafetz 2009, 409; US Senate
2015).

The affront to human dignity and the torture of POWs and detainees at
Guantánamo, in Afghanistan and Iraq, and at black sites all around the world
make it necessary to broaden the frame of what we mean when we speak of
"Guantánamo." Guantánamo is not just a place; it is a discursive formation
that represents the violent detention, interrogation, and torture practices
introduced by the US as a response to the attacks of 9/11 in detention facilities
and military prisons including in Afghanistan, Iraq, and Cuba. As a discursive

---

4   Bush's memo, and the earlier determinations upon which it was based, became part of
     what are now colloquially referred to as the "torture memos" or "torture papers" (Green-
     berg and Dratel 2005). During the first four months after the 9/11 attacks, and in the
     years to follow, employees of the Bush administration also signed and published other
     torture memoranda. Karen J. Greenberg and Joshua L. Dratel have collected and repub-
     lished 28 of these memos, which were revoked by Barack Obama in 2009 (Greenberg and
     Dratel 2005; Obama 2009).

formation, Guantánamo consists of human agents – military or civilian personnel, security agents, contractors, and detainees – and their manifold interactions, as well as various flows of knowledge. Thus, the answer to the question of *where* Guantánamo is extends significantly beyond the geographic location of the Guantánamo Bay Naval Base.

According to *The Report of The Constitution Project's Task Force on Detainee Treatment*,[5] Guantánamo "was a major testing ground for the government's policy of engaging in highly coercive interrogation techniques, practices designed to visit torment on detainees in the expectation or hope they would give up important and usable intelligence to help fight the new style of war in which the United States found itself" (Constitution Project's Task Force on the Detainee Treatment 2013, 25). The techniques "tested" at the Guantánamo detention camp were later deployed in prisons in Afghanistan and Iraq, as well as at CIA black sites. According to the documents collected in the American Civil Liberties Union's (ACLU's) *Torture Database* (ACLU 2022a), these were the epicenters of abuse and torture after 9/11. In these locations, the military expertise accrued concerning brutal interrogation and torture practices was not bound to single individuals or a particular place, but was instead implemented and transmitted on an institutional level.

The relationship between the Guantánamo detention camp, the Abu Ghraib prison, other Iraqi military prisons, and CIA black sites is the most obvious example of this institutional transmission – not only because, at the beginning of 2002, the CIA established two of its black sites at the Naval Base at Guantánamo Bay (US Senate 2015, 140). In addition, 14 men initially held in CIA detention at various locations around the world were later transported to Guantánamo. Another point of connection between these various facilities, prisons, and black sites is the sequence of deployments of higher-ranking military officials. For instance, in 2002, Geoffrey D. Miller took command of the JTF-Guantánamo; in 2004, he became Commander of the Abu Ghraib prison, Camp Bucca, and Camp Cropper. His role in these Iraqi prisons and detention facilities was to implement the "lessons learned" from the Guantánamo detention camp, and to introduce the same "enhanced interrogation techniques" used at Guantánamo in these Iraqi prisons. Human Rights Watch reports that, during an intelligence briefing in the summer of 2003, Secretary of Defense Donald Rumsfeld "[e]xpress[ed] anger and frustration over the application of Geneva Convention rules in Iraq ... [and] *gave an oral order to dispatch MG* [Major General] *Miller to Iraq to 'Gitmoize' the intelligence gathering operations there*" (Human Rights Watch 2022). Soon afterwards, Miller

---

5   This report was written by "an independent, bipartisan, blue-ribbon panel charged with examining the federal government's policies and actions related to the capture, detention, and treatment of suspected terrorists during the Clinton, Bush, and Obama administrations" (Open Society Foundations 2022).

visited Abu Ghraib and other Iraqi prisons to provide intelligence on how to interrogate detainees in a similar manner to the techniques employed at Guantánamo (Trial International 2020). Thus, Guantánamo must be considered a "testing ground," and one of the institutions central to shaping what would take place in Afghanistan, Iraq, CIA black sites, and secret prisons from 2002 on.

The Report of The Constitution Project's Task Force on Detainee Treatment states that "[a]buses in Iraq were not restricted to Abu Ghraib. But attempts to prosecute abuses in other Iraqi prisons were even less successful, due to a lack of resources for investigators and widespread confusion about the rules for prisoner treatment" (Constitution Project's Task Force on the Detainee Treatment 2013, 85f.). Despite the fact that, "unlike Taliban and Al Qaeda suspects in Guantánamo and Afghanistan, detainees in Iraq were protected by the Geneva Conventions" (Constitution Project's Task Force on the Detainee Treatment 2013, 104), accounts by two men, Charles Graner and Ivan Frederick, convicted of crimes during the investigations into the abuse and torture of Abu Ghraib prisoners, reveal that experts trained in interrogation at the Guantánamo detention camp taught them the array of torture techniques they employed at Abu Ghraib (Constitution Project's Task Force on the Detainee Treatment 2013, 108).

The connection between Afghanistan and Guantánamo is substantiated by the fact that many of the captured men were held in Afghanistan before being "shipped" like cargo to the detention facility on Cuba. *The Report of The Constitution Project's Task Force on Detainee Treatment* makes this clear when it calls Afghanistan "[t]he Gateway to Guantánamo" (Constitution Project's Task Force on the Detainee Treatment 2013, 33), revealing that it was "the initial and largest source of the detainees who were sent to the detention center in Cuba" (Constitution Project's Task Force on the Detainee Treatment 2013, 26). The highly networked nature of the different detention facilities in Afghanistan, as well as their ties to the prisons in Iraq, is described in the report as follows:

> The official detention program has been run by the US military during and following the invasion of Afghanistan in the fall of 2001. Estimates on the number of detainees in that program at any one time over the last decade have varied, up to several thousand. The second detention program has involved a secret network of jails, the existence of which was long unacknowledged by US officials, and is believed to have been used to detain only a small fraction of those in the military's detention program. In both programs detainees have been mistreated and some have died.[6] In some

---

6   In 2002, two detainees tortured at the Bagram Airfield in Afghanistan were murdered; in 2003, the unit which interrogated them was moved to Iraq, and conducted further interrogations at the Abu Ghraib prison (Constitution Project's Task Force on the Detainee Treatment 2013, 57).

instances abusive, illegal interrogation tactics utilized in Afghanistan later found their way to Iraq. (Constitution Project's Task Force on the Detainee Treatment 2013, 57)

Alongside the prison facilities that have become public knowledge, there was – and probably still is – a network of detention facilities which has been kept secret, and used to detain a smaller number of people.

Thus, if we want to investigate how what we see and perceive of the Guantánamo detention camp is conditioned and regulated by technological, visual, institutional, and juridical frames, and how one can rupture or break these frames, or cause them and their operations of power to fail, we must acknowledge the networked nature of US detention practices post-9/11, and of the torture committed at Guantánamo, in military prisons in Afghanistan and Iraq, and at CIA black sites. Some of the frames that shape our perception of Guantánamo may not appear to be directly related to the geographic location on the island of Cuba, but they still shape and structure what and whom we can perceive when we turn our attention to the Guantánamo detention camp.

Juridical and Bureaucratic Frames

The legal grounds established by the DoD before January 2002, which were continuously "improved" during the following years, aimed to legiti-mize the use of torture techniques, and resulted in the men detained in the Guantánamo camp being refused fair hearings before juries in US domestic courts. However, Guantánamo was not lawless; instead, the establishment and operation of the detention facility were based on the intertwining of "a space of legal dispute" (Khalili 2013, 74) with a space of military bureaucracy. The popular conception of Guantánamo as being completely without law during its first three and half years of operation, and in the years thereafter, is flawed insofar as the detention facility actually became bound by an "alternate regime of legality" (Khalili 2013, 74). As Safiyah Rochelle incisively notes in her PhD thesis, *Capturing the Void(ed): Muslim Detainees, Practices of Violence, and the Politics of Seeing in Guantánamo Bay*, "[b]oth the choice of Guantánamo and the methods of detention used in this space were, and continue to be, deeply embedded in and coextensive with law, lawfare, and with colonial and imperial projects of past and present" (Rochelle 2020, 29). The negotiations of the legal grounds for establishing Guantánamo and employing the torture techniques described in the previous subsection do not necessarily justify the image of the detention facility as a "legal black hole" (Steyn 2004). The repeated references made by journalists, lawyers, and scholars to Guantánamo being a lawless place may not even be a suitable summary of the legal situation of the detainees during the most precarious period at the camp – the time between its opening in January 2002 and the Supreme Court's rulings on the first

successful *habeas corpus* cases in 2004: *Rasul v. Bush* and *Hamdi v. Rumsfeld*
(*Rasul v. Bush* (2004), 542 US 466; *Hamdi v. Rumsfeld* (2004), 542 US 507).[7]

Even though public discourse repeatedly emphasized the inapplicability of
established legal norms in the camp, the statements and papers written by
lawyers who defended and continue to defend detainees at Guantánamo refer
often to law and semi-legal procedures that uphold the *status quo* in the extra-
territorial detention facility (Denbeaux and Hafetz 2009). In her book, *Time in
the Shadow: Confinement in Counterinsurgencies*, Laleh Khalili rightly points out
that

> [t]he whole complex, and the worldwide network of lawyers, legal
> scholars, advocates, military judges and prosecutors, human rights
> activists, and news reporters, attests to something else again: *a space
> of legal dispute. Not of lawlessness, as it is claimed again and again, but of
> excess of law, rules, procedures, legal performances made by the govern-
> ment to legitimate control*, and contested by those who seek to subject the
> detainees there to an alternate regime of legality. (Khalili 2013, 74; italics
> added)

The fact that Guantánamo's "very creation and reproduction has been steeped
in legal argument and definition" (Khalili 2013, 66) makes it necessary to question our tacit ideas about its lawlessness. Instead, we have to acknowledge
that due to the suspension of established legal procedures in the camp, it was
bound by new forms of law, and that some of the usually applicable laws were,
to a certain extent, replaced by "administrative procedures" (Khalili 2013, 67).
Hence, although Guantánamo falls outside of established legal norms, and is a
space where established legal procedures are suspended or replaced by new
bureaucratic, semi-legal procedures that form part of a different "regime of
legality" (Khalili 2013, 74), it is far from being entirely outside of the law.

Another, broader perspective on this relationship between the legal and
bureaucratic dimensions in the camp can be observed within the larger frame
of how, after 9/11, the US government continuously negotiated the relationship
between sovereignty and governmentality. However, such negotiation does
not imply that these two forms of exercising power are mutually exclusive,
or that one replaces the other. As Michel Foucault outlines in *Security,*

---

7   As Mark Denbeaux and Jonathan Hafetz write, "*Rasul* holds that federal courts have
     jurisdiction to hear *habeas corpus* petitions filed on behalf of Guantánamo detainees.
     Hamdi holds that US citizens must receive a meaningful opportunity to challenge the
     basis for their detention under the Constitution's guarantee of due process" (Denbeaux
     and Hafetz 2009, 407). Before these rulings, trials of the detained men were only carried
     out by military courts, something which became subject to continuous criticism by
     human rights organizations. Furthermore, it was only after the rulings on the *habeas
     corpus* cases, at the end of August 2004, that civilian lawyers were granted access to the
     detainees (Denbeaux and Hafetz 2009, 408).

Territory and Population (2009), sovereignty and governmentality can occur simultaneously, and reciprocally inform one another. In his first lecture from this series, Foucault writes that there was no such thing as "the legal age, the disciplinary age, and then the age of security" (Foucault 2009, 8). The disciplinary and juridical-legal mechanisms that characterize sovereign power were neither replaced by mechanisms of security, nor did they cease to exist. "I am not saying that sovereignty ceased to play a role when the art of government becomes political science" (Foucault 2009, 106) states Foucault, instead, in the 16th and 17th centuries, sovereignty became central to ways of thinking about, and served as a starting point for, the development of theories on the art of government.

In *Precarious Life: The Powers of Mourning and Violence*, Judith Butler, following Foucault, correctly observes how at Guantánamo, sovereignty and governmentality are entangled:

> The new war prison literally manages populations, and thus functions as an operation of governmentality. At the same time, however, it exploits the extra-legal dimension of governmentality to assert a lawless sovereign power over life and death. In other words, the new war prison constitutes a form of governmentality that considers itself its own justification and seeks to extend that self-justificatory form of sovereignty through animating and deploying the extra-legal dimension of governmentality. (Butler 2004, 95)

Thus, the juridical-bureaucratic frame of Guantánamo shows how sovereignty and governmentality can become closely entwined in the management of prison populations. At Guantánamo, sovereignty was – and still is – being revitalized by governmental practices. Butler gets to the heart of this matter when she describes how the Guantánamo detention camp's main purpose is to manage the detained population, and how, in this framework, the military bureaucrat becomes invested with the powers of the sovereign. We might also argue that the power dynamics at Guantánamo reformulate Foucault's observation on the transition which occurred in the exercise of power, initiated in the 17th century, from the "ancient right to *take* life or *let* live" to the "power to *foster* life or *disallow* it to the point of death" (Foucault 1978, 138). The results of this transition – the disciplining of the body in order to optimize and increase its usefulness, and a new biopolitics expressed by various regulatory control mechanisms – may still apply to the circumstances in Guantánamo. However, it is the "extraordinary power over life and death" that was given to "the governmental bureaucrat" (Butler 2004, 59). This reinstatement of the power of the sovereign in the persona of the bureaucrat – a classic agent of governmentality – has direct implications for whom and what (and how) we perceive when we look at Guantánamo.

The management of the lives of the detainees at Guantánamo is not only a question of the legal or bureaucratic frames constructed, expressed, and consolidated in written documents and enacted as policies in the camp. The detention camp was opened by George W. Bush, Barack Obama promised to close it, Donald Trump threatened to refill it with new detainees, and now, Joseph R. Biden Jr. plans to close it yet again. During the course of these four presidencies, 780 detainees have been deported to Guantánamo (Almukhtar, et al. 2022). Some of them took part in four large-scale hunger strikes in 2002, 2005–6, 2009, and 2013–4 to call for due process and humane treatment. The huge number of accounts concerning conditions in the camp given by human rights lawyers and the detainees themselves show that, in addition to being a matter of law and administration, understanding Guantánamo and its management by the DoD is also a matter of representation and visibility.

The bureaucratic dimension of the camp, which came to partially inhabit the space which should have been allotted to the law, has, over the years, supported the US government's efforts to maintain the *status quo* with regard to the public perception of the situation at Guantánamo. Specifically, the "alternate regime of legality" (Khalili 2013, 74) put in place at the camp, coupled with Guantánamo's huge and violent bureaucratic machinery, were intended to keep the detainees' perspectives invisible to the public, and reinforce the idea that these men *don't have legal bodies*. This not only led to the circumstance that the detainees were not, at first, protected by *habeas corpus* law; it also resulted in them not having the right to appear in flesh and blood before a legitimate court. Granting the detainees the right to legal representation and allowing legal challenges to their detention at an early stage would have also meant that the US government would lose control over the visual and discursive representation of these men. Visual, legal, and (self)representation would have rendered the detainees' bodies and lives visible in a manner unaligned with the violent bureaucratization that characterizes the detention practices at Guantánamo. Rather, had they been permitted to appear in US domestic courts, this would inevitably have rendered the detainees' bodies visible – at least in in the setting of a courtroom.

In view of the entanglement of the legal, administrative/bureaucratic, and visual (self)representation of the men held at Guantánamo, this book analyzes the ways in which the DoD and its military have managed the detainees' visibility by establishing perceptual frames grounded in legal and administrative reasoning. As I demonstrate, the US government has deployed media objects in order to control the visibility of the detainees and the public perception of Guantánamo, intentionally seeking to translate the violent language of its administrative and bureaucratic apparatus into images revealing empty camps or views of the detained men from behind. Furthermore, an important aspect of the intertwined legal and the bureaucratic dimensions of Guantánamo that is often overlooked is how both are expressed in visual and written form, including documents, memoranda, and lists, as well as photographs and videos. Following Butler's argument cited in the epigraph, and my interest in the juridical-bureaucratic framework of the detention camp, my aim is to reveal how *seeing Guantánamo* is normatively regulated, and how this norm restricts what we can perceive, which will require constant recourse to the internal objects governing the "staging apparatus" (Butler 2009, 74) deployed by the DoD: namely, to government and military documents relating to the camp.

Thomas Keenan has usefully observed that, whereas the objects we call "documents" appear to function as "truth-claim-making machine[s]" (Keenan and Steyerl 2014, 62), their relation to reality is not, by any means, stable. As Keenan notes, "no document conveys *its meaning unequivocally or speaks for itself*" and, therefore, requires "*an interpreter, a vector … from (before) the start*" (Keenan and Steyerl 2014, 62; italics added). He goes on to reflect on how documents come to co-constitute their interpreter, pointing out that it is not only the interpreter who constitutes the document; the document itself is marked by a certain form of agency. Hence, documents should not be understood as mere "*instruments or tools*" which are subjugated to our use; for Keenan, documents also "*do things to us*" (Keenan and Steyerl 2014, 63; italics added). As a film and media studies scholar analyzing documents and using them as the basis for my investigation into the scope of what is visible and non-visible in the media objects from the Guantánamo detention camp, I am constantly alert to the dynamic outlined by Keenan. My interpretation necessarily leads me to co-constitute the meanings of these documents in significant ways; at the same time, my close readings of the documents carry the threat of ideologically co-constituting me. I see these objects – written documents, but also photographs and videos – as entities not only to be encountered again and again but, significantly, as objects that "work on us" (Keenan and Steyerl 2014, 62). Thus, these media objects are not merely "there" as phenomena to be encountered, presenting a stable, fixed foundation for a visual or cultural analysis; instead, my analysis and theoretical interventions assign meanings to documents, photographs, and videos, meanings which do not align with the meanings assigned to them by the DoD or the JTF-Guantánamo.

Besides being "objects we think with" (Turkle 2007, 5), documents, photographs, and videos from Guantánamo regulate our perception and apprehension of the detention camp, and are embedded in the state's broader ideological operations. As Louis Althusser writes, "an ideology always exists in an apparatus, and its practice, or practices," and "[t]his existence is material" (Althusser 1971, 166). The material existence of photographs, videos, and documents from the Guantánamo detention camp and the manifold visual practices undertaken there make it clear that the task of rendering their ideological operations visible must go far beyond understanding these objects as mere representations, or as tools which restrict the field of what is visible. Although these objects and practices often embody their underlying ideologies in ways that make it difficult to comprehend their effects or what these objects are actually intended to express, as I demonstrate in this book, the DoD cannot determine the ways in which they are now perceived, nor how they will be perceived in the future.

Media Objects, Frames, and Operations

Each of my four chapters focuses on one broader operation of the DoD – *stabilizing interpretation, invisibilizing faces, obscuring knowledge, concealing visibility* – related to a particular media object from the Guantánamo detention camp and follows the same basic dramaturgy. I begin by drawing on government and military documents. This allows me to discuss the broader institutional frames, as well as the practices related to photography, regulation, documentation, and torture carried out by military and intelligence personnel at large. This opening discussion is followed by a more detailed analysis of the minor media object that has inspired the chapter and lies at its core, as well as that object's frames, operations, and effects. Each chapter then concludes by focusing on how the operations and effects of these objects have subsequently been reframed by journalistic, legal, and artistic discourses, and how these discourses can direct our attention to ruptures in the objects' initial, institutional frames.

In the first chapter, "Stabilizing Interpretation," I analyze one of the earliest published collections of images from the Guantánamo detention camp: the photographs taken by the Combat Camera (COMCAM) photographer Shane T. McCoy, which depict the arrival of the first 20 detainees at Camp X-Ray on January 11, 2002. Scholarly debates around these images have been conducted in a broad range of fields, including visual and cultural studies, social studies, and philosophy. These debates have been concerned with the question of why these photographs were published, as well the nature of the discussion they generated in the national and international press. For example, in his article, "X-Ray Visions: Photography, Propaganda and Guantánamo Bay," Bruce Bennett (2012) focuses almost exclusively on two photographs from the series, describing how, though they display the violent treatment of the detainees, the photographs were actually supposed to construct an image of the US as a powerful nation. Bennett makes the compelling argument that McCoy's photographs blur the boundaries between propaganda, publicity, and photojournalism; however, he only briefly touches on the history of their reception. By contrast, in "Between Ethics and Aesthetics: Photographs of War during the Bush and Obama Administrations," Katrin Dauenhauer (2013) discusses in greater detail the responses made by the US government to news-media criticism of these photographs, expanding Bennett's perspective. Uniting both these approaches, in "Captured by the Camera's Eye: Guantánamo and the Shifting Frame of the Global War on Terror," Elspeth S. Van Veeren not only engages with questions about the various institutional and perceptual frames operating in the photographs, as well as their production, perception, and reframing by the news media and government officials, but also places them in the much broader context of other images of the Guantánamo detention camp (Van Veeren 2011a, 1725).

Analyzing these photographs, the contexts in which they were produced and distributed, and the subsequent debates in the news media and scholarly circles, has led me to undertake a more detailed exploration of their institutional frames by focusing on the history of COMCAM. Thus, my first chapter expands the discussions which have been pursued in various fields, from both historical and theoretical angles, by arguing that in order to understand how these images were intended to function and be perceived by the public, we must go beyond what was stated or written by the DoD or the photographer himself following their publication. Whereas Van Veeren places the photographs in the context of the broader picture of Guantánamo's visual culture, I instead focus on documents belonging to the "staging apparatus" (Butler 2009, 74); that is, on memoranda, instructions, and military manuals related to COMCAM which date back to 1953. As I also show, rather than reinforcing the perspective on the circumstances at the camp that the DoD intended the photographs to mediate, journalistic frames were crucial to the failure of the government-sanctioned frames imposed by these photographs. The discourses initiated by the news media, human rights organizations, and lawyers, and the DoD's responses to these discourses, suggest that these photographs are inherently open to being reframed – not only through humanitarian discourses, but also by individuals and organizations dealing with issues of legal and social recognition.

The photographs taken by McCoy, and their worldwide distribution, were supposed to establish the first impression of Guantánamo and the treat-ment of the detainees. At the time of their publication, it was feared that the negative responses by the news media and human rights organizations to these images would lead the DoD to limit media access to the camp. What actually happened, however, was the reverse. Rather than denying access, from January 2002 onward, the JTF-Guantánamo organized an incredible number of guided tours *in situ* for contractors, government officials, and journalists, among others. In the second chapter, "Invisibilizing Faces," I focus on this phenomenon of guided tours for journalists through the Guantánamo detention camp, and how these tours came to be framed by the DoD's claim that Guantánamo is a transparent detention facility. I argue that, rather than contributing to the understanding of what was, and still is, really happening in the camp, images taken during these tours, as well as videos published by the JTF-Guantánamo of virtual visits to the camp for the general public, actively work to ensure that the true circumstances at the camp remain incomprehensible to the viewers. Hence, instead of helping us to understand what kind of practices are actually taking place at Guantánamo, and revealing the real living conditions of the detainees, the images taken at the camp have become part and parcel of what I call the DoD's strategic deployment of opacity, intended to make the circumstances at Guantánamo unintelligible.

Due to the carefully curated media image of the detention camp – of which the guided tours are a part – in "Guantánamo Does Not Exist: Simulation and the Production of 'the Real' Global war on Terror," Van Veeren proposes to understand Guantánamo as a "telegenic spectacle … [f]iltered through the 'triple screen' of manufactured tour, selected spectator and mediation" (Van Veeren 2011b, 202). More recently, Daniel Grinberg has described the guided media tours in great detail in his article, "Some Restrictions Apply: The Exhibition Spaces of Guantánamo Bay" (2019). However, while these articles do an excellent job of describing, analyzing, and rendering visible the very conditions which have restricted visibility of Guantánamo, as well as the aesthetics of the resulting images, these same articles fail to ask how we might engage in an ethical and critical manner with what and who, in the end, *can* be perceived in those images (beyond merely questioning the various restrictions). By further expanding my frame of inquiry, and analyzing a wide range of media objects – including the contract journalists are obliged to sign prior to arriving at Guantánamo, videos of virtual visits to its various camps, and an artistic intervention by the photographer Debi Cornwall into the ways in which the DoD restricts or denies visibility to the detainees – I propose an ethical approach to the highly curated "image of" Guantánamo. This approach focuses on the dialectical relationship between the absence and presence, as well as the appearance and disappearance, of the detainees in images from Guantánamo. Thus, although the DoD denies visibility to these men, I argue that the absence which results from the various restrictions the Department imposes actually provides us with the opportunity to perceive the haunting, non-visual presence of the detainees precisely in their visual absence.

While the photographs taken by McCoy or the videos of the virtual visits to the camp are part of what can be visually perceived of the Guantánamo detention camp, in the third chapter, "Obscuring Knowledge," I turn my attention to the photographic archive that cannot be accessed by the public. Specifically, I explore how the DoD has not only withheld images of the faces of the detainees – as is the case with the videos and photographs taken on the guided media tours – but also how it has obscured knowledge about its photographic practices, and actually denied knowledge of the existence of certain photographs at all. The US government's denial of visual representation shows that when we think about Guantánamo, we must also reflect on the objects which are not visible or accessible to us, and which remain in the DoD's *"shadow archive"* (Sekula 1986, 10) largely consisting of detainees' photographs taken in the course of forensic, medical, and administrative procedures. By analyzing SOPs and other documents, I not only seek to reveal which photographs have been denied to the public, but also describe the legal arguments that the US government has pursued to secure this denial. Covering up or obscuring knowledge about photographic practices and photographs from the camp continues the work of making the circumstances at Guantánamo, and the lives and experiences of the detainees, incomprehensible and opaque. However, in this chapter I reframe the denial of these photographs, as well as the manifold redaction practices undertaken by the US government, with recourse to what Peter Galison has called "antiepistemology" (Galison 2004, 237), that is, the practice of covering up and obscuring knowledge.

In order to be able to speculate about which parts of the Guantánamo photographic archive have been obscured or withheld from the public, I will reconstruct parts of this archive by referring to the *Camp Delta SOPs* (JTF-Guantánamo 2003; 2004) and other texts which set out the photographic procedures undertaken by the US military to document the bodies of the detainees, as well as the surveillance infrastructure at the detention camp – both practices which have undoubtedly resulted in an enormous but inaccessible photo and video archive. Importantly, documents like SOPs are not only guides for Guantánamo personnel on how to conduct their daily operations – they should also be understood as operational records and bureaucratic artifacts. The idea that many of the documents produced and published in relation to Guantánamo are expressions of both the violent apparatus put in place after the attacks of 9/11 and of military bureaucracies in general only emphasizes the phenomenon I have referred to previously as the entanglement of legal and bureaucratic frames at Guantánamo. By reframing these documents as bureaucratic records, I will argue that the photographic practices deployed at the Guantánamo detention camp should also be considered as part of its violent bureaucratic machinery. Despite denying and obscuring knowledge about photographs of the detainees that were produced as part of military documentation practices, the antiepistemic agenda of the DoD has not been successful – the very fact that I am discussing a part of this "secret" archive in this book counters this antiepistemology. By reconstructing a lawsuit between the ACLU and the DoD, I am also looking at how an independent organization rendered knowledge about obscured torture photographs visible. This lawsuit, which concerned photographs of detainees and POWs shot at various extra-territorial detention facilities and military prisons, arose from the ACLU's FOIA request submitted in 2003 (ACLU 2003). In Chapter 3, I am specifically interested in how the ACLU rendered knowledge about obscured and censored photographs visible in tabular form – in a Microsoft Excel spreadsheet – which has not been previously discussed in the fields of film and media studies (ACLU 2022b).

The ACLU's efforts to challenge the legal grounds put forward by the US government for the abuse and torture of people detained after 9/11, along with its many FOIA requests, which have led to the publication of a significant amount of military, legal, and bureaucratic documents, take a central position in the third and fourth chapter. In the last chapter, "Concealing Visibility," I deal with an operation undertaken by the DoD in connection with the lawsuit discussed in "Obscuring Knowledge," but one that would appear to be the exact opposite of denying the existence of or access to photographs – namely, their publication. In 2016, then-US Secretary of Defense Ashton Carter certified under the *Protected National Security Documents Act* (US Congress 2009) approximately 2,000 photographs documenting the torture and abuse of people detained after 9/11. This led the DoD to declassify 198 photographs and subsequently publish them in a single PDF file (DoD 2016). At the beginning of 2016, this PDF file sparked a large amount of debate about whether or not the DoD had adhered to Judge Alvin K. Hellerstein's order to produce the "cache of photographs … , which depict individuals apprehended and detained abroad after September 11, 2001" (*ACLU v. DoD* 2017, 04. Civ 4161 (AKH), 1). In the subsequent discourse, the interpretation of the PDF file, and the scans of the photographs it contains, was rather an ambiguous one: although it could be said that its publication was a success for the ACLU in their sustained legal efforts to force the DoD to publish evidence of torture, the photographs themselves were consistently downplayed by the press as showing only minor bruises, close-ups of indistinct body parts, and redacted faces. The publication of these photographs initially prompted the desire to see other images, particularly photographs which would resemble the iconography of the Abu Ghraib torture scandal. The photographs that had actually been published were deemed irrelevant and were described as not showing anything that approached the real consequences of torture. This, as I argue, is not only factually wrong; it also reveals that the popular understanding of what torture is fails to adequately grasp how torture techniques were designed in the aftermath of 9/11.

Hence, in the fourth chapter, I reframe these photographs in order to understand them as traces of so-called "clean torture" (Hilbrand 2015; Rejali 2007), a set of torture techniques which was specifically designed to leave no traces on the bodies of the tortured detainees and POWs. By learning anew how contemporary democracies devise and employ torture practices, and by unlearning what we think we know about torture, it becomes clear that these photographs do not just show bruised bodies – they also show tortured lives. Nevertheless, the manner in which these photographs were published, without any context or additional explanation, was intended to convince their viewers that, while the images could be read in many different ways, reading them as traces of torture would be farfetched. It initially appeared that the DoD had been successful in making these photographs incomprehensible as torture photographs, and had prevented the viewers from engaging in any meaningful relationship with the people portrayed in them. However, in the final subsection of this book, I subvert the DoD's distribution practices, and propose a way for how we, and future viewers, can engage critically with what and whom these photographs depict. By reading one particular photograph of a burnt foot in the context of the letter written by the man who experienced the torture this image traces, I show how, despite the DoD's sustained success in erasing the stories of tellable lives from torture photographs, we can re-inscribe these stories back into the photographs (al-Ani 2004; DoD 2016, 71).

To summarize, although the four chapters deal with different media objects, frames, and operations, they are united not only by the fact that they all address Guantánamo, either as the geographic location of the camp, or as a discursive formation relating to the networked nature of US government torture practices and detention facilities. In this book, I show that, when engaging with the question of how state power regulates and controls the public perception of such a hermetically sealed environment as a detention facility, it can be highly productive to use the perspective of the state apparatus as a starting point for analyzing how this state envisions certain media objects to function, as well as how it is possible for its "ideological projects … [to] fail" (Kellner 1995, 5). I have assigned to these operations and larger frames the terms *stabilizing interpretation*, *invisibilizing faces*, *obscuring knowledge*, and *concealing visibility* to differentiate the manifold ways in which the DoD publishes and withholds images of the detainees and of the circum-stances in the Guantánamo detention camp. As my book argues, the various media objects produced, published, and withheld since 2002 are still open to responses and to being reframed today and in the future. This makes Guantánamo, and the violence inflicted upon the detainees, a particularly relevant and current case. Although only 36 of the 780 men remain imprisoned in the camp, the continuing urgency to write about Guantánamo shows that there is still a belief that it can become a "transformative event" (Berlant 2007, 670). Some may argue that the fact that Guantánamo has not been closed, despite the outrage it has sparked over the years, makes it appear to be a "case that didn't matter" (Berlant 2007, 670). However, the ongoing debates surrounding the camp confirm that it is not only an open case, but that there is still a shared belief among scholars that Guantánamo is potentially a "transformative case-event" (Berlant 2007, 671). In this vein, my book aims to sustain these discussions about the "case of" Guantánamo, and to reframe anew what we can see when we look in the direction of this extra-territorial detention facility. In this way, I seek to contribute to "[t]he growing stock of new and better arguments about what the revelations [about Guantánamo] meant and mean [, which is also] a tribute to the urgency to maintain the information for a potentially transformative event" (Berlant 2007, 670).

By refocusing our attention on Guantánamo frames, and on the subsequent reframing these frames have undergone, this book shows how our idea of Guantánamo becomes ever more complex as we continue to respond to its media objects.

[Fig. 1] A photograph showing the arrival of the first detainees at the Guantánamo detention camp taken by the COMCAM Photographer Shane T. McCoy on January 11, 2002, and published on January 18, 2002, by the DoD (Source: Shane T. McCoy and the DoD). The appearance of US Department of Defense (DoD) visual information does not imply or constitute DoD endorsement.

Detainees in orange jumpsuits sit in a holding area under the watchful
eyes of Military Police at Camp X-Ray at Naval Base Guantánamo Bay,
Cuba, during in-processing to the temporary detention facility on Jan.
11, 2002. The detainees will be given a basic physical exam by a doctor,
to include a chest x-ray and blood samples drawn to assess their health.
DoD photo by Petty Officer 1st class Shane T. McCoy, U.S. Navy.

– The caption released with fig. 1 by the DoD, according to Wikimedia Commons.

Taliban and al-Qaida detainees in orange jumpsuits sit in a holding area
under the watchful eyes of military police at Camp X-Ray at Naval Base
Guantánamo Bay, Cuba, during in-processing to the temporary detention
facility on Jan. 11, 2002. The detainees will be given a basic physical exam
by a doctor, to include a chest x-ray and blood samples drawn to assess
their health, the military said.

– The caption released with fig. 1 by the DoD, with AP's adjustments for its distribution.

1

Stabilizing Interpretation: Photographs Showing the Arrival of the First Detainees

The photograph is a high-angle shot depicting men in orange clothing and headgear, kneeling in a yard surrounded by mesh and barbed wire [fig.1]. The men's gloved hands are fastened together in front of them, restricting their movements; their mouths are covered by masks, supposedly to protect those around them from contagion. The kneeling men are also wearing blackened goggles and ear protectors, the former making it impossible for them to see what is happening to them and around them, the latter muting every sound from the outside world. All these measures seem designed to discourage, confuse, and strip the men of agency. Furthermore, they prompt us to draw the conclusion that these men are detainees. All of this is shot from above. Apparently floating in the air, the camera captures not only the men we have no doubt identified as detainees, but also those around them. Thanks to the latter's uniforms, we can recognize these people as soldiers. The photograph not only reveals soldiers inside and outside the cage, but also the location in which the scene is set. One element of the nearby architecture that figures very prominently in the photograph is the barbed wire, which is positioned in the foreground, dividing the depicted scene into smaller segments. The perceived proximity of the wire to the viewer's eye creates the feeling that, like the detainees, we too are threatened by it. The silver, shiny, sharp razor wire seemingly endangers our eyes and our gaze. It may prompt us to look away.

The photograph reveals the infrastructure directly around the detainees – such as mesh and barbed wire – as well as a more distant building, and events not directly connected to the foregrounded scene. Even though the camera lens is clearly focused on the detainees, we, the viewers of this image, are given a wide range of visual access: the photograph seems to hold the promise that, rather than just showing a single element or an excerpt, it is revealing the entire story. Thus, if we resist surrendering our perception to the compositional regime of the photograph, we may, for a brief moment, overlook the foreground constellation of the detainees and soldiers, and focus instead on what is visible in the background. Perhaps, then, we might notice the other people depicted in the photograph, and begin to speculate about who they are, and what they are doing. We might then notice three people on a construction site in the upper-left corner. Perhaps they are construction workers, or soldiers, or both? We might also observe three people standing on a hill in the upper-right corner; the architecture in the background may awaken our interest and inform us about how the photograph was taken because, if we look closely, we can make out a surveillance tower in the upper-left corner, next to the construction site. The tower is draped with the US flag. Perhaps, then, we do not simply see two soldiers in the tower, but two US soldiers who are observing and overseeing the situation before them. Or, we might simply contemplate the beauty of the natural environment surrounding the scene.

Hence, without any context or additional explanation, we are invited to make deductions, and to speculate about what the photograph depicts (Sontag 2008, 23). Looking at photographs like this allows us to grasp only parts of the story; to obtain a complete story by means of a photograph alone is mere fantasy. The photograph neither tells us where or by whom it was taken, nor does it explain who the men depicted in it actually are. Ultimately, what we are able to deduce remains mere speculation.

But this photograph was not published without context. From the moment it appeared on the US Department of Defense (DoD) website, on January 18, 2002 (Van Veeren 2011a, 1728), it was accompanied by an explanatory caption cited in the epigraph to this chapter.[1] The caption explains to the viewer who the men depicted in the photograph are and summarizes briefly what is happening in the scene. The published photograph was also accompanied by an image credit which identified the image's creator as the Combat Camera (COMCAM) photographer Navy Petty Officer Shane T. McCoy who, in 2002, was assigned to the Expeditionary Combat Camera Atlantic 0293 (Naval Reserve) unit, and the DoD. Thanks to the caption and other context provided by the international news media, we know that the photograph documents the inauguration of the detention facility at the Guantánamo Bay Naval Base. On January 11, 2002, exactly four months after the attacks of 9/11, the US military transported the first detainees to the Guantánamo detention facility. The series of photographs taken by McCoy documented this new detention facility as it became operational. In addition to documenting a military event, the distribution of this photograph to the general public was intended to establish

1   An AP Archive employee sent me the caption of [fig. 1] from their database (Susan Munns, July 30, 2019).

the first visual frame of the detention facility. However, only "[s]oon after their release, the Pentagon took them off its own Web sites [*sic*] and labeled them 'For Official Use Only'" (Rosenberg 2008) – which did not prevent the news media from further distributing McCoy's photographs.

In this chapter I argue that thinking about this photograph and the way it was intended to frame the public's perception of Guantánamo necessitates a reflection on the history of its institutional framing, because, as I demonstrate, it was the institutional transformation processes within the US military's approach to "Visual Information" which allowed McCoy's photographic frame to be produced and distributed. I will thus shed light on the ways in which COMCAM has transformed itself over the years, on the drawn-out nature of the learning processes that led to this transformation, and the role of military documents such as memoranda and manuals in these processes. I will also analyze McCoy's photographs from 2002 in reference to military manuals, and, more specifically, to the *Joint Combat Camera (COMCAM) / Visual Information (VI): Smart Book* (Defense Visual Information Joint Combat Camera Program 2015).[2] Thanks to this manual, we can develop a better idea of the processes behind the distribution and perception of COMCAM photographs, including those taken by McCoy.

I will then go on to distinguish COMCAM practices from those employed in the field of professional photojournalism. Contrasting COMCAM photography with photojournalism allows me to further delineate its specific nature by simultaneously acknowledging the flows of knowledge between those two fields, and, specifically, how they inform each other with regard to the writing of captions. I will show that the military considers the captions provided by COMCAM photographers – such as the one provided along with McCoy's photographs – to be a crucial aspect of the images' presentation, since they are intended to inform the viewer what each photograph depicts.

I end this chapter with the discussion of how McCoy's photographs were reframed by newspapers, as well as how Secretary of Defense Donald Rumsfeld responded to this reframing. I demonstrate that, in spite of the substantial effort the DoD expends on controlling the production and post-production of official images, the meanings assigned to McCoy's photographs via their captions failed to restrict the newspapers who featured them to a single interpretation of the images. Consequently, I argue against the US military's apparent belief that it can successfully govern the viewers' perception of the photographs it produces, and instead make the opposite case: the DoD's attempts to stabilize the meaning and interpretation of McCoy's photographs have spectacularly failed. As I also show, despite the circumstances depicted in the photographs, and the ways the DoD deliberately denies recognition to

---

2   In the following subsections, I will reference this document as *Smart Book*.

the detainees, the US government was unable to secure this denial in situations where viewers came to perceive the photographs in new frames, such as those provided by the newspapers.

The Frame of Combat Camera

Institutional Learning and Military Transformation

Is it possible to eat soup with a knife? The short answer is "no." The longer one, however, is more complicated. In relation to military institutions, an example of the latter can be found in John Nagl's study, *Counterinsurgency Lessons from Malaya and Vietnam: Learning to Eat Soup with a Knife* (2002), which focuses on institutional learning processes within the US military. But let me first clarify what I mean by "learning" in this particular context. In the following discussion, I base my understanding of "institutional learning" on Colonel Richard Downie's definition in *Learning from Conflict: The US Military in Vietnam, El Salvador, and the Drug War*, where he describes it as "a process by which an organization uses new knowledge or understandings gained from experience or study to adjust institutional norms, doctrine, and procedures in ways designed to minimize previous gaps in performance and maximize future success" (Downie 1998, 22). Along with providing insight into what "learning" means for the military apparatus, both Nagl's study and Downie's book argue that, crucially, the US military learns rather slowly, and that it has repeatedly failed to learn from the past wars in which it has been involved.

In order to understand what the DoD's internal learning processes looked like at the beginning of the 21st century, we can begin by analyzing the institution's own attitude towards its epistemic capabilities. Hence, we can look at what the DoD thought it knew or acknowledged that it did not know, the methods it privileged for acquiring knowledge, and how this attitude was expressed at a specific point in time during the institution's history. In a news briefing held only two weeks after the detention facility at Guantánamo was inaugurated, Secretary Rumsfeld provided the public with a summary of the DoD's view on presumed epistemic realities at the beginning of 2002 (DoD 2002c). In this briefing, Rumsfeld presented the journalists with three categories of knowing, which were apparently guiding the DoD's actions with regard to the acquisition of actionable intelligence:

> Reports that say that something hasn't happened are always interesting to me, because as we know, there are *known knowns*; there are things we know we know. We also know there are *known unknowns*; that is to say we know there are some things we do not know. But there are also *unknown unknowns* – the ones we don't know we don't know. (DoD 2002c; italics added)

Rumsfeld's statement was a reply to a question posed by one of the journalists at the briefing about the lack of evidence supporting the assumption "that Iraq has attempted to or is willing to supply terrorists with weapons of mass destruction" (DoD 2002c). Nevertheless, one can also understand the categories of "known knowns," "known unknowns," and "unknown unknowns" (DoD 2002c) as broader guiding principles of the DoD's strategy of information acquisition after the 9/11 attacks, and as guidelines which influenced the internal workings of the institution. In the context of the detention facility at Guantánamo, the US government, at least under the presidency of George W. Bush, has used these categories to justify the "enhanced interrogation techniques" that were deployed there. However, I am not concerned with how these categories came to govern the interior workings of the detention facility; instead, my interest here lies in the question of how they accelerated institutional learning processes related to visual information and COMCAM.

Rumsfeld's revelation of the three epistemic categories, or guiding principles, of the DoD is interesting not only because it rationalizes uncertainty. It is also closely related to a major transformation that US military forces had been undergoing since the mid-90s, a process which was intensified after 9/11. A paper published by the DoD in 2003 stated that the US military is "transitioning from an industrial age to an information age military" (DoD 2003, 3). Such transformations are unlikely to be easy, and it can take a long time to introduce major institutional changes. However, faced with the 9/11 attacks and the war in Afghanistan, the Bush administration recognized the necessity of accelerating the learning processes already occurring within the US military's institutional culture. In his address to the cadets at The Citadel – The Military College of South Carolina on December 11, 2001, Bush emphasized the urgency of introducing innovation into the US forces in the face of "shadowy, entrenched enemies – enemies using the tools of terror and guerrilla war" (Bush 2001a). He stated that "[t]he need for military transformation was clear before the conflict in Afghanistan, and before September 11th ... What's different today is our sense of urgency – the need to build this future force while fighting a present war" (Bush 2001a; italics added). The "military transformation" mentioned by Bush focused on developing tactics and weapons better suited to the "new" fighting environment. As Christopher Daase writes, in the mid-90s, military transformation became the guiding principle for the DoD, who adopted a strongly critical stance towards the persistence of the doctrine of "*Overwhelming Force*" (Daase 2008, 256).[3] The lengthy process of formalizing a new doctrine, accompanied by the US military's respect for historical precedents, meant that challenging the current

---

3   A doctrine is a result of the formalization and codification of a military's institutional memory; it determines the allocation of resources, and is the "common language and a common understanding of how Army forces conduct operations" (as cited in Nagl 2002, 7; US Department of the Army 2001, 24).

doctrine would not only prove to be a lengthy process; it was also one that was not necessarily welcomed by the US military itself (Hediger 2016, 250f.; Nagl 2002, 8).

The larger aim of changing the doctrine to make it a better fit for the so-called "information age" resulted in the development of the concept of "Network-Centric Warfare" (Force Transformation, Office of the Secretary of Defense 2003b). Supposedly, a major advantage of this concept is that a well-net-worked military is able to share higher-quality information, and thanks to its "shared awareness" (Force Transformation, Office of the Secretary of Defense 2003b, 3) it can increase the effectiveness of its military missions. This concept was supposed to be gradually implemented by the Office of Force Trans-formation (OFT), an institution that focused exclusively on the US military's adaptation to the technological advancements of the 21st century. The OFT was established within the Office of the Secretary of Defense about six weeks prior to Bush's address at The Citadel. Rumsfeld and the newly established office shared the broader idea of transforming three key aspects: how US forces fight, how they "Do Business," and how they "Work With Others" (DoD 2003, 6f.). The US military's official definition of "transformation" reads as follows:

> [Transformation is] a process that shapes the changing nature of military competition and cooperation through new combinations of concepts, capabilities, people and organizations that exploit our nation's advantages and protect against our asymmetric vulnerabilities to sustain our strategic position, which helps underpin peace and stability in the world. (DoD 2003, 3)

In *Military Transformation: A Strategic Approach*, we read that the aim is to change the entire culture of the US military, and that this transformation should be built on four pillars: "Strengthening Joint Operations," "Exploiting US Intelligence Advantages," "Concept Development and Experimentation," and "Developing Transformational Capabilities" (Force Transformation, Office of the Secretary of Defense 2003a, 21–7). However, to prevent the transformation from becoming dogmatic, the US military is required to experiment, and to update ideas in accordance with "operational lessons learned" (DoD 2003, 15), as the *Transformation Planning Guidance* document makes clear. The acquired knowledge "should be systematically captured, analyzed, and incorporated into ongoing experimentation and concept development" (DoD 2003, 19). Both these papers show that institutional learning, or the concept of the US military becoming a learning institution, was central to the transformation endeavor of the DoD under Rumsfeld's leadership.

Thus, between 2001 and 2003, the US military began to learn anew "how to build military organizations that can adapt more quickly and effectively to future changes in warfare" (Nagl 2002, xiii). It is no coincidence that the result of Nagl's aforementioned study of the Vietnam War and his diagnosis of the US military's repeated failures to learn and change was published in 2002. As I have shown, following the 9/11 attacks, the Bush administration viewed the necessity of radically transforming the US military as even more urgent, and came to rely on the insights of such studies. However, as the title of Nagl's study suggests, transformation in such a large institution is a lengthy process, and not one that can be implemented from one day to the next. In the next subsection, I will put forward arguments that support this thesis by focusing on studies, recommendations, and directives in the more specific context of institutional learning and transformation related to visual information and COMCAM. I will demonstrate how lengthy these processes were, and emphasize how much effort it takes for the DoD to introduce long-lasting procedural and institutional changes.

Institutional Learning and Change Within COMCAM[4]

The US military's institutional learning processes related to visual information were initiated long before the news media criticized McCoy's photographs taken at the detention facility at Guantánamo. In fact, institutional efforts to understand how the production and distribution of audiovisual material could be improved took place as early as October 1, 1953 (Crocker 2013, 1). On this day, the Secretaries of the US Military Departments sat down to review the military production of visual material. As Sean Crocker discusses in his paper, *Defense Visual Information History*, during the next thirty years, the US military would conduct various additional studies on how to optimize its internal processes pertaining to the production and distribution of images (Crocker 2013, 1). However, the implementation of the recommendations arising from such studies was not as efficient as may have been expected. It was only in 1975 that eight of the previously conducted studies on audiovisual activities were compiled and compared in one single report, entitled *Audio-Visual Management Task Force Report* (Crocker 2013, 13; Assistant Secretary of Defense (Manpower and Reserve Affairs) 1975). This report revealed that four persistent issues remained in the findings of the different studies:

- Lack of management information and control
- Duplication of services
- Proliferation and under-utilization of facilities
- Lack of software and hardware standardization.

(As cited in Crocker 2013, 13)

4   The historical reconstruction of the developments within COMCAM in this subsection is largely based on this unpublished document which I received in May 2019 from Nicholas Dean Sherrouse, then manager of Joint Combat Camera. I would like to express my deepest gratitude for his assistance, and for forwarding this document, which afforded me insights into the institutional history and documents of COMCAM.

The consistency of these findings prompted the authors to express their astonishment at the lack of progress made in this area, especially since the "subject [has] ... been studied so much" (as cited in Crocker 2013, 13). The main recommendations in the 1975 report were similar to the ones in the previous eight studies. The DoD was advised to 1) establish a "Directorate for Audio-Visual Activities" as an oversight organ; 2) develop an "automated management information reporting system"; 3) prepare evaluation standards for units and guidelines with regard to staffing; 4) establish an "DoD Audio-Visual Master Plan" (Crocker 2013, 13f.).

Four years later, "nearly thirty years of studies and recommendations calling for a single DoD AV manager finally culminated in the issuance of DoD Directive 5040.1" (Crocker 2013, 24). Hence, it took the DoD nearly thirty years to implement long-lasting changes to their audio-visual activities – changes which, as we will see, were followed by still others – and to develop new policies. Directive 5040.1 from 1979 (DoD 1979a) led to the establishment of a new body, the Defense Visual Agency, which was supposed to manage all aspects of the DoD's audiovisual material, such as its "production, acquisition, distribution, and depository" (Crocker 2013, 24). Unsurprisingly perhaps, the agency had a short lifespan. As early as 1985, it was disestablished by the Secretaries of the Military Departments because it was "only minimally meeting the operational requirement to accomplish its mission" (Crocker 2013, 31; Weinberger 1985), and was apparently experiencing major problems at the level of management. As a result, most of the agency's activities were reassigned to different departments. The DoD's Directive 5040.3, "DoD Joint Visual Information Services," published on December 5, 1985, made the reassignment official and cancelled Directive 5040.1 (Crocker 2013, 34; DoD 1985a, 1). This time, the oversight function was given to the newly established Joint Visual Information Services, "operated and maintained by a DoD Component" (DoD 1985a, 1).

The term "Visual Information," as used in the subject line of the 1985 directive, was, at the time, a novelty. As Crocker writes, it was first mentioned in a new version of Instruction 5040.2-R,[5] and was initially "coined as a means of taking photography, graphics, library distribution, and archiving off the table for reporting of expenditures to Congress" (Crocker 2013, 34). Hence, this term was meant to refer solely to the production of moving images, and was introduced in response to the demands for the DoD to outsource more of its audiovisual productions to the US film industry (Crocker 2013, 34). Later, however, the term "Visual Information" also came to encompass photography. In a field manual, *COMCAM: Multi-Service Tactics, Techniques, and Procedures for Joint Combat Camera Operations*, from 2003, we read the following updated

---

5   The original instruction was published in 1979 (DoD 1979b) and was later on amended in 1982, 1984, and 1999.

definition: "Visual Information (VI). The use of one or more of the various visual media, with or without sound. Generally, VI includes still imagery, motion media, video or audio recording, graphic arts, visual aids, models, display, visual presentation services and the support processes" (Air Land Sea Application (ALSA) Center 2003, I-2).

In order to understand McCoy's photograph [fig. 1], it is particularly interesting to focus on the historical developments in the COMCAM units' production and distribution of visual information. The history of the US military's use of photography is nearly as long as the history of the medium itself. For instance, the US military regards the photographers commissioned by Abraham Lincoln during the American Civil War to be the precursors of COMCAM (Air Force Public Affairs 2022). As the US Air Force website states, the history of the 1st COMCAM Squadron dates back to the First Motion Picture Unit – a unit composed of professional photographers active during World War II (Air Force Public Affairs 2022). The website goes on to reveal that apparently, after World War II, many units specializing in the production of audiovisual material were established, and then again dissolved. A detailed reconstruction of COMCAM's "storied history" (Air Force Public Affairs 2022) could be a project for an entire book in itself, and exceeds the scope of this subsection. Instead, I will emphasize the length of time the US military required to learn from its studies on audiovisual production, and to put "theory" into "practice."

1986 was an important year for the aforementioned efforts to consolidate the various activities related to visual information and the improvement of workflows within COMCAM, in that it saw the US Congress pass the *Goldwater-Nichols Department of Defense Reorganization Act* (Public Law 99-433 (October 1, 1986)). The *Goldwater-Nichols Act* focused on the reorganization of the entire DoD. Its main concern was the improvement of the Department in the following areas: "effectiveness, economy and efficiency" (Crocker 2013, 35). In order to achieve these goals, all military operations were designated to be "joint," and the command structure was changed in order to limit the rivalry between the different services. The *Goldwater-Nichols Act* also had a significant impact on the activities of COMCAM photographers. Before 1986/7, field photographers submitted visual material to their own services, with the result that the Joint Chiefs of Staff and Combatant Commands only acquired this material after a considerable delay – there was no standardized procedure to enable a swift exchange of material between the services.[6] This made the production and distribution of COMCAM materials in some cases ineffective, inefficient, and no doubt also expensive. Discussions about a joint COMCAM began in 1987, and were led by the Special Issues Visual Information Working

6   Up until 2018, each branch of the US military – the Air Force, Army, Navy, and Marine Corps – had its own COMCAM unit to produce and distribute photographs and films in support of "strategic, operational, and tactical mission objectives" (DoD 1996, 2).

Group (Crocker 2013, 36). As a result, in the same year, the DoD published Directive 5040.2, "Visual Information (VI)," outlining its visual information policy (DoD 1987). This directive stated that "VI activities shall … [b]e consolidated into as few activities as possible" and "[b]e operated in the most cost-effective manner, and support all DoD organizations and major commands within a geographic area" (DoD 1987, 3). It not only ordered that DoD agencies and military services should provide "[r]apid deployment [of] Combat Camera teams to support military operations and emergencies, including documentation of force deployments and activities before, during, and after military engagements," but also the maintenance of "[c]entralized DoD still and motion media records centers," and "[c]entralized DoD VI product distribution facilities" (DoD 1987, 3f.).

Efforts to centralize COMCAM activities reached their peak in 1988. In that year, the three services signed a *Memorandum of Understanding* (1988) which focused on improving the internal distribution of visual material by establishing a central receiving center in the Pentagon – the Joint Combat Camera Reception and Distribution Center, later renamed the Joint Combat Camera Center – and improving coordination between the services (Crocker 2013, 38).

In 1990, the DoD issued Instruction 5040.4, "Joint Combat Camera (COMCAM) Program" (DoD 1990); each service has had also their own additional instructions pertaining to their individual COMCAM units. This was also a result of the discussions led by the Visual Information Working Group, and was republished as a directive in 1996 (Crocker 2013, 42; Reader 1990; DoD 1996). Of significance to the question of whether the negative responses to the Guantánamo photographs contributed to the intensification of institutional learning processes of the US military is the fact that the directive was reissued in August 2002, only a few months after McCoy's images were published (DoD 2002a). In 2003, Rumsfeld and Raymond F. DuBois, then Director of Administration and Management in the DoD, certified this directive, as well as the 1985 Directive 5040.3, "Joint Visual Information Services," as being current (DuBois 2003, 52). They ordered the revision of Directive 5040.2 (DuBois 2003, 52), "Visual Information (VI)," which, after initially being published in 1985, was reissued in 1987, with a revised version published in 2005 (DoD 1985b; 1987; 2005b). Although they also certified the Directive 5040.4, "Joint Combat Camera (COMCAM) Program" (DoD 2002a), as current (DuBois 2003, 52), it was reissued in 2006 as a formal instruction which established the DoD Joint Combat Camera Planning Group (DoD 2006a). This group would meet annually to "[d]iscuss, explore, develop, propose, and provide recommendations to and advise and assist the ASD (PA) [Assistant to the Secretary of Defense (Public Affairs)] on matters pertaining to COMCAM" (DoD 2006a, 9).

This brief reconstruction of how single directives pertaining to either visual information or to Joint COMCAM were published, republished, and so on, demonstrates that there was a significant increase in the consolidation of knowledge gained over the previous decades, starting in the end of the 80s and continuing throughout the 2000s. I also illustrated how significant institutional changes in the US military in general, and particularly in relation to visual information, took place over a lengthy period of time. The "institutional learning processes" started with "the recognition of short-comings in organizational knowledge or performance" (Nagl 2002, 6) in the 50s but – even though these shortcomings were repeatedly acknowledged – a consensus regarding the implementation of the recommendations only came much later. Significantly, the restructuring of the entire DoD in 1986 was an important impetus for the changes affecting COMCAM. Another aspect I want to emphasize here is the complexity and multilayered nature of the history regarding single documents published by the DoD, such as directives and instructions. As I have shown above, many directives tend to be reissued and adjusted over the years, and, interestingly, these documents always relate to their own lifecycles by referring to their previous versions.

Considering the time it takes the US military to introduce changes to its structures or policies and to make these changes official via the publication of directives or instructions, it is also interesting to look at the similarities between the drawn-out nature of these processes and the processes of codifying knowledge that US forces acquire from "lessons learned." In the latter context, field manuals are of particular significance. On a basic level, military manuals are "document[s] containing procedures for performing specific tasks" (US Joint Chief of Staff 2020, 31). They consolidate and codify practices which have been actively employed up to the point of the manual's publication, and thus do not necessarily contain only elements of innovation. Furthermore, as in the case of directives or instructions, field manuals and smart books also refer to and reflect upon their own histories.

As I have suggested, in the US military, the review and production of knowledge, as well as its subsequent codification, can be accelerated due to extraordinary circumstances (armed conflicts, technological innovation, *et cetera*). The production and consolidation of knowledge can also be accelerated in response to significant "mistakes," and from the perspective of the DoD, the publication of McCoy's photographs depicting the shackled detainees at Guantánamo was likely one such "mistake." Hence, it does not appear entirely coincidental that the first field manual for Joint Combat Camera Operations – entitled *COMCAM: Multi-Service Tactics, Techniques, and Procedures for Joint Combat Camera Operations*[7] – was published in 2003, about seven

---

7   I was told by US forces employees that *COMCAM: Multi-Service Tactics, Techniques, and Procedures for Joint Combat Camera Operations* was the first field manual. A reference

years after the Joint Combat Camera Program was established, and approximately one year after McCoy's images were released (ALSA Center 2003).
This timeframe supports the thesis that it takes the US military a significant
amount of time to learn new things, and to codify and standardize the
acquired knowledge. It also supports my speculation that the visual coverage
of the inauguration of Guantánamo, amongst other things, accelerated
institutional learning processes in COMCAM. This field manual is designed
to complement the Joint Services doctrine with regard to COMCAM (ALSA
Center 2003, i). Interestingly, the manual positions the modern COMCAM and
its functions in relation to the 9/11 attacks and to the visual coverage of that
event, stating that between 2001 and 2003, COMCAM photographers had consistently documented the US military's response to those terrorist attacks:

> No American can forget the horrific images of the terrorist attacks on the
> United States on September 11, 2001. These graphic scenes, captured on
> still and motion imagery, told a vivid story and brought to life the reality
> of the day's events. These memorable images, and others like them
> over the years, have brought to *the forefront the impact of visual imagery.*
> COMCAM forces captured still and motion imagery of America's military
> response to these acts, *documenting the destruction of terrorist forces in
> Afghanistan and further emphasizing the value of visual imagery.* (ALSA
> Center 2003, I-1; italics added)

*COMCAM: Multi-Service Tactics, Techniques, and Procedures for Joint Combat
Camera Operations* identifies 9/11 as a caesura that shifted the public's
perception of the importance of visual information, and the distribution of
officially authorized images. However, it is difficult to sustain this argument
historically, because the US military has a long history of embedded
journalism – wherein journalists accompany military units, and their coverage
has to be cleared by the military before being released – and, as previously
mentioned, even Abraham Lincoln commissioned photographers. Nevertheless, the events of 9/11 certainly had a major impact on COMCAM – for
instance, by accelerating certain knowledge consolidation processes.

This particular manual provides a wide range of "planners" (ALSA Center 2003,
i) with an overview of COMCAM, its history, definition, and mission objectives.
Furthermore, it defines the roles and responsibilities of COMCAM assets,
the Joint COMCAM Center, and of the Joint COMCAM Manager. It also contains an overview of Joint COMCAM Operations, and the various procedures
related to them. Significantly, the manual does not describe how COMCAM

librarian employed at the Navy Department Library confirmed that this was probably
the first field manual for Joint Combat Camera Operations. Prior to the publication
of the 2003 manual, an entire chapter was dedicated to Combat Camera in the *Visual
Information Operations* manual from 2002, published a week after McCoy's pictures were
released (US Department of the Army 2002).

photographers should conduct their daily operations, but instead focuses on the broader structure of the joint operations, and addresses "planners and commanders at all levels" (ALSA Center 2003, i). In relation to the aforementioned protocol in military documents to reflect on their own histories, and to this being an integral part of these types of documents, I want to point out that *COMCAM: Multi-Service Tactics, Techniques, and Procedures for Joint Combat Camera Operations* (2003) is no exception, and contains a list of references to other documents produced for the various military services and joint operations (ALSA Center 2003, References-1). Both of the directives discussed in this subsection – Directive 5040.4, "Joint Combat Camera (COMCAM) Program" from 2002, and Directive 5040.2, "Visual Information (VI)" from 1987 – are mentioned in the field manual (ALSA Center 2003, References-1). Recalling the complex, convoluted histories of these directives, it is fair to say that this manual is a result of a much longer history of institutional learning and transformation.

The complex history of COMCAM, and institutional learning processes pertaining to visual information, can contribute to our understanding of military manuals, their roles, and functions. As I have shown, manuals are the result of, and responses to, processes of institutional learning which usually occur over a period of many years. They are also objects documenting the institutional histories to which they belong, by which they are framed, and which they serve to consolidate. Rather than dramatically changing the *status quo*, many of these manuals function as a codification of previously established procedures and practices. Furthermore, these manuals render visible the networked nature of military knowledge and operations by referring to a broad range of other documents. Despite the many manuals which I could have discussed here, I have focused in this subsection on the 2003 field manual because it is the one released closest to the time when McCoy took his photographs. Referring to the period between 2001 and 2003, this manual highlights the fact that its publication is a result of events and actions taken by COMCAM during those years. At the same time, by acknowledging the various preceding directives and instructions (amongst other documents), the manual also evokes at least 50 years of the US military's institutional history.

Procedural Templates and the Five C's

In the previous subsection, I illustrated the amount of time it can take the DoD to introduce changes and to consolidate knowledge that has already been in use for some years. In this subsection, I will return to McCoy's photographs shot in 2002 and analyze them in relation to the *Joint Combat Camera (COMCAM) / Visual Information (VI): Smart Book* (2015), which was actually published 13 years after the images were taken. This *Smart Book* refers to, and cites from, nearly all the directives, instructions, and manuals discussed in the previous subsection. However, it diverges from these other military documents in that it neither establishes policies nor is designed solely for "planners and com- manders at all levels" (ALSA Center 2003, i). Instead, the *Smart Book* "is meant only as a reference/guide for the Service Member at the customer/user/ tactical level" (*Smart Book* 2015, 4). Hence, the *Smart Book*'s intended reader- ship is military personnel on active duty in COMCAM. Although analyzing images taken and released in 2002 by means of a document published 13 years later could be seen as historically contentious, I believe the arguments I put forward in the previous subsections demonstrate the value of this analysis, and support the thesis that a large amount of the knowledge codified in the *Smart Book* of 2015 would have already been present in 2002. Furthermore, the *Smart Book* positions itself as a consolidation of past practices by stating that "[i]t highlights commonly used practices and formats for deployed operations" (*Smart Book* 2015, 4), and thus could be regarded as an expression and consol- idation of around 50 years of COMCAM's institutional history.

Though the *Smart Book* positions itself as a manual discussing "practices and formats" (*Smart Book* 2015, 4) commonly used by COMCAM photographers, I suggest that it is better described as furnishing *templates*: on the one hand, the manual from 2015 functions as a templating tool in itself, since it describes how to successfully plan and carry out operations concerning military photography, and how COMCAM photographers are on each occasion expected to repeat the steps described therein; on the other hand, the *Smart Book* includes graphic templates to be used by its photographers during the planning phase. Importantly, I understand templates to be *tools that promote repetition, precision, and standardization*. In principle, a template reduces or minimizes the scope for deviation in what is being produced, and establishes repetition in both form and content. Moreover, templates are as much about following established patterns as they are about establishing and following certain standards. In the context of photography, a brief look at the medium's history reveals that certain patterns function as if they were templates. For instance, when looking at the repetitiveness of early family portrait photography, we can extrapolate a template or a certain visual regime when such portraits are arranged next to each other. A more contemporary example is biometric photography for identification documents, where we often use photo booths which display clear guidelines – e.g., in the form geometric shapes displayed on the screen – to help us position our heads and faces correctly before the photograph is taken.[8] In both these examples, the tem- plate governs the image's composition and the arrangement of objects within

8   In her book, *Our Biometric Future: Facial Recognition Technology and the Culture of Surveillance*, Kelly A. Gates writes about the efforts taken by scientists to stabilize images of the face. In the context of pattern recognition, Gates speaks of "'facial templates'" (Gates 2011, 19). The "[c]omputer scientists" to whom she refers "have developed a variety of different techniques designed to translate an image of the face into a 'facial

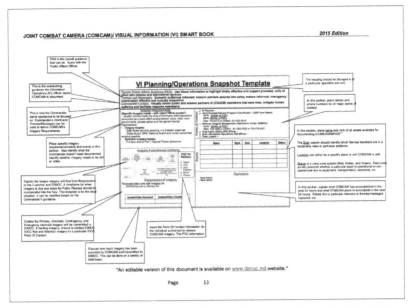

[Fig. 2] The "VI Planning/Operations Snapshot Template" accompanied by explanations of the sections and headings published in the *Joint Combat Camera (COMCAM) / Visual Information (VI): Smart Book* (Source: *Smart Book* 2015, 13). The appearance of US Department of Defense (DoD) visual information does not imply or constitute DoD endorsement.

the photograph. And, in both cases, the type of object/subject captured in the photographs remains the same.

In contrast to the repetition of objects and composition in the aforementioned examples, the "VI Planning/Operations Snapshot Template" [fig. 2] from the *Smart Book* acknowledges the variability of situations and subject matters which COMCAM photographers are likely to capture. Here, the notion of a template as a device to ensure a certain repetition refers to the complex procedures connected to taking the images themselves, rather than to the repetition of a compositional pattern. The standards that the COMCAM template seeks to establish are designed to ensure that the process of taking a photograph comprises the same steps regardless of the variability of the events or subjects being documented. Hence, it could be identified as an operational pattern "producing other similar things" (*Cambridge Dictionary* 2022a), where "things" are not to be confused with photographs.

The key focus of the "VI Planning/Operations Snapshot Template" is on the relationship between the COMCAM practices of production, post-production, and distribution. It is broken down into seven sections, some of which refer

template,' a smaller amount of data that can be compared against existing images stored in a comparison database" (Gates 2011, 17).

to considerations to be made by the photographer before capturing an image, while others focus on the subsequent distribution processes. In the upper section of this template, the photographer is required to write down the specifications received from the Public Affairs Officer, the Information Operations Officer, and the Commander concerning what they have been instructed to document.

The "Commander's Intent" heading demonstrates that, even before COMCAM photographers encounter an event, they may already have been informed of the desired interpretation their photographs should support (*Smart Book* 2015, 12 and 13). The "Imagery Requirements" section is the place where the photographers write down what they are permitted to capture, and here, they write down the requirements of the images and "identify what the Commander *doesn't want documented*" (*Smart Book* 2015, 13; italics added). These two sections summarize what the photographer has been instructed to document and list the restrictions concerning this documentation. Together, they demonstrate that, according to the *Smart Book*, a best-case scenario is when COMCAM photographers do not actually encounter events in a spontaneous or immediate way. Instead, the events themselves are defined prior to the act of photography, and thus are mediated even before they are captured. In addition to summarizing what should and should not be photographed, the "Imagery Requirements" section probably also allows the photographer to infer the preferred compositional and aesthetic features of the photographs they will be taking. Collectively, the prescriptions and restrictions listed in the "VI Planning/Operations Snapshot Template" seem to express the US military's desire to minimize any contingent elements in the production of COMCAM photographs.

In the context of other policies that determine how the US produces official images of armed conflicts, the process of defining and characterizing an event by means of a photograph that then becomes evidence of the event itself is not uncommon. In fact, Susan Sontag already reflected upon the counterintuitive nature of this process in relation to the photographic documentation of the Korean War (1950–3), when writing that "[t]he public did not see such photographs [showing the devastation of Korea] because there was, ideologically, no space for them" (Sontag 2008, 18). Decisions determining which photographs were distributed and viewed were highly dependent on the characterization of the Korean War by a handful of people working for the state apparatus. Sontag summarizes this idea as follows:

> Though an event has come to mean, precisely, something worth photographing, it is still ideology (in the broadest sense) that determines what constitutes an event. There can be no evidence, photographic or otherwise, of an event until the event itself has been named and characterized. And it is never photographic evidence which can construct

– more properly, identify – events; the contribution of photography
always follows the naming of the event. (Sontag 2008, 18f.)

That an event should first be characterized, and only then documented –
hence, providing evidence that it has actually happened – is also the view
taken by the authors of the *Smart Book*. The coincidence of the *Smart Book*'s
view with Sontag's is striking: both appear to present the idea of so-called
"pseudo-events" (Boorstin 1992) in relation to war or military photography.

Importantly, however, not every event is a "pseudo-event." Thus, I must take
issue with Sontag when she writes that what photography contributes to an
event "*always* follows the naming of the event" (Sontag 2008, 19; italics added).
This might be the case when photographs are used by the state apparatus to
present a certain perspective on an event, or to substantiate their characterization of it. But a photograph can do much more. Besides documenting a previously defined event, a photograph may have an event-like quality, or might
even constitute an event in itself. In his discussion of the 9/11 terror attacks,
Jean Baudrillard suggests that representations of the planes striking the Twin
Towers constitute just such an "image-event," which he defines as an "image
[that] consumes the event, in the sense that it absorbs it and offers it for
consumption" (Baudrillard 2003, 27). "Image-events" reverse the succession
identified by Sontag. In this case, the fascination lies from the start not in the
real event, but in its image (Baudrillard 2003, 27ff.). Nevertheless, the idea of
restricting or censoring an event even before it is captured by a photographer
is particularly relevant to the context of McCoy's photographs [fig. 1 and 3].

When reproducing McCoy's photographs, some journalists listed the
restrictions which may have applied to them. However, we learned about
these restrictions only *post factum*, and this information was not revealed by
the photographer himself. Exemplarily, following the news media's critiques
of these images, the DoD sought to justify the blackened goggles and facial
masks worn by the detainees by stating that this equipment was deployed
to comply with restrictions imposed by the Geneva Conventions on what
images of Prisoners of War are permitted to show (DoD 2002b), which state
that "prisoners of war must at all times be protected, particularly against acts
of violence or intimidation and against insults and public curiosity" (*Geneva
Convention III* (August 12, 1949), 87). Carol Rosenberg writes that the masks
were given to the detainees as part of the Pentagon's efforts to comply with
international law: "Pentagon policy to this day dictates that by shielding a
Guantánamo detainee's face from view – blurring it, chopping him off at his
beard, or in that instance, hidden beneath a cap, surgical mask and blindfold
– *spares a captive humiliation banned by the Geneva Conventions*" (Rosenberg
2008; italics added). I cannot say for certain whether McCoy was instructed not
to reveal the detainees' faces prior to taking the images, or if it was only during

[Fig. 3] A photograph showing the arrival of the first detainees at the Guantánamo detention camp taken by the COMCAM Photographer Shane T. McCoy on January 11, 2002, and published on January 18, 2002, by the DoD (Source: Shane T. McCoy and the DoD). The appearance of US Department of Defense (DoD) visual information does not imply or constitute DoD endorsement.

the final selection of the photographs that DoD officials took these restrictions into consideration – if, indeed, they did at all.

Whether or not McCoy used a template identical to the one in the *Smart Book* is not the question that I want to answer here; what I am primarily interested in is the high degree of attention COMCAM photographers are expected to pay to the image requirements *before* they take their photographs, attention we can presume McCoy paid to the instructions he no doubt received regarding his photographs. The significance of these requirements becomes particularly clear if we look at the "Imagery Flow/Release Authority" flowchart [fig. 4], which is also reproduced in the bottom left corner of the "VI Planning/ Operations Snapshot Template."

The requirements are positioned at the top of the flowchart, and thus serve as a starting point for all the subsequent steps taken by the photographer. The flowchart makes it clear that the imagery requirements are deployed as tools to control the meaning and interpretation of COMCAM photographs. Furthermore, the focus of the "VI Planning/Operations Snapshot Template" lies on the informational value of photography; thus, it is not a coincidence that

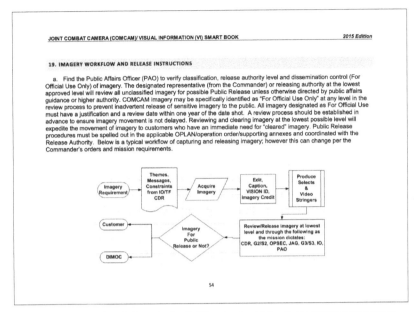

[Fig. 4] The "Imagery Flow/Release Authority" flowchart published in the *Joint Combat Camera (COMCAM) / Visual Information (VI): Smart Book* (Source: *Smart Book* 2015, 54). The appearance of US Department of Defense (DoD) visual information does not imply or constitute DoD endorsement.

the template's title contains the term "snapshot," rather than "photograph."[9] This is the only section in the manual where this term is employed, and hence may appear to be a minor matter. However, I will argue that this terminological decision is highly relevant – I believe it reveals a great deal about the understanding of photography within COMCAM itself, and within the DoD more generally. The *Merriam-Webster Dictionary* defines a "snapshot" as either "a casual photograph made typically by an amateur with a small handheld camera," or "an impression or view of something brief or transitory" (*Merriam-Webster Dictionary* 2022). A similar definition can be found in the *Cambridge Dictionary*, which describes a snapshot as "an informal photograph" (*Cambridge Dictionary* 2022b). In epistemic terms, however, a snapshot is "a piece of information or short description … [or] the way that a particular figure or set of figures gives an understanding of a situation at a particular time" (*Cambridge Dictionary* 2022b). The term also promotes the idea of photographs being

---

9 This is also the term used by Richard Chalfen in his book *Snapshot Versions of Life* to define photographs that belong to the "home mode [of] communication" (Chalfen 1987, 8).

candid and undistorted depictions of reality, which stands in stark contrast to the staging practices sometimes employed by COMCAM photographers.[10]

Clearly, McCoy's images [fig. 1 and 3] have nothing in common with informal photographs and, as I have discussed, it is highly probable that many of the steps in their production process were formalized. However, the definition of a snapshot as a certain configuration of knowledge appears to be highly relevant to the US military's understanding of photography. This definition aligns with the inclination demonstrated by both COMCAM and the DoD to value photographs primarily for their capacity to mediate information, where the aesthetic features of the images are secondary to their informational value. It would, nevertheless, be wrong to say that the US military regards aesthetic features as wholly irrelevant: such features are, indeed, valued, if they encourage the viewer to adopt the preferred interpretation of the information shown in the image.

Thus, one might also read the *Smart Book* in terms of a theory of photography. This theory might appear rudimentary because the manual neither acknowledges nor reflects upon what it is doing with it. Furthermore, rather than regarding photographs as aesthetic objects, the *Smart Book* explicitly reduces photography to mere functionality or instrumentality. The view of photography as a container for visual information might indeed be accurate in cases where photographs are used as internal briefing tools by generals and officials. However, when images produced by COMCAM, such as the ones taken by McCoy, are distributed to the wider public, then their aesthetic dimension comes into play as well. This also applies to my own perception of McCoy's photographs. Only moments after I grasped the subject of the high-angle photograph [fig. 1], I was thinking about its aesthetic features, such as its composition, lighting, perspective, and so on. Crucially, the *Smart Book*'s authors are interested in both these aspects: on the one hand, they consider the information which a photograph is intended to transmit; on the other, they look at the ways in which a photograph informs the viewer.

The *Smart Book* addresses the question of the "how" and the photograph's aesthetic features in a condensed form, summarizing its aesthetic guidelines for photography and video in the form of "Five C's": "Camera Angles, Continuity, Cutting, Close-ups, and Composition" (*Smart Book* 2015, 22). I will discuss these "Five C's" in connection to two of McCoy's photographs, the aforementioned high-angle image, and a second one depicting the same scene from a different angle [fig. 3].

10   Staging scenes is described in the *Smart Book* as a potential strategy when the action can be controlled. Due to the "uncontrolled environment" in which COMCAM photographers usually work, the photographer is advised to "[u]se a Wide or Establishing Shot during the initial part of the event" (*Smart Book* 2015, 21), which probably also allows the photographer to crop the image in the post-production phase.

The first C, the camera angle, is described as the relation between the camera and the subject(s) (*Smart Book* 2015, 22). The angles deployed in both of McCoy's photographs are listed in the *Smart Book* and exemplified by one photograph for each angle (*Smart Book* 2015, 22).

The second C is the requirement to provide a "continuous, smooth logical flow of visual images, depicting the event in a coherent manner" (*Smart Book* 2015, 23). If we look at McCoy's photographs in relation to one another, we can recognize a fluent depiction of a single, continuous event, reflecting this logic. The viewers ability to montage his photographs as part of a single series is especially important when considering their production circumstances and the second C of the *Smart Book*. It appears that McCoy first sought to establish an overview of the scene [fig. 1], and then immersed himself more deeply in it [fig. 3].[11] This sense of immersion is effected thanks to the camera's perspective in the second photograph, which creates the impression that McCoy is one of the soldiers assigned to surveil the detainees from outside the cage.

The third C is concerned with the post-production phase of COMCAM photographs. The term "cutting" (which the *Smart Book* also calls "culling") describes the process of deleting certain shots or images which are of poor quality, contain "superfluous information," or are duplicates (*Smart Book* 2015, 24).

The fourth C, the close-up, which is also designated as belonging to the camera angle, is singled out as "a tool … transport[ing] the viewer into the image or scene," and adding an emotional layer to the photograph (*Smart Book* 2015, 25). Thus, instead of being simply one of the many field sizes available, the close-up is described as especially useful when it comes to telling the viewer the whole story. Close-ups are basically intended to reveal a detail of a scene, or to explain an event. The *Smart Book*, however, makes it clear that the close-up should never be employed as the "only tool during documentation," despite its ability to "tell the entire story"; instead, it must be presented in relation to other photographs (*Smart Book* 2015, 25). Hence, even though the second image [fig. 3] is not a close-up in technical terms, according to the logic of the *Smart Book*, it comes to function as one when viewed in relation to the high-angle photograph.

In the framework of storytelling, when the two images are combined, they enhance the feeling of a virtual space. Writing about the perception of space in film, Vinzenz Hediger argues that when film viewers combine the three dimensions of filmic space – the architectural space, the image-space, and

---

11   At this point, I want to reflect upon the way in which I have presented McCoy's photographs. I intuitively placed fig. 1 before fig. 3 because the former shows an overview of the arrangement of subjects, objects, and architecture, while the latter zooms into the scene and provides the viewer with a closer look through the wire.

the space imagined by the spectator – this space acquires the features of a virtual space (Hediger 2015, 61). According to Hediger, the virtual space is not only intended to be comprehended, but also becomes a space that can be walked through. What Hediger defines as virtual space in film applies equally to photographic sequences. In the case of McCoy's photographs, the camera movement is perceivable thanks to a mental montage [fig. 1 and 3], which moves the viewer "virtually" from a position seemingly floating in the air to one on the ground, next to the soldiers. The experience of movement engendered by photography would thus appear to be productively informed by theories of filmic perception, and specifically, by the technique of montage. The *Smart Book* makes this explicit when it mentions that "[s]equencing photographic moments in much the same manner videographers use scenes tells the complete story" (*Smart Book* 2015, 21).

The fifth and final C focuses on the aesthetic composition of a single shot. The aim of the composition is described as creating "a unified, harmonious whole" (*Smart Book* 2015, 26). Interestingly, this composition rule is informed by the media-specificity of photography and video/film, respectively, highlighting the fact that photography arrests a moment solely in space, whereas video is composed of both space and time.[12] According to the *Smart Book*, the photograph can compensate for the lack of a perceivable progression in time by utilizing a compositional technique that indicates movement (*Smart Book* 2015, 26). The composition is also identified as being of central importance in the determination of the relationship between the viewers – who are described as desiring to "see a story" (*Smart Book* 2015, 26) – and the photograph. A "good composition," according to the *Smart Book*, is capable of keeping the viewers interested in what is depicted in a photograph and, in the context of still images, is also capable of virtually moving them through space and time (*Smart Book* 2015, 26).

As I have demonstrated, both the "VI Planning/Operations Snapshot Template," and the "Five C's," are tacitly concerned with the issue of contingency, which, according to the *Smart Book*, should be reduced by the templates and the aesthetic principles deployed by COMCAM photographers. On the one hand, the "VI Planning/Operations Snapshot Template" stabilizes the procedure of taking a photograph, so that it can be reproduced even in the vastly divergent situations these photographers may encounter. The standardization provided by such templates is designed to minimize procedural contingency and to ensure that each photographed event is mediated in line with the specifications formulated by higher-ranking military officials. On the

---

12   The first four C's apply to videos and photographs alike; the fifth rule is formulated solely for photography: "The four previous C's can be interchanged between photography and videography almost without exception. Composition, however, has unique attributes when independently applied to photography and videography" (*Smart Book* 2015, 26).

other hand, the five C's appear to be built around the idea of minimizing contingency altogether. However, here it is not the contingency of the production processes alone that is in question, but also of the future interpretation of the images produced. Hence, another key issue is how the aspects of COMCAM's photographic practices discussed in this subsection are geared towards a strict governance of the viewers' perception of the images created and distributed by COMCAM photographers.

The Frame of Caption Writing

Photojournalism, COMCAM, and News Images

Up to this point, I have discussed the techniques of governance brought into play during the production process of COMCAM photographs. According to the *Smart Book*, the guidelines established by the "VI Planning/Operations Snapshot Template" and the "Five C's" do not suffice to ensure and stabilize a single, privileged interpretation of the information transported in an image. This stability must be further enhanced by a written caption, which accompanies the photograph when it is distributed to higher-ranking officials or the news media – a practice also common in the fields of photojournalism and art photography. Importantly, photographs released by the DoD are nearly always accompanied by captions intended to stabilize their meanings,[13] although, as I will later demonstrate, newspapers do not always simply reproduce these captions in their articles. Before going into a detailed discussion of the captioning practice within COMCAM and the captions written by McCoy, I will describe how the fields of photojournalism and COMCAM inform each other with regard to captioning. McCoy's photographs, and McCoy himself, set these fields in relation to each other, and we can identify at least three points where they clearly intersect with regard to the 2002 DoD photographs.

Firstly, if the viewer does not realize that McCoy is a military photographer – for example, because the newspaper in which his images are reproduced fails to clarify their source – they might assume that the photographs were taken by an independent photojournalist, by which I mean, one who is not working for the US government. Such an assumption does not feel far-fetched, since McCoy's images have shed a negative light on the US military's detention practices and had an extremely unfavorable effect on its media image. It would thus seem reasonable for some viewers to conclude that the images could not have been produced and distributed by the DoD. Here, I am also speaking from my own experience, since I was very surprised when I learned the provenance of these images, and felt certain they must have been

---

13   In Chapter 4, I will discuss cases where the DoD does exactly the opposite, and instead increases the polysemic nature of photographs.

taken by an independent photojournalist. Confusion over the photographs' origin and the motivation behind their publication was also shared by some politicians. For instance, in a statement during a sitting of the House of Lords in the British Parliament on January 21, 2002, Lord Howell of Guildford summarized this paradox quite sharply: "If those pictures were not really a true depiction of the way in which those people are being held, I am slightly left wondering why a US Navy photographer took them and why they were circulated world-wide. I do not understand the motive for doing that. They certainly gave the situation a very ugly appearance" (UK Parliament 2002).

Secondly, classifying the first photographs from the Guantánamo detention facility as potentially photojournalistic corresponds with McCoy's self-description on his LinkedIn profile as a "Combat Photojournalist" (McCoy 2022) and not as a COMCAM photographer. This job title suggests that photo-journalism is one of the main discursive fields to which he refers when placing his profession in a broader context. The way McCoy describes his job below this title, however, complicates the situation by revealing that he is also an internal documentarian or archivist for the US military. McCoy writes that, between May 1999 and December 2002, he "had the responsibility of shooting a variety of high interest events including the burial at sea of JFK Jr. and detainee operations at GITMO [Guantánamo], Cuba" (McCoy 2022). He adds that his photographs were "used to brief the Joint Chiefs of Staff and high-level government employees" (McCoy 2022). This job description mirrors the answer which McCoy gave in an interview with Rosenberg, where he claimed that the initial reason for the production of photographs in question was to inform DoD officials of what was occurring at the Guantánamo detention facility, and to reveal whether or not the operation involving the arrival of the first detainees was a success (Rosenberg 2008). Apparently, it was only later that the DoD decided to publish a couple of McCoy's images on their official webpage.

Thirdly and lastly, the *Smart Book* refers to documents and guidelines on captioning styles written by the Associated Press (AP) for photojournalists, which I will elaborate on in more detail in the next subsection. COMCAM thus connects its own practices directly to the established discourses within the field of photojournalism.

While I have identified the potential points of connection between McCoy's photographs and photojournalism, I have also implicitly distinguished the pro-fession of COMCAM photographers from that of photojournalists and the field of military photography from photojournalism. A closer look at this distinction might help us to understand the various functions, production circumstances, and institutional and discursive framings at play in McCoy's photographs. Whereas the DoD provides a clear definition for the profession of a COMCAM photographer, I have found it much more difficult to derive a coherent

definition of the profession of a photojournalist from scholarly and professional discourses. I suggest that there are at least two reasons for this: on
the one hand, there have been a series of shifts or ruptures in the history of
the term "photojournalism," and, on the other, the field of photojournalism is
heterogenous in itself. Although photojournalistic practices existed before the
50s, it was only in the beginning of that decade that the term was popularized
(Paddock 2017, 77). Furthermore, what was, or is, considered to be photojournalism – as well as what has been retrospectively defined as photojournalistic practice – has been subject to many changes over time. For instance,
"[t]he concept of a photographer as an individual practitioner of photojournalism did not always exist. Until the early 1950s, the photographer was
a camera operator. It was the picture editor who practiced photojournalism"
(Paddock 2017, 77).

Although it is difficult to formulate a coherent definition of photojournalistic practices, one way to define concepts or a set of practices is by way of
contrast. Hence, photojournalism could be defined in opposition to another
"photography genre." For example, the conclusion of Thierry Gervais' book,
The Making of Visual News: A History of Photography in the Press, relates photojournalism to art photography (Gervais 2017, 181–6). Gervais points out that the
terminological confrontation between these two photographic fields, which
have now become closely related to each other, is not solely the concern of
academics, but also of practitioners themselves. More specifically, Gervais
refers to a statement made by Jeff Wall in his discussion with Roy Arden, published in 1999 (Gervais 2017, 185). Wall stated that if a photographer wants to
situate their photographs in a specific field, they need to adopt a clear stance
towards photojournalism:

> But photojournalism was, and is, such a *dominant social institution*
> that it seemed that everyone positioned themselves in relation to it.
> Photojournalism makes use of photography the way it makes use of
> written language or television or now the Internet. It uses any medium.
> In that sense, photojournalism has nothing necessary [*sic*] to do with
> photography. But reportage derives from the medium. Pictures in the
> vernaculars of photography are acts of reportage that are not codified in
> advance, not subject to the rhetorics of *the institution of journalism*. (Arden
> and Wall 1999, 17; italics added)

Instead of focusing on the notion of photojournalism, Wall and Arden focus
on *vernacular photography* that "is more inclusive" (Arden and Wall 1999, 16)
than the former. In this conversation, Wall pointedly differentiates between
photojournalism, an "art-concept of photojournalism," reportage – and, what
is important to note here is that the citation works in reverse: rather than
photojournalism being defined in contrast to other photographic practices, it
is instead described as the dominant institutional discourse of photography in

the 90s. Artists had thus to actively dissociate themselves and their practices from photojournalism if they did not want their photographs to be perceived as photojournalistic. Arden responds to Wall by arguing that photojournalism "is largely governed by economic interests," and that reportage has an actual place in art photography (Arden and Wall 1999, 17). Both criticize the way in which photography is used in the institution of photojournalism, and compare it to the use of written language or television. For them, it is important that photography should be free from such obvious illustrative uses and institutional pressures.

I have emphasized Wall's idea of photojournalism as a "dominant social institution" (Arden and Wall 1999, 17) because it helps to draw a line between the work of a COMCAM photographer and that of a photojournalist by looking more closely at institutional frameworks. It is true that COMCAM photographs stand in opposition to "[p]ictures in the vernaculars of photography" (Arden and Wall 1999, 17), since they are clearly subject to the institutional rhetoric of the DoD. However, the institutional frameworks of COMCAM photographers and photojournalists can also overlap – for instance, in the educational backgrounds of people working in both fields. Whereas the introduction of photojournalism courses in US journalism schools played an important role in the institutionalization of photojournalism, such courses are also provided for COMCAM photographers by the DoD through the Defense Information School, which teaches "public affairs, print journalism, photography, video production, broadcast journalism, broadcast equipment maintenance, and various forms of graphic design and digital media" (Defense Information School 2022). COMCAM photographers themselves have also revealed that they learned about photographic practices at photojournalism schools. For example, COMCAM photographer Derrick Goode – who was a photojournalism instructor at the Defense Information School from 2012 to 2015 – stated in a documentary that he actively employed knowledge acquired in photo-journalism school: "I look for detail and I look for the moment, which is, you know, what *we're taught in photojournalism school*, just trying to capture the moment" (MAHARBAL5022 2015, 9:33–42; italics added).

Along with the question of education, the issue of authorship is also crucial. For Gervais, proof of the establishment of photojournalism as an institution is the "subjective involvement by the photographer, a specific aesthetic and the circulation of the images" (Gervais 2017, 182). Gervais shows that, at a certain point in time, photojournalists came to be understood as *auteurs*:

> This legitimation mechanism draws on the figure of the *auteur* as sym-
> bolizing the achievement of a status as creator and cultural producer
> whose pictures are henceforth disseminated in a variety of forms. The
> photographer is now an *auteur*: while not relinquishing the use value of
> his images, he aspires at the same time to cultural recognition by the

traditional structures of legitimation, and thus subverts the habitual status of his photographs. This shift notably hinges on the photographer's personality and subjectivity. (Gervais 2017, 182)

The notion of authorship would appear to be one of the central aspects distinguishing photojournalists from COMCAM photographers. When the news media publish images shot by COMCAM photographers – for example, as part of an official handout – they are often credited either to the DoD, or to the image agencies responsible for distributing them. In contrast, photographs taken by independent photojournalists are more often credited with the photographer's name, alongside that of the agency.[14]

A strong argument for the irrelevance of the concept of authorship within COMCAM has been made by McCoy himself. In his interview with Rosenberg, he emphasized the automatism of the camera by revealing that he was not even looking through the viewfinder while shooting the infamous Guantánamo photographs (Rosenberg 2008). Apparently, it was not important to him to be identified as the author and producer of these images. In addition, the military discourse about COMCAM explicitly excludes the idea of COMCAM photographers being the owners of their photographs. A document published by the Defense Information School illustrates this by contrasting them with freelance photographers (The Defense Information School 2020, 3). While the latter are defined by a commercial intent, and by being the copyright holder of their images, the images taken by the former belong to the US government: "COMCAM forces are not freelance photographers competing for commercial use of imagery obtained while in the line of duty. The imagery belongs to the US government, not the individual" (The Defense Information School 2020, 3).

Historically, the emergence of the figure of the *auteur* in photojournalism has also been related to the notion of authorship in art photography.[15] Gervais illustrates the close relationship between photojournalism and art photography by discussing James Nachtwey's photographs of the Balkan conflict taken in the 90s (Gervais 2017, 182). The photographs were initially commissioned by *Life* magazine; however, after appearing there, the images went on to be exhibited all over the world, and they have also been republished in form of photo books. Nachtwey's images have been distributed by

14 Of course, there is also the huge field of commissioned photography in which the name of the photographer often remains unmentioned. Many famous art photographers have been commissioned for various jobs – some of which were credited to them, while others remained anonymous.

15 The understanding of photographers as *auteurs* is closely related to legal frameworks, and to the question of the regulation of copyright. In Germany, for instance, it was only in 1907 that photography came to be protected by copyright law, and that "the photographer's achievement [was recognized] … beyond the purely mechanical" (Blaschke 2016, 35).

many different institutions, and this has not only potentially changed the ways in which they have been perceived, but also their categorization and function. As the discussion of Wall's photographs by Gervais emphasizes, distribution channels play a relatively powerful role in the entire process of defining and delineating types of photographs, or ascribing them to genres. In fact, it is common for photographs originating in the field of photojournalism or taken for the press to have many other afterlives in galleries and books of "art." Conversely, in his book, *The Spoken Image: Photography and Language*, Clive Scott advocates an even more radical view when he writes that every photograph, regardless of its production context, can be transformed into a photojournalistic image:

> Photographic genres – photojournalism, documentary photography, the family snap, the nude, etc. – may be said to exist, but photographs do not belong to them by any inherent right. Rather, a context is expressly created for the photograph, often and predominantly through language, which of itself assigns the photograph to a genre. *No photograph is necessarily, say, photojournalistic; photojournalistic photographs are photographs used by newspapers.* (Scott 1999, 99; italics added)

Scott stresses that genre classifications are highly dependent on the publishing context, and in particular, the language of the caption accompanying a photograph, rather than any aesthetic features or the circumstances under which they were taken. I agree with Scott's emphasis on the importance of distribution channels; however, I also believe a photograph's production context is of equal importance. Supporting my perspective, Mary Angela Bock writes that "[t]he context of a photograph's production is intrinsic to its meaning. There is a limit to what can be said of a photograph or video clip without learning of its inception" (Bock 2008, 170). The importance of the production context contradicts Scott's thesis that every photograph becomes photojournalistic by virtue of being printed in a newspaper (Scott 1999, 99). My own hesitation about conceding everything to publishing context lies in the inescapable intentionality, whether institutional or personal, which I would assign to some photographs. For example, photographs produced for propaganda purposes usually construct ideologically coherent worldviews, and their production contexts are crucial to the ways in which we come to understand their meanings.

Caption Writing in Photojournalism and COMCAM

Due to the instability of interpretation, and the dependence of a photograph's meaning on its context, many different practices have arisen with the aim of stabilizing an image's meanings through context – particularly, the addition of a caption. As I have mentioned, when the DoD published McCoy's photographs on their website, each image was accompanied by a short text, which we can presume McCoy wrote himself, since he explicitly mentioned in his interview with Rosenberg that writing captions was part of his job (Rosenberg 2008). Nevertheless, it is unclear whether the caption cited in the epigraph to this chapter, released with the high-angle photograph [fig. 1], is an exact repro- duction of the caption initially written by McCoy – it may have been edited for the press release by someone else. Despite this uncertainty, considering what McCoy said in his interview, coupled with the information from the *Smart Book*, I will argue that, within the US military, photographs are configured from the start in relation to written text. The range of texts associated with COMCAM photographs includes the specifications given to the photographer with regard to what they are instructed to capture, and the caption written by them after they have taken their "snapshot." The discourse within the US military reveals that captions are regarded as a central element in the configuration of an image: no photograph speaks to the viewer, or tells the story, all by itself.[16] Major Matthew Yandura stated that "a Well-Focused [*sic*] Combat Cameraman can tip the scales in the battle for words, deeds and images" (Soldier Media Center Videos 2010, 0:03–12), which emphasizes the equal importance the military attaches to these three different elements.

Considering Sontag's view on the inability of photographs to explain anything (Sontag 2008, 23), and the close relationship between words and images put forth in military documents, it is imperative to analyze photographs dis- tributed through the official channels of the DoD in terms of both the visual and the textual configurations within which they appear. Specifically, with regard to print media, this analysis should focus on the various configurations of photograph, written caption, and text in the article. Since my reading of the *Smart Book* has demonstrated that the US military perceives photography and video to be media that cannot necessarily be trusted, primarily because of the uncertainty ascribed to their final interpretation, it is crucial to analyze how COMCAM photographers (re)frame their images during the post-production process. Thus, I will focus on the way the *Smart Book* presents captioning and, more specifically, analyze how captioning, as a practice of reframing or consolidating the given frames governing a photograph, figures as part of the attempt to stabilize the viewers' interpretation of images.

The *Smart Book* describes captions as a standardized element in the processes of production and distribution. The chapter entitled "DoD Captioning Style Guide" provides COMCAM photographers with clear guidance about how to caption an image (*Smart Book* 2015, 80–90). The rules are given as an addition

---

16   Some scholars have argued that not all images necessarily require captions. See, for
      example, *No Caption Needed: Iconic Photographs, Public Culture, and Liberal Democracy*
      (2017), in which Robert Hariman and John Louis Lucaites argue that photographs which
      have acquired a so-called "iconic status" do not need captions.

to the "Associated Press (AP) Style Guide" (*Smart Book* 2015, 80),[17] and thus act as an annex to the established rules of captioning for photojournalists. Importantly, while the *AP Stylebook*'s rules on caption writing apply to all sorts of images circulating in the news media; the *Smart Book* updates them for the requirements of COMCAM operations. The *AP Stylebook* encourages the photographer or photojournalist to restrict the caption to two sentences. "The first sentence of the caption describes *what* the photo shows, in present tense, and states *where* and *when* the photo was made"; the second "gives background on the news event or describes *why* the photo is significant" (AP 2000, 380; italics added). The person submitting the caption along with the photograph is advised to bear in mind what will be regarded as the most important information for the reader. In a similar way, the *Smart Book* enumerates five W-questions that should be answered in a caption written by the COMCAM photographer: Who? What? When? Where? Why? (*Smart Book* 2015, 80–2). The *Smart Book* reframes these rules for the military context, adding further details that are of importance if the caption's subject is a military employee. Section H, "Constructing a Caption," gives a brief overview of the practice of captioning:

> (1) The first sentence contains the 5 W's and is always written in the present tense using active voice. A caption describes the moment the image is captured, not what came before or after, so the first sentence will be written as if from that moment. (2) The second sentence should almost always be written in past tense. This sentence gives background information on the image. It explains why the image is significant and places it in a larger context. When providing background information in a caption, include information that explains the significance of the action in the image. (*Smart Book* 2015, 82)

Bearing in mind the largely negative reactions to McCoy's photographs by the news media and human rights organizations, a comprehensive analysis of these images necessitates a discussion of the accompanying caption, not just of what the images themselves show. Consequently, with regard to the five W-questions, it becomes evident that McCoy's caption answers the final question – *Why?* – in only a rudimentary fashion, as I will discuss later. The "non-compliance" of this caption with the guidelines stands in stark contrast to the importance which the *Smart Book* authors ascribe to answering this question. The *Smart Book* mentions at least twice that, when creating a caption, the photographer must describe the significance of what is depicted in the image, and that the caption should "place ... it [the photograph] in a larger context"

---

17   The "Associated Press (AP) Style Guide" probably means *Associated Press Stylebook and Briefing on Media Law* (AP 2000), a guide that is generally published on an annual basis by the AP. In the following passages, I will abbreviate the full title of this publication as follows: *AP Stylebook*.

(*Smart Book* 2015, 82). The caption is ultimately expected to explain what a photograph is showing and to stabilize its preferred interpretation.

The various responses to McCoy's photographs demonstrate the dynamic relationship between the meanings of these photographs and the context within which they were published. Discussing the relationship between meaning and context, Jan Baetens is right to argue that there is a "difficulty with limiting 'meaning' to itself, that is, with keeping 'meaning' safe from 'context'" (Baetens 2007, 54). With regard to photography, this results in the circumstance that one and the same image is capable of evoking different meanings and understandings – in other words, the photographic image is *polysemic*. Within literary studies, the majority of discussions regarding the polysemy of photographs have historically focused on the semantic instability of photography in negative terms. It has often been stressed that the ontology of the photographic image made it "vulnerab[le] to the characteristics of its seemingly opposite pole: the text and, more broadly speaking, the time-based arts" (Baetens 2007, 60). This pessimistic view on the dominance of the written word over the photographic image is not only questionable; it is also linked to a disciplinary bias.[18] In the context of the discussion of McCoy's photographs, it is necessary to shift the focus from a relationship of dominance to an understanding of the relationship between photography and the written word as a dynamic one marked by kinship. When discussing the images produced by COMCAM, neither the notion of dominance of the written word over images, nor its reverse, is particularly helpful. In light of the *Smart Book*'s view that a written text can help define, fashion, and stabilize the meaning and interpretation of a photograph, we need to open up this discussion by abandoning the idea of dominance, and shifting our focus to the dynamic aspects of the relationship between text and image.

In other contexts, however, captioning may have different aims from those of COMCAM, and not all of them are supposed to ensure a stable interpretation of the image. Historically, since the emergence of photography, scientists and artists have employed captions in a variety of ways and forms; for example, captions have been used to describe what given photographs depict, but they have also provoked viewers to challenge photographs' proposed meaning. Sometimes, captions have nothing to do with the photographs

18   Baetens shows that many prominent theories of photography have been written by scholars with a background in literary studies, and that this has led to a focus on the discrepancies and similarities between the written word and the photographic image (Baetens 2007, 60). It is important to acknowledge that there have also been significant historical changes within the discipline of literary studies. For instance, by referring to the "linguistic turn" in 1994, Gottfried Boehm introduced the discussion of the "iconic turn" (Boehm 1994). Debates on the "iconic turn" have, in a certain sense, rehabilitated the position of images in this historical discussion. Another prominent position is that taken by W. J. T. Mitchell. In his book, *Picture Theory: Essays on Verbal and Visual Representation*, he developed the idea of a "pictorial turn" (Mitchell 1994).

themselves, leaving it up to the viewer to make the connection, or to playfully acknowledge that there simply is none. Due to the variety of captions, there is also a scholarly desire to systematize their different styles and aims, but the plethora of published photographs and captions makes the fulfillment of this desire nearly impossible. Despite the many difficulties in undertaking a historical systematization of captions, Scott identifies two types of captions and three functions in the titles assigned to photographs. On the one hand, he argues that a title can function

> a) as destination, as that which explains and synthesizes the image, gives it its coherence – this is particularly the function of allegorical or descriptive titles; (b) as point of departure, something minimal and non-interfering, which orientates the spectator and then leaves the image to do its work; (c) as parallel but displaced commentary, set at a distance from the picture, so that the meaning is neither in the picture nor in the title, but in their point of convergence. (Scott 1999, 47)

A caption, on the other hand, assumes either the form of a "rebus" or a "quote/direct speech" (Scott 1999, 49 and 52). The rebus strengthens the dependency between meaning and context: in this case, the meaning of a photograph is highly dependent on the photographer, or the newspaper editor, who is in charge of captioning. The "quotational or direct-speech caption" (Scott 1999, 52) functions differently, since it addresses the viewer directly, and creates a straightforward connection between the photograph, the newspaper editor, and the viewer.

If we recall McCoy's caption which was provided with fig. 1, we will discover it is difficult to assign it to one of these types. This caption contains additional information that, in a certain sense, "complements" what is depicted in the image: it mentions what will happen next, and explains why the detainees are kneeling on the ground. Its language is one of military simplicity, directness, and specificity, which moves it far from the rebus caption, and puts it closer to the "quotational type." But McCoy's caption does not create a direct link to the viewer either – if there is any straightforward connection between the viewer and McCoy's photograph, it is created by the perspective taken by the camera. Nevertheless, the precision with which McCoy describes the depicted scene resembles that of a quotation and thus I would hesitantly place his caption in Scott's second category. On a further note, because the photographs were not given titles by the DoD, or by the AP, the texts that accompany them serve a twofold function: on the one hand, as captions, and, on the other, as titles – it appears to me that McCoy's caption for the high-angle photograph functions as a destination, since it seemingly "explains and synthesizes the image" (Scott 1999, 47).

If we want to understand the relationship between meaning and context of McCoy's photographs, we also have to analyze the significant differences between the original captions, and the captions written for them by the newspapers. It would appear that the way COMCAM and the DoD attempt to regulate captioning differs from the manner in which the newspapers actually used their captions. Alan Sparrow, the Chairman of the UK Picture Editors Guild, told me in a brief conversation that it is very unlikely that a newspaper would reproduce the caption provided by the image agency or photographer word-for-word. The caption is usually rewritten in the form of a two or three-liner by a subeditor who primarily deals with text, and not by the photo editor. Notably, many print newspapers only published parts of the original caption; some of the newspaper captions did not include the photographer's name and/or failed to mention the DoD as the releasing authority, instead naming the image agency that distributed the image.

Reframing Combat Camera Photographs

The Newspapers' Responses to McCoy's Photographs[19]

I will now take a closer look at some of these newspapers to demonstrate the crucial discrepancies in the captions that I have described above, and explore how Rumsfeld subsequently responded to the critical reframing of McCoy's photographs. On January 21, 2002, *The Guardian* published a cropped version of the high-angle photograph [fig. 1] with the following caption: "The picture that caused the storm: Al-Qaeda suspects, manacled hand and foot and wearing masks, kneel before their guards. The photograph is one of the series released by the Pentagon" (Burkeman, Norton-Taylor, and Watt 2002, front page). This caption does not identify the photographer, although it does state that the photograph was released by the US authorities. The *Boston Globe* also published the same photograph on the same day, printing the following caption beneath the image: "In this photo from the US Department of Defense, made available Friday, prisoners suspected of Taliban and Al Qaeda ties sit in a holding area at Camp X-Ray in Guantánamo Bay, Cuba. The photos raised concern in Britain about treatment of the men" (Gardiner 2002, A8). Here, AP Images is identified as the news agency distributing the photograph.[20] The

---

19   I am particularly interested in the relationship between the photograph and the written caption and thus my focus lies primarily on newspapers. Although television also played an important role in the circulation of McCoy's photographs, it is rather uncommon for news broadcasters to include a caption with an image. In the following analysis, I focus on examples from the US newspapers with the largest circulation including the *Boston Globe*, the *Los Angeles Times*, and the *Chicago Tribune*; I also include the front page from *The Guardian* since it is one of the more critically engaged international newspapers.

20   Since this photograph was part of a handout from the DoD, the AP was not selling its copyright. An employee of the AP told me that these photographs and their captions

Chicago Tribune published one of McCoy's photographs on January 19, 2002. Their caption reads: "Al Qaeda and Taliban detainees kneel under close guard last week as they are checked in at the US prison camp in Guantánamo Bay, Cuba. The photo was released by the Pentagon on Friday" (AP 2002, 4). The image is credited with the name of the photographer and reveals his affiliation to the US military. The final example comes from the *Los Angeles Times* which closely covered the arrival of the first detainees at the camp. For example, on January 26, 2002, eight days after McCoy's photographs were released, the *Los Angeles Times* published his second photograph [fig. 3]. The text to which the photograph was linked was a short letter from one of the newspaper's readers entitled "Treatment of Detainees is Justified" (Sobin 2002, B18). The caption named the AP as the image agency and titled the photograph: "Detainees at Guantánamo Bay" (Sobin 2002, B18).

Interestingly, some of the cited newspaper captions and titles refer explicitly to how McCoy's photographs were discussed in the British press and Parliament (UK Parliament 2002), informing the reader that "[t]he photos raised concern in Britain about treatment of the men" (Gardiner 2002, A8), identifying "[t]he picture that caused the storm" (Burkeman, Norton-Taylor, and Watt 2002, 1), or entitling the accompanying article "Prisoner Photos Trouble British" (Gardiner 2002, A8). These captions and titles reframed the photographs with an alternative narrative – one that was less concerned with what followed the moment in which McCoy took the photographs, and more with the ensuing public debate on the images. Some of the captions and titles are also referring to the January 20, 2002, edition of the British tabloid, the *Mail on Sunday*, which published McCoy's second photograph on its front cover [fig. 5]. In the upper part of the reproduced photograph, the newspaper's readers were confronted with a one-word headline in capital letters: "TORTURED" (*Mail on Sunday* 2002). The editorial staff photoshopped the image and partially superimposed the silhouettes of the soldiers over the letters of the headline. This superimposition breaks the frame of McCoy's photograph and creates the impression that the military guards are emerging out of the image. In the bottom right-hand corner of the cover page, readers were provided with a longer text, a commentary that also acquires the function of a caption: "They can hear nothing, smell nothing, feel nothing. Manacled hand and foot, they kneel in submission. Is this how Bush and Blair defend our civilisation?" (*Mail on Sunday* 2002).

The superimposition of this text over the image is a second rupture of the photographic frame. The use of such visual techniques on McCoy's photograph has powerful consequences for the way in which the viewer perceptually experiences the image. Scott succinctly summarizes such perceptual

were probably included in a newswire provided to subscription clients. Unfortunately, I have not been able to verify this, since the newswires are only archived for one month.

[Fig. 5] The context provided by the title story of the January 20, 2002, edition of *Mail on Sunday* shed a critical light on the treatment of the detainees visible in the photographs taken by Shane T. McCoy. As the cover page makes clear, the practices depicted in these images were identified as torture (© dmg media licensing).

consequences in terms of an "eye … [being] constantly harassed by images lifting off the page, goaded into a promiscuous assimilation of the news" (Scott 1999, 108). Even on its own terms, McCoy's photograph might already harass the viewers if they feel that a soldier's point of view is being imposed on them by the camera's perspective, especially if it is a view to which they are ideologically opposed. The *Mail on Sunday* further emphasizes the photograph's three-dimensional quality by means of the added headline and the superimposed text. This suggests that, in the tabloid format, McCoy's photograph is not only intended to be looked at; it also immerses the viewer by encouraging them to virtually walk through the scene in the image. This kind of immersion could potentially be experienced by the viewer as harassing not only their eye but also their body.

On page two and three readers were provided with two further photographs and an illustration of the detention cages at Camp X-Ray. The related article entitled "Horror of Camp X-Ray," written by Rosenberg and William Lowther, appeared with the following subtitle: "First Pictures Show Use of Sensory Deprivation to Soften up Suspects for Interrogation" (Lowther and Rosenberg 2002, 2f.). The longer texts printed on or directly beside the photographs seem to assume the function of distinct commentaries, neither naming the copyright holder nor the author of the images, as a COMCAM caption would usually do. The source of the photographs, and McCoy as their creator, however, are mentioned in a very small, barely readable, caption in the right bottom corner of the image reproduced on the front page: "SHANE T. MCCOY / US NAVY." Hence, instead of providing the readers with the production context of the images, these longer captions function as a straightforward commentary on the subjects and practices depicted in the photographs, and deliver a strong interpretation of them. Meanwhile, the text appearing on the *Mail on Sunday*'s front page [fig. 5] seems to refer directly to the caption written by McCoy and, more specifically, to the part where he mentions the orange jumpsuits. The *Mail on Sunday*'s text elaborates in even greater detail on the equipment given to detainees and, in addition, mentions the consequences for their perception of the outer world by stating that the detainees cannot hear, see, smell, or feel anything. The text emphasizes the fact that the detainees have been stripped of nearly all agency. Chief Medical Officer of Amnesty International, Jim West, made an important comment on the use of this equipment as a means to humiliate the detainees when he pointed out that, because the men had already left the airplane, there was no reason for them to keep the gear on; thus, the only grounds for doing so was "an attempt to degrade the man" (as cited in Lowther and Rosenberg 2002, 3).

The accusations of torture brought by the journalists and editorial staff of the *Mail on Sunday*, alongside other contributions in newspapers and the broadcast media, fueled a worldwide discussion about the detention practices at Guantánamo. The articles and debates forced Rumsfeld to publicly respond to this criticism. In his appearance at a news briefing on January 22, 2002, he emphasized, on the one hand, the instability of interpretation inherent in McCoy's photographs, and, on the other, the "humane treatment" of the detainees (DoD 2002b). He argued that McCoy's photographs had been wrongly reframed by the news media: "[w]hat happened was, someone took a picture – and we released it, apparently – of them [the detainees] in that corridor, kneeling down while their head pieces are being taken off, and people made a whole – *drew a whole lot of conclusions* about how terrible that was that they're being held in that corridor" (DoD 2002b; italics added).

According to Rumsfeld, because the official narrative accompanying the publication of these images was not detailed enough and/or did not sufficiently narrow down the potential understanding of the photographs, the public, news media, and human rights organizations were unintentionally given the opportunity to re-write or re-imagine the meanings of these images. In his response to a follow-up comment on his statement from one of the journalists, Rumsfeld emphasized the significance of the context and additional information accompanying a photograph:

> Question: Mr. Secretary, *you said it was unfortunate that that photograph was released*. I would just argue that it was unfortunate that it wasn't

released with more information.

Rumsfeld: Maybe. Yeah. That's fair.

Question: The lesson here ought not to be –

Rumsfeld: I mean, I'm not blaming anyone for releasing it, but –

Question: – less information or withholding photographs, but simply *releasing more information* –

Rumsfeld: Fair enough.

Question: – so we can make better judgments. (DoD 2002b; italics added)

The reporter was clearly concerned about a future backlash against these photographs, and was anticipating that the negative responses might lead to the introduction of even harsher restrictions on the media's access to Guantánamo – access that, for journalists at that time, was already minimal – and that the US government might become more hesitant with regard to releasing additional photographs showing the situation of the detainees. Crucially, Rumsfeld described all the media restrictions put in place as actually being an acknowledgment of the detainees' right to be protected from "ridicule" under the *Geneva Convention III* (DoD 2002b).

In reaction to the discussion of the photographs by the news media, Rumsfeld explained what he had been told was depicted in the images, and clarified how the situation shown in the photographs should be understood. Even in the first few minutes of the briefing, Rumsfeld stated: "And let there be no doubt, the treatment of the detainees in Guantánamo Bay is proper, it's *humane, it's appropriate, and it is fully consistent with international conventions.* No detainee has been harmed, no detainee has been mistreated in any way" (DoD 2002b; italics added). The critiques expressed between January 18 and January 22 in "numerous articles, statements, questions, allegations, and breathless reports on television" (DoD 2002b) were formulated by people lacking sufficient information about what the photographs actually depict, as he argued. As to whether he could explain what the photographs actually show, Rumsfeld gave the following answer, which I will cite here at full length:

I will, to the best of my ability. It's probably unfortunate that it was released. It's the tension between wanting to meet the desires of the press to know more and the public to know more. And what that was, I am told, is not a detention area, that is a corridor or a walk-through area that came – my understanding is – goes something like this. When they're on the airplane, they wear earpieces because of the noise. You've ridden on these airplanes; they're combat aircraft, and we've all worn earpieces. That's no big deal. There were a number who had tested – they were worried about tuberculosis, so in a number of instances they were given masks for the protection of other detainees and for the protection of the guards. They come out of an airplane and the back lowers and they walk out. And then they loaded them into, I believe, buses and they took

them down to a ferry. And they were still restrained, their hands and
their feet restrained because of the dangers that occur during a period
of movement. They put them on a ferry, if I'm not mistaken, and the ferry
takes them across to the other side of the Guantánamo Bay. They get off
of the ferry and they get into some – something that then transports them
to the detention area. They get out of that vehicle, and in relatively small
numbers are moved into this corridor that is a fenced area. And they are
asked to get down on the ground. They get down on the ground. And they
take off their ear pieces, they take off their masks, they do whatever they
do with them before taking them in small numbers into the cells, where
they then would be located, at which point the – they are no longer in
transit, and therefore, they are no longer restrained the way they were.
(DoD 2002b)

In his description of the scene captured by McCoy, Rumsfeld takes a step-by-
step approach to explain each element which might catch the attention of the
viewer, or be criticized by the news media and human rights organizations.
He explains nearly all the equipment the detainees were forced to wear by
contextualizing it as a humanitarian effort – as a means of protecting the
detainee or the guard watching over him. This certainly shows that the DoD
regarded the context provided with the initial release of the photographs to
be insufficient and in need of reformulation – a reformulation that was largely
based on humanitarian arguments.

In her memoir, *Lipstick on a Pig: Winning in the No-Spin Era by Someone Who
Knows the Game* (2006), the government's spokeswoman at that time, Victoria
"Torie" Clarke, argues along similar lines to Rumsfeld that the photograph had
been misperceived due to a lack of context. That context, she writes, should
have been provided by the DoD to accompany the release of the images:
"The problem wasn't that we released too much, it was that we explained too
little. We just released the photos with brief descriptions and left it at that"
(Clarke 2006, 82). She adds that the photographs "needed ... *long exhaustive,
detailed captions* and probably, in hindsight, *a full briefing describing the circumstances*" (Clarke 2006, 82; italics added), and that she "was the one who blew
it, but in the Pentagon press briefing on January 22, 2002, Rumsfeld took the
heat" (Clarke 2006, 83). Furthermore, Clarke, too, reframes the critiques by
emphasizing the safety and humanitarian aspects, and deflecting accusations
that the ear protectors were part of an intentional "'sensory deprivation'"
effort (Clarke 2006, 82). Thus, echoing Rumsfeld's response, in her memoirs
Clarke employs a twisted rhetoric of "care" and "protection" to explain what
these images were supposed to show. She also directly criticizes the way
the *Mail on Sunday* commented on these pictures by stating that: "Instead of
showing the care and concern with which we treated the detainees, the photos
served as high-octane fuel for our critics and doubters. *'Torture' ran across the*

top of lots of foreign tabloids. 'Images Raise Concerns over Detainee Treatment,' blasted others" (Clarke 2006, 82; italics added).

Katrin Dauenhauer analyses Rumsfeld's and Clarke's responses to the news criticism in her essay "Between Ethics and Aesthetics: Photographs of War during the Bush and Obama Administrations" as well (Dauenhauer 2013). She interprets Clarke's response "as a prime example of rhetorical warfare which attempts to strategically employ the polysemous potential of pictures by means of verbal interpretation" (Dauenhauer 2013, 629). She argues that the US government and military in this case actually welcome the semantic insta-bility of photography. I do not entirely agree with Dauenhauer's argument – to me Rumsfeld's and Clarke's statements show how the US government and the DoD actually blamed the captions for the negative reactions by the news media and human rights organizations. As I have previously demonstrated, a COMCAM photographer is expected to provide a caption along with the pho-tograph that addresses five W-questions: Who? What? When? Where? Why? (*Smart Book* 2015, 80–2). The potential blame allocated to the (lack of) context provided by the caption in this case emphasizes the importance which the DoD ascribes to the written text, or the written/oral discourses in relation to images. According to Rumsfeld and other government officials, a more extensive explanation of McCoy's photographs and the practices they reveal would have convinced the public that the circumstances they depict were "humane," and in accordance with the *Geneva Convention III*.

Significantly, the caption published on the DoD homepage mentions the day – January 11, 2002 (when?); the detainees and military police (who?); a description of the situation (what?); and the Naval Base Guantánamo Bay, Cuba (where?) (see the epigraph to this chapter). What is not clearly explained is the most relevant question with regard to this photograph, namely the "why?" The caption explains that the detainees are being "in-processed" and that they are awaiting "a basic physical exam by a doctor... [that] include[s] a chest x-ray and [drawn] blood samples ... to assess their health." One could argue that this sentence figures as a basic answer to the why-question. However, this question could also be formulated in other terms: *Why is this happening? Or, Is there a good reason for why this is happening? Is it justifiable?* Indeed, from the perspective of the DoD, the five W-questions that guide the captioning of the photograph have failed, and the news media were seemingly invited to "deduc[e] ... , speculat[e], and fantas[ize]" (Sontag 2008, 23). According to both Rumsfeld and Clarke, the photographs, combined with their captions, did not explain enough, and failed to stabilize the interpretation of the images and the situation they depict.

Despite Rumsfeld's and Clarke's critiques of the shortcomings of the caption/ context, I want to emphasize that the US government, as the target of this criticism, and the news media and human rights organizations who were expressing the critiques, both reframed the photographs with reference to humanitarian discourses. In the official US government narrative, represented here by the statements made by Rumsfeld and Clarke, each element of the image that was suspected of being evidence of inhumane treatment is given a humanitarian explanation. For example, the masks are explained to have been provided for protection from tuberculosis, and the earpieces for protection from noise. Furthermore, the official narrative emphasized that all this was only temporary – the detainees were in transit; shortly after the picture was taken they were moved to their cells, where the equipment was removed. Thus, the DoD discursively reiterated the function of these photographs, framing them within a strange rhetoric of recognition – as if they had published these images to provide evidence of the "humane treatment" of the detainees, of this treatment being "consistent with the Geneva Convention" (DoD 2002b), and of the (at least partial) recognition of the detainees in legal terms.

But how are we to square the violent and brutal treatment of detainees visible in McCoy's photographs – where they were prevented from perceiving or interacting with their environment – with the rhetoric of recognition deployed by Rumsfeld and the DoD that emerged in response to the negative news media reactions? The answer is brief: *we cannot*. These practices, and the fact that photographs that reveal them were produced and distributed, actually stand in opposition to Rumsfeld's claims, and were based in an institutionally grounded denial of legal and social recognition to the detained men.

The Perspectives of the Participant and the Observer

Analyzing the newspaper discourses prompted by McCoy's photographs has shown that, despite the highly regulated production and distribution process, the DoD was unable to ensure a single, privileged interpretation of these images. Instead of being read as images of victory or as showing humane treatment, the photographs were rightfully discussed by national and foreign news media as depicting torture practices and providing evidence of the DoD's denial of legal recognition to the detainees. This subsection is dedicated to the discussion of another form of instability connected to the scene depicted in McCoy's photographs – an instability that stems from the DoD's attempt to persuade the viewers of these images to share the government's position and to take part in the denial of legal and social recognition to the detainees. My initial intuition with regard to McCoy's photographs was that they were intended to force the viewer to apprehend the detainees as reified things, rather than persons.[21] My own response to these images, however,

---

21   The idea of reification and alienation will be discussed in greater detail in the last chapter of this book.

required me to find an alternative to the strictly Marxist notion of reification. Significantly, Axel Honneth's (2008) re-reading of Georg Lukács' thoughts on reification as a theory of recognition unites the Marxist understanding of this term with my wish to develop a framework for discussing what it means to respond to these photographs in a way that not only recognizes the violence being enacted on the detainees, but also acknowledges the implications behind the way the DoD used these images to modulate the public's feeling of distance from or proximity to the detainees.

Lukács, Honneth argues, puts forward a binary model that opposes involvement or participation, seen as the ideal human behavior, to observation or contemplation seen as a transgressive one (Honneth 2008, 33f). Honneth terms the former "recognition" and describes the latter as the "forgetfulness of recognition" (Honneth 2008, 34). I believe that Honneth's focus on the issue of observation and participation can inform a reading of the situation depicted in McCoy's images, as well the larger question of how a photograph negotiates proximity and distance between viewers and its subject(s). My chief argument is that, although the photographs depict a situation in which the detainees are being denied recognition by those who appear to be in physical proximity to them, and by the institution that produced these photographs, the viewer's response to these photographs is not necessarily pre-determined by this dynamic.

In his book, *Reification: A New Look at an Old Idea* (2008), Honneth describes recognition as a mode how human beings relate to each other, feel close to an object of perception, become involved in, and participate in what or whom we are seeing. He thus defines recognition as a perceptual mode where one person is capable of taking on the perspective of the Other (Honneth 2008, 34). His emphasis on the "'perspective of the participant' in contrast to the perspective of a mere observer" (Honneth 2008, 34) distinguishes Honneth's later model of recognition from his earlier writings, where recognition is tied to the imperative of intersubjectivity and reciprocity.[22] In his later work, Honneth also considers one-sided recognition as more than a pathology, as he had defined it in his previous writings. Discussing this crucial shift in Honneth's theory of recognition, Dirk Quadflieg writes:

> Because Honneth now connects intersubjective recognition to the capacity for affective participation, it is no longer conceptualized as a necessarily reciprocal relationship, as it was in *The Struggle for Recognition*. Putting oneself into other people's places also remains possible in situations where the Other does not (or does not visibly) assume the same

22   In *The Struggle for Recognition: The Moral Grammar of Social Conflicts*, Honneth distinguishes "three patterns of reciprocity," or three "Patterns of Intersubjective Recognition," which he identifies as love, rights, and solidarity (Honneth 1996, 94 and 92).

stance – for instance, because of the ... forgetfulness of recognition. (Quadflieg 2019, 89; my translation)

Significantly, Honneth argues strongly for the priority of recognition. Drawing from arguments formulated by Martin Heidegger (1993) and John Dewey (1981a; 1981b), Honneth sees recognition as an act that takes place even before the subject engages in cognitive activity – thus, for him, recognition precedes cognition. Taking Heidegger's reflections in *Sein und Zeit* (Eng. *Being and Time*) as his starting point, Honneth develops the argument that the subject is characterized by "Sorge" (Eng. "care"); the human mode of existence is not one of objectivity or neutrality but, instead, of participation and involvement (Honneth 2008, 30).

Human beings, as Honneth puts it, are capable of inhabiting the point of view of the Other, and simultaneously feeling or being involved in what this Other is experiencing. Dewey, too, sees the individual being involved in the perspective of the Other as a primordial mode (Dewey 1958). For him, an objective or rational position towards reality does not take priority, rather, precedence is given to engagement with, and proximity to, the object or subject of perception (Honneth 2008, 37f.). Proximity and distance, as well as involvement and contemplation, are central ideas in Honneth's 2008 study. Further developing Lukács' thoughts about reification in capitalist societies as being a transgression of human practices, and a mode of distanced contemplation of the Other, Honneth proposes to understand reification as forgetfulness of recognition, and as such, a transgression.[23] Honneth argues that "the *contemplative* nature of man under capitalism" (Lukács 1972, 97) is, for Lukács, a kind of transgressive behavior:

> The concept of 'contemplation' thus indicates not so much an attitude of theoretical immersion or concentration as it does *a stance of indulgent, passive observation*, while *'detachment' signifies that an agent is no longer emotionally affected by the events in his surroundings, instead letting them go by without any inner involvement, merely observing their passing.* (Honneth 2008, 24; italics added)

This idea of contemplation as a transgressive practice leads Honneth to engage with another idea formulated by Lukács that becomes central to his reconsideration of reification as the forgetfulness of recognition. Honneth writes that Lukács already postulated a better form of human behavior, one in which subjects actively witness and form an organic unity. Reification could thus be understood as a deviation from what Lukács describes as the original

---

23   According to Honneth, recognition takes place prior to the subject's cognitive capacity; reification takes the form of forgetting this initial recognition towards the other person. Nevertheless, if this initial recognition is forgotten, we might well recognize the other person again, and, hence, can de-reify what or whom we perceive.

and desired relational mode between two persons, as "a deviation from a kind of human praxis or worldview essentially characteristic of the rationality of our form of life" (Honneth 2008, 21).

Referring to the ways in which Heidegger, Dewey, Lukács, and Stanley Cavell (1976) discuss intersubjective relationships, Honneth not only highlights the fact that some of their theories overlap, but also discusses how this "genuine' or 'proper' stance toward the world" (Honneth 2008, 20) can be understood. According to Honneth, Lukács – in a way similar to Heidegger and Dewey – did not comprehend the subject's position towards the world as being neutral; instead, he defined it as a participatory mode. Honneth thus reinterprets Lukács' notion of reification, arguing that Lukács understood it as a "false interpretive habit with reference to a 'correct' form of praxis that is always given in an at least rudimentary fashion" (Honneth 2008, 33). For Honneth, we "participate in social life by placing … [ourselves] in the position of … [our] counterparts, whose desires, dispositions, and thoughts … [we] have learned to understand as the motives for… [their] actions" (Honneth 2008, 34). In contrast to this, if we do not take on the perspective of the other person, and instead have *"a merely detached, contemplative stance toward the other, then the bond of human interaction will be broken*, for it will then no longer be maintained by their *reciprocal* understanding of each other's reasons for acting" (Honneth 2008, 34; italics added). To participate in what another person experiences, and to thus recognize them, would mean taking on the perspective of that person and, by means of this change in perspective, reaching an understanding of the motivation behind this person's actions.

Honneth's binary model, although thought-provoking, is problematic for a number of reasons. The most important issue is that not every form of participation affirms the other person positively; conversely, not every mode of observation results in the denial or forgetfulness of recognition. A major critique of his model has been expressed by Judith Butler who, in her essay "Taking Another's View: Ambivalent Implications" (2008), incisively raises issues with defining the distinction between a participatory and observational perspective as being central to the distinction between recognition and the forgetfulness thereof. Butler argues against the binary nature of Honneth's model, writing that "[i]t would seem that, according to this scheme, our choice is either to be merely observational (and hence reifying) and fail to take up the position of the other, or to be participatory, by which we mean, among other things, taking up the position of the other" (Butler 2008, 102). I agree with Butler's critique and her argument that the participatory and observational perspectives are far more complex than the manner in which Honneth describes them, and that it is possible for them to appear in combination with one another or in different gradations. Since Butler's major interest in the past few years has centered on debates around precarious life in the context of military conflicts, it is unsurprising that her criticism of Honneth's binary model evolves from the fact that violence or aggression can also be regarded as an affective and participatory mode. Butler demonstrates that aggression immediately throws into question the validity of Honneth's binary model – although an aggressor is in an emotionally engaged state, they would certainly not appear to be striving to recognize the other person.

Butler writes: "[i]n fact, if we look at modes of rage that seek to eradicate the other, that is, to physically harm and kill the other, then we have *a mode of highly affective engagement that in no way seeks to affirm the existence of the other; rather, it seeks to eradicate the existence of the other*" (Butler 2008, 103; italics added). What Butler describes here is an intense affect that is connected to emotions such as rage, anger, and aggression. In contrast to Honneth's description of distinct perspectives that relate to recognition and the forgetfulness thereof, respectively, Butler demonstrates that intense participation and engagement do not necessarily aim at, or result in, the recognition of the Other. Quite the opposite, in fact: violence is, in most cases, an "affective engagement" that seeks to kill the Other (Butler 2008, 103). This, however, is not necessarily bound to the dehumanization of the other person, and might actually result from an acknowledgment of the significance of the Other's existence. In this vein, Paul Bloom is right when he points out that "our best and our worst tendencies arise precisely from seeing others as human" (Bloom 2017).

Returning to the situation depicted in McCoy's photographs: if we interpret the intense manner in which the soldiers are gazing at the detainees as an expression or revelation of aggression and anger, then it is more difficult to determine, on the basis of Honneth's arguments and Butler's counter-arguments, whether the soldiers are, in fact, recognizing or reifying the detainees. It is possible that the soldiers are highly engaged or affected by the arrival of the detainees, and yet still do not recognize them as human beings or persons who should be recognized legally or socially. Alternatively, we can look at statements made by the guards themselves in which they reveal that they were trying to distance themselves from the situation of the arrival, and from the detainees, a disclosure which supports Honneth's view. As Karen J. Greenberg writes, the detainees' arrival was staged and designed in such a manner as to ensure that the guards and military personnel would not become emotionally involved in what they were doing, or feel what the detainees were experiencing:

> Shimkus [the Commanding Officer and JTF-Guantánamo surgeon at the US Naval Hospital from 2002 to 2003] explained that a certain degree of roughness was an inescapable part of maintaining security. 'It may have been perceived as rough. But I don't think it was any more rough than maintaining positive control.' Shimkus, Carrico [the first Commander at

the Guantánamo detention camp], and the guards insist that they were handling the detainees professionally, without anger or emotion of any sort. As one guard explained, he had dealt with hardened criminals before and knew 'how not to allow myself to think about what they might have done, but just to treat them according to the rules.' (Greenberg 2009, 79f.)

In light of the statements made by the guards, alongside Honneth's views on the perspectives of the participant and the observer, and the difficulty of determining how the soldiers were acting in relation to the detainees, I will now reframe and further complicate the discussion of the scene shown in McCoy's photographs. I will consider how viewers might respond in an ethical manner to these photographs as well as how the photographs may not necessarily impose "the perspective of a mere observer" (Honneth 2008, 34) on them.

Since its emergence, the medium of photography has negotiated the spatial and physical unity between the perceiving and the perceived. Generally speaking, in spatial terms, a photograph usually depicts a different space from the one in which the perceiving person is physically located; in most cases, there is no phenomenological unity between the space depicted in the photographic image, and the space in which the perceiving subject actually is.[24] Nevertheless, the cognitive capacity of the perceiving person can help them to (re)construct such a unity; or, perhaps more accurately, to smooth away the experience of spatial and temporal distance. Going back to the photographs taken by McCoy, this means that since they are characterized by a break in the phenomenological unity between the persons depicted and the viewer, the perception of temporal and geographic distance or proximity is dependent on the viewer's perceptual capabilities.

These photographs further complicate Honneth's binary model of the perspective of the participant and the observer. Both perspectives presuppose an initial object of perception, and most of us will never encounter the men detained at Guantánamo in person. Nevertheless, their recognition in affective, legal, and social terms is crucial if there is to be any hope of changing the violent detention policies undertaken at the facility. Hence, in the context of Guantánamo, reflecting on the role of mediation, and how it might influence whether these types of recognition are afforded to the detainees, takes on a higher level of complexity. The DoD's restrictions of access to images and the strict procedures put in place at Guantánamo raise immediate questions about whether, and in what manner, such restrictions might be understood as media operations, which play a significant role in the structural denial of

---

24 With the rise in digital technologies, it has become possible for the viewer to perceive the photograph in the instant it is taken. An extreme case of such simultaneity is the selfie taken by a mobile phone, where the instant the image is being shot it is perceived by the photographer.

recognition. Restricting viewers' ability to see, to perceive, or forcing them to look away, may transform their initial recognition of the detainee's life into a perception of him as a reified entity. Another question arising from McCoy's photographs is how specific forms of mediation – ones that make objects and subjects visible – may be used not to participate in or help to initiate the act of recognition, but rather to encourage the viewer's denial of recognition to the detainees. Thus, I will extend Honneth's recognition theory to include situations where we can perceive the Other only by means of a photograph.

As the previous analysis of the news media reactions to McCoy's images has demonstrated, rather than creating a consensus among viewers about the acceptability of the humiliating and degrading treatment visited upon the detainees, the photographs failed to instill in the people who viewed them a denial of recognition to the detainees. The multifaceted responses to McCoy's photographs clearly raise an issue that intertwines media and recognition theory. In the following discussion, I will argue that, due to the polysemy of photographs, the instability of their interpretation, and the different and multiple futures inscribed in and initiated by a photograph (Schneider 2018), images such as those taken by McCoy are characterized by an inherent openness towards future processes of recognition. In the context of McCoy's photographs, this means that, even though they both depict and participate in processes that might initially promote the denial of recognition, they demonstrably came to function, conversely, as gestures encouraging the recognition of the detainees.

Although a photograph itself might not depict a scene of recognition, it can potentially help to initiate or intensify recognition processes in those viewing it; to do so, however, the photograph must be embedded in, and reframed by, effective discourses. The *Mail on Sunday*'s article entitled "Horror of Camp X-Ray: First Pictures Show Use of Sensory Deprivation to Soften Suspects for Interrogation," published two days after the photographs were officially released, is especially helpful in understanding the role which the discursive reframing of McCoy's photographs played in the context of mediated recognition (Lowther and Rosenberg 2002). By listing all the senses that were "robbed" from the detainees, and comparing these men to "animals" and "slaves," the article clearly interprets the scene depicted as one that denies recognition to the detainees. It also raises the issue of recognition as being at the core of the images. On the one hand, the authors draw a comparison between detainees and animals: in the opening sentences of the article – "SHACKLED like wild animals, deprived of sight, sound, smell and touch. Al Qaeda terrorists kneel before their American guards in the Guantánamo Bay prison camp" (Lowther and Rosenberg 2002, 2) – they highlight the violence to which the detainees were subjected, and reveal that they were being treated as "living figure[s] outside the norms of life" (Butler 2009, 8). Even though life is not restricted to human life, the comparison to "wild animals" emphasizes the fact that the detainees were being denied legal recognition and human rights. On the other hand, by writing that the handcuffs and leg-irons are "a term that survives from slave-trading days" (Lowther and Rosenberg 2002, 3), the article makes a direct connection between the history of slavery and the detainees' situation in the 21st century. Rumsfeld's reply on January 22, 2002, to the critiques such as those found in the *Mail on Sunday* article also circled around the idea of the recognition of the detainees in terms of international human rights (DoD 2002b). He not only referenced the instability of interpretation with regard to the images, but also emphasized a partial legal recognition of the detainees. In a certain sense, the discursive reframing undertaken by both sides – the US government and the news media – indicates that the recognition of the detainees, and the denial thereof, is one of the central issues related to Guantánamo and the detained men. McCoy's photographs certainly played an important role in the initiation or intensification of these debates, and this reveals the necessity of reflecting upon the role of media in recognition processes.

Although Honneth himself shows little interest in visual culture as such in his writings on recognition, his essay entitled "Invisibility: On the Epistemology of 'Recognition'" (2001) implicitly invites us to reflect on the role that media can play in the act of recognition. In this essay, Honneth distinguishes between "recognition" and the act of "cognition." For him, this difference lies in recognition's visible expression as an affirmative act:

> In contrast to cognizing, which is a non-public, cognitive act, *recognizing is dependent on media that express the fact that the other person is supposed to possess social 'validity.'* On the elementary level on which we have up to now been operating in regard to the phenomenon of social 'invisibility', *such media may still be regarded as equivalent to physically based expressions.* (Honneth 2001, 115; italics added)

The act of recognition, according to Honneth, is strongly dependent on media that are understood as "physically based expressions," and "positive expressive gestures" (Honneth 2001, 115 and 117). Although his use of the term "media" has nothing to do with the media of photography or film, and instead refers to "actions, gestures or facial expressions" (Honneth 2001, 116), his argument opens up his theory to situations where we are only able to encounter the Other via a photograph. To extend this argument, we need to rethink the way in which the context and frames given to photographs emphasize the gestural quality of these media, and acknowledge that gesture is not necessarily bound to human agents alone. According to Honneth, however, a gesture is primarily a physiological act that communicates meaning and is, in a certain sense, bound to the concept of a language system.

Gestures typically take place in public, where external third parties can observe the act of communication, and even take part in it. As Honneth writes, "[t]o this extent, recognition possesses a performative character because the expressive responses that accompany it symbolize the practical ways of react- ing in order to 'do justice' to the person recognized" (Honneth 2001, 118). The act of recognition is, thus, not restricted to the person recognizing and the one being recognized: the involvement of a third party to perceive the social situ- ation is crucial to the act itself. The same goes for the act of misrecognition.[25] Consequently, as media of recognition, gestures are performative in nature and, because of this, are characterized by a certain openness in the com- municative field. This openness is also directed towards potential spectators who perceive the gesture and may, by means of that perception, participate in processes of recognition.

In spite of Honneth's limited interest in (or understanding of) the various media in which recognition may be expressed, or media that participate in processes of recognition, his emphasis on gestures can be highly productive when thinking about recognition from the perspective of media theory in general, and theories of photography in particular. Specifically, Rebecca Schneider's view on gestures in photographs provides us with a way to rethink the relationship between photography and recognition. In her essay, "That the Past May Yet Have Another Future: Gesture in the Times of Hands Up," Schneider presents the case for a potentiality of different and multiple futures inscribed in, and initiated by, the photograph due to a "response-ability" (Schneider 2018, 287) towards gestures.

Importantly, gestures can be understood both literally and metaphorically. Literal definitions of gesture usually resemble the one provided by Honneth, understanding the gesture to be a codified, bodily movement that com- municates meaning. If we wish to understand gesture in metaphorical terms, however, and detach it from the human body, then it can also signify a broader spectrum of practices or objects. In this vein, we can agree that ges- tures are, in a certain sense, acts of address. To use a less ideologically loaded terminology, we might align ourselves with Schneider's view on gestures and, alternatively, see them as invitations to respond (Schneider 2018, 294). As I have demonstrated, McCoy's photographs have been, and remain, such invitations; furthermore, the multifaceted responses to them are ongoing. Thinking about gestures in this way also directly embeds the photograph into questions of ethical "response-ability" (Schneider 2018, 294). In her essay,

25   With regard to what Honneth terms "social invisibility," he emphasizes the capacity of other persons to observe and comprehend the injustice inflicted on the person who is not being recognized, or is being misrecognized, by means of this intentional invisibility: "not only the affected subject, but also the other persons present in the room, can normally establish that the overlooking or ignoring is of a humiliating kind" (Honneth 2001, 115).

Schneider uses the term "response-ability" to clarify the issue of address in relation to gesture, photographs, and ethics:

> For me, an idea of response-ability is embedded in gestural engagements that function as call and response. Gestures caught in or as documents such as film and video or composed of paint on surfaces or in sculptural form are taken up by other bodies, things, or surfaces and passed along, body to body, as call meets response becomes call again. As such, gesture can be considered to both inaugurate and cross intervals that extend it across time and space. A photograph itself, regardless of whether it depicts a literal gesture in an image form, can be said to gesture toward a future viewer: 'Hey, you there, look at me!' Rather than approaching an image simply as representation, trace, documentation, art, or evidence of the bygone (a conventional approach to photography as trace document), might we think of it as resonance, reverberation, or ongoing call? (Schneider 2018, 299)

Schneider criticizes our habit of perceiving a photograph, and the gesture captured in it, as evidence of something that has passed and is no longer happening. She argues that such readings have severe ethical implications, and highlights the fact that conceiving the photograph as a mere trace of past events inevitably distracts us from – and perhaps relieves us of – our apparent complicity in what we are perceiving. Regarding McCoy's photographs merely as evidence of the past would thus mean avoiding the fact that we, the viewers, are intended to be complicit in the denial of recognition to the detainees.

Hence, in addition to documenting or providing evidence of a situation relegated to the past, the photograph opens itself up to another reading: one that expands the dominant theories of the photograph as a trace (Barthes 1982; Didi-Huberman 1999; Kittler 1986; Sontag 2004). On the level of content, the photographs of the first detainees at Guantánamo and the responses they elicited appear to not only provide an account of the past, but also to function as gestures for future uses. Such gestures are not limited to the repetition and reenactment of the denial of recognition to the detainees; they also open up the viewers' perception of the detainees to processes of recognition. This double reading of gestures and photographs, and the emphasis on seeing them as invitations to respond, is central to understanding how photographs can participate in recognition processes of the persons depicted in them. A photograph is not a gesture *per se*, but it does possess gestural qualities, by which I mean that some photographs prompt their viewer into a response which is not only a cognitive, but also embodied form of "response-ability" (Schneider 2018, 299). Viewers are thus required to reframe the photograph and to hold themselves to account for their own reading of it and the meanings they assign to it. Thus, we might also say that the gestural dimension also lies in the particular *subversive reframing* that our responses to images from the Guantánamo detention camp produce.

Furthermore, if we understand gestures in the way Honneth does, as intentional acts of communication, then the gestural quality of photography would appear to be highly dependent on the context in which such photographs appear. The discursive frames of McCoy's photographs, as has been shown, have emphasized one or more specific aspects of the images that are intended to be communicated to the viewer. These photographs address the viewer in many different ways, but I cannot imagine a situation in which a person looking at them does not respond at all. McCoy's photographs "gesture toward a future viewer: 'Hey, you there, look at me!'" (Schneider 2018, 299), and, if they appear within the discursive frames formed by institutions, they are also gesturing: 'Hey, you there, look at me *in a certain way*!' Due to the way that the photographs were framed by the *Mail on Sunday* article, for example, the newspaper's readers were asked to look at these images as expressing the denial of recognition – which contributed to the initiation or intensification of recognition processes towards the detainees. This reframing thus encourages us to respond to the images in a way that bridges the distance between "us" and "them," the distance co-produced by McCoy's photographs.

Summary and Conclusion

In this chapter, I have discussed the phenomena of learning and transformation in the US military, specifically with respect to visual information. Of course, learning is much more multifaceted, and occurs at many more points of intersection than I was able to discuss here. But to make my point, I focused on documents that established and described broader policies, such as the directives and instructions discussed in the first section. Furthermore, I illustrated the time it took the DoD to learn from the various studies it had commissioned, and to consolidate the knowledge from "lessons learned" in the form of policies. My broader claim is that many of the military documents I discussed here represent the accumulated sediments of lengthy processes of institutional learning and change, and do not necessarily symbolize sudden moments of innovation. Visual information acquisition by the US military in general, and COMCAM in particular, is a prime example of how, at times, the US military learns to eat soup with a knife (Nagl 2002). It took the DoD over 30 years of studies, recommendations, and lessons learned to introduce long-lasting changes – changes that were expressed and consolidated in the form of overarching policies.

Manuals, more broadly speaking, complement directives and instructions insofar as they establish overarching procedures. They also provide insights into the administrative side of military operations. Hence, the field manual complements the procedural information that "planners and commanders at all levels" (ALSA Center 2003, i) would require. In the third subsection of this chapter, I discussed in detail the *Joint Combat Camera (COMCAM) / Visual Information (VI) Smart Book*, published in 2015, in relation to McCoy's photographs. I set out to show that every procedural and aesthetic aspect of COMCAM's operations is geared towards restricting and governing the various elements of image production, distribution, and perception. I also looked at the template used by COMCAM photographers when shooting still or moving images, and demonstrated that, even before they encounter an event, they already have been briefed on what should and should not be recorded. On the one hand, the standardization of the procedure of taking a photograph aims to regulate the process; on the other, it tries to ensure that the event is mediated in line with the specifications formulated by higher-ranking military officials. Finally, I analyzed the way in which COMCAM and the DoD appear to perceive photographic media, emphasizing the priority these bodies give to an image's ability to transmit information over its aesthetic dimension.

In order to position COMCAM photography within the broader field of news-media images, I also drew a distinction between the fields of photojournalism and COMCAM, as well as between photojournalistic images and COMCAM photographs. Nevertheless, I argued that, depending on the context given to COMCAM photographs and on their distribution channels, military photographs may also be understood as belonging to the genre of photojournalism. Hence, the "genre" ascription given to photographs is not guaranteed by their production or distribution context; instead, the many afterlives of photographs can redefine how they are perceived. Therefore, as I noted, COMCAM puts a lot of effort into regulating the context of images, and evidence of these efforts can be found at each stage of the production and distribution process. Being especially interested in captioning as one such stabilizing practice, I discussed how it is performed by photojournalists and COMCAM photographers alike, elaborating on this practice in these two institutionally different fields, as well as conducted a close reading of the caption that accompanied the high-angle photograph [fig. 1] taken by McCoy.

In the last section of this chapter, I illustrated how the newspapers have changed the DoD's captions. Despite the US government's various efforts to shape and stabilize the interpretation of the images it produces, it has proven unable to ensure the dominance of one privileged interpretation of COMCAM photographs like McCoy's. The force with which some journalists and human rights organizations responded to McCoy's photographs – accusing the US military of torturing or degrading the detainees – shows that the perception of one and the same photograph can deviate drastically from the way it was intended to be read and perceived. McCoy's photographs rightfully sparked an international debate about the treatment of detainees at Guantánamo, and were by no means unilaterally perceived as images of victory, or as showing "humane treatment" (DoD 2002b). Significantly, I also demonstrated that the responses by news media were followed, in turn, by responses from the DoD, and that many years later, ex-government officials and McCoy himself commented on this image-event.

I then expanded my analysis of the potential forms of instability related to McCoy's photographs. On the one hand, I analyzed how the scene the photographs depict might be understood in the context of Honneth's recognition theory. On the other hand, I explored how a photograph itself can participate in processes of recognition and the denial thereof. There, I focused on Honneth's later study, *Reification: A New Look at an Old Idea* (2008), in which he reflects on non-reciprocal and non-mutual forms of recognition. Honneth's definition of recognition, and of reification as the forgetfulness of recognition, in terms of modes of relatedness opens up his theory to a consideration of the role played by visual media in such processes. I have broadened his recognition theory by discussing the potential scope of what we understand to be the "media" in which recognition is expressed or which contribute to processes of recognition, and reflected upon what happens when photographs appear in new frames. Honneth's idea that, on a basic level, media of recognition are to be understood as embodied, expressive gestures opens up a possibility to think about how different forms of visual media can potentially express, contribute to, or even initiate processes of recognition. Consequently, I put forward the argument that not only embodied gestures, but also photographs, can come to participate in processes of recognition. If we understand gestures as invitations to respond (Schneider 2018, 294), then photographs – such as the one taken by McCoy and distributed by the DoD – might also contain gestural qualities, thanks to the way they place the viewers in relation to themselves.

This chapter itself could also be seen, in a certain sense, to be a response. However, it is a response not only to these photographs, but also to some parts of the institutional history of the DoD and COMCAM. By reframing these photographs, and discussing the institutional discourses associated with them, I have shown how the DoD's publication of these first visual frames from Guantánamo and their captions were unable to control the ways in which future viewers will perceive them, nor whether these future viewers would be joining the DoD in refusing to recognize the detainees as legal persons and bearers of human rights.

C. Protected Information

1. Protected Information necessarily includes classified information. Protected Information also includes (i) information the disclosure of which could reasonably be expected to cause damage to the national security, including intelligence or law enforcement sources, methods, or activities, or jeopardize the physical safety of individuals, and (ii) information subject to a properly-issued protective order by an official authorized to issue such orders by law or regulation.

2. NMRs shall not publish, release, publicly discuss, or share information gathered at GTMO, or in transit to or from GTMO on transportation provided by DoD (or other U.S. government entities), that is Protected Information for purposes of these ground rules.

3. A NMR will not be considered in violation of these ground rules for re-publishing what otherwise would be considered Protected Information, where that information was legitimately obtained in the course of newsgathering independent of any receipt of information while at GTMO, or while transiting to or from GTMO on transportation provided by DoD (or other U.S. government entities).

4. While at GTMO, and in transit to and from GTMO, NMRs may be exposed to aspects of detention and base operations the disclosure of which must be avoided for reasons of national security, force protection and compliance with international treaty obligations. These operations are part of the base operations that the general public is not invited or permitted to view. As a result, JTF-GTMO has designated aspects of these operations whose disclosure is not permitted, and NMRs at GTMO will be required, as a condition of their visits, to safeguard this information, which will be deemed Operational Protected Information. Operational Protected Information, as determined by JTF-GTMO, is identified in these ground rules.

D. General Photography and Video Limitations

1. At no time during a media visit is communication (verbal, written or other) with a detainee allowed. Attempting to communicate with a detainee and photographing or taking video of a detainee's attempts to communicate with members of the media are prohibited. If detainees become agitated at the presence of media, the media may be asked to leave for the safety and security of the detainees, NMR and the guard force.

2. Photographs or video shall **not** be taken of the following:

a. Frontal facial views, profiles, ¾ views, or any view revealing a detainee's identity.

b. Identifiable JTF-GTMO personnel, without their consent.

c. Deliberate views of security protocols including security cameras, metal detectors, locks, keys, gates, reinforced doors or other security measures.

10 Sept 2010   Initials_____ Page 4

[Fig. 6] Page four of the *Media Policy at Guantánamo Bay, Cuba: Agree to Abide*, which is a document signed by journalists prior to their participation in the guided tours through the Guantánamo detention camp. The DoD defines here what is considered to be "protected information," and describes their censorship of photography (Source: DoD 2010, 4). The appearance of US Department of Defense (DoD) visual information does not imply or constitute DoD endorsement.

2

Invisibilizing Faces: Photographs and Videos Taken During Guided Tours

"Few spectacles in the 21st century war on terror could be stranger or more disquieting than the ghostlike figures that are displayed behind glass to visiting media," writes David Smith (2016) in his report of a two-day guided tour he participated in at the Guantánamo detention camp. In his article on how Guantánamo personnel stage and frame such media tours, Smith emphasizes the strangeness of this visual spectacle; a spectacle that leads to encounters ghostly in nature, rather than showing the visitors the violence happening behind closed doors. He begins with a description of how he was watching a detainee walking around a cellblock: "A man with grey beard, loose white T-shirt and sandals silently paces around the cellblock, *appearing and disappearing from our view with the regularity of a comet*. He is reading a book; his gait is slow; he seems oblivious to *the visitors watching him like a zoo animal*, through a one-way mirror and mesh fence" (Smith 2016; italics added). Smith's description of the detainee's circling, pacing, or quiet restlessness, and his comparison of his encounter and viewing position to how Sunday visitors see animals in zoos, are descriptions that have been present ever since the very first tours were provided for news-media representatives at the detention camp. Whereas Smith compares the situation to a visit to a zoo and recounts that he has seen "ghostlike figures," as early as 2002 – only shortly after the arrival of the first detainees at Guantánamo – the detention camp also became "essentially … a national-security tourism hotspot" (Greenberg 2009, 90). While the association of Guantánamo with tourism might appear strange, it feels highly accurate when considering the large number of guided tours provided by the Joint Task Force-Guantánamo (JTF-Guantánamo). From the start, such tours were organized for "government VIPs, military personnel, journalists and intelligence officials from the United States and abroad" (Van

Veeren 2011b, 198). In 2009 alone, one hundred visitor groups were shown around the facility (Van Veeren 2011b, 198).

In this chapter, I explore the perceptual frames created by such guided media tours, and how these frames were, and still are, intended to shape the public image of Guantánamo. I also examine how the US Department of Defense (DoD) regulates these tours, and what we can perceive from them. I argue that, instead of contributing to the transparency of Guantánamo, as the Department has claimed (DoD 2010, 3), the tours for journalists and the images taken during these visits actually make the circumstances in the detention camp ungraspable and opaque to the public.

The first section of this chapter is thus dedicated to the question of how such guided media tours have been institutionally framed by the JTF-Guantánamo, and, more specifically, how they were scripted for independent journalists. Thus, rather than focusing on visits staged for military officials or politicians, I will investigate the possibilities given to – and the limits imposed upon – journalists. My emphasis will lie on the contractual stipulations journalists are obliged to accept if they want to report on the situation in Guantánamo from within the facility itself. Moreover, I will reflect on how these contractual stipulations are intended to determine the public perception of the men detained at the facility as well as of the circumstances in the camp. In particular, the document that provides the framework for these tours explicitly forbids visitors to capture the detainees' faces or profiles in photographs, with the result that images produced during these staged events show only empty spaces in the camp, and the backs of so-called "compliant" detainees (DoD 2010, 3). This raises the question of how institutional frameworks like such a contract condition the visibility, or indeed, non-visibility, of the detained men.

Importantly, journalists, contractors, and government officials have not been the only ones allowed to visit the camp. Over time, the target audience of these tours has been significantly expanded: today, even the general public can access the camp virtually via online videos. Thus, I will also discuss how these online videos of virtual visits have made Guantánamo visually accessible, albeit in a restricted form, to non-journalists including scholars like myself, a fact which extends the question of the visibility or non-visibility of the detainees via such tours. I will analyze two virtual visit videos which were uploaded to YouTube in 2008 (The Broadcast Report 2008c; 2008d), and were distributed with the logo of the JTF-Guantánamo. Although these videos were not produced by independent journalists, they appear to follow similar restrictions to those imposed on external visitors to the camp, which suggests that the rules structuring (or rather restricting) Guantánamo's visual culture apply to different types of visual productions. Both these tours – the first showing Camp X-Ray, the second Camp 6 – negotiate, in a striking manner, the relationship between absence and presence, as well the appearance and disappearance of bodies, objects, and practices in images shot in the camp. Despite the many years during which the detainees were continuously denied visibility, individual identification, and visual representation of their faces, I will argue that these videos indicate and emphasize the opposite: the haunting phenomenological presence of the detainees in their visual absence.

The last section of this chapter focuses on artistic interventions into these mediated and highly censored guided tours which have been undertaken by the American photographer, Debi Cornwall. Cornwall, who worked as a lawyer focusing on wrongful convictions before becoming an artist, has visited Guantánamo and participated in the tours on three occasions. Her exhibition, entitled *Welcome to Camp America*, first shown in 2017 at the Centre de la Photographie Genève, and her photo book containing, amongst other things, photographs taken during the guided tours, embody sharp reflections on Guantánamo's highly controlled and restricted visual culture. In addition, Cornwall's artistic practice pays strong attention to the various juridical frameworks which condition our engagement with the complex relationship between the non-visibility of the (released) detainees and the image of the detention facility produced by the JTF-Guantánamo and the DoD. In addition to the photographs taken during the guided tours, Cornwall's exhibition and photo book include a series of images entitled "Beyond Gitmo | ما وراء خليج غوانتانامو" which were not actually taken at the US Naval Station. This series is a result of Cornwall's interest in the lives of the released men after Guantánamo, and makes it painfully clear that the trauma of the detention camp is not limited to the period during which the men were deported to and detained on the island of Cuba; it continues to mark and haunt their lives following their release.

The Frame of Guided Tours

The "Tourist Gaze" and Military Tourism

To understand the participation of journalists in the guided tours at the Guantánamo detention camp, we must view these tours within the larger practice of military tourism, and consider how tourism functions as a mode of experiencing reality. Tourists are people in transition, temporarily present in a particular space. Conventionally, tourism is considered a leisure activity, associated with large numbers of people travelling during holidays. However, there is a much wider range of tourist experiences beyond those that bring pleasure alone. For instance, you can be a tourist and still not enjoy the travel or stay in a foreign country. In addition, you can come to perceive yourself as a tourist even if you are living in a particular place. Due to the multiple ways in which tourism or tourist experiences are formed, shaped, and interpreted, rather than searching for an ontological commonality among these experiences, it is more useful to discuss them in relation to what John Urry has termed the "tourist gaze" (Urry 1990; 2002; Urry and Larsen 2011). Focusing on this "gaze" allows us to understand tourism as a particular way of experiencing reality; that is, as a perceptual phenomenon.

In the introduction to the first edition of *The Tourist Gaze: Leisure and Travel in Contemporary Societies*, Urry acknowledges "the historical and sociological variation in this [tourist] gaze" and emphasizes that "there are some minimal characteristics of the social practices which are conveniently described as 'tourism'" (Urry 1990, 2). He summarizes the shared qualities of historically and sociologically different formations of this gaze, consolidating the fundamental experiences of tourism in nine points (Urry 1990, 2f.), though this edition does not yet include a discussion of such phenomena as military tourism, the entanglement between military violence and/or occupation and "tourist events" (Stein 2008, 647), or "thanatourism." In such contexts, tourism cannot be defined solely as "a leisure activity which presupposes its opposite, namely regulated and organized work" (Urry 1990, 2). There are forms of tourism that are part of the paid work of the traveler, as in the case of journalists visiting Guantánamo. The phenomenon of the guided tours at Guantánamo and the wide range of people from different professions who have participated in them demonstrates that, in this specific case, it would be wrong to call these tours a leisure activity.

Despite the difficulties of relating Urry's definition of the "tourist gaze" to the guided tours at Guantánamo, in the second edition of his book, published in 2002, he added a new chapter entitled "Globalising the Gaze," in which he addresses some of the issues I have just raised (Urry 2002, 141–61), and, in the most recent publication, co-authored with Jonas Larsen, he also reflects upon the role of vision and photography in tourist practices (Urry and Larsen 2011, 155–88). In "Globalising the Gaze," Urry mentions that, in the period between the publication of the first and second edition, tourism and the tourist gaze had been subject to a wide range of infrastructural changes, and became localized in the "unlikeliest of places" (Urry 2002, 142). Tackling the issues of colonialism, violence, the military, and so-called "dark tourism," Urry observes that

> [s]ome destinations now significantly included in the patterns of global tourism include Alaska, Auschwitz-Birkenau, Antarctica especially in the Millennium year, Changi Jail in Singapore, Nazi occupation sites in the Channel Islands, Dachau, extinct coal mines, Cuba and especially its 'colonial' and 'American' heritages, Iceland, Mongolia, Mount Everest, Northern Ireland, Northern Cyprus under Turkish 'occupation,' Pearl Harbour, post-communist Russia, Robben Island in South Africa, Sarajevo's 'massacre trail,' outer space, Titanic, Vietnam and so on. (Urry 2002, 142f.)

Tourist practices at many of these locations have been described in detail in scholarship dealing with the phenomenon of "dark tourism" or "thanatourism," which consists of tourist practices at sites historically associated with violence and death (Oleson 2020). Adding to Urry's list, the guided tours at Guantánamo and through other, still-operational, prisons worldwide provide an opportunity to further expand on a phenomenon which Urry only mentions briefly. In "Gazing on History," he writes about the Lancaster Castle, a destination which until 2011 functioned both as a museum and an operational prison (though the prison part was inaccessible to museum visitors) (Urry 2002, 108). Urry observes that there is "something inappropriate about tourists gazing upon a building which functions as a prison" (Urry 2002, 108). Considering that historical, and even contemporary, tourist practices did and still do allow visitors to gaze upon such buildings, and not only from the outside but also from within, this "inappropriateness" takes on a whole other dimension.

Tours of incarceration centers are nothing new: as early as the 18th century, the US was providing visitors with the opportunity to visit detention facilities. One of the more prominent accounts based on such tours was written by Charles Dickens in *American Notes for General Circulation*, published in 1842 (Dickens 1942; Oleson 2020, 544). Although carceral tours of operative prisons are not usually considered to be tours of death sites and in most cases fall outside of the definition of "thanatourism," the guided tours of Guantánamo evoke the impression that the detention camp is uninhabited, despite the fact that it continues to be an operational facility. Considering the violence that is taking place behind closed doors at the camp, these tours – and the media objects (such as photographs) resulting from them – might also evoke the sense of mourning that Urry defines as being an integral "part of a reflexive process" (Urry 2002, 143) experienced at thanatourist sites. That said, any processes which might occur during guided tours of operational prisons or detention facilities tend to be highly regulated by a wide range of institutional scripts. As James C. Oleson remarks in "Dark Tours: Prison Museums and Hotels," during carceral tours "the visitor's gaze is limited to a handful of spaces: the front gates, the parking lot, the security checkpoint, the waiting room, the visitation room. Most of the prison remains unseen" (Oleson 2020, 544). Justin Piché and Kevin Walby make a case for the benefit of carceral tours for pedagogical and research purposes – albeit also acknowledging that the scripts followed by such tours "reduce their research and pedagogical value" (Piché and Walby 2010, 579). The guided tours through the Guantánamo detention camp figure as a pedagogical tool in a different sense: whereas the DoD and the JTF-Guantánamo emphasize the pedagogical purposes of these tours, perhaps the most salient fact to be learned by journalists participating in them is that the US government is creating a strictly regulated misrepresentation of the reality experienced by the detainees.

Military tourism – the category to which I would assign these tours – might indeed be a leisure activity in accordance with Urry's definition of the "tourist gaze," and there are many examples in which governments provide guided tours through military bases. Nevertheless, the function of the guided media tours at Guantánamo, as well as the kind of experiences usually associated with military tourism in general, precludes them from being "a specific form of holiday" (Hrusovsky and Noeres 2011, 87). "When people think of the military they are likely to associate it with for example war scenes, noise, danger or cruelty. A normal tourism product is usually designed to avoid all those things" (Hrusovsky and Noeres 2011, 92f.), write Michael Hrusovsky and Konstantin Noeres in their definition of military tourism. They continue their description of the paradoxes inherent to military tourism as follows: "A jet flight, for example, might be a product for a customer from the adventure tourism sector, who might also enjoy skydiving or driving a race car for recreational purposes. The same jet flight might be an interesting product for somebody who has a genuine interest in the military itself" (Hrusovsky and Noeres 2011, 93). Here, Hrusovsky and Noeres simplify or break down the many paradoxes of military tourism, which may be a result of their rather sparse discussion of the rich history of tourist experiences that have been provided by various military organizations.[1]

Importantly, tourist practices related to the military have also been introduced and shaped by other governments and militaries alongside those of the US. An interesting case study is tourist practices of Israelis in Palestinian territories. Rebecca L. Stein observes that "[f]rom the occupation's beginning, Israeli tourist practices functioned as cultural companions to, and alibis for, the more repressive work of military rule" (Stein 2016, 546). The guided tours at Guantánamo appear to target a similar goal as these "cultural companions" (Stein 2016, 546) described by Stein in the context of Palestinian territories – they represent the effort to legitimize an extra-legal and extra-territorial detention facility. Hence, the "tourist gaze" at Guantánamo inscribes itself in a much broader ideological apparatus that normatively frames the guided tour and its outcomes. In relation to Israel – and also to the US – "the interplay between tourism and military occupation has a considerable legacy … , functioning as yet another illustration of the postcolonial axiom that the

---

1   The complex history of the relationship between the military, industry, and entertainment has been acknowledged and described in detailed ways in film and media studies, two disciplines which have always been interested in analyzing how institutions such as the military mediate their activities. In this context, particular attention deserves to be paid to the edited volume *Cinema's Military Industrial Complex* that "explores the ways in which this uniquely powerful globe-spanning institution [the US military] began to use 'cinema' as industry, technology, media practice, form, and space to service its needs and further its varied interests" (Grieveson and Wasson 2018, 1). When it comes to the guided tours at Guantánamo, we might also speak more broadly of a US military-entertainment complex that could be regarded as part of its industrial complex.

histories of colonialism and colonial violence are intimately entangled with the history of leisure travel" (Stein 2016, 545). The guided tours through the camps of Guantánamo are, so to speak, also one of the many expressions of the ongoing colonial and racial violence perpetrated by the US government.

As Amy Kaplan writes, "Guantánamo Bay had been a strategic colonial site since the arrival of the Spanish in the fifteenth century" (Kaplan 2005, 834); the US occupation and lease of this region goes back to the Cuban war of independence against Spanish rule in 1895. In 1898, the US decided to aid Cuba in its efforts to fight the Spanish. However, following a three-month war that ended in a Cuban victory, the US refused to accept Cuban independence, and instead occupied the island for almost three years. The US withdrew its troops from the island only after signing the *Platt Amendment* in 1901, which granted the US the right to undertake military intervention in Cuba, as well as to take control of the Cuban economy, and "guaranteed the lease or purchase of coaling and naval stations, a provision that would lead to leasing Guantánamo Bay in 1903" (Kaplan 2005, 835). Though the *Platt Amendment* was subsequently canceled in 1934, the US lease of Guantánamo Bay was extended indefinitely, until both countries could reach a bilateral agreement to cancel it. The contemporary detention facility at the Guantánamo Bay Naval Station continues this colonial and imperial history, as well as prolonging the various uses which the US has made of the territory over the years. Of particular note is the historical role played by Guantánamo at the end of the 20th century, when Haitian and Cuban refugees were prevented from entering the US, and ended up being "quarantined" at the Naval Base. In 1991, following the military *coup d'état* in Haiti, the US initiated "Operation GTMO" / "Operation Safe Harbor," and built a tent city at the Guantánamo Bay Naval Base which was able to house around 10,000 Haitians who were waiting under uncertain circumstances for transfer to the US. Subsequently, between 1994 and 1996, when around 50,000 Haitian and Cuban citizens were seeking political and economic asylum in the US, the US government initiated "Operation Sea Signal" at Guantánamo.

A trenchant example of how the guided tours constitute a prolongation of the colonial and racial violence perpetrated by the US government at this site can be found in early 2002, when the main and only detention infrastructure was the "provisional" Camp X-Ray. In 2002, the organized group tours were associated not only with the experience of tourism – as the citation from Karen J. Greenberg's *The Least Worst Place* in the introduction to this chapter suggests – but also, in the words of Major Tim Nichols, with visits to a "petting zoo" (Greenberg 2009, 91), a phrase which expresses the racializing and speciating function of these tours, while also echoing the association of its infrastructure with "dog cells" (Greenberg 2009, 18). During the first 100 days after the official opening of the detention facility, the tours were largely improvised, much like everything else occurring in the camp during that period. Due to the new circumstances at the Guantánamo detention facility, and the camp not being based on a known military precedent, "command decisions about nearly every aspect of detainee life, including medical policies, legal considerations, press relations, and religious observances" were to a large degree improvised (Greenberg 2009, 90). Over the course of time, however, the tours became more and more rigid in their scripts and institutional frameworks. In the case of the guided media tours, which differ from tours for military officials or politicians, one of the institutional frameworks guiding and restricting the conduct of visitors to the camp is the document entitled *Media Policy at Guantánamo Bay, Cuba: Agree to Abide* (DoD 2010). This document, published online as late as 2010, (but very likely to have existed in an earlier version) and republished in 2021 (DoD 2021), states the ground rules to be followed by independent journalists participating in the guided media tours. The DoD describes these tours as being part of the "effort to encourage open reporting and promote transparency" (DoD 2010, 3). Their claim reiterates the JTF-Guantánamo's motto: "Safe, Humane, Legal, Transparent," a motto that contradicts everything the detention facility actually is.

Transparency and Opacity

The notion of "transparency" is key to analyzing the "image of" the camp projected through the *Media Policy* document as well as the broader institutional discourses surrounding the camp. First, we must acknowledge that transparency itself is an effect which is produced rather than simply being a given. Nevertheless, the circumstances of this production are usually rendered invisible to the viewer. The notion of "transparency" thus can never keep its promise; the promise to provide an unhindered and unmediated view of the objects and subjects. One reason for this is that transparency itself is dependent upon – and can only come into being through – processes of mediation. Every form of transparency is established and shaped by a broad range of human and non-human agents. The "case of" Guantánamo intensifies the difficulty of defining what transparency actually means. The conceptual opacity of transparency thus makes it necessary to offer a preliminary definition of this term before applying it to what we actually see when we look at Guantánamo and its images. In this way, I want to establish the link between forms of highly restricted seeing and the DoD's claim of transparency.

In recent years, the concept of "transparency" has become an intense subject of public debate, widely discussed in the news media, as well as in media and cultural studies. Nevertheless, our understanding of this term can be as opaque as the phenomenon it is meant to signify. In their introduction to the edited volume *Transparency, Society and Subjectivity*, Emmanuel Alloa and his co-editor Dieter Thomä ask the crucial question: "what does 'transparency' refer to?" (Alloa and Thomä 2008, 2). Significantly, to foster a working definition of transparency, Alloa and Thomä use a metaphor that frequently crops up in the field of film and media studies – that of the window:

> The metaphoric level of the notion [of transparency] seems to strangely mirror its literal meaning: the perfectly transparent window is one which completely diverts the attention from itself. *The less we see the windowpane, the more we see through it.* But having seeing-through be synonymous with overlooking, makes it easy to understand why transparency – as an operative concept – rarely is an object of reflection in its own right. (Alloa and Thomä 2008, 3; italics added)

The metaphor of the window is particularly productive for describing the phenomenon of transparency, as well as for thinking about how institutional discourses came to guide and frame the perception of Guantánamo. Importantly, the less viewers see the ways that the image of Guantánamo is mediated and controlled, the more transparent the detention camp appears to them. A similar observation can be made regarding a person looking through a windowpane, which is, by necessity, framed.

In his own chapter in the same volume, Alloa takes up a more detailed discussion of the significance of the window frame with regard to the concept of transparency. In "Transparency: A Magic Concept of Modernity," Alloa states that "[a]ny form of phenomenal transparency *requires certain framings*, just as a windowpane is *not unrestrictedly transparent, but only within a certain given frame*" (Alloa 2008, 52; italics added). Of interest here is not only the question of what it means to look through a windowpane without noticing it, but also how its frame conditions the transparency effect.[2] The work of Judith Butler (2009), or earlier writings such as Erving Goffman's *Frame Analysis* (1974), call into question Alloa's observation that "[s]o far, the specific *interventions of framing are hardly ever analyzed*, when it comes to psychological, moral and social framings" (Alloa 2008, 52; italics added). Nevertheless, Alloa highlights an important point: the effect of transparency exists only in relation to a given frame, and such frames are not only visual, but also social, moral, or even psychological. A frame is thus not only a means of facilitating an unhindered view of the objects the viewer is supposed to be looking at; it is also a structuring device that arranges elements. Significantly, the frame produces "an optic continuity between things in a row, but it also underscores, by visually superposing them, their unanticipated interconnections" (Alloa 2008, 52). The window, windowpane, and window frame are helpful visual metaphors for thinking about transparency. However, if we approach the phenomenon via the claim made by the DoD that it is seeking to make Guantánamo (appear)

2   Although Alloa uses the metaphor of the window to define how we might understand "transparency," it is important to note that window glass is almost never fully transparent.

transparent, then we must consider how such framing extends far beyond the visual dimension. Following Alloa's suggestion, we must comprehend the broad variety of frames that influence the perception of Guantánamo and the men detained therein.

Nonetheless, to reach these broader dimensions, we must first deal with the visual, material frames of images – perhaps the edge of a photograph, or the *cadrage* of a video "illustrating" the situation at the detention facility. Most of the time the viewer is not supposed to recognize these frames as restrictions, excluding that which has no place in the image. Rather, the frame encourages us to look merely at the surfaces of the images. Secondly, we must consider institutional frames. It is not only the DoD or its military that impose such frames; news media and human rights organizations also provide us with multilayered alternative frames. Other institutions of control include written documents such as manuals, memoranda, or directives. Finally, when dealing with media objects from Guantánamo and the way they restrict our view of the detainees, we need to attend to the social and moral framings imposed by the military apparatus as well. This apparatus is put relentlessly to work when it comes to what or whom we can perceive in images from Guantánamo.

Returning to the *Media Policy* document, the rules and procedures described therein are framed by the statement that the DoD "will facilitate media access to the maximum extent possible, in an effort to encourage open reporting and promote transparency" (DoD 2010, 3). If we analyze these provisions in detail, however, they turn out to be working in favor of anything but a transparent detention facility. Instead, the rules and procedures appear to be an expression of what I will subsequently term "a strategy of opacity." The notion of "opacity" has been assigned quite a positive connotation in post-colonial studies. However, when considering the difficulties imposed on the viewer with regard to understanding or "*grasp[ing]*" (Glissant 1997, 191) what is happening at Guantánamo, opacity can also be interpreted in a different way. Édouard Glissant, one of the most prominent theoreticians of opacity, writes in *Politics of Relations* that the opacity of subjects functions as a poetic force that opposes the established structures of power (Glissant 1997, 189ff.).[3] He states that

> [i]f we examine the process of 'understanding' people and ideas from the perspective of Western thought, we discover that its *basis is this requirement of transparency.* In order to understand and thus accept you, I have to measure your solidity with the ideal scale providing me with

3   I am aware of the vast literature published on the notion of "opacity" in the fields of philosophy, cultural and media studies, however, I will focus primarily on Glissant's view in the following discussion since his work continues to be a central reference point for contemporary thinkers working on these issues.

grounds to make comparisons and, perhaps, judgements. *I have to reduce*. (Glissant 1997, 189f.; italics added)

In relation to subjectivity, Glissant defines transparency as a strategy that makes subjects understandable and measurable to the persisting structures of power. Transparency is thus understood as a reductive power that annihilates differences between subjects, or does not permit such differences to exist. By contrast, opacity makes subjects unreadable to the structures of power, and thus works against the reductionist aspects of transparency. "It [the opaque] is that which cannot be reduced, which is the most perennial guarantee of participation and confluence" (Glissant 1997, 191), writes Glissant. The opaque evades the aim of transparency, which is "*to grasp*" (Glissant 1997, 191) subjects, or to make them graspable and, hence, manageable.

As a critical concept that undergirds the acknowledgement of difference between subjects, and the corresponding possibility of opposing the unifying and reductive aspects of power, opacity can be regarded in a positive light. At Guantánamo, however, the DoD and the JTF-Guantánamo appear to have appropriated these positive effects and maneuvered them in a totally different direction. The objects and subjects that the public perceives in images shot on the inside of the detention facility are rendered opaque and unreadable. But this is not undertaken with the aim of opposing the power relations put in place at Guantánamo; instead, it is designed to reinforce or consolidate them.[4] Under the cloak of transparency, Guantánamo, and the practices carried out by its personnel, are made visible only in such a manner that someone outside of the US military or security apparatus would not be able to comprehend or grasp them. Rather than being employed by the DoD to evade the pre-existing structures of power, the effects of opacity are instead used to enforce them. Thus, while opacity of subjects makes it difficult for state power to exercise control or restraint and for the oppressed opacity can be liberating, when implemented by the state power, opacity allows for a perverted kind of liberation: an unchecked power evading public monitoring.[5]

Both concepts – of opacity, on the one hand, and transparency, on the other – are central to the strategies employed by the Department concerning Guantánamo's visual culture. In the next subsection, I will argue that Guantánamo is a strategically opaque detention facility, rather the transparent one it claims to be. More specifically, I will focus on the role of journalists whose visits to the detention facility are described by the US government as making a significant contribution to Guantánamo's

4   In the next chapter, I will show how the situation is diametrically different within the detention facility and the military apparatus itself, and how military personnel seek to make the detainees epistemically available for inside parties. In relation to Glissant's critique, this can also be seen as an effort to enforce transparency on the detainees.
5   I would like to thank Dan J. Ruppel for sharing with me his thoughts on this passage.

transparency (DoD 2010, 3). In fact, as my discussion will show, the guided media tours are staged in such a way that both the tours themselves and the resulting photographic objects are simultaneously transparent and opaque.

The *Media Policy* and its Denial of Visibility

The *Media Policy* document provides an essential perspective into how the Guantánamo media tours are designed and regulated (DoD 2010). Journalists are obliged to acknowledge and sign this document – which is, more precisely, a contract between visitors and the DoD – prior to their arrival at the base, and only after they have successfully undergone an extensive background check. The document discloses that the DoD is the "sole release authority for all military information contained in all media" (DoD 2010, 3), and lays out the types of information journalists are forbidden to write down, forward, discuss, or publish in any form:

> Protected information necessarily includes classified information. Pro-
> tected Information also includes (i) information the disclosure of which
> could reasonably be expected to cause damage to the national security,
> including intelligence or law enforcement sources, methods, or activities,
> or jeopardize the physical safety of individuals, and (ii) information sub-
> ject to a properly-issued protective order by an official authorized to issue
> such orders by law or regulation. (DoD 2010, 4)

The document does not clearly define the specific nature or even the material constitution of the information which is protected. Hence, it might be the kind of information related to the methods and routine activities of military personnel that journalists might witness during their visit to Guantánamo; it might also be a photograph showing a glimpse of the surveillance infrastructure. Rather than being accidental, this lack of precision is intentional: by being formulated in such a vague way, the document enables the photographic material and information gathered by news-media representatives to be assessed on a case-by-case basis, giving the DoD absolute freedom when it comes to censoring the output of the tours.

As the document progresses, however, the rules become more precise, especially when it outlines the limitations with regard to photography and video [fig. 6]. In particular, the section entitled "D. General Photography and Video Limitations," demonstrates how the detainees are being denied forms of visibility, framing what we will be able to see of Guantánamo (DoD 2010, 4f.). In this section, the DoD includes a list of objects and subjects that are prohibited from being recorded on camera. This begins with the prohibition of photographs showing "[f]rontal facial views, profiles, 3/4 views, or any view revealing a detainee's identity" (DoD 2010, 4). In relation to military personnel, it also prohibits the recording of "JTF-GTMO personnel, without their consent" (DoD 2010, 4). Apart from the restrictions applying to the human beings who are either detained or employed at Guantánamo, the list largely focuses on inanimate objects, particularly those belonging to the facility's infrastructure (DoD 2010, 4f.). Although a large part of these prohibitions are standardized restrictions for detention facilities and military bases, the inclusion of human subjects and non-human objects in one single list evokes the impression that the DoD does not differentiate here between, or create a hierarchy of, "threats" that may potentially arise from the different subjects or objects being filmed or photographed. The document attributes an equalizing function to the camera and photographic images: the possibility that different objects and subjects can be captured by a camera establishes a certain equivalence between them, as well as the types of "threats" that might result from the distribution of their images. However, within the discourse shaped by the US government, not all of these restrictions are framed by the rhetoric of "threat" or "national security." The official reason given for the restrictions on depicting the faces of the detainees or producing any image that would disclose their identity is, instead, grounded in the rhetoric of the "protection" of the detained men.

The US government has continuously argued that the denial of visibility to, and visual representations of, the detainees is a result of efforts to comply with the *Geneva Convention III*, which protects Prisoners of War (POWs) from "public curiosity" (*Geneva Convention III* (August 12, 1949), 87). At this point, it is difficult to ignore the fact that granting the detainees visibility could have led to the identification of these individuals early on, and might have accelerated the process of them acquiring legal representation by human-rights lawyers. Nevertheless, the US government has consistently argued that the *Geneva Convention III* prohibits any kind of humiliation of captives, and that identifying individuals would have necessarily resulted in their stigmatization. This is, of course, true to a certain extent – and, as the cases of detainees rejecting appearances in documentaries or photographs also show, sometimes the detainees themselves have refused to be depicted. However, the US government's justifications of these restrictions deserve to be seen in a critical light. As I discussed in the previous chapter, the official discourse that employs humanitarian arguments to justify the denial of identification demonstrates how the DoD instrumentalizes the rhetoric of "protection" and "care." Thus, instead of giving the detainees the opportunity to decide for themselves whether or not they want to be photographed, this regulation has been applied with such rigor that it has indeed, in some cases, obstructed judicial overview, legal representation of the detainees, and insight into what is really happening at Guantánamo. Furthermore, over the long-term – from approximately 2002 to 2006 – the US government not only succeeded in withholding the names and photographs of the majority of the detainees but, in some cases, even managed to keep secret the names and the fact that they were detaining certain persons at all.[6] We now know from diaries, autobiographies, official reports, and statements made by lawyers that the abduction and "rendition" of men was a common practice in the US "Global War on Terror" (GWoT). Special attention should be paid to the Central Intelligence Agency's (CIA's) Rendition, Detention and Interrogation Program, to which many of the men were subjugated before arriving at Guantánamo.

One of the better documented cases from the camp is that of Abu Zubaydah, who is still detained at Guantánamo, and whose abduction and torture were described in detail in *The Official Senate Report on CIA Torture: Committee Study of the Central Intelligence Agency's Detention and Interrogation Program* (US Senate 2015). His case, and this report, illustrate the CIA's extreme secrecy when it comes to disclosing the location of men abducted within the framework of the Rendition, Detention and Interrogation Program. When Zubaydah was detained at the "DETENTION SITE GREEN" (US Senate 2015, 24), one of the CIA's so-called "black sites," CIA officers repeatedly checked who knew his precise location. The report states that, as soon as the "CIA learned that a major US newspaper knew that Abu Zubaydah was in Country ████████," CIA officials and Richard B. "Dick" Cheney not only asked the "the newspaper not to publish the information," but also decided "to close the DETENTION SITE GREEN" (US Senate 2015, 24). In similar cases, the relatives of abducted persons and the lawyers who should have been permitted to offer them legal protection were not only denied knowledge of the men's locations, but were sometimes even denied the information that the subject was in CIA custody. Making people disappear by abducting them and placing them in CIA black sites would appear to be the US government's way of saying: "we won't confirm whether someone is here." In contrast, the denial of identification in spite of visibility is equivalent to them saying: "here is someone, but we cannot say who this someone is." Because my focus is on the images released from Guantánamo, and on the question of what we see when we look at them, I am more interested in the latter. However, it is important to bear in mind other related practices that resulted in the disappearance of men all over the world.

The denial of identification via visual representation has significantly obstructed the right of the detainees to legal representation, undermining the oversight function of the judicial branch. To a certain extent, it has also functioned as a frame facilitating the denial of social and legal recognition to the detainees (see Chapter 1), which has helped the DoD to establish a dehumanizing and depersonalizing norm at Guantánamo. Nevertheless, as stated, the DoD argued that it served the opposite function: that it was a

6   In the next chapter, I describe the *Associated Press v. DoD* lawsuit that led to the publication of two lists containing detailed information about the detainees, including their names, citizenships, and places and dates of birth. Photographs of the detainees were also subject to this request. However, Judge Jed S. Rakoff ruled in favor of the DoD and ordered that these photographs should remain sealed for security and privacy reasons.

"humane" practice. Government discourse repeatedly claimed that the frame that facilitates this denial of recognition actually acknowledges the humanity – in terms of the human rights granted to POWs by the *Geneva Convention III* – and vulnerability of the detainees. As Elspeth S. Van Veeren rightly points out, the "effacement may be done in the name of 'humane treatment' and 'in the spirit of Geneva,' [nevertheless] it succeeds again in stripping detainees of an important part of the connection between the viewer and the subject in these images – their ability to return a gaze" (Van Veeren 2011a, 1742). Indeed, the *Media Policy* document also regulates in-person contact between visitors and detainees with the following rule:

> *At no time during a media visit is communication (verbal, written or other) with a detainee allowed.* Attempting to communicate with a detainee and photographing or taking video of a detainee's attempts to communicate with members of the media are prohibited. If detainees become agitated at the presence of media, the media may be asked to leave for the *safety and security of the detainees*, NMR [news-media representatives] and the guard force. (DoD 2010, 4; italics added)

While the rule prohibiting photographs of the detainees' faces disrupts the connection or potential for communication between viewers of the photographs and the detainees they show, this rule restricts face-to-face communication at the facility, as well as further limiting what or whom people viewing the photographs or videos shot at Guantánamo will be permitted to perceive.

An important insight gained by analyzing the officially approved photographs taken during these organized media tours is that the detainees' faces have been largely excluded or are "missing" throughout the many years that this detention facility has been in operation. This does not mean that there are no images depicting the detainees or infrastructure. Quite the opposite, in fact: a plethora of images has contributed to the camp's highly curated form of visibility. But, in spite of this excess of images, the representations of faces of the detainees have been often withheld; in addition, the viewer is unlikely ever to encounter the names of the depicted detainees in most of the news media captions accompanying the images. This remained the case even after the names of the detainees were released in 2006.[7]

---

7   In 2011, WikiLeaks released secret documents, the so-called "JTF GTMO Detainee Assessment[s]," that were issued between 2002 to 2008 at Guantánamo, some of which (besides the personal information) also contain mugshots of the detainees that were subject to the assessments (WikiLeaks 2011). Furthermore, also the *Guantánamo Docket* project of *The New York Times* includes portraits of the detainees (Almukhtar, et al. 2022). The photos are credited to a wide range of human rights organizations, image agencies, and to the detainees themselves (Almukhtar, et al. 2022).

In "Captured by the Camera's Eye: Guantánamo and the Shifting Frame of the Global War on Terror," Van Veeren categorizes the plethora of photographs from Guantánamo into three groups: the orange series, the white series, and the empty-cells series (Van Veeren 2011a, 1729). She writes that, in contrast to other detention facilities, such as Camp Bucca and Camp Nama, both located in Iraq, "there are thousands of photos of Guantánamo from inside the wire, many of which since 2007 have been available on the JTF-Guantánamo website" (Van Veeren 2011a, 1728). The large number of photographs available from inside the detention facility would seem to support the US government's avowals of transparency about what is happening in Guantánamo. However, we must bear in mind that a complex apparatus of censorship pre-frames the release of any visual representation of the detainees, and that we have been presented with images which deny them visibility and make it difficult to identify them as individuals. Thus, the enormous number of images available to the public actually contributes to the difficulty in grasping what is happening in Guantánamo, contradicting the DoD's claim of transparency. Nevertheless, these images do permit us to see the various tactics taken to render the identities of the detainees invisible. The denial of visibility in the so-called "orange" and "white" series is achieved by obscuring the detainees' faces, either by the addition of objects such as masks and goggles, or by permitting photographers to only take pictures of the detainees' from behind. For example, in the photographs taken by the military photographer Shane T. McCoy [fig. 1 and 3], identities are concealed by blackened goggles, ear protectors, and masks. The photographs from the "white series" – so named by Van Veeren because the detainees are wearing white rather than orange jumpsuits, indicating that they are "compliant"[8] – depict only views from behind. In the third and last series identified by Van Veeren – the empty-cells series – the effacement of the detainees is even more extreme: in these photographs, viewers can only see the camp's infrastructure, with a complete visual absence of the detainees. The images of empty cells are supposed to shift the viewers' focus from the detained men to the operational side of the facility – but, in spite of this, they actually evoke the feeling of Guantánamo as a place haunted by the ghostly apparitions of the detainees.

---

8   The detainees were not suddenly all given white clothing to wear. At a certain point, orange clothing was reserved for detainees assessed to be non-complaint. By contrast, "tan-and-white" clothing came to signify cooperative detainees (Van Veeren 2016b, 126). According to Juliet Ash, there were also "brown [jumpsuits] for those who were segregated in solitary confinement" (Ash 2010, 159).

The Frame of Virtual Visits

Absence and Presence of the Detainees

It is not only news-media representatives who can be "Guantánamo tourists" – anyone who goes to the website of the Defense Visual Information Distribution Service, or even goes to YouTube and searches for videos of media tours at the detention camp or virtual visits to the facility, will receive a fragmentary glimpse of what is happening "over there." In this section, I will focus on two videos of virtual visits (The Broadcast Report 2008c; 2008d) that the general public can access via YouTube, and which pertain to the camps, their histories, and the living conditions of the detainees held there. In "Captured by the Camera's Eye: Guantánamo and the Shifting Frame of the Global War on Terror," Van Veeren writes that virtual visits to Guantánamo – with exception of the "Platinum Camp" – were also available on the JTF-Guantánamo homepage (Van Veeren 2011a, 1728).[9] In this and the next subsection, I will analyze how military personnel and the DoD aim to render the detainees, objects, and certain practices at Guantánamo invisible in those videos by making them (visually) disappear, thereby attempting to force a specific perceptual frame on the viewers. I will argue that, despite the visual absence of the detainees, the viewers can still perceive their phenomenological presence, and discuss how the DoD has consequently failed to impose its perceptual frames.

One virtual visit is particularly interesting. In June 2008, Lance T. Cagnolatti, who received the nickname "Mr. Broadcast" during his deployment to Guantánamo "work[ing] in media relations and broadcasting," uploaded a video entitled "Guantánamo Bay Detention Facility – Virtual Visit Camp X-Ray" to his personal YouTube channel (Cagnolatti 2022; The Broadcast Report 2008d).[10] In contrast to the infamous images taken by McCoy in 2002, discussed in the previous chapter, Cagnolatti's video reveals the camp after it had become inoperative, showing that by 2008 the camp's initial infrastructure had already become overgrown by grass and was uninhabited by humans. The following caption was provided with the video:

> Camp X-Ray was built in the early 80's. Originally, the government used it to hold delinquent migrants. Enemy combatants captured during United States operations in the Global War on Terror were brought to Camp

---

9   The link www.jtfgtmo.southcom.mil/vvvintro.html no longer works (Van Veeren 2011a, 1728). Therefore, here I will discuss the videos which are still available on YouTube.

10 On the Defense Visual Information Distribution Service website, the public can access videos that reveal how journalists were guided through the inoperative Camp X-Ray in 2009 (Wolff 2009a), as well as through Camps 5 and 6 of Camp Iguana (Wolff 2009b). Cagnolatti has also published two further virtual visits that might be of interest in relation to Richard Wolff's videos (Broadcast Report 2008a; 2008b).

X-Ray in January 2002. They were held here until Camp Delta opened a few months later in April 2002. *JTF Guantánamo conducts safe and humane care and custody of detained enemy combatants*. JTF Guantánamo conducts operations *ethically*, *legally* and *transparently*. For more info visit www. jtfgtmo.southcom.mil. (The Broadcast Report 2008d; italics added)

But what is it that we actually see when we watch this video? On the simplest level, the video depicts nothing more than the abandoned detention facility. With the opening of Camp Delta in April 2002, just three months after the arrival of the first detainees at Guantánamo, the DoD closed Camp X-Ray. However, although it is no longer used for detention purposes, the efforts of human rights lawyers mean its infrastructure still exists. These lawyers requested that Camp X-Ray be maintained because, at a future date, it could function as potential proof of the crimes committed by the US government. As a result, in 2005 a US court ordered that this camp should remain protected rather than being torn down (Rosenberg 2018). Under the Trump administration, the existence of this part of the detention camp was again at risk. The administration planned to replace the physical infrastructure with an "interactive, simulated three-dimensional, digital virtual tour of Camp X-Ray that shows all areas of the camp where detainees were held, interrogated, or otherwise present" (Warden as cited in Rosenberg 2018), as Andrew Warden, a Justice Department attorney, stated in an interview. This interactive virtual tour was to be created by the Federal Bureau of Investigations and was supposed to be released after the demolition of the initial detention facility. Nevertheless, for the time being, Camp X-Ray is still standing, and, until 2016, journalists and other visitors were guided through it during the media tours. As Carol Rosenberg reports in the *Miami Herald*, between 2016 and 2018 "Navy admirals in charge of the prison" decided that "the site was no longer part of the story … [they] wanted reporters telling" (Rosenberg 2018).

The YouTube video "Guantánamo Bay Detention Facility – Virtual Visit Camp X-Ray" thus shows moving images of the "emptied out" Camp X-Ray accompanied by a male voice-over – whereas the Camp itself is marked by a stillness resembling the stillness of ruins. Most of the time, the narrator comments on what the viewers can see in the video; at the beginning, he recalls that the facility was used for "delinquent migrants," and reiterates the information contained in the caption that is provided with the video. He goes on to inform the viewer that, from 1994 to 1996, the base was used for "Operation Sea Signal, when over 50,000 Haitian and Cuban migrants sought out both political and economic asylum" (The Broadcast Report 2008d, 00:25–33). Then, there is a jump in the timeline to 2002, and the narrator recounts that this part of the detention facility was used to detain men captured in the course of the US GWoT. At this point, the camera moves through the outdoor infrastructure of mesh and barbwire, and the indoor architecture of the wooden sheds.

[Fig. 7] Screenshots of the YouTube video "Guantánamo Bay Detention Facility – Virtual Visit Camp X-Ray" showing the overgrown, empty Camp X-Ray, the site where McCoy took the infamous photographs discussed in Chapter 1 (Source: The Broadcast Report 2008d). The appearance of US Department of Defense (DoD) visual information does not imply or constitute DoD endorsement.

An important aspect of the video's storytelling strategy is that the narrator formulates his sentences in the past tense, which, in combination with images depicting only minimal barbwire, and revealing wild flora climbing up the now invisible fences, evokes the feeling that this recounted history must have happened a very long time ago [fig. 7].

Furthermore, the images are accompanied by sounds of nature, and what I would like to call the sound of abandoned infrastructures. The viewer can hear birds tweeting and the occasional sound of metallic objects colliding, possibly caused by the silent wind; the most prominent sound is the chirping of grass-hoppers and crickets cooling down from Guantánamo's heat in the long grass. Of equal importance, however, is what the viewer does not hear: all sounds of the human lives being lived while the video was shot – from detainees and guards alike – are inaudible. But although the place might seem to be uninhab-ited on a visual level, it does indeed become populated by the detainees and guards, thanks to the narration and the viewer's imagination. The narrator evokes the iconography of Camp X-Ray, and comments that the second screenshot in fig. 7 shows the place where McCoy took his photographs [fig. 1 and 3]: "This main alley is the site of the camp's first photographs, the notorious images. Here and the road were the only authorized areas for any media personnel to take photos or video. When the detainees arrived, everyone wore the same orange suit. Now they're dressed according to com-pliancy" (The Broadcast Report 2008d, 01:17–32). Interestingly, the evocation of the photographs to which I dedicated the previous chapter stands in stark contrast to the images displayed in the video itself. It is as if, by means of juxtaposition, the video is telling us a story about events that happened long ago; at the same time, its main intent seems to be to increase the distance between the present – both the present of 2008, when the video was pub-lished, and the future presents when it will be viewed – and the history of Camp X-Ray, without necessarily having to deny this history altogether.

The video then cuts from the main alley to pan over the detention cages, followed by an image of a green tarpaulin [fig. 7]. The voiceover reveals that these tarpaulins "were placed throughout the perimeter of the camp to prevent any unauthorized pictures" (The Broadcast Report 2008d, 01:34–8). Apparently, "the tarps also blocked the hot sun and protected them [the detainees] from the weather" (The Broadcast Report 2008d, 01:38–43). Here, we find a similar rhetoric to the one employed by Secretary of Defense Donald Rumsfeld back in January 2002, when he explained to the public the reasoning behind the equipment which the detainees were forced to wear during the arrival procedure at Camp X-Ray. Instead of acknowledging that it was part of the technique of sensory deprivation, Rumsfeld argued that it was deployed for the detainees' protection and safety (DoD 2002b). Here, the voiceover lends the tarpaulin a similar ambiguity: on the one hand, it prevented the media and other parties from being able to record the horrendous living conditions in Camp X-Ray; on the other, its role was to protect the detainees from the heat of the Guantánamo sun.

Viewers also learn from the online video that the now "desolate camp" previously had guard towers, non-electronic locks, a commandant and administrative section, a cinder-block structure accommodating shower units for the detainees, and "eight by eight [sic] cells" (The Broadcast Report 2008d, 00:10–1 and 02:17–9). Later on, the cells were equipped with hand/foot washers as well as gravity pipes to replace the buckets for excrement. The camp also had an internal hospital for the detained men. As the video reveals exterior and interior images of the now empty wooden architecture of the hospital, the narrator describes it as follows:

> Upon arrival, all detained enemy combatants were screened for any possible medical conditions. Anticipating battle wounds, infections, mild forms of TB [tuberculosis], and other various ailments, the Marine Corps Hospital inside Camp X-Ray operated 24 hours a day, observing the physical health of the detainees. This hospital was equipped with x-ray machines, MRI [Magnetic Resonance Imaging] scanners, and other equipment used to help diagnose medical conditions. (The Broadcast Report 2008d, 02:50–03:14)

Hence, the viewer is guided through the various elements that once formed the "provisional" detention camp, and while the narration causes the images to become populated by human agents, objects, and practices, the images themselves express an absence that will persist long into the future.

However, when watching this video, the following questions arise: what kind of absence is this? Is it an absence which is limited in its geographical and temporal span? What is the camera panning across weedy landscapes of metal and wood, devoid of people, prisoners or guards, expressing? And, what is the relationship between presence and absence, when the only sounds that fill Camp X-Ray are the narrator's voice and the subtle noise of flourishing animal and plant life? Although prompted by a close analysis of this particular video, these questions are also relevant to the other images released from Guantánamo, once again prompting the query: what do we see, when we look at these images?

At the core of these images of abandoned structures, I argue, lies a negotiation of the relationship between the absence and presence of the detained men. While the military apparatus used the restrictions discussed above to regulate the representation of the detainees and to try to render them invisible, the absences produced by these restrictions in fact reveal – and emphasize – the exact opposite phenomenon: *the acute presence of the detainees in their visual absence*. The decision to emphasize the absence of subjects, objects, and practices at Guantánamo in the framework of virtual visits evokes something else – a haunting, non-visual presence of the detainees.

In his essay "Portrait of Absence: The Aisthetic Mediality of Empty Chairs" (2016), Tomáš Jirsa presents a persuasive argument about the shifts between visual absence and phenomenological presence in relation to portraiture, which can easily and productively be applied to images showing the now-deserted buildings and infrastructure of Camp X-Ray. Jirsa asks the following, crucial questions: "[W]hat happens if a *disappearing subject is replaced by an object*; does it become its mere substitute? Does the object left after the subject *embody its invisibility*, its absence or a desire for it?" (Jirsa 2016, 14; italics added). For Jirsa, it is the empty chair that "[in a remarkable way] embodies but also *mediates* and *materializes* this absence [of the subject]" (Jirsa 2016, 14). Chairs, as Jirsa tells us, play an important role in the history of portraiture, since they are the material entity on which the body of the portrayed person was usually rendered visible. He writes that the absence of a subject is *"perform[ed]"* (Jirsa 2016, 20) by an empty chair. Similarly, in the case of Guantánamo, it is the uninhabited, unused infrastructure that takes on this role. Jirsa bases his reflections on the relationship between the trace, absence, and presence on Sybille Krämer's book, *Medium, Messenger, Transmission: An Approach to Media Philosophy* (2015). Krämer argues that, even though we might be dealing with a visible trace – exemplarily in or as photographs – "what produced it remains withdrawn and invisible" (Krämer 2015, 174). According to her, the relationship between presence and absence – between the trace and what it indexes – is multilayered, because "the presence of the trace visualizes the non-presence of what left it behind" (Krämer 2015, 174). Importantly, at the same time, this non-presence is actually made present to the viewer; it is "not the absent thing itself, but rather its absence" (Krämer 2015, 174) that the trace stands for. Hence, for a trace to be a trace, there must be a "fundamental *asynchrony*" (Krämer 2015, 174) between the moment it was produced and the moment it is perceived. This temporal discrepancy is certainly present on many levels when viewers take a virtual tour of the now inoperative Camp X-Ray and hear the story told by the narrator interspersed with the sounds of the animal life now present at the site.

Whereas Jirsa's focus lies mainly on absent human subjects, the empty infrastructure depicted in the video appears to trace a broader range of absences. The absence of the detainees in "Guantánamo Bay Detention Facility – Virtual Visit Camp X-Ray" is performed not only by the inanimate objects which are visible in the images, but also by the narrator, who appears to complicate their absence on an acoustic level. This narrator refers, on more than one occasion, to the presence of the detainees and military personnel, however, he does so in a way which suggests to the viewer that this is a presence from a very long time ago and that, today, the detainees who once were caged there can only ever be absent. Thus, the images, intertwined with the narrator's story-telling, make present the absence of subjects such as the detained men, and the military and medical personnel; the absence of objects such as buckets, MRI scanners, and X-ray machines, *et cetera*; and the absence of daily events such as the physical restraint of detainees, guards feeding the detainees through the bean hole, or detainees throwing buckets filled with excrement at the guards. The video also supports the thesis that the "absence … is not and cannot be definitive," and is instead "in a state of oscillation between presence and absence, between appearing and disappearing" (Jirsa 2016, 19). While por-traiture in its traditional form is not accompanied by sound, but still has the ability to speak to us despite the absence of an acoustic voice, the voice of the narrator in the video – who makes the infrastructure and its history speak – and the sounds of animal life effect a perceptual shift from a mode of reading into a mode of listening to traces.

In her book, *Listening to Images* (2017), Tina M. Campt presents a cogent argument that listening is an important alternative to perceiving images by sight alone. Campt writes that to listen to images is "a method of recalibrating vernacular photographs as quiet, quotidian practices that give us access to the affective registers through which these images enunciate alternate accounts of their subjects" (Campt 2017, 5). As a method, accessing images via listening has the ability to disrupt the normative frameworks that guide how images like those of the empty facilities at the Guantánamo detention camp are produced and disseminated. Campt argues that listening to images "opens up the rad-ical interpretive possibilities of images and state archives we are most often inclined to overlook, by engaging the paradoxical capacity of identity photos to rupture the sovereign gaze of the regimes that created them by refusing the very terms of photographic subjection they were engineered to produce" (Campt 2017, 5). In a similar vein, Laliv Melamed argues that we should read traces "through the ear" (Melamed 2018), rightly pointing out that in this mode of listening or "reading through the ear … something else can resonate" (Melamed 2018). In the virtual visit to Guantánamo and its Camp X-Ray, this "something else" resonates if we pay special attention to the sounds made by insects and birds – the remaining inhabitants of the abandoned camp. By listening to them, and to the narrator, we gain a different perceptual access to what we see in the images themselves, allowing us to approach the depicted phenomenon in a way that exceeds the rationale of knowing through the sense of sight alone. In a Glissantian sense, listening might operate differently and push against the reductive, rational visibility produced by the DoD. Thus, rather than reading the traces of absence in a visual and cognitive sense, we might find ourselves listening to them in order to oppose the ideological effects created by their production contexts. The mode of listening or reading through the ear provides a point of access to different perceptual dimensions;

more specifically, we gain access to appearances – perhaps ghostly in nature – which have only little to do with what we can see or perceive on the surfaces of images.

Thinking about what it means to listen to the traces of Camp X-Ray in light of the speculation with which Jirsa ends his essay – whether "there is such a thing as an empty chair at all" (Jirsa 2016, 28) – we might also wonder whether there is such a thing as a totally empty detention camp. It is possible that "desolate camp[s]" (The Broadcast Report 2008d, 00:10–1) are always populated, or even inhabited, by the now-absent detainees, as well as by their stories. To go even further, the mode of listening opens up dimensions of recognition beyond the field of the visible and allows us to resist the perspective that the video imposes on its viewers with regard to the circumstances at the camp. In contrast to the efforts of the DoD and the JTF-Guantánamo, the video tells us that the infrastructure, abandoned cells, and wooden sheds continue to index subjects, objects, and practices – all of which were once present and are now absent, or which are still present in their absence.

The Disappearance and Reappearance of Detainees

The aesthetics of empty cells and interiors can also be found in virtual visits to other parts of the detention camp that are still in operation and inhabited by human subjects. Even though men are still being detained, and practices are carried out on a daily basis in the operational parts of the detention camp, the aesthetic strategies adopted in these virtual visits evoke the feeling that there is only little or no life taking place there. This effect is most striking in the video entitled "Guantánamo Bay Detention Facility – Virtual Visit Camp 6" (The Broadcast Report 2008c). In this video, which is approximately two minutes in length, we are guided through a part of Camp Delta that, when the video was published in 2008, was still being used to detain men, and which continues to be maintained by military and civil personnel to this day. The impression the video leaves behind is not so different from the one evoked by "Guantánamo Bay Detention Facility – Virtual Visit Camp X-Ray," since the images of the cells and corridors in the virtual visit to Camp 6 are also marked by the dialectic of presence and absence. An important visual difference between the two videos, however, is that the images of Camp 6 neither reveal an infrastructure overgrown by plants, nor one that appears to be uninhabited or abandoned [fig. 8].

The two videos also differ in terms of the temporal structure connected to the oscillation between absence and presence: while the Camp X-Ray video vocalizes a presence which was supposedly already lying in the past during the moment when this representation of absence was produced, the video of Camp 6 shows the absence of a presence that was still in place at the moment

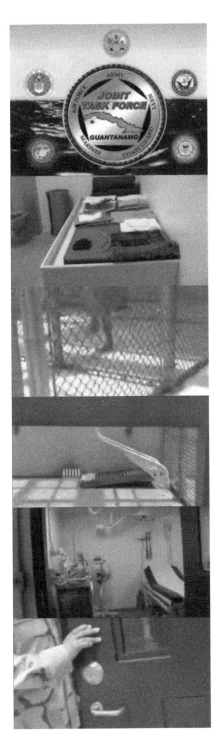

[Fig. 8] Screenshots of the YouTube video "Guantánamo Bay Detention Facility – Virtual Visit Camp 6" showing the inhabited and operational Camp 6 (Camp Delta) (Source: The Broadcast Report 2008c). The appearance of US Department of Defense (DoD) visual information does not imply or constitute DoD endorsement.

the video was shot. Rather than being framed as a history long since passed, the virtual visit to Camp 6 is accompanied by information about the costs of this particular facility, and the fact that it was completed in November 2006. A different male voice narrates the images of this camp, informing viewers that Camp 6 can take up to 160 detainees, has several interrogation rooms and rooms where detainees can meet with their lawyers, as well as four recreation facilities with soccer balls, a treadmill, and roll mats in which the detainees can socialize; a medical clinic, and a dental examination room (The Broadcast Report 2008c). Another significant difference is that the "Guantánamo Bay Detention Facility – Virtual Visit Camp 6" video does not completely exclude shots of human subjects: in some images, viewers can identify silhouettes or body parts including the hands of military personnel opening doors to various rooms, or the legs of the detainees kicking a soccer ball (as the third and sixth screenshot in fig. 8 show). However, these human subjects are filmed in such a way that it is nearly impossible to distinguish any individual features besides the fact that they are either military personnel or detainees. Thinking about Van Veeren's categorization of images from Guantánamo in three groups – the orange series, white series, and the empty-cells series – this video mainly contains material from the two latter categories; images belonging to the white series revealing the backs of "compliant" detainees, as well as those from the empty-cells series showing images of empty interiors (Van Veeren 2011a, 1729).

Whereas the virtual visit to Camp X-Ray is interested in the details of the detainees' living situation in 2002, the visit to Camp 6 is more invested in the economic and administrative aspects of the facility, despite showing incidental glimpses of human lives. At the end of the video, the narrator reveals that

> Camp 6 was built to better withstand the elements as well as to provide a climate-controlled environment making it easier for the JTF-guard force to provide security, to reduce the numbers of troopers necessary to care for the detainees, better JTF-guard force working conditions and to improve the living conditions for the detainees. (The Broadcast Report 2008c, 01:45–02:03)

Thus, the facility is framed not only by economic or administrative facts but also, in a certain sense, by details that correspond to the living conditions described in the virtual visit to Camp X-Ray. In contrast to the cells in Camp X-Ray – which, in 2008, were populated by flora and fauna, and probably are to this day – the empty cells visible in the Camp 6 video are protected from the outside world and the actions of nature by more than mere tarpaulins. The "show cell" we see in the Camp 6 video is not in any way "provisional" like the detention cells in Camp X-Ray. It is constructed from solid concrete and is completely separate from the outside world (see second screenshot in fig. 8).

In contrast to Camp X-Ray, there is only artificial lighting, with no windows to allow daylight into the room.[11]

When the camera in "Guantánamo Bay Detention Facility – Virtual Visit Camp 6" enters the cell, the viewers see a toilet and a bed in an empty room without any detainee present. On the bed, everyday objects are laid out in a very precise manner. The camera only briefly focuses on the bed, making it difficult for the viewer to recognize or identify all these objects without pausing the video. The narrator does not help viewers to grasp the scene, for instance, by describing and naming the objects they can see in the image.[12] Instead, this narrator says that "Camp 6 was envisioned as a medium-security detention facility, but during its construction in June 2006, Camp 6 was modified with safety in mind of guards and detainees alike" (The Broadcast Report 2008c, 00:28–42). The very precise organization of objects shown for a brief moment suggests that viewers are being presented with a cell that has been staged as a photo opportunity for visitors: it is a cell in which no one is actually living. Such "show cells" – which have now become part of Guantánamo's iconography – are usually prepared by Guantánamo personnel for the sole purpose of being presented to visitors. Thus, it is impossible to encounter traces of individual lives within them. The items displayed on the bed may be read as present or past traces of their potential uses by detainees, but their arrangement suggests that these particular items are not being used, and probably never will be – they have been removed from their context of daily use and displaced into the framework of a peculiar military exhibition.

The materiality and physical presence of objects such as shoes, shirts, and religious items tell us, in an uncanny way, stories of haunting: stories of bodies which are being made disappear, and which reappear to us through the representation of such everyday objects. In *Ghostly Matters: Haunting and the Sociological Imagination*, Avery F. Gordon writes that "[t]o confront those who become *desaparecido* (disappeared) under the auspices of state-sponsored terror in Argentina … is to contemplate ghosts and haunting at the level of the making and unmaking of world historical events" (Gordon 2008, 63). Although the "ghostly matter" of Gordon's analysis differs in its geographic specificity and the violent regime which caused it, I believe it still makes sense to think about such representations as the empty cells at Guantánamo through the prism of haunting. The idea of a haunting reiterates, in a different way, the phenomenon I described before as the dialectic of presence and absence.

---

11   For detainees, this means they cannot estimate the time of day by means of natural light. A good description of how detainees developed different strategies for telling time can be found in Sebastian Köthe's dissertation (Köthe 2021, 224–9).

12   At the beginning of the "Media Tour of Joint Task Force Guantánamo" video published on the Defense Visual Information Distribution Service website, the person guiding the journalists through Camp Iguana takes them into the show cell and describes the laid-out objects in more detail (Wolff 2008b).

According to Gordon, the "ghost" is not invisible but its "whole essence … is that it has a real presence and demands its due, your attention"; it "is one form by which something lost, or barely visible, or seemingly *not there to our supposedly well-trained eyes, makes itself known or apparent to us, in its own way, of course*" (Gordon 2008, xvi and 8; italics added). However, in relation to the images of empty cells and the abandoned infrastructure analyzed above, the ghosts are not only the visually absent detainees. The violent detention practices which were – and still are – employed at the Guantánamo detention camp are also ghostly appearances, which should draw a great deal of our attention. "Haunting," as Gordon writes, is a modality which "registers the harm inflicted or the loss sustained by a social violence done in the past or in the present" (Gordon 2008, xvi). Significantly, the visual material made available to the public from Guantánamo aims to preemptively negate such ghostly appearances the viewer might in fact perceive when being confronted with these images. The DoD's framing thus seeks to refocus the viewer's attention by (over)emphasizing the legality, transparency, and humanity of the practices carried out in this particular military detention facility.

Gordon's idea of disappearance diverges in a small but important way from Jirsa's argument, discussed above, about representations of empty chairs. According to Gordon, disappearances can only exist if they are "apparitional" "because the ghost or the apparition is the principal form by which something lost or invisible or seemingly not there makes itself known or apparent to us. The ghost makes itself known to us through haunting and pulls us affectively into the structure of feeling of a reality we come to experience as a recognition" (Gordon 2008, 63). In the case of Guantánamo, disappearance can be understood as a special form of knowing or anticipating: a "[h]aunting recognition [which] is a special way of knowing what has happened or is happening" (Gordon 2008, 63). Combining ideas about the presence and absence of the detainees, their appearance and disappearance, with the haunting recognition of what is happening at Guantánamo can help us to access the available material in a different manner. By reframing what we actually see when we look at Guantánamo in light of such haunting, the viewer can disrupt the logic which governs how these images are produced and distributed.

Thus, in spite of the restrictions and intense efforts made by the DoD to efface the faces and identities of the men detained at Guantánamo, what we can see and perceive in the photographs and the two videos discussed above fails to make the detainees absent or disappear. We may perceive the invisibility of the detainees alongside the efforts of the DoD to exclude them from the visual field, but the result of these efforts is the reappearance of the detainees in their disappearances, highlighting their presence in their absence. The photographic material and videos continuously negotiate the absence of the detainees, rendering it non-definitive. Even though these images try to make the detainees and practices disappear, they end up indicating the existence, presence, and appearance of subjects, objects, and practices which either once were, or still are, present in the detention camp. As the inanimate objects and empty infrastructure speak to us, a subversive reframing of these images requires us to simultaneously look at and listen to them – and to acknowledge the haunting presence of the detainees and their experiences of violence in images of their visual absence.

Reframing Invisibilized Faces

Empty Chairs and the Violence of Guantánamo

Not only journalists, but artists, too, have been confronted with the multilayered censorship apparatus deployed at the Guantánamo detention facility. For some of them, the censorship of the detainees' faces, and the regulations at Guantánamo, have even come to function as a point of departure for their work. In this and next subsection, I will focus on the work of Debi Cornwall, and in particular, her photo book entitled *Welcome to Camp America: Inside Guantánamo Bay* (Cornwall 2017g).[13] Cornwall, who has participated in three guided media tours at the detention camp, provides the viewer with a different perspective on Guantánamo, one which also reflects the legal and aesthetic frameworks imposed on external visitors. Moreover, she engages in a critical manner with the regulations laid out in the *Media Policy* document (DoD 2010), and her work makes a case for an ethical approach to representations of the men who are still being held at Guantánamo or who have been released from the detention camp.

In light of my previous analysis of the aesthetics of empty chairs, it is worth highlighting that Cornwall chose a photograph of an empty armchair for the front cover of her photo book [fig. 9]. The photograph – or rather, the left-hand side of it – indicates what we will see, and also what we will not see, in Cornwall's photo book. Firstly, it suggests that viewers will be confronted with various forms of absence of the detainees in the broad range of images compiled in the book. Secondly, the cozy, homely, and unremarkable appearance of the empty chair on Cornwall's book cover, made of materials that appear to offer its occupant a comfortable and relaxing seat, also refers to the violent regime that frames most of the photographs in the book. The empty armchair, however, does not highlight this frame in itself: the viewer's gaze has to wander across the surface of the image to discover the shackles attached to the floor in front of the chair. Significantly, without further information, this image cannot explain the use of the chair, since there are no people in the image to illustrate it. Nevertheless, the shackles suggest that

13   Camp America houses the American troops stationed at Guantánamo.

[Fig. 9] An image showing the front cover of Debi Cornwall's photo book entitled *Welcome to Camp America: Inside Guantánamo Bay*, published in 2017 by Radius Books. The photograph Cornwall chose for the jacket of the book is entitled *Compliant Detainee Media Room, Camp 5*, and was taken during her visit to the camp in 2014 (© Debi Cornwall).

those sitting in the armchair will not usually be Guantánamo personnel, and that it is most likely designated for detainees. Building on Jirsa's argument about how empty chairs evoke absent sitters, and keeping in mind the way the videos of virtual visits uploaded to YouTube indicate not only the visual absence of detainees, but also the violence inflicted on them, the shackles attached to the floor become a key element in accessing and understanding what Cornwall's cover photograph actually depicts.

Whereas the armchair emphasizes a practice of sitting, and maybe even relaxation, which is absent from the image, the shackles remind the viewer of the visual absence of violent restraining practices. Hence, the shackles disturb the impression of coziness evoked by the material constitution of the armchair, and remind the viewer of the chair's location, as well as of the necessity of questioning what is being presented to us in the center of the image. Our gaze must not only wander across the entirety of the cover image, but perhaps also beyond its frame (or inside the book) for us to understand what we are seeing when we look at this photograph. By "looking beyond the visual frame" of Guantánamo photographs we become attentive to their particular contexts, institutional and discursive frames, and, although the shackles point us in the direction of those frames, as discussed above, the photograph does not tell us by itself when and for which purpose the armchair was or is used. However, its title, *Compliant Detainee Media Room, Camp 5*, as well as various accounts from journalists and released detainees themselves, help us to understand this peculiar scenography: the armchair is located in the media room at Camp 5 in which the so-called "compliant" detainees are permitted to watch movies and play video games. Carol Rosenberg writes that "TV time is spent alone, each man shackled by an ankle to the floor of an interrogation room, always under the watch of a special guard force" (Rosenberg 2011). The armchair has also been used to force-feed detainees pursuing hunger strikes. Jason Leopold, exemplarily, mentions in an article for *Vice* the existence of video-tapes showing detainees being force-fed while sitting in it (Leopold 2015). That the force-feeding procedure would take place while watching films or playing video games was only reserved for a few detainees (Rosenberg 2014). In an interview, a female corpsman said that "if not fed in groups ... cooperative captives are allowed to play video games or watch TV while restrained in a reclining chair as they receive their nourishment" (Rosenberg 2014).[14] Never-theless, this was the exception rather than the rule. Starting from 2005, when the JTF-Guantánamo acquired the so-called "Emergency Restraint Chairs," most hunger-striking detainees were immobilized in the type of chairs deployed in psychiatric clinics to restrain patients (Golden 2006). The force-feeding procedures have been described by survivors as being so brutal and painful that many detainees actively fought against them; their resistance was then used to legitimize again the acquisition of these restraint chairs (Lennard 2014). In her book, Cornwall also included a photograph she took of an empty restraint chair that evokes these brutal procedures [fig. 10].

To return to the primary function of the armchair as a TV chair, in "Some Restrictions Apply: The Exhibition Spaces of Guantánamo Bay," Daniel Grin-berg refers to Jean-Louis Baudry's arguments about the "Ideological Effects of the Basic Cinematographic Apparatus" (Baudry 1974–5; Grinberg 2019, 62). To Grinberg, the situation of being confined in the armchair while watching movies highlights Baudry's thesis of the extreme passivity of the audience within the cinematographic apparatus. Viewers, as Baudry argues, "find themselves chained, captured, or captivated" (as cited in Grinberg 2019, 62). Whereas this thesis, as various theories on spectatorship and Grinberg him-self have shown, has been disputed, the viewing situation arranged in one of the rooms at Camp 5 is described by Grinberg as a more literal and violent translation of Baudry's observations. The detainee restrained in the media chair inhabits both positions: he is the one watching moving images, but he is also the one being watched. This is not the case for cinemagoers, who are not usually surveilled as they watch a film. Nevertheless, there is a commonality

14   I would like to thank Sebastian Köthe for pointing me toward articles discussing the force-feeding procedures.

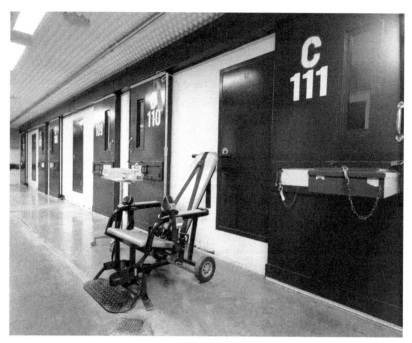

[Fig. 10] During her visit to the camp in 2015, Debi Cornwall took a photograph of an empty emergency restraint chair and entitled the photograph *Feeding Chair, Camp 5* (© Debi Cornwall).

between these two groups: cinemagoers can choose to watch a movie and leave the theatre at any time; this is also the case for the detainees. Although "TV time is spent alone" (Rosenberg 2011), it is also usually requested time and, even if they are shackled to the ground while in the room, it is the detainee who can make the decision to both enter and exit.

Regarding Cornwall's photograph of the armchair, the question of the ideological effects of Guantánamo – in terms of an apparatus that produces, archives, and distributes media objects – is not only highlighted by the practice of movie watching among the detainees, but also by the composition of Cornwall's photograph itself. The manner in which she has captured the chair and had it reproduced on her book's cover, for which she has also chosen and had printed the title *Welcome to Camp America*, focuses our attention on the power of some of these effects. The image of the armchair on the cover conceals something which only becomes clear when both sides of the photograph are put together: the strangeness of the media room's architecture. It appears to be a triangular-shaped room, in which the armchair is placed in the apex. Just above and behind the empty chair is an interior window, darkened and mirrored to obscure the surveilling authorities on the other side.[15] The photograph and architecture suggest that the JTF-Guantánamo wants us to assume that there is nothing else we should or could look at in this particular room – just the emptiness of the chair. Hence, one of the ideological effects of the image is introduced by prompting us to believe that all our attention should go to the armchair; or, to put it more precisely, we are supposed to focus our attention on the absence of the detained men.

The subject of an absent presence of detainees and practices at Guantánamo is a recurring motif in Cornwall's work. Her photo book not only reflects on the denial of visibility and visual representation to the detainees, and the absence of their representation in photographs shot during the guided tours; it also includes written essays by several authors. In her own essay, entitled "Safe, Humane, Legal and Transparent," quoting the JTF-Guantánamo's motto, Cornwall provides the reader with a detailed description of her response to the experience of taking part in the guided media tours, describing them as "a spectacular diversion from what happens behind closed doors, the things that will never make the media tour" (Cornwall 2017e). In the essay, Cornwall guides us through the talking points prepared by Guantánamo personnel, the photo opportunities, and the scripts of the tours – as she herself was guided through the camp. She also shares her subjective impression of the tours with the reader when she writes that "[t]he impression is of zoo animals, not people. There is no privacy here; these men have no control over being seen" (Cornwall 2017e). This formulation is reminiscent of Major Nichols' description of the early days of the guided media tours at Camp X-Ray: to him, they resembled a "petting zoo" (Greenberg 2009, 91). Thus, even though the detention facilities had been improved in terms of living conditions and infrastructure, the later media tours still evoked similar impressions to those created by tours of Camp X-Ray over a decade before Cornwall visited Guantánamo.

Along with sharing her impression of such showcases and photo opportunities, Cornwall also reflects on the conditions and regulations applied to the media coverage at the base. She provides the reader with further information about the circumstances of production, the censorship applied directly after the tours are completed, and the possible consequences for anyone in breach of the rules of conduct set out in *Media Policy* (DoD 2010).[16] Returning to this document, and reading it through the prism of Cornwall's account, it can be argued that the prohibition of photographing the detainees' faces is a form of anticipatory censorship, in that it preemptively restricts the field of the visible, and regulates what the public will be permitted to see. However, the document – and Cornwall's essay – also disclose a second round of censorship,

15   I would like to thank Debi Cornwall for this information.
16   This is also the version that Cornwall signed prior to her visit to the Guantánamo Bay Naval Base.

one which ensures that journalists have adhered to the rules and prohibitions. These censorship procedures take place directly after the photographs and videos have been created, usually on the same day. Before departing from Guantánamo, journalists are obliged to submit all (audio)visual material they have captured during the tour to the so-called "Operational Security Review ... to be screened prior to upload into any laptop and prior to release" (DoD 2010, 5). Still and moving images are thus submitted directly on memory cards and cameras, or visitors must provide military personnel with compatible playback devices. If an image violates the prohibitions, there are two potential consequences: it is either deleted, or it is cropped, and a "record of every deleted or cropped file would be stored on military computers for future reference" (Cornwall 2017e). Cornwall goes on to share the fact that any violation of the *Media Policy* rules could lead to a "temporary suspension of access, expulsion and unspecified other 'adverse action'" (Cornwall 2017e).

In addition to the photographs taken at the Guantánamo detention camp – the two series shot at the facility are entitled "Gitmo at Home, Gitmo at Play," and "Gitmo on Sale" – *Welcome to Camp America* contains a third series of images which were taken all over the world: "Beyond Gitmo | ما وراء خليج غوانتانامو" (Cornwall 2022b). Each of the series differs in its focus, dealing with different aspects of the camp and the lives of the (released) detainees. "Gitmo At Home, Gitmo at Play" primarily features photographs of empty architectures – such as the so-called "show cells," a recreation pen for detainees, a band room for military personnel, a children's paddling pool and playground, the sergeant's quarters, the base's driving range, a hospital room, a tiki bar, and the Marble Head Lanes food court – as well as objects of daily use: the aforementioned armchair in the media room, a prayer rug, a broad range of so-called "comfort items" for the detainees – including shoes, clothing, towels, toothpaste, *et cetera* – and barracks cleaning equipment. "Gitmo on Sale" consists of photographs of memorabilia which visitors could have acquired at the Naval Station's tourist shop (Cornwall 2022a). "Beyond Gitmo | ما وراء خليج غوانتانامو" is a series of portraits of the released detainees, which I will discuss in more detail in the next subsection.

Portraits of the Detainees' Backs

Given the absence of faces in the images from the detention camp that were officially approved for release, it is interesting to study the way in which Cornwall took the portraits in her photographic series featuring former detainees. The series, entitled "Beyond Gitmo | ما وراء خليج غوانتانامو," explores what has happened to these men since their release, asking: if there is such a thing as a life beyond Guantánamo, what does it look like? The fourteen portraits of Djamel Ameziane, Mourad Benchellali, Hisham Sliti, Hussain al-Adeni, Murat Kurnaz, Mamdouh Habib, Sami al-Hajj, Moazzam Begg, Rustam Hamidova,

[Fig. 11] Debi Cornwall's portrait of the German-Turkish citizen Murat Kurnaz taken in 2015 is accompanied by the following caption: "Murat, Turkish; Refugee Counselor; Containerdorf, Refugee housing; Bremen, Germany: Held 4 years, 7 months, 22 days; Released August 24, 2006; Charges never filed" (© Debi Cornwall).

and anonymous Uzbek and Chinese Uyghurs depict the men in various public spaces, and are all taken from behind, showing only their backs (Cornwall 2017a). Bearing in mind the previously analyzed restrictions set out in the *Media Policy* document, the aesthetics of these images [fig. 11] implicitly evoke the ground rules for media visitors to Guantánamo – specifically, the rule that it is forbidden to show the detainees' faces. This reference is made explicit by Cornwall on her homepage, where she provides the following description of the photographs constituting the "Beyond Gitmo | ما وراء خليج غوانتانامو" series:

> Beyond Gitmo offers an unprecedented view of 14 men held as alleged terrorists at the US Naval Station in Cuba – after they have been cleared and freed – to nine countries, from Albania to Qatar. Gitmo's [Guantánamo's] inmates are reviled as the 'worst of the worst,' but many were innocents kidnapped and sold to American forces. Hundreds of men held for years at Guantánamo without charge or trial have now been released home or displaced to foreign countries as unlikely permanent tourists. *The military prohibits photographing faces at Guantánamo Bay. Beyond Gitmo replicates this 'no faces' rule in the free world; their bodies may*

be free, but Guantánamo will always mark them. (Cornwall 2022b; italics added)

If the viewer is not provided with this short description, and only has access to the images, it is possible that they could evoke the impression that it was the choice of the former detainees to remain anonymous. This is actually true in the case of the portraits of the Uzbek and the Chinese Uyghurs (Cornwall 2017a). But the other portraits are accompanied by the following detailed information: the former detainee's forename (their full names are included in the acknowledgments at the end of the book), current location, period of being detained at Guantánamo, date of clearance and release, and usually also the information that "charges [were] never filed" (Cornwall 2017d).

In her description of the images on her homepage, Cornwall makes explicit what is already implied in the photographs' composition, spelling out the tacit reference in her portraits to the normative frames surrounding the aesthetics of Guantánamo's visual culture. Her photographs go beyond being a mere reference, however: by repurposing or even appropriating these normative frames, they appear to express the fact that there is no such thing as "beyond Guantánamo" for the detainees – "beyond" in the sense of an event that has passed and is no longer occurring.

The portraits in Cornwall's photo book were printed on loose pages (or inserts, as Cornwall calls them), not bound into the book. Each portrait was printed on one side of an A4 page with the reverse side containing the afore-mentioned details about the person portrayed in two languages: English on the right, and Arabic on the left [fig. 12]. In the case of at least three of the por-traits – namely, those of Djamel, Hisham, and Murat – Cornwall has included additional texts, such as email conversations between the released detainees and herself (Cornwall 2017b); excerpts from the protocols of the Combatant Status Review Board (Cornwall 2017d); and statements about how the men are being treated in their country of release (Cornwall 2017c). The status of these loose pages in relation to the photo book is a fascinating one and offers a theoretical argument to the reader, since a bound book usually appears as a whole, while any additional material or unbound pages do not seem to belong to, or to be an integral part of, the whole. We might think of flyers or other promotional materials that can occasionally be found between the pages of a book – papers and pages to which we do not usually ascribe much importance, and perhaps discard. However, there are also other genres of loose pages that are highly relevant to the core text of a book: for example, *errata*, slips of paper added to the book after printing by its editors or the publishing house to correct mistakes or errors. Thinking about the loose-sheet-portraits from Cornwall's photo book as *errata* allows us to read them against the suggestion that they are disposable. In this case, the loose sheets indicate that we must adjust our perception of what can be seen at Guantánamo, and reflect on the

[Fig. 12] The image shows the back side of the loose sheet with Debi Cornwall's portrait of Murat Kurnaz, on which she has printed passages from his hearing by the Combatant Status Review Board (© Debi Cornwall and Radius Books).

established discourses as being incomplete and fragmentary. The portraits allow us to look beyond the highly restricted and censored visual culture produced by the DoD, and to complete, at least partly, the fragmentary image of what it means to have survived Guantánamo.

Loose pages like fig. 11 and 12 emphasize how fragile and unstable memories can be. In my own case, the loose pages had me worried that, if I am not careful, I will lose them someday. This sense of anxiety in relation to the unanchored nature of these portraits could be loosely connected to the permanent mobility of the detainees, and their status of "permanent tourists" (Cornwall 2022b). As Cornwall writes in her accompanying text, to reiterate the previous citation: "[h]undreds of men held for years at Guantánamo without charge or trial have now been released home or displaced to foreign countries as unlikely permanent tourists" (Cornwall 2022b). However, not all the released men photographed by Cornwall for "Beyond Gitmo | ما وراء خليج غوانتانامو" were deported to foreign countries or were forbidden to rejoin their families. Whether or not we assign the status of "permanent tourist" to a released detainee depends on the specific circumstances of his release and on whether he was sent back to his country of origin, or to a third country.

A good example to illustrate this point is the portrait of the German-Turkish citizen Kurnaz [fig. 11 and 12]. Cornwall photographed a view of his back at a refugee housing complex in Bremen, Germany, surrounded by green living containers. The containers visible in Kurnaz's portrait appear to speak of the continuous mobility forced on both refugees and some of the released detainees, and also to the fact that both groups are refugees and "permanent tourists" alike (Cornwall 2022b). Nevertheless, Kurnaz's case is different. After being released from Guantánamo, he was permitted to return to Germany; he has since dedicated his life to supporting refugees as a counselor. Furthermore, his story has been widely covered in the German and international press: he has given video interviews, posed for photographers, and has even written an autobiography, entitled *Fünf Jahre meines Lebens: Ein Bericht aus Guantánamo* (Eng. *Five Years of my Life: A Report from Guantánamo*), which in 2013 was adapted for the screen (Kurnaz 2007; Schaller 2013). With regard to his return to his country of origin and the press coverage it has generated, it would appear that he does not actually belong on a loose sheet, having escaped the status of a permanent tourist.

Thus, Kurnaz's portrait carries a different resonance, and might also be read in a different way. In relation to the widespread coverage of his story, even someone with no knowledge of the regulations governing guided tours at Guantánamo could deduce from the photograph itself that it was the artist's intentional decision to photograph Kurnaz from behind. Here, the intentional reproduction of the regulations outside of the geographic and institutional frames of the detention camp appears to implicitly question the possibilities and limitations of opposing the DoD's strategic deployment of opacity. Cornwall's photographs subvert the established discourse by appropriating some of its mechanisms, but, they are also at risk of becoming (re)inscribed into the very discourse they are tacitly criticizing. Without the provision of captions and further information, the aesthetics of the portraits of the other released men are indistinguishable from the aesthetics of photographs taken under the supervision of the JTF-Guantánamo. In her comment on the late draft of this chapter and in response to this passage, Cornwall has emphasized the importance of the captions: "This is why the inserts have the caption … information on them, unlike most of the other images in the book. You can't encounter the portrait without also seeing the captions. It was important to me to place the anonymous photographs in the context of this information" (Debi Cornwall, January 9, 2022). Nevertheless, as I have already discussed in the previous chapter, images can acquire many afterlives and circulate without their initial captions. In these particular cases, without the foreknowledge that these photographs were created by an artist, and that they are referring to the normative apparatus of censorship imposed upon journalists who are reporting from inside the detention facility, the viewer might be unable to recognize these images as critical interventions into Guantánamo's visual culture. Thus, also Cornwall's photographs "cannot themselves explain anything, [and can become] … inexhaustible invitations to deduction, speculation, and fantasy" (Sontag 2008, 23), as well as are at risk of being inscribed into the plethora of images taken at the Guantánamo detention facility.

However, I concur with Zack Hatfield's view that "Cornwall's decision also endows her faceless subjects with an awkward universality that denies each man's individuality" (Hatfield 2018). He describes these portraits as an "attempt to evoke an *empathic presence* without a face," and goes on to observe that "their anonymity … is bestowed not by the camera, but by circumstance and indifference" (Hatfield 2018; italics added). It is true that Cornwall's aesthetic choice emphasizes the continuing nature of the violence perpetrated by withholding the detainees' faces, as well as their voices and stories, and renders this visible as a gap within public discourse. This withholding, or absence, concerns both the detainees still being held in Guantánamo, and the men who have been released to a wide range of countries. Cornwall's portrait of Kurnaz also shows that, even if individual stories about the detainees have become well known to the public, ultimately, these stories have not succeeded in providing us with the complete picture of what happened to him and has happened, or continues to happen, to other men.

To support the argument I have put forward in the beginning of this chapter that the denial of visual representation has influenced, and was connected to, the denial of legal representation to the detainees, and to relate it to Cornwall's work, I will briefly refer to a short account written by the Guantánamo lawyer Richard Grigg (2009). The account, included in the edited volume entitled *The Guantánamo Lawyers: Inside a Prison Outside of Law*, not only makes it clear how difficult it has been for human rights lawyers to gain access to the detained men at Guantánamo, but also reveals what it might mean to encounter the face of a detainee. Grigg, who represented the Afghan detainee Mohammad Akhtiar, recounts that it was only after he had submitted a *habeas corpus* petition on behalf of his client that he was able to visit him at the detention facility. As Grigg writes, this visit has

> *put a human face on what had previously been a legal issue*. No longer was I representing a detainee on a *habeas corpus* petition. I was representing a human being, a man about my age who had been uprooted from his family, flown 10,000 miles from his home, and placed in a dog cage. Here was a human being who had never been charged with any crime, a man with very little hope. (Grigg 2009, 19; italics added)

Hence, the issues of visual and legal representation are closely connected to each other – an idea which is also present in Cornwall's portraits. In the case of Grigg's account, the issues discursively overlap in the metaphorical as well as the material face of Akhtiar. Significantly, not only were some of the lawyers representing detainees at Guantánamo denied access and the opportunity to talk face-to-face with their clients; when we look at the thousands of photographs released by the US authorities and journalists, as well as at the videos of virtual visits, we quickly notice that many of them have something in common – they appear to follow the rule of no "[f]rontal facial views, profiles, 3/4 views, or any view revealing a detainee's identity" (DoD 2010, 4).

At the core of both Cornwall's portraits of the released men and her images from the guided tours lies a dialectical relationship between absence and presence, and between appearance and disappearance. To further expand on this idea, although Cornwall intentionally withholds the faces of the detainees from the viewer, it is these faces that are the actual subject of her photographs. Here, I do not intend "faces" to be understood merely on a literal level. In relation to the photographs and videos produced and distributed by independent journalists which depict the detainees' backs, on the one hand, and in the context of Cornwall's aesthetic decision to picture the released detainees' backs, on the other, we should consider what it could mean to ethically encounter the – literal, metaphorical, and maybe also metaphysical – face of the Other.

The reference made by Emmanuel Levinas to Vasily Grossman's description of the back-views of persons in *Life and Fate* is particularly telling with regard to what such an ethical encounter might be like. Levinas writes:

> *Face that thus is not exclusively the face of man.* In Vasily Grossman's *Life and Fate* … there is [a] mention of a visit to the Lubianka in Moscow by the families and wives or relatives of political prisoners, to get news of them. A line is formed in front of the windows, in which they can only see each other's backs. A woman waits for her turn: 'Never has she thought the human back could be so expressive and transmit states of mind so pen-etratingly. The people who approached the window had a special way of stretching the neck and back; the raised shoulders have shoulder-blades tensed as if by springs, and they seemed *to shout, to cry, to sob.' Face as the extreme precariousness of the other.* (Levinas 1999, 140; italics added)[17]

The face, according to Levinas, should not only be understood to be the surface of the human body, the mere frontal view of a person's head. The face is also a metaphysical entity which speaks to us about, and from, the position of the precariousness of the human subject. It is the backs of people in Grossman's story in which Levinas locates the opportunity to encounter the face of the Other. Vocal expressiveness and the ability to speak are thus not only restricted to the mouth, the vocal cords, or expressive eyes. Significantly,

17   The 2006 translation of this passage reads as follows: "Yevgenia had never realized that the human back could be so expressive, could so vividly reflect a person's state of mind. People had a particular way of craning their necks as they came up to the window; their backs, with their raised, tensed shoulders, seemed to be crying, to be sobbing and screaming" (Grossman 2017, 667).

what Levinas takes from Grossman's recollections is the idea that people's backs are also able "to shout, to cry, to sob" (as cited in Levinas 1999, 140). Thus, the ability to be expressive, and to tell stories of pain, injustice, and mal-treatment, is uncannily present in a situation when we can "only" perceive a back.

Cornwall's portraits provide us with a similar opportunity to encounter the detainees' faces in their backs. However, the outcome of this encounter is slightly different from the one described by Levinas above. Whereas, for Levinas, the resulting proximity gained from such encounters "is the responsibility of the *I* for the Other, the impossibility of leaving him alone before the mystery of death" (Levinas 1999, 141), the backs of the released men in Cornwall's photographs tell a different story: a story about the painful indif-ference of the public with regard to the ongoing violence that marks their lives. The photographs also emphasize the viewer's evasion of responsibility and complicity in the situation of the released men. Hence, although it is necessary that we, the broader public, take responsibility for the harm inflicted upon these men, their shoulders and backs seem to express a certain disillusion and hopelessness that this will ever come to pass.

At this point, it is helpful to take up Butler's re-reading of Levinas, and her thoughts about the encounter of the face in the back of the Other, as well as the (de)humanizing nature of representation. Following Butler, we might think that what we can actually perceive in these portraits are "scene[s] of agonized vocalization" (Butler 2004, 133). In her reading of the same passage from Levinas, Butler makes an important remark with regard to the productivity of thinking with Levinas about a contemporary ethic of non-violence, and a theory of representation.[18] She writes that Levinas

> gives us a way of thinking the relationship between representation and humanization, a relationship that is not as straightforward as we might think. If critical thinking has something to say about or to the present situ-ation, it may well be in the domain of representation where humanization and dehumanization occur ceaselessly. (Butler 2004, 140)

Significantly, the depiction of the face is not always necessarily a means to achieve the humanization of the depicted person. Conversely, the denial of faces, as well as the denial of the visual identification of the detainees, does not solely result in the dehumanization of these men. Here, to reiterate a

---

18   Anna Szörényi, who draws in "Facing Vulnerability: Reading Refugee Child Photographs Through an Ethics of Proximity" (2018) on Levinas' and Butler's proximity arguments, makes an important observation about what it means to be faced with the vulner-ability of the Other via a photograph. She argues that "a photograph might give us an encounter not only with a (mediated) other, but with our own exposure to and depend-ence on relations with others; an attitude that can remind us that the attempt to keep others at a distance is both futile and violent" (Szörényi 2018, 164).

thought I formulated previously in a slightly different way: *the absence of the face might indeed evoke its presence, and vocalize the issues at stake*. Cornwall's decision not to show the faces of the released detainees evokes a haunting presence of the face which can be understood "as the extreme precariousness of the other" (Levinas 1999, 140), a face that vocalizes the experience of pain, injustice, and indifference – a face which requires from us to be willing to encounter it in an ethical manner.

Listening to the portraits of the detainees' backs means to listen to ourselves, and to our reflections in those faces encountered in the backs, and thus holding ourselves accountable and co-responsible for the situation of the detainees. In this way, listening might be a mode which will allow us to overcome the distance between ourselves and the detainees, a distance which was put in place and continues to be maintained by the DoD, so that we can finally come to acknowledge our co-responsibility for the situation of these men. Thus, an ethical approach to the perception of photographs such as those taken by Cornwall, an approach that would acknowledge the perceptual dimensions beyond the sense of sight, and would be more inclined to listen to the vocalizations made by the depicted backs, should be based on an ethics of proximity rather than emphasizing geographical and experiential distance between "us," the viewers, and "them," the detainees.

Summary and Conclusion

In this chapter, I have focused and elaborated on how "outsiders" – such as journalists, the general public, and myself – have the opportunity to visit the Guantánamo detention facility, either physically or virtually. I described how the DoD and the JTF-Guantánamo pre-framed visits for journalists by establishing a contract entitled *Media Policy at Guantánamo Bay, Cuba: Agree to Abide* (2010), and stressed that the DoD's claim included in this contract, that the guided tours for news-media representatives form part of the US government's effort to encourage transparency with regard to Guantánamo, is merely a fantasy. I went on to argue that the reverse is actually true, and that a strategically employed form of opacity would be a more appropriate frame for the theoretical discussion of what we see when we look at the images produced in the course of the guided tours through Guantánamo. This strategic deployment of the effects of opacity aims to hinder the viewer's ability to use their epistemic capabilities when attempting to understand what is happening to the men detained at the camp.

I went on to analyze the online video tours which offer even non-journalists a glimpse of the various camps at Guantánamo. By discussing two examples, I set out to demonstrate how the bodily absence of the detainees, practices, and objects in these videos actually indicates the opposite, creating an acute presence of the detained men – a phenomenological presence intrinsically connected to their visual absence. With regard to my claim that Guantánamo's visual culture is intentionally designed to be opaque to the public, thus rendering the circumstances at Guantánamo ungraspable to outsiders, it is important to bear in mind the dialectical relationship between the absence and presence, or appearance and disappearance, of subjects, practices, and objects in the photographs and videos. A critical engagement with what the virtual visit video tours and photographs from the guided tours *in situ* actually show, and the manner in which they show it, requires us to adjust the way in which we perceive the visual material made available to us from the detention facility. I argued that if we also listen, rather than just see, we – the viewers – can open ourselves to other, perhaps more ethically sensitive perceptual and epistemic dimensions of the Guantánamo detention camp.

In the last section, I returned by means of a detour to ideas about the critical form of opacity put forward by Glissant (1997). Cornwall's photo book, *Welcome to Camp America: Inside Guantánamo Bay*, suggests that an encounter with the faces of the detainees in the photographic representations of their backs could make it possible to gain a better understanding of the injustice experienced by these men, and how the trauma of Guantánamo continues to haunt their lives. In contrast to the strategic deployment of opacity undertaken by the DoD, Cornwall's decision to photograph the released men from behind makes a case for the positive effects of opacity, while also acknowledging the inaccessibility of their subjectivity and their experiences at Guantánamo. Whereas the DoD uses opacity as a strategy to disable the viewer's epistemic access to what is actually happening at the facility, Cornwall has appropriated and reframed the opacity inscribed in the officially released photographs and videos in order to bring us closer to an understanding of what it might mean to have survived Guantánamo. In her depictions of the detainees' backs, we might encounter the men's faces, and listen to what they are telling us.

"[T]here is the seen and then there is the unseen at Guantánamo" (Smith 2016), writes Smith in his report cited in the introduction to this chapter, speaking to my core arguments with regard to the guided tours through the camp. This chapter was specifically dedicated to images of incarceration, or, more precisely of the detention infrastructure, that were taken in the course of guided media tours – images that are marked by appearance and disappearance of detainees, just like the detainee in Smith's story who comes and disappears like a comet (Smith 2016). Despite the fear that the DoD would restrict access to the camp following the publication of McCoy's photographs and the negative responses towards them by the news media, I have shown the ways in which the guided tours and virtual visits have provided the public with a multitude of opportunities to encounter the detainees and to acknowledge the violence inflicted on them in an ethical manner. I hope that this chapter will inspire its readers to listen to images from the Guantánamo detention camp – be they taken by military personnel, journalists, or artists – so that they begin to hear the stories told by the detainees in their absence, or rather, in their phenomenological presence in their visual absence.

PHOTO

DENIED IN FULL

EXEMPTION

6&7

DOD JUNE 2542

ACLU-RDI 2479 p.2

DOD056358

[Fig. 13] Page two of the "DOD Hospital Patient Record re: Incident at Guantánamo Hospital" document showing a redacted photograph published by the US Department of Administration (2004a) and included in the ACLU's *Torture Database* (© American Civil Liberties Union, Inc. 2006).

3

Obscuring Knowledge: Photographic Practices of the "In-Processing" Procedure

"There was nothing in it [the memorandum] that threatened national security" (Galison, et al. 2010, 1030), recalls the American Civil Liberties Union's (ACLU) director Anthony Romero. The memo "just gave instructions on how to take photographs of detainees in a way that complied with the Geneva Conventions. It didn't reveal their identities; it didn't talk about how to destroy photographs. *It explained how to do it right*" (Galison, et al. 2010, 1030; italics added). The US Department of Justice and the US Attorney's Office saw it differently, however. When they realized that the classified memo had been distributed to a number of lawyers, they began to investigate who might have it in their possession, and filed a subpoena requesting its immediate return and deletion from the lawyers' computers. The ACLU filed a motion to quash the subpoena, won, and published the memo on that same day (Galison, et al. 2010, 1030). My own experience of researching this initially classified memo adds another layer to Romero's anecdote. After not being able to find it online, I contacted the ACLU and sent them the link to an interview with Romero, asking if they could forward the PDF file. This is the answer I received: "Thank you for your interest in reproducing ACLU content. Unfortunately, I am not aware that such a memo exists. Since this interview is from 14 years ago, it's likely the memo was once published on our website, but over the years, has been lost or removed" (Chloe Rasic, March 12, 2020). These anecdotes are telling, because, on the one hand, they reveal as much about the US government's efforts to cover up or obscure knowledge about how photography is employed at Guantánamo as they do about the absurd dimensions of the desire to overclassify information. On the other hand, they also suggest that to reflect upon what it means to look at Guantánamo means to engage with documents and photographs that have been lost, removed, or censored. If we want to understand what the US Department of Defense (DoD) ultimately permits us to see, as well as their reasons for publishing certain images and withholding others, we have to think about how the US government actively contributes to a situation of disinformation and intentionally deceives the public by creating an image of the camp that, while false or incomplete, creates an impression of providing the complete truth.

Since the very beginning, the Guantánamo detention camp has been an open secret, surrounded by an extensive legal discourse. From the moment that Shane T. McCoy's photographs [fig. 1 and 3] were published, we have known that the detained men were being treated in an unacceptable and violent way. Yet the government has effectively deployed a disinformation campaign with regard to Guantánamo by publishing such a large amount of information that it has become difficult to comprehend what is actually being published, and what is being withheld. Moreover, on many occasions, the published material has not even come close to providing a true portrayal of the actual living conditions of the detainees, thereby creating a false impression of the situation in the camp. As Don Fallis writes, the deployment of disinformation is nothing new, and does not only pertain to "[n]ew information technologies [though they] are making it easier for people to create and disseminate inaccurate and misleading information" (Fallis 2015, 402). For instance, some of the disinformation strategies mentioned by Fallis, including "government propaganda, doctored photographs, forged documents, and fake maps" (Fallis 2015, 402), apply to the objects analyzed in the previous chapter. Both the photographs taken by journalists under military supervision in the context of the guided tours through the camp, and the videos of virtual visits produced by the Joint Task Force-Guantánamo (JTF–Guantánamo) have had an active role in creating a false idea of the detention camp.

In this chapter, I will argue that the ways in which the DoD redacts documents or withholds them completely serve to make the circumstances at the camp difficult for the public to grasp, presumably on the premise that making something ungraspable limits the possibility of effectively opposing it. Thus, disinformation is present not only in the instances where a document is completely withheld, but also when the DoD chooses to publish it, releasing some parts, while others remain hidden by means of black lines or white fields. I will thus reframe the issue of opacity discussed in the previous chapter, arguing that the efforts of the DoD to make Guantánamo, along with everything that took and takes place there, incomprehensible can also be understood as a form of "antiepistemology." As Peter Galison writes in his essay "Removing Knowledge," in contrast to epistemology, which "asks how knowledge can be uncovered and secured … [,] [a]ntiepistemology asks how knowledge can be covered and obscured" (Galison 2004, 237). The argument that the DoD has designed and carried out an antiepistemology with regard to the perception of

Guantánamo is intertwined with its deployment of a strategic form of opacity, insofar as its operation of fragmentation – on the one hand, by publishing visual fragments, and, on the other, by censoring and denying information – attempts to establish an opaque visual culture surrounding the camp. In contrast to the previous chapter, in which I discussed what kind of visual material the DoD has chosen to publish, here, I am focusing on photographs which we cannot or are not permitted to perceive. Specifically, I will try to reconstruct parts of this inaccessible archive by analyzing military and government documents that have either been officially published by the relevant authorities, or leaked to the public by independent bodies.

This close analysis of certain declassified or leaked documents, however, also requires me to explain why such an emphasis is particularly productive. I will, therefore, begin with a discussion of how the US military regards and performs documentation practices, focusing on its bureaucratic and recordkeeping procedures. I argue that in order to understand the institutional frameworks of the Guantánamo detention camp, it is essential to contextualize the photographic practices undertaken there, as well as the documents pertaining to these practices, within the larger context of the US military's internal bureaucratic procedures.

Following this, I will turn my attention to a set of indexical techniques employed when new detainees arrive at the camp, and the photographic objects these techniques produce. I will speculate on objects such as photographs, X-rays, and fingerprints, which remain largely withheld from the public, via a close reading of the *Camp Delta Standard Operating Procedures (SOP)* (JTF-Guantánamo 2003; 2004). I will also dwell on the question of how military personnel use these techniques in their attempt to acquire knowledge about what they assume that the detainees are hiding from them, and thus to epistemically access the imagined insides of the detainees. In the spirit of the aforementioned antiepistemology, however, making the detainees' bodies epistemically available to the military and security apparatus goes hand-in-hand with covering up and obscuring the knowledge aquired. Thus, I argue that, although the government documentation practices transform the detainees' bodies into visual archives for future uses, the US government ensures that the resulting archives remain obscured, unclear, and not-fully-graspable to those outside of the military apparatus.

In the final section, I discuss what I call "counter-archival practices" in the context of the legal efforts undertaken by the ACLU to access the obscured photographic records depicting detainees and Prisoners of War (POWs). In 2003, six months prior to the publication of the torture photographs from the Abu Ghraib prison, the ACLU filed a *Freedom of Information Act* (FOIA) request to see the photographs redacted from a wide range of documents (ACLU 2003). The subsequent, well-documented lawsuit, initiated in 2004 by a complaint from the ACLU, continued over the course of three presidencies. The lawsuit reveals crucial aspects of the way the US government perceives torture photographs, while also laying out the legal grounds for why, in spite of FOIA, the DoD was permitted to keep information about the photographs hidden (*ACLU v. DoD* 2017, 04. Civ 4161 (AKH)). The final subsection of this chapter is dedicated to the analysis of a Microsoft Excel spreadsheet entitled *TorturePhotos*, which was created and published by the ACLU in response to the US government's refusal to provide detailed information about the photographs the ACLU had requested (ACLU 2022b). This spreadsheet renders visible, in a structured way, the nature of the photographs of detainees, which, in 2015, continued to be withheld from the public. I argue that this case is an example *par excellence* of how independent bodies have been successful in their efforts to transform the DoD's antiepistemology into an epistemology, revealing via alternative frames the (visual) knowledge which the Department renders obscure.

The Frame of Documentation

Military Bureaucracy and Standard Operating Procedures

To understand the various functions of photography and the different levels of censorship at work in Guantánamo, one has to focus on military documents, because they are the primary means by which the DoD regulates the conduct of its military personnel in, and visitors to, the detention camp. Furthermore, military documents represent the institutional frames which regulate daily activities at the camp, notwithstanding the important fact that, as accounts by some military personnel deployed at Guantánamo have made clear, the rules laid out in these documents are not always followed. One of the most prominent firsthand accounts demonstrating the various breaches of the rules of conduct by Guantánamo personnel is that of Staff Sergeant Joseph Hickman. Deployed for a year at Guantánamo, Hickman was stationed at the camp during the period when three detainees allegedly took their lives. In his book, *Murder at Camp Delta: A Staff Sergeant's Pursuit of the Truth about Guantánamo Bay* (2015), Hickman reveals that the camp basically became a laboratory or testing ground for torture techniques – or "Counter-Resistance techniques" (Haynes II 2002, 1), as the US government euphemistically termed them. Although the *Camp Delta SOPs* clearly forbid any form of maltreatment of detainees, stating that soldiers should "[r]espect all detainees as human beings and protect them against all acts of violence" (JTF-Guantánamo 2003, 1.3), it could be argued that, in parallel to this written document, there is a tacit, unwritten SOP which encourages acts of violence towards the detainees.

When considering one of the key research questions of this book – namely, what do we see when we look at Guantánamo? – an analysis of the *Camp Delta SOP* document is of particular relevance, albeit with the provision that it is necessary to cross-check its contents with contradictory reports coming from military personnel and the detainees themselves. The importance and centrality I am ceding to military documents in my attempts to understand how Combat Camera (COMCAM) photographers operate (Chapter 1), and in my reconstruction of photographic practices at Guantánamo (which I will undertake in the next subsections), is partly a result of the emphasis given to such documents within certain images released by the US military itself – such as that of the sheet of paper held by the soldier walking between the rows of detainees in McCoy's photograph [fig. 1]. Rather than a gun or other weapon, the soldier is holding a sheet of paper that completely absorbs his attention. Even if the image's viewers cannot see the contents of this particular document, by focusing on this sheet we are redirected towards something we cannot see or access: to the *off* of the photograph. More specifically, the sheet directs our attention to the fact that this particular scene was designed and framed by various written documents produced by the DoD and the JTF-Guantánamo, some of which disclose how Guantánamo personnel are employing photographic media in their daily routines.

In addition, my focus on documents stems from my own perspective on how they operate in relation to antiepistemology. The antiepistemology introduced by the DoD with regard to the public perception of Guantánamo is not only achieved by the refusal of access to knowledge. Significantly, it also relies on making knowledge available in the form of documents. These documents promote a kind of antiepistemology not only in relation to the photographic practices conducted at the camp, but they themselves can also be perceived as pieces of fragmented knowledge that "cover[s] and obscure[s]" (Galison 2004, 237). My own experience of reading military documents has often resulted in the feeling that they represent only a fragment of an indefinable whole. This observation is closely connected to the argument I made in Chapter 1, when I described my personal experience of reading documents written for COMCAM photographers, and my difficulties tracing their various histories and references. There, I argued that documents produced and distributed by the DoD for their personnel are complex sources of operational information which simultaneously express and reflect on their own histories, making for a complex reading experience. Military documents have multilayered histories; they contain a wide range of references to other documents and media objects, which in turn, refer to yet other documents. This makes it difficult for someone outside of the US military apparatus to comprehend, analyze, and create an overview of the information contained within them.

Hence, a critical inquiry into the antiepistemology pertaining to the public's perception of Guantánamo necessitates a closer look at the documents that regulate the operations conducted at the detention facility. The US military attaches particular importance to its internal archival or documentation practices, as well as to bureaucratic procedures. As my analysis of its institutional discourses will demonstrate, it perceives these practices and procedures to be essential to the success of its operations. Not only does the success of procedures – such as those pertaining to the arrival of the detainees at the camp – depend on such documents; such bureaucratic procedures are also crucial to the smooth running of the US military as a public institution.

Taking a historical perspective, Cornelia Vismann demonstrates that recordkeeping is an essential task of modern-day bureaucracies. In her analysis of how "[p]ublic records facilitated a file-based administration – in other words, a bureaucracy" (Vismann 2008, 59), Vismann refers to Max Weber's monumental work, *Economy and Society: An Outline of Interpretive Sociology* (1978), noting the historical developments that led to a situation where "expropriated, socialized files deposited in archives shaped governmental administration in the modern sense of the word. No office without an archive" (Vismann 2008, 59). In the third chapter of her book *Files: Law and Media Technology*, entitled "From Documents to Records," Vismann draws our attention to what Weber has called the principle of "Aktenmäßigkeit" (Vismann 2008, 91), which in the 17th century, saw the establishment of the practice that "[a]dministrative acts, decisions and rules are formulated and recorded in writing" (Weber 1978, 219), even if they originated in oral form. Furthermore, "the central focus of all types of modern organized action" is, according to Weber, "[t]he combination of written documents and a continuous operation by officials [that] constitutes the 'office' (*Bureau*)" (Weber 1978, 219). As I will demonstrate, this idea also applies to the bureaucracy of the contemporary US military. The practice of recording matters in writing is, as Vismann argues, "an indispensable element of bureaucratic rule" (Vismann 2008, 91), and one that also applies to historic and 21st century militaries. Here, it is interesting to note Weber's observations on the significance of bureaucracies to military bodies when he states that "the modern higher-ranking officer fights battles from the 'office'" (Weber 1978, 1393), a passage also cited by Vismann, and that in the "modern state the actual ruler is necessarily and unavoidably the bureaucracy, since power is exercised neither through parliamentary speeches nor monarchical enunciations but through the routines of administration. This is true of both the military and civilian officialdom" (Weber 1978, 1393). An early example of a "fully bureaucratized military" (Vismann 2008, 127), identified by someone writing from within the military apparatus, namely General Field Marshal Alfred von Schlieffen, dates back to 1909 (von Schlieffen 2003).

Another, more contemporary perspective from within the US military is given by Major Zachary Griffiths, a Special Forces Officer and American Politics Instructor in the Department of Social Sciences at West Point Military Academy. In his essay, "In Defense of the Military Bureaucrat," he notes that the DoD should be considered the "biggest federal bureaucracy" (Griffiths 2018) in the US. Defending bureaucratic procedures, Griffiths states that "[s]uccessful bureaucracies aren't where expertise dies, however, but where it *lives* in the government" (Griffiths 2018). This military perspective on the position of expertise within a government not only allows us to reframe the US military as a bureaucracy, it also helps us to understand some of the procedures carried out at Guantánamo as bureaucratic or archival practices. Writing from within the military apparatus, Griffiths connects two points of view: those of daily practices, and a theoretical, historical perspective. Referring to James Q. Wilson's book of 1992, *Bureaucracy: What Government Agencies Do and Why They Do It*, Griffiths enumerates Wilson's five principles of successful bureaucracies:

> The first principle Wilson identifies is that critical tasks guide bureaucracies ... Second, successful bureaucracies inculcate a sense of mission ... Third, bureaucrats must exercise autonomy ... Fourth, successful bureaucracies judge themselves by their results ... Fifth, bureaucracies must manage their standard operating procedures (SOPs). (Griffiths 2018)

In relation to the first principle, Griffiths identifies a significant commonality between the US military and other bureaucracies, since the employees of both are "familiar with critical tasks" (Griffiths 2018). In Chapter 1, I described and analyzed a potent example of this type of bureaucracy: the "VI Planning/Operations Snapshot Template" (*Smart Book* 2015, 12f.) provided to COMCAM photographers before they document an event. This template contains a section entitled "Commander's Intent," where military photographers are expected to write down the specifications they have received from a higher-ranking officer with regard to what they wish to be documented (*Smart Book* 2015, 12f.). The importance given to the Commander's intent in this template, and in the photographic practices carried out by COMCAM, is reflected in Griffiths' first principle for a successful military bureaucracy. He argues that understanding and executing the "commander's intent" is vital for the survival of military structures, and goes on to state that this understanding of critical tasks should be combined with "personal expertise ... to guide their decision making" (Griffiths 2018).

In the context of military bureaucracies, the second principle listed by Griffiths is supposed to ensure that the commitment and engagement of soldiers and other employees does not result from fear of repercussions or disciplinary measures. Instead, "[t]o accomplish their critical tasks, military leaders must inspire their soldiers to put aside other concerns and complete the mission" (Griffiths 2018).

The third and fourth principles refer to the autonomy of a bureaucracy and its capacity for self-evaluation, which allow the military "to redefine key problems and then build a sense of mission around the tasks that are key to solving those new problems" (Griffiths 2018), as well as having its accomplishments evaluated by those with military expertise. Griffiths thus understands military bureaucracy as a closed-circuit entity, an organization that evaluates its actions *from* the inside and *for* the inside, with very little input from external bodies. This in-sourcing of checks and balances is highly problematic in the US "Global War on Terror" (GWoT), since, following the events of 9/11, we have seen a significant expansion in the powers of the executive at the expense of the oversight function of the judicial branch. It appears that the 21st century US military, and perhaps also the military that preceded it, understands itself as the sole keeper of expertise on military actions, as well as on the bureaucracies that govern these actions.

Significantly, documentation practices are crucial to the functioning of military bureaucracy. In order to be able to oversee and organize "complex processes" (Griffiths 2018), the military – like other big organizations – establishes what are known as "SOPs" which are at the core of Griffiths' fifth principle. SOPs enjoy a prominent and important status within the US military as management and governance tools. They will also be of particular importance to this chapter, especially in its second section. A major source for my analysis of the Guantánamo archive are two SOP documents, one from 2003 and one from 2004, published by WikiLeaks in 2007 (JTF-Guantánamo 2003; 2004). These *Camp Delta SOP* documents, written by the JTF-Guantánamo, meticulously describe the daily operations conducted at Camp Delta. Because they include sections dedicated to photographic practices and to rules for internal recordkeeping procedures, these two SOP documents are extremely helpful in responding to the central question of what we see when we look at Guantánamo – a question which includes *how* as well as *why* we see something from the camp – and to comprehending the various frames which restrict and structure the field of the visible.

As the *Army Tactical SOPs* manual from November 2011 makes clear, standardization and recordkeeping are considered to be vital to the functioning of the US military (Headquarters, Department of the Army 2011). Consequently, a great deal of emphasis is given to compliance with SOPs such as the ones designed for Camp Delta. SOP documents are described in the manual as "a type of operational record," and a contribution to the standardization of internal processes, "reduc[ing] operational turbulence and confusion between units when force tailoring occurs" (Headquarters, Department of the Army 2011, 1-2). The manual provides the following definition of "SOPs":

A *standard operating procedure* is a set of instructions covering those
features of operations which lend themselves to a definite or standardized procedure without loss of effectiveness … A SOP is both standing
and standard: it instructs how to perform a prescribed and accepted
process established for completing a task. Features of operations that
lend themselves to standardization are common and usually detailed
processes performed often and requiring minimal variation each time.
(Headquarters, Department of the Army 2011, ii)

To return to an argument I first formulated in Chapter 1, SOPs function as templates to promote repetition, precision, and standardization. The basic idea
behind the production and distribution of these documents is to reduce possible deviations in "recurring task[s]" (Headquarters, Department of the Army
2011, 2-1), to improve processes so that there is minimal or no friction between
units, and to limit uncertainty experienced by military personnel.

Although the terms "standard" or "standardization" imply a certain immobility
and consolidation of SOPs, the *Army Tactical SOPs*, along with both versions
of the *Camp Delta SOPs*, make it clear that the reality is quite different (Headquarters, Department of the Army 2011; JTF-Guantánamo 2003; 2004). SOPs
are not fixed once they are written down. Rather, they are updated on a
regular basis to encompass newly encountered challenges and solutions to
problems that arose only after the documents were distributed to military
personnel. In his defense of military bureaucracy, Griffiths writes that "the
Army also knows that they must change, sometimes rapidly, as environ-
ments or missions shift. Military professionals, with their expertise built
on education and practical experience, recognize when our SOPs must change
and work to shift them" (Griffiths 2018). This is certainly the case with regard
to the *Camp Delta SOPs*. Whereas in the first leaked version, drawn up in March
2003 by the JTF-Guantánamo, we read that "[p]olicies and procedures will be
reviewed every 120 days" (JTF-Guantánamo 2003, ii), only a year later, in March
2004, the update period had been shortened to 30 days (JTF-Guantánamo
2004, iii).

Hence, in contrast to the long periods of time necessary for the introduction
of major changes to the structures of the DoD and its military, as discussed
in the first chapter, SOPs are constantly improved and changed. For the
purposes of this chapter, and my inquiry into what is made available and what
of the visual material from the detention facility is withheld, it is important
to note that the *Camp Delta SOP* documents do not represent my sole source
for investigating the documentation practices at the Guantánamo detention
camp: in the next subsection, I will refer to a wide range of other documents
issued by a variety of governmental bodies.

Documentation of Interrogations and Guantánamo's Archive

When it comes to the documentation practices employed at Guantánamo
– such as written records, photographs, and video footage – there is a wide
range of (redacted) documents and other media objects which can help us
to see beyond the information published by the DoD. On the basis of various
reports, we can speculate about the amount of footage of detainee interrogations that has been withheld from the public. For example, the final report
of a 2005 inquiry conducted by the Federal Bureau of Investigations (FBI) into
the alleged abuse of a detainee at Guantánamo discloses significant information about the vast video archive at the camp (DoD 2005a). This document
reveals that, between 2002 and 2008 alone, the CIA and other bodies conducted around 24,000 interrogations (Denbeaux, et al. 2011, 1308). As was confirmed in a report issued by the Office of the Surgeon General of the United
States Army (US Department of the Army, Office of the Surgeon General 2005),
"all interrogations conducted at Guantánamo were videotaped" (Denbeaux,
et al. 2011, 1309). Nevertheless, there is a persistent doubt about whether the
tapes documenting the interrogations are being properly archived, or whether
some of them have already been destroyed or overwritten. In "Captured on
Tape: Interrogation and Videotaping of Detainees in Guantánamo," we read
that "many videotapes documenting Guantánamo interrogations do or *did*
exist" (Denbeaux, et al. 2011, 1309; italics added).

In this article, Mark Denbeaux and his co-authors identify several occasions
when the tapes of Guantánamo interrogations have been destroyed. The
article's authors also discuss how the mere mention of a tape's destruction
can become a starting point for an investigation into the inaccessible
archive of Guantánamo's surveillance infrastructure. For instance, the CIA's
destruction of at least two interrogation videotapes in 2005 resulted in one of
the most extensive investigations into the torture and abuse of detainees that
took place in the context of the US GWoT:

> The destruction of these two tapes occurred not only after the orders
> ['mandating that 'all evidence and information regarding the torture, mis-
> treatment, and abuse of detainees now at the United States Naval Base at
> Guantánamo Bay' be preserved' (Denbeaux, et al. 2011, 1307)] were issued,
> but also after the United States Supreme Court ruled that individuals
> detained at Guantánamo could pursue *habeas corpus* actions. Attempting
> to ward off judicial inquiry into the destruction of the tapes, the govern-
> ment argued that inquiry by the courts would compromise the Justice
> Department's investigation of the matter. On January 24, 2008, however,
> United States District Court Judge Richard W. Roberts issued an order
> which became the first to require that the government provide infor-
> mation regarding the tapes' destruction. (Denbeaux, et al. 2011, 1308)

The legal inquiry into why these tapes were destroyed and what they depicted sparked an investigation by the US Senate into the conduct of the CIA and the torture of detainees, not only in 2005, but during the entire period from 2001 to 2009.

Dianne Feinstein, at that time chair of the Senate Select Committee on Intelligence, writes in the foreword to the published, but shortened and censored, version of *The Official Senate Report on CIA Torture: Committee Study of the Central Intelligence Agency's Detention and Interrogation Program* that "[t]he Committee, through its staff, had already reviewed in 2008 thousands of CIA cables describing the interrogations of the CIA detainees Abu Zubaydah and Abd al-Rahim al-Nashiri, whose interrogations were the subject of the videotapes that were destroyed by the CIA in 2005" (Feinstein 2015, 4). Feinstein describes the review process of CIA documents as a very complex one, since the small team investigating the Agency's conduct was confronted with "more than six million pages of CIA materials, to include operational cables, intelligence reports, internal memoranda and emails, briefing material, interview transcripts, contracts, and other records" (Feinstein 2015, 5).

The shortened and redacted version of the report published by the committee reached a wide audience when Senator John McCain's Senate floor statement was screened on C-Span on December 9, 2014, five days after the final declassification revisions had been made (McCain 2014). In his statement, McCain – himself a victim of torture during the Vietnam War – shared his views on the use of torture techniques, and on the unreliability of information gained through them, as well as expressing his moral objections towards such practices:

> I know from personal experience that the abuse of prisoners will produce more bad than good intelligence. I know that victims of torture will offer intentionally misleading information if they think that captors will believe it. I know they will say whatever they think their torturers want them to say if they believe it will stop their suffering. Most of all, I know the use of torture compromises that which most distinguishes us from our enemies, our belief that all people, even captured enemies, possess basic human rights, which are protected by international conventions the US not only joined, but for the most part authored. (McCain 2014, 04:44–05:34)

In 2019, the report reached an even wider audience when the investigative process, and its revelations of the extent to which detainee abuse was embedded at a systemic level, was adapted for the screen. Following its theatrical release, *The Report* (2019), directed by Scott Z. Burns, was made available on Amazon Prime in the US and Europe. It focuses on the work and personal commitment of Daniel Jones (played by Adam Driver), who is identified in Feinstein's foreword as the person who "has managed and led the Committee's review effort from its inception. Dan has devoted more than six years to this effort, has personally written thousands of its pages, and has been integrally involved in every Study decision" (Feinstein 2015, 6). In the context of my own efforts to understand military documents, one of the most fascinating aspects of this film is the way it depicts Jones' daily work procedures at his desk. The plethora of documents – over six million classified records – formed the basis of his study on the CIA's detention and interrogation program, and resulted in a 6,700-page report, of which 499 pages were declassified. *The Official Senate Report*, published four years prior to the film's release, continues to inform our understanding of the torture and systemic abuse of detainees perpetrated at CIA black sites, as well as the specific role played by Guantánamo.

Alongside feature and documentary films which have reconstructed, sometimes in great detail, events taking place at Guantánamo, and those studies which have published their findings in the form of redacted summaries, there are also other documents available to the public, which disclose information about the infrastructure set up to tape the interrogations conducted at the camp. For example, Denbeaux and his co-authors have recourse to a wide range of military documents and summarize the information they reveal concerning the surveillance technologies at play. At Guantánamo, they write, "[c]ameras are positioned in every interrogation room, and each room is monitored from elsewhere" (Denbeaux, et al. 2011, 1311). They have also confirmed, firstly, that the detainees underwent surveillance by camera, and, secondly, that they suspected they were being filmed (Denbeaux, et al. 2011, 1313). Hence, the panoptic mechanism – where the surveilled subjects know they are being surveilled, and change or adjust their behavior accordingly – has clearly been at work in the interrogation cells at Guantánamo. To support their contentions about the extent of the Guantánamo video archive, the authors refer to at least three documents. Firstly, they mention the contents of the "Memorandum from ▮▮▮▮▮, to ▮▮▮▮▮ (Apr. 28, 2003)," in which a person whose identity has been redacted reports that he and his colleague simultaneously monitored two separate interrogations from a third room. Secondly, they refer to an email written by an FBI agent in which he describes how he used a monitor to watch a detainee praying and preparing for a meeting in his cell (Denbeaux, et al. 2011, 1311). Thirdly, in addition to these individual reports, they refer to the SOPs at Camp Delta:

> In fact, the Defense Department's 'Standard Operating Procedures for Guantánamo's Camp Delta' *mandated* that 'monitors will observe all interrogations' and that monitors 'will be located either in a monitor room that is equipped with two way mirrors and CCTV [closed-circuit television]

or in a CCTV only room.' Thus, an infrastructure for taping exists at Guantánamo. (Denbeaux, et al. 2011, 1311)[1]

Hence, considering the significance placed on documentation practices by military bureaucracies, as well as the other documents and media objects cited in this subsection, there is likely an almost uncountable number of documents and other media objects, which have been created or produced and distributed on a purely internal basis within the Guantánamo detention camp, and which will probably never see the light of day. This argument is substantiated by the fact that a great deal of critical research conducted on the internal processes at the detention camp has been based on leaked documents, such as the *Camp Delta SOPs* (JTF-Guantánamo 2003; 2004). In addition to these leaked documents, and the information about internal documentation practices which they reveal, we can assume that there is an enormous number of records which will never be published, and which can only ever be a source of speculation on my part. In "Removing Knowledge," Galison writes:

> You might think that the guarded annals of classified information largely consist of that rare document, a small, tightly guarded annex to the vast sum of human writing and learning. True, the number of carefully archived pages written in the open is large. While hard to estimate, one could begin by taking the number of items on the shelves of the Library of Congress, one of the largest libraries in the world: 120 million items carrying about 7,5 billion pages, of which about 5,4 billion pages are in 18 million books. In fact, the classified universe, as it is sometimes called, is certainly not smaller and very probably is much larger than this unclassified one. (Galison 2004, 229)

Galison's case study is the "military applications of nuclear weapons" (Galison 2004, 231) and not the US GWoT. Nevertheless, his estimate is also valuable when considering the number of classified documents produced in the context of the operations performed at Guantánamo. Galison notes that "[n]uclear weapons knowledge is born secret," meaning that any knowledge related to nuclear technology "becomes classified the instant it is written down" (Galison 2004, 232). Other documents issued by the DoD usually go through the process of classification by so-called "classifiers," who focus on

---

1   The passages from the *Camp Delta SOPs* referred to by Denbeaux and his co-authors can be found in Chapter 14 of the manual and are entitled "Intelligence Operations" (JTF-Guantánamo 2003, 14.1–4). According to the *SOPs*, the interrogations "require personnel to monitor and to react in the event of an altercation between detainee and Interrogator [*sic*]" (JTF-Guantánamo 2003, 14.2). Thus, the observation by the monitors is a purely visual one and the "monitors" are prohibited from listening to the interrogations: "JIIF [Joint Interagency Interrogation Facility] monitors will observe all interrogations. They will NOT listen to any interrogations. They will NOT discuss any events that occur inside an interrogation room" (JTF-Guantánamo 2003, 14.2).

the level of damage that might be caused should a specific piece of information be released to the public. The classifier must estimate whether the consequences would be "damage," "serious damage," or "exceptionally grave damage" (Galison 2004, 235; DoD 1999, 8). The classification statuses correlating to these three levels of damage are: "Confidential," "Secret," and "Top Secret" (DoD 1999, 8).

The *Camp Delta SOPs* never actually underwent such a classification process (JTF-Guantánamo 2003; 2004). Discourses from within the military apparatus reveal that this is problematic not only in terms of possible leaks, but also because of the confusion this lack of classification might cause among military personnel. The DoD describes the issues related to unclassified documents in its *Handbook for Writing Security Classification Guidance* from 1999 as follows:

> Broad guidance such as 'U-S' meaning Unclassified to Secret does not provide sufficient instruction to users of the guide, unless you also delineate the exact circumstances under which each level of classification should be applied. The exact circumstances may be supplied in amplifying comments, for example, 'Unclassified ('U') when X is not revealed;' 'Confidential when X is revealed;' and 'Secret when X and Y are revealed.' Failure to provide such guidance will result in users of the guide making their own interpretations that may, or may not, be consistent with your intent. (DoD 1999, 13f.)

Although no classifier was instructed to estimate the damage that the release of the *Camp Delta SOPs* could potentially cause, the "document, and any part therein, are classified as 'for official use only' and are limited to those requiring operational and procedural knowledge in the direct performance of their duties as well as those directly associated with JTF-GTMO" (JTF-Guantánamo 2003, ii).

To return to this chapter's aim of seeing beyond the images and information about Guantánamo that are made available to us, it is important to acknowledge the methodological difficulties posed by such a task. Although the context of a work of scholarship permits a certain amount of speculation, it is essential to base this speculation on the analyzed materials. Investigating the fragments not included within the frames of the seeable requires a kind of counter-forensic approach towards those documents or visual materials that can be accessed, such as the *Camp Delta SOPs*. To exacerbate the situation further, the physical locations of the pieces of information produced within the detention facility are scattered across many locations – both physical and virtual – making even a partial reconstruction of Guantánamo's archive an especially difficult task. As with any other archive, the objects constituting Guantánamo's archive are presumably stored in some physical location. I assume that parts of it are kept in electronic form on the Pentagon

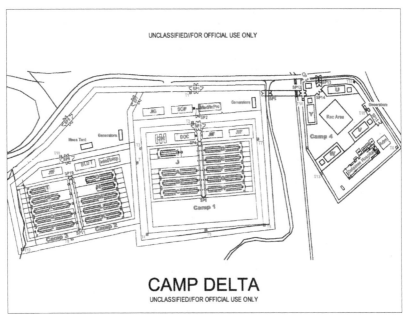

[Fig. 14] *Camp Delta SOPs* include an annotated map of Camp Delta with the SCIF appearing in the upper-center of the image (Source: JTF-Guantánamo 2003, 225). The appearance of US Department of Defense (DoD) visual information does not imply or constitute DoD endorsement.

and FBI servers, but many of the files are supposedly stored directly at the Guantánamo camp. For example, some of the images produced during the "in-processing" of the detainees are sent to the FBI, whereas other images are kept "safe" at Guantánamo (JTF-Guantánamo 2003, 4.3).

The *Camp Delta SOPs* include a map of Camp Delta [fig. 14] where one of the buildings is identified as "SCIF," the abbreviation for "Sensitive Compart-mented Information Facility," a DoD term for "a secure room or data center that guards against electronic surveillance and suppresses data leakage of sensitive security and military information" (SCIF Global Technologies 2022). Although the *Camp Delta SOPs* mention that some data and objects are transferred outside the facility (albeit still within the US security apparatus) it seems safe to assume that many of the files pertaining to the detainees are stored in the SCIF. This appears to be the case for the documentation of particular interrogations. According to an account by an FBI agent, employees at Guantánamo kept detailed records of all interrogations within the detention facility (Denbeaux, et al. 2011, 1316).

The materials stored in the SCIF and the distribution of various images within the military apparatus raise the crucial question of how we can write about archives whose existence is assumed, but to which we have no access.

According to Jacques Derrida, the archive cannot exist *"without a place of con-signation, without a technique of repetition, and without a certain exteriority. No archive without outside"* (Derrida 1995, 14). Derrida defines access to the archive and participation in its constitution and interpretation, as genuinely political issues, when he states in his first and only footnote in *Archive Fever: A Freudian Impression* that *"[t]here is no political power without control of the archive, if not of memory. Effective democratization can always be measured by this essential criterion: the participation in and the access to the archive, its constitution, and its interpretation"* (Derrida 1995, 11). His views on the political nature of the archive are also relevant to the US government's denial of public access to large parts of the Guantánamo archive. To extend Derrida's argument that there cannot be an interiority without an exteriority, I will next pursue a counter-forensic investigation into Guantánamo's archive – a consciously political act – and thus will investigate the "inside" of the Guantánamo archive from such a position of exteriority: from an outside that is crucial to the inside.

The Frame of Archival Practices

Archiving Bodies for Future Uses

Documentation practices carried out by military personnel at the Guantánamo detention camp are manifold. Alongside the written records of daily activities and procedures undertaken there, military personnel use photographs and moving images to visually record and archive events, as well as the bodies of the detainees. Considering the wide range of documentation practices, I have chosen to focus here on indexical practices – such as fin-gerprinting; photographing scars, wounds, tattoos, or bodily deformations; and chest X-rays – which are performed as part of the SOPs during the "in-processing" of the detainees (JTF-Guantánamo 2003, 15.2). I argue that these practices – which are designed to function as recordkeeping, but are also violent tools of control – have played a significant role in transforming the bodies of the detained men into epistemic archives for future use within the military apparatus. Here, I would like to reiterate that photographs of the detainees' bodies taken during the initial documentation at the camp – that is, photographs ostensibly recording the men's health, scars, and tattoos, among other things – remain largely inaccessible to the public and to scholars. However, in spite of the restrictions on access to images, military doc-uments make it possible for scholars to reconstruct the actions performed by military and medical personnel, and to speculate on this important part of Guantánamo's archive.[2]

2   This archive primarily consists of images taken by "insiders" for internal uses. In the con-text of Guantánamo, "insiders" does not solely refer to the personnel stationed at the base. In this chapter, I will also refer to members of the intelligence, security, and state

An analysis of the forensic methods applied to the living bodies of the detainees thus requires a counter-forensic sensibility. The counter-forensic approach in this subsection, however, does not seek to "exhume[e] and identif[y] … the anonymized ('disappeared') bodies" (Sekula 2014, 30), but instead to identify photographic practices and the objects resulting from them. Importantly, the DoD and the military have aimed to make any knowledge of its internal photographic practices and the resulting objects disappear, making it difficult for me to reconstruct the presumed archive of images. Nevertheless, this disappearance is only an illusion, since military and intelligence personnel are prohibited from destroying documents, photographs, and surveillance footage. The apparent disappearance of these media objects is thus usually part of the institutional processes of obscuring knowledge via deliberate overclassification.

The *Camp Delta SOPs* disclose, in a highly detailed manner, many situations in which photographic technologies are employed by military personnel. The first leaked version of the document was finalized over a year after the arrival of the first detainees at the facility; in it, the JTF-Guantánamo describes the "standardized" treatment of the detainees and the uses of photographic media (JTF-Guantánamo 2003). According to a letter written by Geoffrey D. Miller, who was Commander of the JTF-Guantánamo at the time, as well as one of the central figures in the design and implementation of torture techniques on a global scale after 9/11, this SOP document was distributed to the commanders and directors so they could brief their teams (Miller 2003, 3). In its 32 chapters, the *Camp Delta SOPs* cover a wide range of topics and evoke a highly complex image of military operations at the camp, meticulously describing even the smallest procedures, leaving very little room – if any – for interpretation, speculation, and deviation. In the following discussion, I will reconstruct and summarize some of the passages from the *Camp Delta SOPs* designed to inform military personnel about when to use photographic equipment – and when not to.

In section "1–7. US Personnel Standards of Conduct" photographic equipment appears in a list of prohibited items and is referred to as "contraband" (JTF-Guantánamo 2003, 1.2). Military personnel are not allowed to bring such contraband – including cell phones, obscene material, recording devices, and many other things – to the camp for their private use, nor to give it to the detainees. Nevertheless, photographic equipment and recording devices might be "approved by proper authority" (JTF-Guantánamo 2003, 1.2). By contrast, the use of recording devices is explicitly authorized during the "in-processing" of the detainees, and when the Immediate Reaction Force enters a cell in order to "extract" a detainee (JTF-Guantánamo 2003, 24.1). Detailed

apparatus as "insiders." Thus, the demarcation between outsiders and insiders is not designated by the physical architecture of the detention facility alone.

instructions about the use of such devices can be found in the chapters entitled "3. Detainee Reception Operations" and "4. Detainee Processing (Reception/Transfer/Release)." Significantly, when a new detainee arrives at Guantánamo and Camp Delta, he is subjugated to twelve "in-processing" stations, with each station involving a set of specific actions performed upon the detainee by military and medical personnel.[3]

In the "Clothing Removal Room (Station 1)," the detainee's clothing is cut off and thrown away while he remains shackled (JTF-Guantánamo 2003, 4.2). The detainee is obliged to continue wearing his facial mask during this entire procedure. In the second station, the detainee is showered and examined by a medical doctor for "lice, scabies and open wounds that require treatment" (JTF-Guantánamo 2003, 4.2). If any of the above is detected, the detainee is supposed to receive immediate treatment. The third station is located in the "medical exam room" where a "Physician Assistant (PA) performs a quick exam, a body survey check, and a body cavity search" (JTF-Guantánamo 2003, 3.3). This is also the first station where photographic cameras are deployed, with military personnel taking "[p]hotos of scars and tattoos" for the FBI (JTF-Guantánamo 2003, 3.3). In Station 4, the detainee is re-clothed by the escort team. Further recordkeeping practices are conducted in Station 5, where personnel collect a DNA sample from the detainee and record his weight and height (JTF-Guantánamo 2003, 3.3). The Joint Intelligence Group takes further photographs in this station, but the *Camp Delta SOPs* do not specify their nature. In the sixth station, the collected information is entered into the "PWIS database" (JTF-Guantánamo 2003, 3.3). Station 7 again focuses on the documentation of detainees' bodies: here, personnel take another series of photographs, this time for an "identity (ID) bracelet" (JTF-Guantánamo 2003, 3.3), and the so-called "detainee Dossiers" (JTF-Guantánamo 2003, 4.3). Along-side a frontal photograph, instructions are given for five further images. The detainee is placed before a white screen and pictures are taken "[in terms of a clock: 0900, 1000, 1200, 1300, and 1500] for the FBI's image recognition software" (JTF-Guantánamo 2003, 4.3). In Station 8, two military police officers take the detainee's fingerprints (JTF-Guantánamo 2003, 3.3; 4.3). This is followed by medical personnel drawing a blood sample from the detainee in Station 9. In "station 10 ... [d]etainee is moved to x-ray room and receives chest x-ray" (JTF-Guantánamo 2003, 3.3). Stations 11 and 12 are interchangeable, and see the detainee sent to the medical or dental examination room, and vice versa.

---

3   A similar process was probably being implemented on the day of the arrival of the first detainees photographed by Shane T. McCoy. McCoy's caption ends with the statement: "[t]he detainees will be given a basic physical exam by a doctor, to include a chest X-ray and blood samples drawn to assess their health." These steps are also mentioned in *Camp Delta SOPs* as part of the "in-processing" procedure.

Thus, during the "in-processing" procedure, each detainee is photographed on at least three occasions. Alongside photographic cameras, the various documenting technologies include X-rays and fingerprinting, both of which are also indexical practices. The precise documentation of the men's distinguishing features in the (medical) examination rooms, and the entering of their data into the "National Detainee Records Center," the "Detainee Reporting System," and the "PWIS database," as well as the forwarding of five photographs per detainee to the FBI for their image-recognition software, means that the detainee's body becomes archived, recognizable, and searchable (JTF-Guantánamo 2003, 4.1). The visual record of its constituent parts – including the detainee's face, scars, fingerprints, and chest X-rays – is stored for future use.

The photographs intended for the FBI's image-recognition software are part of the extensive surveillance apparatus developed after, and legitimized by, the failure to recognize the men involved in 9/11 – including Mohamed Atta and Abdulaziz al-Omari, who were recorded by surveillance cameras at the airport in Portland (Maine) on the morning of 9/11, but were not apprehended. The image-recognition software seeks to recognize faces in the general population, and is rooted in what Kelly A. Gates calls "the drive to 'know the face'," wherein "facial recognition technology treats the face as an index of identity" (Gates 2011, 8).[4] By contrast, "[t]he X-ray can be seen as an image of you [or the detainee] and the world, an image forged in the collapse of the surface that separates the two" (Lippit 2005, 43). Although X-rays might also be used as a means of visual recognition, they seek to recognize the inside, rather than the outside, of a body. Interestingly, both technologies, facial-recognition software and X-rays, are about making certain bodies epistemically available by means of their penetration via image technologies. Although the facial recognition of the detainees is based on five photographs of the surfaces of their faces, Gates is right when she writes that *the surface of the face [is used] to see inside the person*" (Gates 2011, 8; italics added). X-ray images are also about the desire to see (literally) inside a person, even if their purpose is primarily framed by health, rather than security discourses. While this book is guided by the question, "what do we see when we look at Guantánamo?," in his book, *Atomic Light (Shadow Optics)*, Akira Mizuta Lippit poses a similar question in relation to X-rays: "[W]hat does one see *there*, in the X-ray? ... What is *there* to be seen?" (Lippit 2005, 52). The answer is that we see a "*thereness*, perhaps, that is avisual: a secret surface between the inside and out, the place where

---

4   Fingerprinting the detainees also produces surfaces that come to function as "an index of identity" (Gates 2011, 8). As Peter Geimer writes in "Image as a Trace: Speculations About an Undead Paradigm," "[t]he fingerprint is the personal signature of its creator and accordingly possesses a certain optical similarity to him. This quality, be it actual or speculative, is ultimately what underpinned the use of the fingerprint in criminology" (Geimer 2007, 11).

you are, there, secret and invisible. A spectacle of invisibility, shining, shown, avisual" (Lippit 2005, 52). Lippit suggests that X-rays are about revealing the thing which is located on the "secret surface" (Lippit 2005, 52) separating the inside and outside; it is a technology that collapses this separation before the eyes of the viewer.

Given Lippit's incisive discussion of the ideology underlying X-rays, it is more than coincidental that the name of the initial infrastructure of the detention camp from the 1990s – Camp X-Ray – was retained: a name which, in a certain sense, set the agenda for, and the purposes of, Guantánamo in the 21st Century. If X-ray photography is about collapsing the borders between the external and internal, the detention camp demonstrates the various efforts and techniques employed by military personnel to look inside the detainees' bodies and minds while, at the same time, creating geographical and legal borders, as well as increasing the distance between the inside and outside of the camp.

Generalizing and Anonymizing the Detainees

The meticulous documentation of the detainees' bodies, epistemically accessing their surfaces and even their insides to reveal secrets and confirm their identities in the future, is not new at all. It inevitably inscribes itself into a long tradition of documenting and producing the so-called "criminal body" (Sekula 1986, 6). Efforts to make the bodies of the detainees identifiable by recording their scars, tattoos, and other significant features, coupled with the repetitive nature of photographic practices, present a direct continuation of the procedures undertaken by scientists and police officials in the 19th century. Putting aside the fact that actions designated as crimes in the 19th century are rather different from those of modern-day terrorism, it is productive to analyze the points of connection between these practices. In his essay, "The Body and the Archive," Allan Sekula writes about the historic developments related to the photographic documentation of prisoners, as well as other 19th century methods of recording their identities. He argues that photography is "a system of representation capable of functioning both *honorifically* and *repressively*" (Sekula 1986, 6). While portraiture functions honorifically for the bourgeois self, for example, it operates repressively for a person accused of crimes. In the 19th century, as Sekula writes, "[t]he battle between the presumed denotative univocality of the legal image and the multiplicity and presumed duplicity of the criminal voice" resulted in the definition of two new objects: the "criminal body," on the one hand, and the "social body," on the other (Sekula 1986, 6). Photographic practices, and other forms of documentation, became central tenets of the constitution and recognition of the "criminal body."

As early as 1880, Sekula notes, there were already two systems in place to identify and describe such bodies: the methods developed by the French police official Alphonse Bertillon, and those expounded by Francis Galton, a British citizen and propagator of eugenics (Sekula 1986, 18). Reading the 21st century practices of the JTF-Guantánamo through Sekula's analysis of the relationship between the body and the archive in the 19th century allows us to historicize the "in-processing" procedures at Camp Delta in relation to much older endeavors that strived to produce the body of the criminal and make it epistemically available. The photographs taken of the detainees' wounds, scars, and tattoos during the arrival procedure at Guantánamo – elements perceived to be distinguishing features and, hence, a means of making a body identifiable in the future as belonging to a specific individual – echo Bertillon's interest in corporeal deformations. Historically, these defor-mations were perceived as features of the criminal's individuality, and were used in a similar way in the French penal system as at Guantánamo – as a means of identification. Bertillon actually "invented the first effective modern system of *criminal identification*" by "combin[ing] photographic portraiture, anthropometric description, and highly standardized and abbreviated written notes on a single *fiche*, or card" (Sekula 1986, 18). He also developed a compre-hensive filing system for those cards within the French police force. Galton's composite portraiture is recalled in the systematic approach towards the documentation of the bodies of the detainees, which become racialized and stereotyped through photographic procedures. Galton sought to identify a "biologically determined 'criminal type'" (Sekula 1986, 19) by exposing the same photographic plate during different sessions. However, it is not only the repetitive nature of the photographs of Muslim men that evokes the racialized and standardized image of a "Guantánamo detainee" – this effect of uniformity is also achieved by material practices such as dressing all the men in the same clothing, shaving their heads, and allotting each of them an "Internment Serial Number (ISN)" (JTF-Guantánamo 2003, 4.1) – all of which contribute to an imaginary "composite image" of the presumed "terrorist body."

The generalizing effects of the clothing that the detainees are obliged to wear at the camp is emphasized by the term "jumpsuits" used in much of the scholarly literature and newspaper articles. A jumpsuit is a one-piece garment combining shirt and trousers. However, as Guantánamo photographs show, detainees have also worn separate items of clothing – in some images, for instance, we can see that their shirts have been raised or trousers lowered. The *Camp Delta SOPs* confirm my observation in the instructions in section "4–11. Dressing/Shackle Exchange (Station 4)":

> a. Kneel the detainee down on the floor or chair; remove the Air Force leg irons and place them in the storage box to go back to the Air Force.

b. Place *orange pants* and leg shackles from three-piece suit [feet, hand, and connecting shakles] on detainee.
c. Remove hand irons and place in the storage box.
d. Put the *orange shirt* on the detainee while the guards have positive control of arms.
e. Place handcuffs from three-piece suit on detainee. (JTF-Guantánamo 2003, 4.2; italics added)

Nevertheless, it is the jumpsuit which has become an icon of Guantánamo, with protesters wearing them in front of the White House (Reuters 2013), and military employees holding them while posing for photo opportunities. For instance, in 2002, US Marine Major Steve Cox – then spokesman of the JTF-Guantánamo – held up such a jumpsuit for the reporter's camera; the caption accompanying the photograph revealed it to be the clothing which the detainees would be wearing at the camp (Getty Images and Chapman 2002).[5] Despite the difficulty of determining whether the detainees were in fact wearing jumpsuits, trousers and shirts, or both, it seems telling that the public and scholarly discourse usually refers to their orange clothing as a one-piece item. The clothing effaces the visual specificity of the individual men, with the result that the viewers are unable to visually distinguish one detainee from another. Elspeth S. Van Veeren is right to point out that "through the orange prison jumpsuit individual detainees were subsumed into a larger collective group through its anonymizing and flattening function" (Van Veeren 2016b, 125). What Van Veeren calls the "flattening function" (Van Veeren 2016b, 125) of the jumpsuit is nothing less than the garment's ability to render individuality invisible, and to produce an image of a collective which is solely defined by the presumption of terrorist activity. The emphasis on the jumpsuits in public discourses would appear to suggest that the DoD and its military have partially succeeded in producing an image of the generalized body of the "Guantánamo detainee," not only within, but also outside of the military apparatus.

Using clothing and shaving the detainees' hair (including facial hair) to degrade them and deprive them of individual identities is horrific in itself. However, another "in-processing" procedure further aggravates this issue: the moment when each detainee is allotted an ISN. The detainees are not only stripped of their individuality by means of facial masks and blackened goggles – an argument I presented in the first chapter in relation to McCoy's photographs – but also by being issued a serial number in lieu of their name. It is hard to overlook the historical context in which identity numbers were issued at detention camps; specifically, the numbers tattooed onto the skin of people incarcerated in Nazi concentration camps during World War II. Admittedly, the practice of tattooing an identity number onto a person's skin differs materially

---

5   Elspeth S. Van Veeren refers to this photograph in the pre-publication draft of her essay, "Orange Prison Jumpsuit," published on researchgate.com (Van Veeren 2016a).

from the issuing of an ISN for an identity bracelet. However, in the historical context, the issuing of ISNs also forms "a constituent of the brutal procedure of shaving, disinfecting, clothing and unclothing that marked the entrance in the camp, which is in unison described as an act of dehumanisation" (Därmann 2017, 231).[6] Iris Därmann, in her essay about the numbers tattooed on prisoners in the Auschwitz-Birkenau camp, formulates two theses, both of which tell us also something about the ISNs issued at the Guantánamo detention camp (Därmann 2017). The first is that, for the SS administration, the tattoos "allow[ed] the secure identification of murdered inmates, but also … guarantee[d] the daily routine of the registration and the statistical-managerial census of the living inmates" (Därmann 2017, 232). Her second thesis relates to the fact that the needles used in Auschwitz-Birkenau were not those found in tattoo shops for humans, but instead were actually needles "used in animal husbandry" (Därmann 2017, 232). The intentional refusal to differentiate between human and animal lives leads Därmann to observe that "[t]hese different tattoos of killing, breeding, and life (survival) are thanato- and biopolitical markers and reflect the 'functions' of NS-racism" (Därmann 2017, 232). In the context of Auschwitz-Birkenau, she demonstrates how these tattoos led detainees to be treated as "living corpses," suspended on the border between "life and death" (Därmann 2017, 245; my translation).

Considering the horrific legacy of numbers used for identification in detention camps, it is imperative to inquire about the reasons for the introduction of this practice at Guantánamo. The DoD has not published an official statement about why the detainees were given ISNs. However, we can draw on statements made by guards and the detainees themselves to understand why the JTF-Guantánamo implemented such a system of administration. One of the guards described to a lawyer the consequences of censoring the detainees' names and replacing them by numbers as follows: "'I don't want to know the names, ma'am,' a prison guard once told me when I asked him if he knew our client's name, not just his ISN. 'Why?' I asked. 'It's all about attachment. It's like when you're a kid on a farm and you're told not to name the animals you're going to eat in the future'" (Denbeaux 2009, 324).[7] The guard describes the anonymizing function of the ISN as a way of avoiding any potential attachment which may be felt by military personnel towards the detained men, and perhaps even as a tool to make it more difficult for them to develop a human connection. The issuing of ISNs apparently also redefines or *reframes* the guard-detainee relationship as an inter-species relationship. This account supports Därmann's contention that numerical identification reinforced the biopolitical divide at the heart of Nazi racism, and it is similarly indicative of the forms of racism thriving in the Guantánamo detention camp. The biopolitical

6   I would like to thank Sebastian Köthe for pointing me towards this text and for our intensive exchanges on the following passages.
7   I would like to thank Sebastian Köthe for alerting me to this citation.

argument that underlies the guard's comparison of the detainees to farm animals and the guard's racial distinction between guards and detainees – incisively analyzed by Sebastian Köthe in his dissertation – has been reiterated by many different military actors during the years of Guantánamo's existence (Köthe 2021, 229–45).

However, more than negotiating an animal-human relationship, as I will show in the following discussion of former detainee Shaker Aamer's satire of the *Universal Declaration of Human Rights* (UDHR), the ISNs in fact relocate the border between the world of humans and the world of things, redefining the individual lives of the detainees as "'package[s]'" (Aamer 2014). Aamer, a Saudi citizen, identifies the practice of stripping the detainees of their names and referring to them as numbers rather than people as one that strives to dehumanize them in the eyes of both the guards and the public. His thoughts on the ISNs can be found in an originally classified, subsequently declassified document, in which he recounts how, during his detention, he was permitted to study the 1948 UDHR (UN General Assembly 1948). In a satirical way, Aamer relates his own circumstances of detention to the articles in the UDHR, updating each with an addendum that reflects his interpretation of the US government's view on international human rights, and the situation of the detainees at Guantánamo (Aamer 2014). As Aamer notes (highly ironically) members of the Bush administration continuously emphasized the necessity of updating the international human rights declared after World War II, since they appeared to be "'outmoded'" (Aamer 2014). In his alternative version, which he entitled "The Declaration of No Human Rights," we read the following introduction:

> [T]he longer I have remained in this terrible prison, the more I have come to realise that the US has already amended the UDHR by imposing their own addendum to each Article. Here, then, is a recently declassified copy of the Declaration of No Human Rights (DNHR):
> Article 1.
> ...
> Article 2.
> ...
> [and so on]. (Aamer 2014)

In the context of my discussion of the ISNs, Aamer's addendum to Article 6 is particularly pertinent. Article 6 of the UDHR declares that "[e]veryone has the right to recognition everywhere as a person before the law" (UN General Assembly 1948, 14). Aamer's addendum recasts the dehumanizing practice of the ISNs as making the detainees equivalent to "package[s]": "[e]veryone in Guantánamo Bay should be *recognised only as a number and will be referred to as a 'package'* when being taken from one 'reservation' to the next" (Aamer 2014; italics added). Aamer's invocation of the concept of a "shipment" or "package" is another way of reiterating the phenomenon Därmann has diagnosed as the suspension of the detainees between life and death. Significantly, by referring to them as packages or numbers, the detainees are ascribed the status of things rather than human beings, which complicates the answer to the question of whether the DoD places the detainees on the side of life or death.

Aamer's addendum to the first article of the UDHR is also telling with regard to the status the JTF-Guantánamo afforded to the lives of the detainees at Guantánamo, and resonates with the aforementioned guard's comparison of the detainees to farm animals. The UDHR's first article states that "[a]ll human beings are born free and equal in dignity and rights. They are endowed with reason and conscience and should act towards one another in a spirit of brotherhood" (UN General Assembly 1948, 4). Aamer's addendum begins with "BUT" in capital letters: "BUT, all Muslim men held in Guantánamo Bay are considered to be something rather less than human, the worst of the worst of America's enemies. Indeed, the detainees should have fewer rights than the iguanas that roam the naval base" (Aamer 2014). As Aamer observes, the detainees have been given even fewer rights than some of the animals at the detention camp – such as the iguana, which is protected by the *Endangered Species Act*, and whose killing can be punished by a fine and prosecution (Ito 2008). On the way, Aamer describes the relationship between the legal protection of certain animal species at Guantánamo, and the denial of such protection to the detainees, Köthe writes:

> The declaration exposes the legal form of the violent practices as well as the short circuiting of law and justice. Instead of testifying to the violence in the first person singular – instead of running through the humiliations and violations by means of the example of his own experiences – Aamer allows the law to bear witness by itself. This law expresses the racism and speciesism of tyranny over the lives of prisoners. (Köthe 2021, 232f.; my translation)

This animal metaphor expresses the crucial biopolitical divide which would be reiterated in the Bush administration's discourse on the men detained at the Guantánamo detention camp again and again. Thus, numbers rather than names; orange jumpsuits rather than individual men; body parts rather than biographies – these are the violent operations "of homogenization, totalization and genericity" (Puglesie 2013, 34) put relentlessly to work at the Guantánamo detention camp. Along with the serial repetitiveness of photographic practices documenting the bodies of the detained men, the ISNs contribute to the production of a generalized body both within and outside the military apparatus. And this is in spite of the fact that the detainees are supposed to be individually identifiable, thanks to the archive consisting of images, amongst other objects, taken by military personnel. The historical legacy of these practices cannot be overlooked, and Sekula is right to observe that

> 'Bertillon' survives in the operations of the national security state, in the condition of intensive and extensive surveillance that characterizes both everyday life and the geopolitical sphere. 'Galton' lives in the renewed authority of biological determinism, founded in the increased hegemony of the political Right in Western democracies. (Sekula 1986, 62)

"Bertillon" and "Galton" do not only survive behind the fences of the Guantánamo detention camp; they are legitimized anew and thrive on the anti-terrorist rhetoric of constant threat. Their legacy flourishes in the fantasy that image technologies can be used to epistemically access the detainees' bodies and minds, and archive them for future use.

Reframing Withheld Photographs

The DoD's Refusal to Publish Torture Photographs

Here, I will return to the argument that the DoD's intentional denial of access to Guantánamo's archive can be understood as an antiepistemology which seeks to prevent the public from understanding what is happening at the detention camp. Significantly, many of the military documents and photographic objects end up in "the basements" of the DoD's archives or are buried in the SCIF at the camp. This shows that these objects are not supposed to be available to the public and, as I have discussed, can only be a target of speculation on my part. Clear examples of this include Romero's anecdote about the unauthorized distribution of a classified memo, recounted in the introduction to this chapter (Galison, et al. 2010, 1030), as well as the unauthorized publishing of the *Camp Delta SOPs* by WikiLeaks. Furthermore, these cases illustrate the ways in which the DoD, the JTF-Guantánamo, and other governmental bodies have worked to obscure and deny knowledge even about the mere existence of certain photographs and photographic practices, and how they sometimes fail to do so. Regarding the Guantánamo detention camp, the fact that the public is not even aware that knowledge has been "covered and obscured" (Galison 2004, 237) is the rule rather than the exception. However, along with the unauthorized distribution of documents, which has led to the uncovering of previously hidden knowledge, in certain cases, the US government itself has revealed to the public the ways in which it withholds information. Sometimes, it has even done so in the same moment as it has revealed knowledge by releasing documents.

Of the documents pertaining to the treatment of detainees after 9/11 that were initially classified, and have subsequently been declassified, many contain significant redactions. Personal information that identifies military employees and detainees is not all that is redacted, covered by black lines; most of the associated photographs also continue to be withheld. These photographs are redacted (or censored) not by blackening, but usually by replacing them with a white field and adding the text "PHOTO DENIED IN FULL EXEMPTION 6&7" [fig. 13]. In other cases, the pages containing photographs are simply deleted from the PDF file. Nevertheless, even in these documents, the written text some-times makes it possible to deduce the existence of and even, in particular cases, the contents of the withheld photographs. For example, we can infer that some of these photographs were taken during forensic and medical procedures, and that they document bruises, wounds, and other evidence of harm, potentially resulting from the abuse and maltreatment of detainees at Guantánamo, in military prisons in Iraq and Afghanistan, and at various CIA black sites.

In light of the importance ceded to photographic evidence of torture in the *habeas corpus* cases pursued on behalf of detainees imprisoned at Guantánamo, in which proof of torture has been the grounds for dismissing testimonies given under pressure of physical and psychological duress, it will come as no surprise that the ACLU has tried "to learn everything … [it] could about what the government is hiding" (Relman 2015), and, in particular, to dis-cover what the photographs redacted from documents actually show. Thus, in the following discussion, by reconstructing the legal history of the ACLU's FOIA request "for records, including photos, relating to the abuse and torture of prisoners in US detention centers overseas" (Relman 2015) submitted in 2003 (ACLU 2003), I will consider another dimension of counter-forensics, and demonstrate how an independent human rights institution such as the ACLU sought to transform the antiepistemology resulting from the US government's refusal of access to, redaction, and censorship of photographs, into an actual epistemology for the general public.

In 2004, when the infamous torture photographs from the Abu Ghraib prison were leaked to the media and the ACLU had still not received any of the records mentioned in their FOIA request, the organization decided to file a complaint to the US District Court for the Southern District of New York (Banchik 2018, 1171). The 2004 complaint marked the beginning of the *ACLU v. DoD* lawsuit, which concerned the DoD's ongoing refusal to produce photographs depicting persons detained after 9/11, and which would even-tually last more than a decade (*ACLU v. DoD* 2017, 04. Civ 4161 (AKH)). The images under dispute in this lawsuit were taken at various military prisons and detention facilities abroad, including at Guantánamo and Abu Ghraib, and are estimated to amount to some 2,000 photographs (Relman 2015). The history of this lawsuit and the 2017 summaries of its proceedings by its judge, Alvin K. Hellerstein, reveal the many instruments and arguments through which two US administrations have sought to keep knowledge about the photographs hidden, and in particular, they help us to understand how the DoD has obscured knowledge about the photographs of detainees and POWs.[8] The ACLU's FOIA request was filed as early as six months prior to the publication of the photographs of the tortured prisoners at Abu Ghraib. The latter scandal revealed the scope and extent of the abuse occurring in US detention facilities abroad and increased public pressure on the US government to disclose further photographic evidence of the torture perpetrated on the people it had detained after the attacks of 9/11. According to the ACLU, nearly 6,000 documents in their *Torture Database* referred to the abuse of prisoners; many of them originally included photographic evidence of the traces of abuse and torture of detainees – evidence which was redacted during the declassification process (ACLU 2022a). The *ACLU v. DoD* case, for which an eighth motion was decided at the beginning of 2017, extended over the terms of three presidencies and demonstrates how even the Obama administration – which had proclaimed its intention to close the Guantánamo detention facility – successfully continued to obscure and deny evidence of torture.

Nevertheless, during each administration, the so-called "FOIA exemptions" evoked and official arguments put forward for why these photographs should not be published were formulated in different ways, and were based on either avowed concerns about privacy, or on issues of national security. During the Bush presidency, the lawsuit focused on a substantial set of photographs produced following 9/11 at various detention facilities abroad, including the images taken at the Abu Ghraib prison, which were revealed by whistle-blower Sergeant Joseph Darby. In 2005, the US government requested that it be permitted to "exempt" these photographs from publication, arguing that releasing them "would compromise the privacy of the individuals depicted in the photographs" (*ACLU v. DoD* 2017, 04. Civ 4161 (AKH), 3 and 4). Judge Hellerstein writes:

> After I conducted an *in camera* review of all the Darby photographs and ordered redactions of all personal characteristics, the Government changed its position and instead invoked FOIA Exemption 7(F), which exempts from production records compiled for law enforcement purposes to the extent that disclosure 'could reasonably be expected to endanger the life or physical safety of any individual.' (*ACLU v. DoD* 2017, 04. Civ 4161 (AKH), 4)

Hence, after Hellerstein ordered the redaction of the individual features of the persons visible in those photographs, the US government shifted its argument

---

8   Despite the US government's sustained efforts to fight the publication of the photographs by appealing the court's decision and Hellerstein's order to publish them, in 2016 the DoD decided to publish a set of 198 photographs in one single PDF file (DoD 2016). For a detailed discussion of this PDF file see Chapter 4.

from privacy concerns to those of national security and invoked the FOIA exemption, which applies when the release of documents or photographs would endanger the lives of soldiers. In spite of this change in position, Hellerstein denied the applicability of both exemption requests and, in 2005, again ordered the government to publish the redacted photographs. Significantly, after the US government's appeal of Hellerstein's decision, the so-called "Darby photographs" were leaked to the public in 2006 and published on the *Salon.com* website. This leak led the government to withdraw its appeal.

Despite the publication of this set of photographs, the ACLU again requested the US government to disclose whether or not some of the photographs subject to the motion remained unpublished. In doing so, they discovered that a total of 44 photographs did not make it onto *Salon.com*'s homepage. In two rulings, from 2006 and 2008 respectively, the US government was yet again ordered to publish the remaining photographs; these were supposed to be released in May 2009 (Banchik 2018, 1172).

In her reconstruction of the *ACLU v. DoD* case in "Too Dangerous to Disclose? FOIA, Courtroom 'Visual Theory,' and the Legal Battle Over Detainee Abuse Photographs," Anna Veronika Banchik subdivides the lawsuit's course and arguments into three distinct phases. She places the Bush administration's arguments for the FOIA exemptions between 2003 and 2009 in the first phase (Banchik 2018, 1170ff.). The second begins with Barack Obama's presidency, and with his administration establishing a new basis for the dismissal of Hellerstein's previous rulings ordering the photographs to be published, while the third is the post-*Protected National Security Documents Act* (PNSDA) litigation phase (Banchik 2018, 1172–5). In 2009, the US Congress passed the PNSDA, which introduced a new review process for documents and photographs, and appeared especially applicable to the set of disputed photographs in the ACLU's lawsuit (US Congress 2009). The PNSDA granted the US government an exemption from the FOIA, provided that the Secretary of Defense certified each photograph individually, with the certification having to be renewed every three years. The PNSDA defines a "protected document" as

> any record – (A) for which the Secretary of Defense has issued a certification, as described in subsection (d), stating that disclosure of that record would endanger citizens of the United States, members of the United States Armed Forces, or employees of the United States Government deployed outside the United States; and (B) *that is a photograph that – (i) was taken during the period beginning on September 11, 2001, through January 22, 2009; and (ii) relates to the treatment of individuals engaged, captured, or detained after September 11, 2001, by the Armed Forces of the United States in operations outside of the United States.* (US Congress 2009, 1; italics added)

The first certification of the disputed photographs was undertaken in 2009 by the then Secretary of Defense, Robert Gates. In 2012, Leon Panetta renewed the certification; in 2015, Ashton Carter did likewise. In 2011, Hellerstein upheld the first certification under the PNSDA on the grounds of the political situation in Iraq. However, when it came to Panetta's certification, Hellerstein ruled that the "Government had not satisfied its burden" (*ACLU v. DoD* 2017, 04. Civ 4161 (AKH), 9) of certifying each photograph individually. Panetta only certified three "representative sample[s] of five to ten photographs" (*ACLU v. DoD* 2017, 04. Civ 4161 (AKH), 9) prepared for him by Megan M. Weis, then Associate Deputy General Counsel in the Department of the Army. The first samples went through a complex review process by "senior military leadership and field commanders," and "senior lawyers for the Chairman of the Joint Chiefs of Staff, the Commander of US Central Command, and the Commander, International Security Assistance Force / United States Forces – Afghanistan" (*Declaration of Megan M. Weis* (December 19, 2014), *ACLU v. DoD* 2017, 04. Civ 4161 (AKH), 4) before being reviewed by Panetta himself. Panetta was revealed to have based his decisions on recommendations given by the generals John R. Allen, James N. Mattis, and Martin E. Dempsey (*Declaration of Megan M. Weis* (December 19, 2014), *ACLU v. DoD* 2017, 04. Civ 4161 (AKH), 4f.). Hellerstein's ruling that the US government had not satisfied its burden was obviously right, since the certification was issued only in relation to "representative sample[s]" (*ACLU v. DoD* 2017, 04. Civ 4161 (AKH), 4); Panetta apparently never saw the full scope of images.

In 2015, Secretary of Defense Ashton Carter issued the third certification in relation to the Abu Ghraib images and other abuse photographs, an action which was then subject to Hellerstein's opinion of 2017. The review processes which took place under both Carter and Panetta are revealing of the DoD's understanding of photography. As was the case during the previous certification process, the way the Department reviewed these photographs in 2015 expresses their conviction that a small group of images can represent and illustrate the information depicted in a large number of other photographs, and shows how they discursively established a type of visual equivalence between torture images by means of "[c]ultural techniques of categorization" (Young 2017, 52). Hellerstein's reconstruction of the review reveals the multiple levels of this process and, furthermore, illustrates quite clearly why Carter's certification also did not meet the burden of individual review:

> [An unnamed] attorney sorted the photographs into categories according to what they depicted, and then sorted them again based on the perceived likelihood of harm from publication. The attorney performed this sorting 'on behalf of the Secretary.' *Id*. According to the Government, '[t]he purpose of this sorting was to ensure that a true representative sample that contained the full spectrum of what the full group of

photographs depicted would be created for the Secretary's review.' ... The second review [by commissioned officers], like the first, was of each photograph, and the photographs were again sorted based on the likelihood of harm from production. The purpose of the second review was to 'assess whether the initial sorting of the photographs would ensure a true representative sample.' ... A third-level review was then conducted by four new attorneys ... They reviewed the 'combined work product' of the first two reviews, but it is unclear whether their review was *de novo* or in any way built on or deferred to the first two reviews ... This process led to a recommendation to Secretary Carter: 198 photographs should be released, and the rest, an unspecified number, should be kept secret. (*ACLU v. DoD* 2017, 04. Civ 4161 (AKH), 12f.)

Importantly, despite this clearly delineated review process, the US government denied the court more specific knowledge on the selection criteria and samples: "A 'representative sample' of the remaining photographs was then created. The Government does not disclose the size of the sample, whether the sample was broken down by category, the criteria used to create the sample, or why the third-level reviewers concluded that the photographs should not be released" (*ACLU v. DoD* 2017, 04. Civ 4161 (AKH), 13).

Here, the framework of the legal document and the court's decision encourages, and contributes to, the executive branch conducting itself in a more transparent manner by requesting a detailed description of the review process. However, Hellerstein's remarks indicate the areas of knowledge that remain obscured from both the judicial branch and the general public. Furthermore, the Second Circuit Court of Appeals reversed Hellerstein's 2017 opinion just one year later (*ACLU v. DoD* 2018, Docket No. 17-779). Thus, in the course of this particular lawsuit, the DoD was able to guarantee its antiepistemic agenda to a certain degree. By refusing to disclose more detailed and specific knowledge that could potentially help identify what kind of photographs remain withheld, the DoD continued to hinder the public's understanding of what was, and still is, really happening to the detainees and POWs.

The ACLU's Counter-Archival Practices

The ACLU's archival practices have sought to subvert the antiepistemic efforts embodied in the DoD's strategy of covering up knowledge or making it incomprehensible to the public. In this subsection, I will pay special attention to the epistemic tools which the ACLU has employed in the course of the here reconstructed lawsuit. The difficulty of understanding what the US government is actually hiding led the ACLU to investigate the places where the government had obscured information about torture. In 2015, the organization published an Excel spreadsheet entitled *TorturePhotos* [fig. 15], enumerating and describing censored torture photographs (ACLU 2022b). In this spreadsheet, published prior to Carter's certification of the photographs on November 7, 2015, ACLU employees summarized their analysis of the documents collected in their *Torture Database* which, in spite of significant redactions, disclose information on the actual existence of forensic and medical photographs.

The ACLU divided it into columns under the following headers: Title; Document Description; Description of Photo(s); Document Date; Location of Photo(s); Autopsy photo; Mugshot; Photo of injury or alleged injury; Photo of environment (cell, interrogation room, crime scene); and Notes (ACLU 2022b). The spreadsheet lists the titles of exactly 130 items, including memos, emails, Criminal Investigation Command (CID) reports, and other types of documents hyperlinked to the PDF files from their *Torture Database* (ACLU 2022a). It also reveals that the photographs were taken in various US facilities in Iraq and Afghanistan. Four of the documents listed in the spreadsheet are directly related to Guantánamo, although not to a specific camp: "DOD Hospital Patient Record re: Incident at Guantánamo Hospital, October 7, 2004," "FBI Memo re: Response to Canvass Email Concerning Treatment of Detainees at Guantánamo Bay," "FBI Memo re: Reports on Fingerprint Processing of Military Detainees in Afghanistan and Guantánamo," and "Statements of Guantánamo Hospital Personnel and Military Police re: Oct. 7, 2004 Incident at Guantánamo Hospital" (US Department of Administration 2004a; FBI 2004a; FBI 2004b; DoD 2004). Two further documents relate to events occurring at Camp Delta in 2002 and 2004: "Interview of Guantánamo Bay Detainee re: Detainee's Treatment While at Guantánamo Bay" by the Criminal Investigative Task Force, and "CID Report: 0260-2004-CID023-67287" (Criminal Investigative Task Force 2002; US Department of the Army 2004).

Here, I will analyze two aspects of the spreadsheet in more detail to illustrate how an Excel spreadsheet came to be employed as an epistemic tool, and how it can be understood as a counter-archive in its own right. On the one hand, it is important to look at lists like this in terms of their cultural, economic, and political facets, and to reflect on their various links to a particular episteme. On the other hand, we should compare and contrast Excel spreadsheets with other forms of lists. From its inception to the mid-90s, Microsoft Multiplan, the precursor to Excel, was developed as a calculation tool which already contained a line-column system. Whereas perhaps the most remarkable visual aspect of the contemporary Excel spreadsheet is the grid formed by the thin lines separating the columns and rows, an element which allows the user to move through the file both vertically and horizontally, lists are typically characterized by the movement of the reader's eyes on a vertical axis. The history and contemporary uses of Excel spreadsheets as listing and calculation tools requires us thus to reflect upon the ACLU's *TorturePhotos.xlsx* file as an

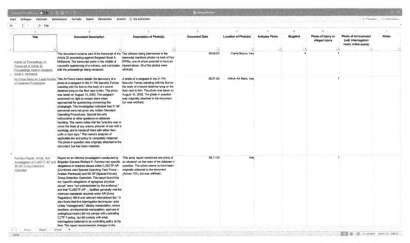

[Fig. 15] A screenshot showing the first entries of the Excel spreadsheet produced and published by ACLU employees. The file entitled *TorturePhotos.xlsx* (ACLU 2022b) figures as a meticulous archive of what the ACLU was able to learn about the redacted torture photographs (© American Civil Liberties Union, Inc. 2006).

administrative, political, and economic media object. Furthermore, we should also understand such spreadsheets to be "scientific instruments" and "visual technologies" (Cubitt 2014, 6).

In his book, *List Cultures: Knowledge and Poetics from Mesopotamia to Buzzfeed* (2017), Liam Cole Young poses a set of questions which are particularly relevant to the ACLU's Excel spreadsheet and are also closely related to my own: How spreadsheets function as a type of storage or an inventory; how they structure and visualize knowledge; and, how they create new ways of making concealed knowledge epistemically accessible:

> By collecting and materializing information, do lists create fields of knowledge? How do they structure the way data and knowledge circulate? What are the ethics of listing, a technique that has been complicit in the administration of human populations and in the 'disenchantment' of the modern world? Does list-making offer opportunities for challenging dominant systems of classification or ways of knowing? (Young 2017, 15)

Significantly, rather than primarily challenging the "dominant systems of classification or ways of knowing" (Young 2017, 15), *TorturePhotos.xlsx* challenges a system of imposed "not-knowing," or a system in which only a few possess knowledge. This is the dominant system of knowing in relation to the torture that has been perpetrated in the course of the US GWoT. However, documents like the ACLU's Excel spreadsheet have the "ability to interrupt the same systems of knowledge production and circulation that they seem, on the surface, only to enforce" (Young 2017, 15). The file's ambiguity lies thus in the fact that it interrupts how the DoD has made published knowledge incomprehensible to the public while, at the same time, it appears to reproduce a system of administrative, political, and economic (not)knowing.

Young writes that lists are "constitutive of epistemology" because they "combin[e] and stabiliz[e] data so that it can be mobilized as knowledge" (Young 2017, 47). Hence, it is not only that lists, as administrative media, solve daily "problems of storing and sharing information": they also influence how we think and act (Young 2017, 46). When I first discovered the *TorturePhotos. xlsx* on the Internet, I could not ignore the feeling that the format of the ACLU file mirrors, or echoes, the way in which the state "sees" these photographs and documents. The Excel spreadsheet replicates, to a certain extent, the DoD's administrative, bureaucratic, and economic processes; it also inscribes itself – or is entangled – in the pre-existing strategies with which the DoD treats the bodies of the detainees.

For instance, we can counterpose the techniques deployed by military personnel at the Guantánamo detention camp during the so-called "in-processing" procedure with the ways in which the ACLU has created a counter-archive – one which includes information on photographs taken at the camp, and on images produced at other black sites and prisons abroad. As I argued above, during the "in-processing" procedure, military personnel at Guantánamo make the bodies of the detained men epistemically available to the military and security apparatus by transforming them into visual archives intended to disclose something about the insides and the minds of the detainees. The ACLU's Excel spreadsheet also seeks to disclose something about an otherwise inaccessible inside – the inside of the military and security apparatus, its censorship procedures, and its abuse of the detained people. Despite the differences in the objects, subjects, formats, and results of the Guantánamo "in-processing" procedure and the ACLU's research, both can be framed by the notion of an economic inventory, or by the practice of taking stock. On the one hand, by documenting the detainees' bodies during the arrival procedure, military personnel have produced both an inventory and the visual materials that are the object of this inventory. On the other hand, the ACLU has created its inventory on the basis of information that has already been produced and disclosed, with the focus on the images which the public cannot access.

Of course, there is a significant difference between what or whom military personnel are inventorying when they produce a series of photographs during the "in-processing" procedure and what the ACLU's Excel spreadsheet is inventorying. Whereas the former focuses on the production of a generalized image of the "Guantánamo detainee," the latter seeks to list acts of abuse, of which the photographs in question function as proof. The latter thus makes an inventory of the misconduct of military or intelligence personnel and other actors involved in the interrogation and torture of the detained subjects. Nevertheless, in both inventories, the "goods" are the photographs of detainees – whether accessible or not – and both rely, to a certain degree, on the cultural techniques of listing (in tabular form). To reiterate, the inventory created on the detainees' arrival at the Guantánamo detention camp consists of the following: frontal photographs or mugshots; five photographs for the FBI's image-recognition software; photographs of scars and tattoos; fingerprints; and X-rays. By contrast, the rows in the *TorturePhotos* Excel spreadsheet are dedicated to incidents of potential maltreatment, protocoled in writing and documented by photographic cameras, with two columns containing descriptions of the documents and the censored photographs. For example, in the entry pertaining to the description of a 2002 interview given by a detainee held at Camp Delta to the Criminal Investigative Task Force, the spreadsheet cites the passage where "[t]he detainee alleged that he was physically abused by an interrogator and that the interrogator 'forcibly took his photograph'" (ACLU 2022b, Row 48, Column B; Criminal Investigative Task Force 2002). In the description of the associated photographs, the spreadsheet lists all of them as being withheld. Significantly, the ACLU spreadsheet simplifies the complexity of the documents it includes in its list, focusing mainly on the knowledge disclosed about the photographs and photographic practices.

If we read the original transcript of this interview, however, we acquire a more complete picture of the circumstances to which this detainee – whose name and ISN have been redacted by a black marker pen[9] – was subjected. He stated that not only was he forcibly photographed, but also that his interrogation by a Special Agent of the US Army was "recorded" (Criminal Investigative Task Force 2002, 1). The form of abuse he underwent is also described in more detail in the original document:

> The ████████ said the United States would put ████████ on trial and it would be better to go back home. ████████ ████████ continued to refuse to answer their questions. ████████ became angry and told him to think about it, when they were leaving the room, one of ████████ turned the Air Conditioner down as low as it would go and left him in the room for approximately 7-8 [*sic*] without food or water. According to

9   In many cases, the redactions are undertaken manually by overwriting the passages of text with a black marker pen. Hence, the files must be printed out, redacted, photocopied, scanned, and uploaded. However, PDF files can also be redacted electronically by using, for example, Adobe Acrobat X Pro. In 2011, the US National Security Agency published a document entitled "Redaction of PDF Files Using Adobe Acrobat Professional X" that teaches personnel how to redact information visually from the surface of the text, and also how to redact it in the metadata of the file, meaning the document does not have to be copied and then scanned (US National Security Agency 2022). / I would like to thank Abram Stern for sending me this document in the course of our conversations at the Visible Evidence XX conference.

██████████ the room became so cold that he was shaking and his mus-
cles hurt. ████████████ stated they did not physically abuse him while in the
interrogation room. (Criminal Investigative Task Force 2002, 2)

Importantly, some of the entries in the spreadsheet specify the form of
maltreatment, whereas others focus mainly on how the referenced documents describe photographs or photographic practices. The spreadsheet
thus appears to function as a register which indexes proof of torture and its
traces on the detainees' bodies, rather than specifying the torture techniques
themselves.

As James C. Scott writes in *Seeing Like a State: How Certain Schemes to Improve
the Human Condition Have Failed*, analyzing the relationship between the state
and scientific forestry as a field of knowledge, "[c]ertain forms of knowledge
and control require a narrowing of vision" (Scott 1998, 11). Scott refers to this
practice of narrowing and focusing on "certain limited aspects of an otherwise far more complex and unwieldy reality" as "tunnel vision," which "makes
the phenomenon at the center of the field of vision more legible and hence
more susceptible to careful measurement and calculation" (Scott 1998, 11).
In the case of the documents listed in the *TorturePhotos.xlsx*, however, the
US government might actually be encouraging the opposite: by releasing a
large number of declassified but redacted documents, the government has
created a complex and opaque information landscape; one which outwardly
complies with – but, in practice, operates against – the "'right to know' doctrine" (Banchik 2018, 1168) introduced by the passing of the FOIA in 1966. The
fact that US government documents are distributed and published by different
bodies and appear in different places and formats makes it even more difficult
to grasp what they are actually about and how they relate to each other, as
well as the specific events and subjects to which they refer. In turn, the ACLU's
Excel spreadsheet appears to be a response to these official techniques of
opacity. The organization's "tunnel vision" – in its technique of collecting and
listing, and also in the layout of the spreadsheet itself – enables it to counteract the state's strategies of making knowledge unreadable and ungraspable.
Thus, the ACLU's "schematic knowledge" allows it to exercise "control" over
an area of knowledge that was formerly monopolized by the US government
(Scott 1998, 11). However, by narrowing down the complexity of the reality to
which it refers, the Excel spreadsheet also reduces the narratives contained in
the original documents.

Of course, the cultural technique of creating lists is not solely a counter-
archival practice. Significantly, daily operations at the Guantánamo detention
camp are framed by an enormous number of (check)lists. In the annex to the
Camp Delta SOPs, I counted over 45 pages containing lists and tables used to
organize the daily tasks performed by military personnel, and also to track
and record the activities of the detainees (JTF-Guantánamo 2003). Echoing the

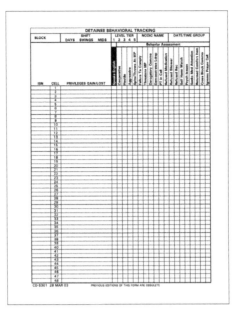

[Fig. 16] Page 174 of the *Camp Delta SOPs* shows a document used by Guantánamo personnel to track the behavior of the detainees. By simply ticking boxes, the guards can document whether a detainee was perceived to be "cooperative," "hostile," or "aggressive" (Source: JTF-Guantánamo 2003, 174). The appearance of US Department of Defense (DoD) visual information does not imply or constitute DoD endorsement.

close relationship between the ISNs at Guantánamo and the concentration camp tattoos from World War II, this practice of creating lists in relation to the detainees could be contextualized in the cultural and administrative techniques of the 20th century, and, more specifically, in those developed by the Nazi regime. The lists created by the JTF-Guantánamo are not so very different from those drawn up by Nazi administrators which were "built into census taking and statistical methods that established subject positions – making up people – that could be observed, calculated, and transported" (Young 2017, 86). For example, the *Camp Delta SOPs* include a list for "Detainee Behavioral Tracking" [fig. 16], and a table in which military personnel can archive the "detainee discipline history for ISN," to name at least two (JTF-Guantánamo 2003, 174 and 179).

The aim of Guantánamo's documentation practices appears to be as much about making up a "generalized body" by means of biological determinism – an argument I put forward previously – as it is about "making up" (Young 2017, 85) the "Guantánamo detainee" through the behavioral tracking practices which appear in the form of (check)lists and tables like the ones mentioned above. As Götz Aly and Karl Heinz Roth write in *The Nazi Census: Identification and Control in the Third Reich*, people under the Nazi regime "were reduced to an entry in a *registration*," where the regime's "bureaucratic abstraction de-humanized individuals and transported them to a new reality – namely, death" (as cited in Young 2017, 85; Aly and Roth 2004, 1). The lists used by military personnel at Guantánamo also abstract the complexity of the lives of the detainees, reducing them, for example, to lists of which activities they refused to undertake, and which kinds of punishment they were forced to endure (JTF-Guantánamo 2003, 179 and 205). In both these cases, the reduction of the narrative quality of the detainees' lives to mere lists and ticked boxes works against the perception of "a life that will have been lived" (Butler 2009, 15).

Furthermore, the fact that one of the most famous lists published from Guantánamo is a register strongly supports the thesis that such listing practices correspond to the administrative techniques of the Nazi regime. In 2006, the Associated Press (AP) made a FOIA request for the release of "basic information about the individuals housed in the detention facility at Guantánamo Bay" (*AP v. DoD* 2006, 06 Civ. 1939 (JSR)), with the result that the DoD was ordered to release the names of, and other biographical information related to, the detainees. This led, on April 20, 2006, to the publishing of the "List of Detainees Who Went Through complete CSRT [Combatant Status Review Tribunal] Process" comprising of the ISNs, names, and citizenships of the 558 detainees whose cases had been reviewed by the Combatant Status Review Tribunal (DoD 2006b). Significantly, the list was presented in a numeric order according to the ISNs, indicating the administrative significance of these numbers. One month later, on May 15, 2006, the DoD published an even longer list which included the names of all the men detained at the camp between January 2002 and the date of publication, not just those whose status had been reviewed (DoD 2006c).[10] In the context of the ACLU's FOIA request, the AP not only requested such information as the names, citizenships, birthplaces, and birth dates of the detainees, but also "photographs identifying past and present detainees, as well as information as to each detainee's weight and height" (*AP v. DoD* 2006, 06 Civ. 1939 (JSR)). This, as I have demonstrated pre-viously, is also the information gathered by military personnel during the "in-processing" procedure following the detainees' arrival at the detention camp.

Although Judge Jed D. Rakoff initially ruled in favor of the AP, ordering the DoD to release the names of the detainees, in an opinion and order dated November 28, 2006, the judge granted the Department the right to continue to withhold the photographs. Paul Rester, then Director of the Joint Intelligence Group for the JTF-Guantánamo, argued that, in contrast to the list alone, the list combined with photographs would lead to the individual identification of the detained men: "[the] release of the photographs coupled with the names (which may be common names) would specifically identify each detainee in

10   This list was ordered alphabetically rather than numerically and, in contrast to the first list, also contained the detainees' places and dates of birth.

a way that a release of *576 names and other biographical information does not" (*AP v. DoD* 2006, 06 Civ. 1939 (JSR)). Rakoff granted the DoD's motion to continue to withhold the photographs because the "disclosure … would both increase the risk of retaliation against the detainees and their families and exacerbate the detainees' fears of reprisals" (*AP v. DoD* 2006, 06 Civ. 1939 (JSR)), which, in turn, would lead to a decrease in the detainees' willingness to cooperate. The AP's FOIA request also reveals another crucial insight into what, according to the US government, a successful identification of the detainees would look like: the combination of biographical and photographic information.

To conclude, the wide range of lists created by the DoD in relation to the detainees at Guantánamo reveals the entire operation to be a huge and violent bureaucratic machine. In his book, Young writes that "lists teach us about the systems of order that surround and enframe us because they simultaneously conceal and reveal, enforce and subvert the contours of such systems" (Young 2017, 15). The Guantánamo lists also teach us about the powers of governmentality that are at work in this detention facility, and about how the DoD redefines the lives of the detainees as objects by subjecting them to a wide range of indexical, managerial, and cultural techniques. As Judith Butler has observed, in Guantánamo, sovereignty and governmentality become so closely intertwined that they are nearly indistinguishable – a fact that might have its most pronounced expression in the form of the various lists used by the military personnel stationed there (Butler 2004, 95). In the detention camp, governmentality revitalizes sovereignty which, according to Butler, represents a rupture in the modern tradition of governance. Reiterating a thought expressed in the introduction to this book, it is "the governmental bureaucrat" (Butler 2004, 59), or, more precisely, the military bureaucrat, who holds the power over life and death, but this bureaucrat also has the power to define life and death anew. If the definition and understanding of life and death in a closed-circuit system like the Guantánamo detention camp is formulated by such bureaucratic agents and their (check)lists, then it has particularly grave implications for the understanding of the lives of the detained men by the camp's personnel. If the detainee is regarded as an object to be managed by agents of governmentality, then to follow this particular logic, life and death are translated into an economic and managerial framework. Consequently, the broad range of cultural techniques present in the detention camp, such as listing, categorizing, and photographing, transform the detainees' lives into metaphorical "goods" in Guantánamo's imaginary inventory.

In light of these observations, and the still-open question of what it is that we can learn from the ACLU's Excel spreadsheet, one answer could be that this spreadsheet teaches us as much about the ambiguous position of lists in the Guantánamo discourse as it does about the obscured or withheld photographs. The spreadsheet not only informs us about the nature and number of censored photographs, but – to follow Young's argument – also about the entire system of documentation, redaction, and the US government's legal history of obstructing access to knowledge. Furthermore, it shows us that we can never know everything: there are more torture images than we can see, and most of the photographs will probably never be published by the DoD. Yet even if these images remain out of view, the ACLU's spreadsheet functions as a witness to a past which is still acting upon the present, "marking absence or loss" (Young 2017, 9) of the documents and the photographs depicting lives that have been tortured and maltreated. Significantly, in addition to referring to the past and present, the spreadsheet is a prognostic tool: it may be simultaneously "retroactive, administrative, or prescriptive" (Young 2017, 16). Thus, in sum, the spreadsheet teaches us as much about administrative and legal procedures of the US government as it does about the torture carried out in the course of the US GWoT – which may still be perpetrated now and in the future. And it does this, by potentially appropriating certain ways in which the DoD collects and visualizes administrative, political, and economic knowledge.

Summary and Conclusion

As I set out to demonstrate at the beginning of this chapter, the production and distribution of documents are a central aspect of the activities undertaken by the US military. Recordkeeping and standardization via a wide-range of documents represent a significant part of the military's daily practices; the documents themselves are simultaneously expressions or results, and an intrinsic part, of military bureaucracy. As Griffiths argues in his defense of the military bureaucrat, bureaucracy is the place where expertise lives and thrives within the military apparatus (Griffiths 2018). Importantly, the act of documenting within the military does not only produce a record of something that has happened in the near or distant past; it also provides templates for the future. As I have demonstrated, in this context, the design of and compliance with SOPs, as managerial and governmental tools, are recognized in military discourses as being vital to the functioning of the military as an institution. As a tool of standardization, these SOPs provide military personnel with templates for how they should act and what they should do in a specific situation, or which exact steps they should take when charged with a task. I have also argued that the Guantánamo detention camp should be understood as a place which follows the US military's rules of documentation, as well as being framed by SOPs which, among other things, set out the rules of recordkeeping pertaining to the detainees. I also introduced the idea that documents from Guantánamo play an important role in what I have termed – in reference to

Peter Galison's work (2004) – the US government's antiepistemic agenda, since the information contained in such documents is subject to both classification processes and/or is being completely withheld from the public. The scattered locations, and the redaction of certain parts of documents, coupled with the complete removal of photographs, significantly hinder the ways in which the public can access and understand the situation of the detainees in the Guantánamo detention camp. The difficulty of grasping what particular documents from Guantánamo are telling us and the vast number of documents which remain hidden from the public raise methodological issues, or rather, questions with regard to how we can access such a fragmented archive, as well as how we can investigate or speculate about objects that remain obscured or inaccessible.

Building on this examination of documentation and recordkeeping practices, I went on to investigate the information contained in various documents to reveal the surveillance infrastructure put in place for recording detainee interrogations and discussed three indexical practices deployed during the "in-processing" of newly arrived detainees at the detention camp: photography, fingerprinting, and X-raying. I argued that these practices are designed to enable the US military "*to grasp*" (Glissant 1997, 191) the detainee via his body; or, more precisely, via the representations of his body, making it epistemically available in the form of a visual archive. Despite the DoD withholding the objects produced during this process, I was able to outline and infer what we could potentially expect to see in some parts of the Guantánamo archive by analyzing the *Camp Delta SOPs* (JTF-Guantánamo 2003). I further elaborated on how these photographic practices, along with other material practices conducted during the "in-processing" procedure at the Guantánamo detention camp, serve to generalize and anonymize the bodies of the detainees. By connecting the practice of issuing detainees with ISNs and stripping them of their names to the practice of tattooing numbers onto the skin of people incarcerated in the Nazi concentration camp of World War II, I sought to criticize this violent practice by indicating its historical legacy.

In the final part, I analyzed how the ACLU recognized the obfuscation and refusal of knowledge on photographic practices and objects as an antiepistemology, and how they sought to oppose it. As I have shown, their efforts "to learn everything ... [they] could about what the government is hiding" (Relman 2015) were framed by a lawsuit which extended over more than a decade and the terms of three different presidencies. I wanted to discover what it looks like when an independent body seeks to transform an antiepistemology created by a government which denies documents or publishes them only in a redacted form, into an epistemology for the public, and, furthermore, to analyze the epistemic and visual tools which such a body might use. To do so, I focused on the unfolding of the lawsuit, and on how legal documents such as the *Order and Opinion* written by Judge Hellerstein in relation to *ACLU v. DoD* have contributed, in rather significant ways, to the transparency of the executive branch. Nevertheless, in spite of the pieces of information Hellerstein rendered visible in his *Opinion and Order* of 2017, such as the individual steps of the PNSDA certification process, and the flexibility and transformation of the DoD's counter-arguments to the ruling in which he ordered the detainee photographs to be published, the US government managed, to a degree, to follow its antiepistemic agenda. It has neither disclosed the criteria used to certify the photographs, nor revealed which types of images were placed in the categories it certified as protected documents.

As a response to the refusal of knowledge about which kind of photographs are still being withheld, the ACLU's *TorturePhotos.xlsx*, containing a list and descriptions of the redacted photographs, reveals what the organization has learned about the obscured archive (ACLU 2022b). Despite the prominence enjoyed by the cultural techniques of listing and categorization within the detention camp, by appropriating the way in which the state sees and applying a kind of "tunnel vision" (Scott 1998, 11) to documents, the ACLU has succeeded in rendering visible the torture which has already occurred, and the torture photographs of detainees that have already been taken, but which remain withheld.

At the same time, this Excel spreadsheet sheds light on an uncertain future – a future in which the past lives on and might one day become public knowledge.

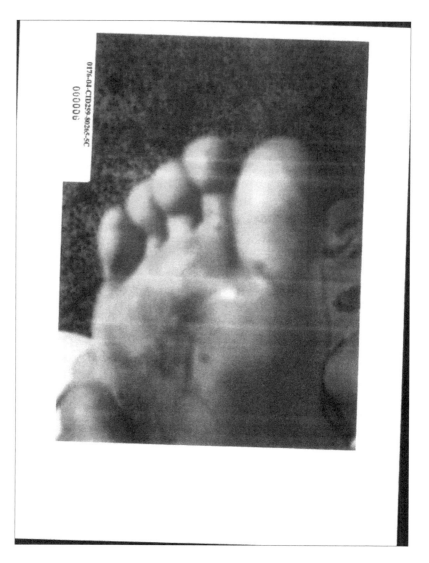

[Fig. 17] A torture photograph (DoD 2016, 71) showing Ibrahim Khalid Samir al-Ani's burnt foot which was published in 2016 by the DoD in a PDF file along with other 197 images (© American Civil Liberties Union, Inc. 2006). In al-Ani's letter we read: "[The American] put his foot on my back and started screaming and cursing me in English, which I do understand. And after 15 minutes, I felt that one side of my belly and thigh started to burn due to the heated air that was coming out of the car. And the back of my feet started to burn. I asked the responsible to be careful but he did not care" (al-Ani 2004, 2).

Honorable Sir,

I am asking your honor, to take some time and read my letter. I would like to inform you that my blind trust in your laws and your fair justice has encouraged me to write to you and ask you kindly to hear my case. Additionally, your kind treatment to me and my fellow prisoners detained in this camp, where your conducting and performance abide by the American and international laws, has urged me today to write to you and ask you to hear my case based on my lawful rights and my familial situation as well as my health conditions. Please receive my sincere thanks.

1- March 10/2004, I was informed officially that based on all the information provided I am considered as a prisoner of war (POW) according to the international convention of Geneva dated on 12 August 1949. I thoroughly agree and respect you decision, but I would like to clarify the following matters:

A- I worked with the secret services as an (officer). As you might know that the former Iraqi secret services is a civil institute. And has no relationship whatsoever with the military work. Its law is totally civilian. Its ranks and functional posts are civilian and have no relationship with the military law.

B- the ranks varies between a (clerk, assistant superintendent, executive administrator and director manger) while the functional post varies between an (officer, division manager, province manager and general manager). And all these positions are congruent with civilian ranks in other countries.

C- institute or college graduates are entitled to officer titles by definition while a high school graduate or less than that is called an employee. In the secret services, more than 6000 employees are called officers while 1500 are being considered as directors based on their years of service. Moreover, more than 250 others are being division managers. So, since I served more than 24 years in that job I was a division manager.

D- I have a college degree (university of law and politics). I have never attended any military school or institute. And I was never granted any military rank. Sometimes, even if one is a graduate of military school, police academy or school of national security, once he or she joins the secret services his ranks are not applicable anymore, and he or she abide by the civilian codes and laws.

According to what I have stated above, I was not a soldier, and I was never granted a military rank. Nor have I ever attended a military school. The duties of secret services are limited to the usual daily job description. In case of emergency, the secret services main job is to maintain order in the country, and has no deal with military operations in defending, attacking or networking with the different bodies of the military. I would like to state the fact that I have never worked or served in any military post or any job that might have military traits. I was never asked or executed any military order. And my duty during the last war was to defend the organization where I used to work as division manager at the secret services. I was captured in my house after the end of the war 2003/7/2. Thus I believe, according to the definition of prisoner of war in article 4 (A&B), that the nature of my job does not fall under the conditions stated in the convention. Plus, I think if I had been able to defend my case in front of you, your honor,

[Fig. 18] Page one of Ibrahim Khalid Samir al-Ani's letter (al-Ani 2004, 1) describing the torture he experienced at the hands of US forces in Iraq, which caused the burns visible in fig. 17 (© American Civil Liberties Union, Inc. 2006).

4

Concealing Visibility: A PDF File with 198 Torture Photographs

At the beginning of 2016, a PDF file containing precisely 198 images depicting close-ups of body parts, redacted mugshots, and crime scenes was published on the Pentagon's "Reading Room" website (US Department of Defense (DoD) 2022a). As Vincent Iacopino from the Physicians for Human Rights (PHR) organization observed, "[t]hese photos fail to show a single act of abuse which the government's own records describe as having taken place" (as cited in PHR 2016). The release of the photographs, which were taken at the Abu Ghraib prison, Mosul Airfield, Baghdad Airport, Camp Bucca, Camp Cooper, Bagram, and other, unspecified locations, was authorized by Ashton Carter who, as the US Secretary of Defense in 2015, reviewed and certified approximately 2,000 photographs of people detained by the US forces after 9/11 (*American Civil Liberties Union (ACLU) v. DoD* 2017, 04. Civ 4161 (AKH), 1f.). This certification process, and the *ACLU v. DoD* lawsuit which prompted it, led the US government to publish this PDF file in 2016, a disclosure which, according to the ACLU, should have provided proof of the maltreatment of prisoners in detention facilities and military prisons abroad. The fact that the released photographs and their content did not even come close to complying with Judge Alvin K. Hellerstein's order to produce the "cache of photographs ... which depict individuals apprehended and detained abroad after September 11, 2001" (*ACLU v. DoD* 2017, 04. Civ 4161 (AKH), 1) suggests that what Iacopino identifies as a failure and "obstruction of justice" (as cited in PHR 2016) might have been seen as the direct opposite by the DoD: namely, as a spectacular success in their strategy of obscuring knowledge about torture.

In the previous chapter, I focused on how, during the aforementioned lawsuit, the DoD sought to obfuscate knowledge about the existence of certain photographs by withholding them from the public, while the ACLU successfully rendered this knowledge visible in a Microsoft Excel spreadsheet. In this chapter, I am interested in how, even as the DoD published 198 images from a much larger set of photographs, it simultaneously sought to make them unreadable to the public. More specifically, when the ACLU submitted its FOIA request and sued the DoD for withholding images that provided proof of torture, the Department responded by publishing these 198 photographs without context, thus concealing the violence of "clean torture" (Hilbrand 2015; Rejali 2007) and rendering the experiences of torture incomprehensible to the general public. By doing so, they also hid the identities of the perpetrators, and protected them from criminal or disciplinary proceedings.

To understand the specific ways in which this PDF file conceals information, rendering it invisible via its visibility, I will outline the broader political and legal framework around discourses on torture and the impunity of perpetrators in the aftermath of 9/11. I will discuss not only how the techniques of clean torture deployed by US troops and CIA agents are intended to render such acts of torture invisible, but also the way in which the legal discourses on the definition of torture produced by the DoD further aggravated the invisibility of the perspectives of torture victims. I will then reconstruct some of the ways in which the Bush and Obama administrations ensured that no person employed in or professionally connected to the DoD would be held accountable or punished by US courts for having committed or facilitated criminal acts of torture. I will also explore how the so-called broader "justification narrative" (Forst 2013; my translation) of torture post-9/11 has significantly contributed to the ongoing impunity of the perpetrators, and look at how this narrative is composed of a broad web of storytelling. I will pay special attention to a filmic actualization[1] of this narrative by analyzing the opening sequence of Kathryn Bigelow's film, *Zero Dark Thirty* (2012), and how it supports the idea that, under certain circumstances, torture is a justifiable means to an end.

I will further analyze how the covert nature of clean torture practices is mirrored by the purported visibility produced by the PDF file – a visibility that actually hides and blurs the ways in which the published photographs are connected to these practices, the pain and suffering endured by the victims, and the identities of those who tortured them. By discussing how the DoD stripped these photographs of context, and thereby rendered them incomprehensible as evidence of torture, I demonstrate that the PDF file produces a form of contorted visibility which deploys visual representation to conceal

---

1   The term "actualization" is a one-to-one translation of the German "Aktualisierung" used by Jochen Schuff and Martin Seel in their introduction to the edited collection *Erzählungen und Gegenerzählungen: Terror und Krieg im Kino des 21. Jahrhunderts* (Eng. *Stories and Counter-Stories: Terror and War in 21st Century Cinema*) (Schuff and Seel 2016a, 3). I could have translated it as "updating," which is also used in German but has a different resonance.

what it is actually documenting. I will argue that the DoD's decision to publish the photographs in this format increases their polysemic nature, obscuring the specificity of individual experiences of torture and the identities of the victims and perpetrators. By releasing only visual fragments of indistinct body parts, the DoD continued to withhold evidence of torture even as it apparently made it visible – a violent operation in and of itself. It also reiterated the invisibility of the victims' perspective in the associated legal debate, and ensured that past, current, and future employees of the military and intelligence apparatus involved in the torture of Prisoners of War (POWs) and detainees would not face trial or punishment.

However, in contrast to the position taken initially by the ACLU and news media who claimed these photographs did not depict the consequences of torture, I will argue that it may indeed be possible to read traces of clean torture in these images and others like them, however minimal or insignificant these traces at first appear. This expands our understanding of post-9/11 torture practices, which until now has been dominated by the imagery of the torture photographs taken at Abu Ghraib. It will also render visible the processes by which torture has been concealed in this PDF file, processes which have perpetuated the violent legal framework within which it was published and which has, in turn, secured the impunity of the perpetrators. The PDF file carefully avoids the gruesome imagery associated with the torture photographs from the Abu Ghraib prison by chiefly revealing only minor injuries on indistinct body parts. However, coupling the legal and journalistic discourses around the camp with a greater understanding of clean torture techniques shows how torture can again become perceptible and phenomenologically present in these images. I also argue that the manner in which the DoD published these 198 photographs, stripping the depicted bodies of any social context and separating them from the situations in which they were injured, expresses and intensifies the processes of reification already present in the act of torture. Categorizing, archiving, and then publishing this set of photographs in a single PDF file redefines the subjects as "things" rather than lives, alienating them from the viewer.

In response to this reification, in the final subsection of this book, I will describe the implications of restoring the initial contexts of the photographs. There, I will emphasize the importance of reframing the images by acknowledging the stories told by the people whose abused bodies appear in them. Despite the initial difficulty of understanding what these images actually show, and of recognizing them as images of torture, we can reveal the traces of the torture and abuse of detainees and POWs that these photographs contain by undertaking investigative efforts of our own. Beyond reconstructing the "stories behind" the photographs, I will also, whenever possible, place these images in the context of stories told by the tortured persons themselves, and thus tell the stories of the photographs from a perspective which is usually proscribed by the DoD and deemed "impermissible to show" (Butler 2009, 73). Restoring these stories, and hence the perception of the lives of the people depicted in the photographs, recovers these "tellable lives" (Arendt 1998). That is, by considering these perspectives, rendering them visible, and emphasizing them, we can not only reveal the ways in which the broader justification narrative of torture is constructed and how it functions, we can also oppose the narrative structures that normalize it. Bringing these stories to light ruptures, if only a little, the broader frame of the justification narrative.

The Frame of Clean Torture

Post-9/11 Torture and the Impunity of Perpetrators

Before embarking upon a detailed analysis of what we actually see in the 198 photographs, and how the news media and human rights organizations responded to these images upon their release, I will first look at the broader legal and political framework within which the PDF file was published. Whereas the photographs analyzed in the first chapter and the videos of the virtual visits to the camps at Guantánamo discussed in the second chapter were released under the Bush administration, the lawsuit analyzed in the previous chapter stretched itself over the course of three presidencies, and it was under President Barack Obama that the DoD finally distributed the torture photographs in question. As we may recall, Obama promised to close the Guantánamo Bay detention camp, and raised the hopes of many human rights organizations and torture victims that his administration would hold torturers, politicians, contractors, and diverse other actors accountable for the violent treatment of people detained in the course of the US "Global War on Terror" (GWoT). What actually happened could not have been further from this promised outcome. Admittedly, the Obama administration publicly acknowledged that the US forces and CIA agents had committed what is legally deemed to be criminal acts of torture. However, rather than initiating trials of the perpetrators, lawyers, and politicians who "legalized" and systemized the torture of detainees and POWs around the world, the administration went to great lengths to ensure that none of these actors would ever face trial, nor suffer any repercussions or punishments.

In his book, *Torture and Impunity: The US Doctrine of Coercive Interrogation*, Alfred W. McCoy is right to point out that the "[i]mpunity [of perpetrators] begins at the site of torture" (McCoy 2012, 218). Here, McCoy refers to the way in which the US government designed torture techniques under the Bush presidency and the ways that intelligence and military personnel deployed them in the course of the US GWoT in a manner intended to leave the "most permanent scars on the psyche rather than the body" (McCoy 2012, 217). As McCoy observes, "these [torture] techniques are like disappearing ink, their visible trail rapidly fading" (McCoy 2012, 217). Scholars often refer to such techniques as "clean torture," since they do not leave any visible traces on the bodies of the victims and are thus presumed to be unrepresentable. In his introduction to *Torture and Democracy*, Darius Rejali provides us with the following brief description of this term: "There exist many painful physical techniques of interrogation or control that leave few marks. I call these *clean* techniques in contrast to *scarring* techniques of torture" (Rejali 2007, 4).[2] Rejali's definition makes it clear that, despite being largely traceless, the pain inflicted on the tortured person by clean torture techniques is not just psychological in nature; it can also be deeply and gravely painful in a physical sense (Rejali 2007, 4). Thus, clean torture might be (mostly) traceless, but it can still be as physical and brutal as other "*scarring* techniques of torture" (Rejali 2007, 4). Another peculiarity of these "cleaner" techniques is that they are not deployed separately; instead, they are often combined with other torture techniques, with each amplifying the pain caused by the other (Rejali 2007, 4).

Carola Hilbrand writes that clean torture does "not leave any visible traces in form of wounds or scars, but consist of practices of sensorial and mental disorientation that strive to break the detainees psychically" (Hilbrand 2015, 11; my translation). "As a phenomenon of absence, clean torture is not only characterized by tracelessness and invisibility, but also by speechlessness and silence" (Hilbrand 2015, 12; my translation), she adds. It is usually impossible to find traces such as open wounds, bruises, or amputation scars in victim photographs, or to recover traces from "attempts of its [clean torture's] verbal mediation" (Hilbrand 2015, 12; my translation). This is what Hilbrand describes as the failure of representation with regard to clean torture – that is, the inability to prove it by means of photography, other indexical practices, or oral testimonies – a view which, as I will show, is problematic for a number of reasons. The tracelessness of clean torture, the difficulty of showing its painful consequences, is supposed to make it difficult, if not impossible, to use forensic evidence commonly used in disciplinary or criminal investigations to prove such techniques were actually carried out. The deliberate design of torture techniques used by US forces to ensure the invisibility of the violence inflicted upon tortured persons has often led to situations where "[e]ven when such torture is [or was] discovered, this invisibility has also enabled its perpetrators and their protectors to escape prosecution" (McCoy 2012, 217f.). As Rejali observes, it is precisely the "stealthiness ... [that] makes these clean techniques desirable to torturers" (Rejali 2007, 5). Consequently, lawyers

2   Sebastian Köthe pointed me towards this extraordinary book, and also shared with me his reading and critique of Carola Hilbrand's observations on clean torture.

and journalists who seek to challenge the abuse and torture of detainees or POWs encounter difficulties in acquiring forensic or medical evidence, forcing them to find alternative ways to prove the brutality of these interrogation techniques – for instance, by referring to detainee testimonies or interviews.

"Democracies torture, but they torture differently, favoring cleaner techniques to avoid scandal and to boost their legitimacy. The history of modern democratic torture is part of the history of stealth torture," writes Rejali (2007, 405). In the context of the torture committed by US forces on foreign soil in the aftermath of 9/11, Rejali identifies a close relationship between democracy and the use of clean torture techniques during interrogations. He argues that dictatorships which torture prisoners do not feel the pressure to cover up the traces torture leaves; indeed, often the exact opposite is the case – the traces are intentionally made to be visible to others as a form of intimidation (Rejali 2007, 2). In contrast, according to Rejali, *"public monitoring of human rights"* (Rejali 2007, 8) in democracies forces these governments to develop and deploy a set of techniques that leave no traces on the bodies of their victims, so neither the perpetrators nor the government can be held accountable for this torture. Rejali explains this connection as follows:

> But *why* do clean torture and democracy appear to go hand in hand? … My explanation for this pattern generally is this: *Public monitoring leads institutions that favor painful coercion to use and combine clean torture techniques to evade detection, and, to the extent that public monitoring is not only greater in democracies, but that public monitoring of human rights is a core value in modern democracies, it is the case that where we find democracies torturing today we will also be more likely to find stealthy torture.* (Rejali 2007, 8)

In the case of the Guantánamo detention camp and the public debates about torture that began immediately after the attacks of 9/11, the fact that the US government was torturing the camp's detainees became public knowledge, at the latest, four months after the attacks, when the DoD published Shane T. McCoy's photographs of the first detainees arriving at the camp [fig. 1 and 3]. However, due to the role played by the US public in monitoring its government's actions, the institutional training and legal discussions within the DoD focused on how to inflict the maximum amount of pain on detainees without leaving visible traces on their bodies.

It is not just the invisibility of the effects of these clean torture techniques that underpins the ongoing impunity and lack of accountability of the perpetrators. The idea of impunity which, as Alfred W. McCoy writes, is integral to torture practices conducted post-9/11 (McCoy 2012, 218), was additionally grounded in a legal debate initiated by the Bush administration directly after 9/11. Faced with the restraints on torture put in place after World War II by the *Geneva Convention III* (August 12, 1949), and by the US ratification of the United Nations' (UN) *Convention Against Torture and Other Cruel, Inhuman or Degrading Treatment or Punishment* (UN General Assembly 1987) in 1994, the US was bound by international standards which banned and criminalized torture. After various countries signed the *Convention Against Torture* in 1987, each of them was required to ratify the text into their domestic law. As McCoy writes, the ratification process, which was initiated by the Reagan administration and finalized by Bill Clinton in 1994 injected a certain flexibility and lack of precision into the legal interpretation of torture (McCoy 2012, 230). The ratified text in *18 US Code §2340A* emphasizes that, in order for an act to be torture, the investigation must prove that it was the perpetrator's intent to torture and inflict severe physical and mental pain on another person: "'[t]orture' means an act committed by a person acting under the color of law specifically *intended to inflict severe physical or mental pain or suffering* (other than pain or suffering incidental to lawful sanctions) upon another person within his custody or physical control" (*18 US Code §§2340* (April 30, 1994); italics added).

One of the main tools the Bush administration used to exploit the vagueness of this legal language was a series of legal memoranda, of which one of the most important was written by Jay Bybee, Assistant Attorney General from 2001 to 2003, with the help of then-Attorney General John Yoo (Bybee 2002).[3] In their memorandum of August 1, 2002, Bybee and Yoo concluded that *§2340A*

> proscribes acts inflicting, and that are specifically intended to inflict, severe pain or suffering, whether mental or physical. Those acts must be of an extreme nature to rise to the level of torture within the meaning of Section 2340A and the Convention. We further conclude that certain acts may be cruel, inhuman, or degrading, but still not produce pain and suffering of the requisite intensity to fall within Section 2340A's proscription against torture. (Bybee 2002, 1)

Proposing a shocking interpretation of the definition of torture, and a reevaluation of the standards for interrogations, Bybee and Yoo focused on the interpretation of three phrases from the definition provided in the ratified law: "specifically intended," "severe pain or suffering," and "severe mental pain or suffering" (Bybee 2002, 3–7). Bybee's and Yoo's interpretation of the first term – "specifically intended" – aggravated the invisibility and legal insignificance of the perspective of torture victims, and emphasized the perspective of the perpetrator, shifting the focus from the experience of torture by the victim to the question of a person's intent in committing a violent act:

---

3   As Sebastian Köthe shows, Bybee's and Yoo's memo was intended to provide legal cover for the torture of one particular person, Abu Zubaydah, which was being carried out in CIA black sites (Köthe 2021, 42f.).

Thus, *even if the defendant knows that severe pain will result from his actions, if causing harm is not his objective, he lacks the requisite specific intent even though the defendant did not act in good faith.* Instead, a defendant is guilty of torture only if he acts with the express purpose of inflicting severe pain on a person within his custody or physical control. (Bybee 2002, 4; italics added)

Hence, according to this memorandum, if an interrogator were to argue that they had acted in "good faith" (Bybee 2002, 4) and claim that their primary aim was not to inflict severe pain on the other person, they could not be held accountable under §2340A.

Bybee's and Yoo's legal interpretation of the second term, "severe pain or suffering" (an interpretation which would later be taken up by the Bush administration when drafting a set of "legalized" torture techniques (Haynes II 2002, 2)), significantly restricted the spectrum of injury or harm from interrogation techniques which would qualify as evidence of torture. As such, severe pain or suffering came to be defined as a form of "damage that must rise to the level of death, organ failure, or permanent impairment of significant bodily function" (Bybee 2002, 1). In view of the broad set of torture techniques which the US government used to force detained people to disclose information in the course of its GWoT, techniques deliberately designed to leave no visible traces on the bodies of the victims, as well as to avoid causing death, organ failure, or permanent impairment, would fall outside this legal understanding of torture.

The descriptions of pain and suffering expressed by victims of torture, and of the consequences for their physical and psychological well-being, show quite drastically the perversity of the definition of torture codified in §2340A and its 2002 interpretation. The legal interpretation by Bybee and Yoo is not only a failure of the legal system to acknowledge the wide range of ways that individuals experience violence and pain in the context of imprisonment or interrogation, but also demonstrates "failings of spirit" (Das as cited in Rejali 2007, 31; Das 1997, 88). As Rejali writes, "[t]o know I 'have pain' is to invoke linguistic and social conventions that help us make sense of what words mean" (Rejali 2007, 31). Bybee's and Yoo's memorandum, and their interpretation of what counts as "severe pain or suffering" (Bybee 2002, 5f.), demonstrate that these "conventions [which] we count on to express ourselves breakdown, as they do in stealth torture" (Rejali 2007, 31). Beyond this, the experience of pain does not only seek expression in words. The subjects who suffered due to clean torture techniques encounter difficulties in describing their experiences because their testimonies fall outside of the legal frames, such as the ones constructed by Bybee and Yoo in their memorandum (Bybee 2002). Torture seeks a "home in the body" (Das as cited in Rejali 2007, 31; Das 1997, 88) which "[s]tealth torture denies" to the victims by "tangling … [them] and their communities in doubts, uncertainties, and illusions" (Rejali 2007, 31).

In their memorandum, Bybee and Yoo further enhance the uncertainties intrinsic to clean torture techniques when they narrow down the spectrum of potential experiences of pain and suffering to these three phenomena, all of which might render the victims speechless. Significantly, the interrogation techniques approved by Secretary of Defense Donald Rumsfeld on December 2, 2002, were chosen precisely on the grounds of their physical untraceability (Haynes II 2002). The original list consisted of the following: "[y]elling at a detainee," "deception," "use of stress position" and "falsified documents or reports," "interrogating the detainee in an environment other than the standard interrogation booth," "[d]eprivation of light and sensory stimuli," placing a hood "over his head during transportation and questioning," "use of 20-hour interrogations," "[r]emoval of clothing," "[f]orced grooming," "[u]sing detainees individual phobias (such as fear of dogs) to induce stress," "[u]se of isolation facility up to 30 days" (Phifer 2002, 1f.).

The third and final term specified by Bybee and Yoo in their memorandum – "severe mental pain or suffering" – was also defined on the basis of the perpetrators' intent and their perception of what they did:

> A defendant could negate a showing of specific intent to cause severe mental pain or suffering by showing that he has acted in good faith that his conduct would not amount to the acts prohibited by the statue. Thus, if a defendant has good faith belief that his actions will not result in prolonged mental harm, he lacks the mental state necessary for his actions to constitute torture. (Bybee 2002, 8)

Here, as with the interpretation of the first term, the perspective of the tortured person is rendered invisible within framework of the legal evaluation of whether an act amounted to torture. The whole emphasis is placed on the intent of the perpetrator who, in order to be charged with the crime of torture, must explicitly admit that the aim of their actions was to cause "prolonged mental harm" (Bybee 2002, 8).

As I have shown so far, the impunity of perpetrators was not only facilitated by the way that torture was designed, perfected, and employed, but also by the legal framework which offered protection to those who perpetrated the torture of detainees and POWs. Especially between 2001 and 2004, when the US was facing enemies which the Bush administration described as difficult to catch, hold, and force to disclose "life-saving intelligence," there seemed to be a broad political and social consensus in the US about the necessity of torture. Nevertheless, when the CBS program *60 Minutes II* broadcast the infamous torture photographs from the Abu Ghraib prison at the end of April 2004, triggering their widespread distribution and discussion in the news media, public opinion in the US dramatically shifted (Leung 2004). The images, and the subsequent public debate, created a climate of mistrust towards the self-proclaimed moral authority of the US in the MENA region, and "drained American credibility around the world" (Baker 2010). Due to the decisive role this particular image-event played in the US government's decision-making about the Iraq conflict, and in the public's perception of torture, it is crucial to highlight the importance of these images and how they reframed the torture discourse. As McCoy writes, when viewers were confronted with the torture committed at Abu Ghraib prison, with images showing sodomized prisoners, mock executions, and techniques of sensory deprivation, the apparent consensus around the necessity of torture "evaporated with surprising speed" (McCoy 2012, 237). Having said this, despite the visibility of torture in this particular case – where it was not only acts of torture themselves that were caught on camera, but also smiling soldiers standing over or next to the bodies of dead or tortured prisoners – and the international outrage sparked by these images, the investigations which followed their publication did not put an end to torture practices. In fact, they were part of the effort to safeguard the future impunity of perpetrators and the many architects of the torture network. As McCoy observes, the "military inquiries [into the torture committed at Abu Ghraib] were, in effect, the first step in a slow slide toward impunity" (McCoy 2012, 238).

It was not only that certain torture practices were "legalized" by the US government, as is shown in Bybee's and Yoo's memorandum; after the Abu Ghraib torture scandal, the legal efforts of the Bush administration increasingly began to focus on how to ensure impunity for a wide range of people involved in the torture network that had been developed after 9/11. Instead of introducing changes and sanctions at an institutional level and holding generals, politicians, and lawyers to account for facilitating the violence inflicted on the people in the Iraqi prison, the Bush administration punished only a few, lower-ranking soldiers who were captured on camera or who had taken the photographs, as well as a single higher-ranking officer – Janis Karpinski, who commanded the forces at Abu Ghraib and other prisons in Iraq at the time of the abuses. In order to explain what had occurred in the Abu Ghraib prison, the government employed the rhetoric of a "few bad apples," repeatedly emphasizing that it was a few rogue soldiers who had acted on their own account when they were torturing prisoners. In doing so, the US government consistently denied the fact that what happened in Abu Ghraib was enabled and facilitated on an institutional level, and that it was common practice throughout detention facilities controlled or overseen by the DoD post-9/11. Thus, the distribution of the infamous Abu Ghraib torture photographs did not prevent the US government from further torturing prisoners and detainees in Afghanistan, Iraq, Guantánamo, and CIA black sites in the following years. Instead, many of the political and legal efforts undertaken by the Bush administration after 2004 focused on laying the groundwork for the legal impunity of torturers, lawyers, politicians, and contractors involved in the post-9/11 torture network. An example of this is the passing of the *Military Commissions Act* in 2006 by the US Congress, which again emphasized the loopholes in the ratified version of the *Convention Against Torture* and reiterated Bybee's and Yoo's findings (McCoy 2012, 243; US Congress 2006). The main purpose of this act was to shield CIA agents and others involved in the torture of POWs and detainees from potential prosecutions and convictions for war crimes. By reiterating the stance on torture expressed by Bybee and Yoo in their interpretation of *18 US Code §2340A*, the *Military Commissions Act* is regarded as a milestone in the process of eliminating any accountability for torture that might be demanded in the course of a legal action.

Preemptively negating the possibility of holding government employees accountable for torturing detainees and POWs is one of the many ways in which the US government sought to protect its personnel from being convicted of criminal acts in US courts. The focus on protecting military and intelligence personnel from prosecution was extended by the Obama administration. Despite being obliged by the outcome of an ACLU lawsuit to publish four torture memos in 2009, memos which proved the systemic nature of torture post-9/11 and the involvement of high-ranking officials, the Obama administration continuously withheld evidence of torture which might have implicated individual employees. Due to Obama's advocacy for closing Guantánamo, many thought that his administration would "correct … [the] excesses [of the legal system] through the legal process," and thus reassure "the principle of legality" (Finkelstein and Lewis 2010, 204). In contrast, this administration actually invested great effort into making it legally challenging, if not impossible, for government employees to be punished and held to account for the post-9/11 torture of detainees and POWs in US courts. Obama did in fact acknowledge that the Bush administration tortured detainees, famously stating in his briefing of August 1, 2014, in response to *The Official Senate Report on CIA Torture: Committee Study of the Central Intelligence Agency's Detention and Interrogation Program* (US Senate 2015), that the US "tortured some folks" (The White House, Office of the Press Secretary 2014).

However, his administration neither held higher-ranking officials or politicians to account, nor (publicly) punished any of the perpetrators who had actually tortured detainees. Instead, even as Obama admitted that US forces had employed torture techniques, he rationalized and justified these practices by employing the rhetoric of persistent fear following the 9/11 attacks:

> With respect to the larger point of the RDI [Rendition, Detention, and Interrogation] report itself, even before I came into office I was very clear that in the immediate aftermath of 9/11 we did some things that were wrong. We did a whole lot of things that were right, *but we tortured some*

folks. We did some things that were contrary to our values. I understand why it happened. I think it's important *when we look back to recall how afraid people were after the Twin Towers fell and the Pentagon had been hit and the plane in Pennsylvania had fallen, and people did not know whether more attacks were imminent, and there was enormous pressure on our law enforcement and our national security teams to try to deal with this ...* And when we engaged in some of these enhanced interrogation techniques, techniques that I believe and I think any fair-minded person would believe were torture, we crossed a line. And that needs to be – that needs to be understood and accepted. *And we have to, as a country, take responsibility for that so that, hopefully, we don't do it again in the future.* (The White House, Office of the Press Secretary 2014; italics added)

In this statement, Obama emphasized that, rather than prosecuting criminal acts (which seemingly lay in the past anyway), the US public should look to the future and simply prevent such acts from happening again. Hence, his acknowledgment that US forces and Central Intelligence Agency (CIA) agents "crossed a line" by torturing detainees did not lead to the legal prosecutions within the US, as such a public acknowledgment of unlawfulness would imply.

Obama's actions and statements in 2009 already anticipated what he would say in 2014. As I briefly mentioned above, in 2009, in the course of a lawsuit initiated by the ACLU, Obama's administration was forced to release four of the so-called "torture memos," one of which was Bybee's and Yoo's legal interpretation of the ratified definition of torture (The White House, Office of the Press Secretary 2009; Bybee 2002), initially leaked to the public in 2004 by *The Washington Post* (Priest and Smith 2004). The release of these documents was announced in a statement by Obama on April 16, 2009, in which, referring to the issue of state secrecy, he stated that his administration would not be prosecuting anyone involved in torture:

> In releasing these memos, it is our intention *to assure those who carried out their duties relying in good faith upon legal advice from the Department of Justice that they will not be subject to prosecution.* The men and women of our intelligence community serve courageously on the front lines of a dangerous world. Their accomplishments are unsung and their names unknown, but because of their sacrifices, every single American is safer. *We must protect their identities as vigilantly as they protect our security, and we must provide them with the confidence that they can do their jobs.* (The White House, Office of the Press Secretary 2009; italics added)

Here, Obama publicly admitted that US personnel had perpetrated acts of torture, and signaled the end of the use of "enhanced interrogation techniques" by US forces. However, ultimately no one would be held account-able for the torture committed prior to 2009. As the ACLU lawyer Jameel Jaffer rightly observed: "[t]he Bush administration constructed a legal framework for torture but the Obama administration is constructing a legal framework for impunity" (as cited in McCoy 2012, 245 and *The New York Times* 2009).

In 2009, before the release of the four torture memos, Obama also issued the Executive Order 13491, "Ensuring Lawful Interrogations," and revoked the Bush Executive Order 13440, "Interpretation of the Geneva Conventions Common Article 3 as Applied to a Program of Detention and Interrogation Operated by the Central Intelligence Agency" (Obama 2009; Bush 2007). He furthermore revoked "[a]ll [other] executive directives, orders, and regulations inconsistent with this order, including but not limited to those issued to or by the Central Intelligence Agency (CIA) from September 11, 2001, to January 20, 2009, concerning detention or the interrogation of detained individuals" (Obama 2009, 199). The Executive Order decreed that the CIA should close any detention facilities it was operating abroad to detain and interrogate people. Furthermore, Obama ordered that the International Committee of the Red Cross should have immediate access to anyone detained by US forces. Nevertheless, this presidential document also contained major loopholes. For instance, it did not mention the network of secret prisons in Afghanistan in which many detainees were being subjected to torture (McCoy 2012, 251). Hence, the idea that Obama would correct the ways the Bush administration had deployed legal discourse to "legalize" war crimes proved to be no more than a vain hope. To echo Jaffer's observation, Obama significantly co-shaped the legal framework that provided impunity to perpetrators, lawyers, and politicians.

As McCoy argues, "[i]n President Obama's first three years in office, the United States moved, via a mix of bipartisanship and bitter political in-fighting, through … five tactics to reach a state of impunity" (McCoy 2012, 246). The first tactic focused on blaming a few so-called "bad apples," in a similar vein to the arguments put forth by the Bush administration to explain what had occurred at the Abu Ghraib prison (McCoy 2012, 246). The second involved invoking national security concerns, and Obama also proved to have strong views on this issue (McCoy 2012, 246). Despite his promise to reduce presidential recourse to state secrets, "[t]he Obama administration disappointed its civil libertarian constituencies by invoking the [state secrets] doctrine in several high-profile cases" (Pious 2011, 276). When considering the broad network of people involved in the torture of detainees and POWs, and the network of lawyers who "legalized" such practices after 9/11, it is crucial to understand how the Obama administration came to shield so many of the agents involved in the design, conduct, and legitimization of torture post-9/11. An example *par excellence* is what happened when David Margolis, who served as Associate Deputy Attorney General for 25 years, assessed the role of lawyers in providing misleading legal advice on torture (Margolis 2010). His report "concluded that former Office of Legal Counsel (OLC) attorneys John Yoo and Jay

Bybee engaged in professional misconduct by failing to provide 'thorough, candid, and objective' analysis in memoranda regarding the interrogation of detained terrorist suspects" (Margolis 2010, 1). Despite this determination, and the glimmer of hope it offered that lawyers, and possibly other agents, might be held accountable for their involvement in "legalizing" violent and brutal torture techniques, Margolis' finding was reversed only one month later, in February 2010. Obama's administration thus consistently shielded government employees from civil suits initiated by the detainees (Pious 2011, 279). The third tactic identified by McCoy involved addressing the issue of "national unity" (McCoy 2012, 246), with the Obama administration urging the US public not to focus on issues which could divide the government and military. "To these three, we must add two more," writes McCoy, "a political counterattack by perpetrators and their protectors, who excoriate human rights reformers for somehow weakening the nation's security; and, finally, revision of the historical record to justify the use of torture" (McCoy 2012, 246).

As McCoy suggests, the final event that has consolidated the impunity of perpetrators under the Obama presidency was the assassination of Osama bin Laden in May 2011, and the speculation by Republican politicians that it was the "enhanced interrogation techniques" used on Khalid Shaikh Mohammed that secured the first clue leading to bin Laden's whereabouts (McCoy 2012, 254ff.). Hence, with bin Laden's assassination, the idea that torture works and is a necessary evil was again revived – legitimizing the past, current, and perhaps even future torture of detainees.

The Justification Narrative and its Actualization

It was not only the assassination of bin Laden which was deployed as a powerful story to justify torture; a web of storytelling contributed to, in Rainer Forst's words, a much broader justification narrative of torture. The stories supporting and co-constituting the state-sanctioned narrative of the necessity of torture after the attacks of 9/11 – such as Obama's aforementioned statement during his 2014 press conference in which he relativized the crimes committed by military and intelligence personnel; the legal document denying people captured during the US GWoT the status of POWs; the DoD's internal document negotiating the definition of torture; and, finally, also the PDF file with the torture photographs – are all part of a much larger, discursive formation (The White House, Office of the Press Secretary 2014; Bush 2002a; Bybee 2002; DoD 2016). In order to show how analyzing these torture photographs and telling the stories behind them can rupture the dominant, state-governed justification narrative of torture – as I will do in the final subsection of this chapter – it is first crucial to look at how the notion of "justification narratives" relates to forms of storytelling. In his article, „Zum Begriff eines Rechtfertigungsnarrativs" (Eng. "On the Notion of the

Justification Narrative"), Forst writes that "the justifying reasons for normative orders are not simply connected to stories, but, without them, these orders cannot be fully understood" (Forst 2013, 12; my translation). Importantly, normative orders are not simply a given, instead, they "are grounded in basic justifications," and they should be understood in terms of *"justification orders"* which "presuppose justifications and [which], at the same time, generate them" (Forst 2013, 13; my translation).

When thinking about the question of how the idea of a justification narrative relates to the use of torture following the 9/11 attacks, Jochen Schuff and Martin Seel provide a few helpful observations on the relationship between stories, storytelling, justification narratives, and media (Schuff and Seel 2016a). In their introduction to the collection of essays, *Erzählungen und Gegenerzählungen: Terror und Krieg im Kino des 21. Jahrhunderts* (Eng. *Stories and Counter-Stories: Terror and War in 21st Century Cinema*), Schuff and Seel are right to point out that "[o]ne should understand such [justification] narratives in their own right as a solid basis of normative orders: as knowledge, memory, and value judgments to which every justification, and also every critique of prevailing circumstances, must at least implicitly refer" (Schuff and Seel 2016a, 20; my translation). In essence, the normative orders pertaining to torture which were shaped and justified by the US government are highly dependent on storytelling, and on a broader justification narrative. Furthermore, with regard to Schuff's and Seel's observations, my own efforts to criticize how the US government has continuously shielded its employees, and has disregarded the pain experienced by detainees, also relate to normative orders which are not only based on justifications, but which also generate them, as previously mentioned. Schuff and Seel write that "[o]n a basic level – besides convictions – actions are essentially related to justifications" (Schuff and Seel 2016a, 30; my translation). They go on to argue that justification narratives are much more powerful than other forms of storytelling, defining their power as lying in their ability to legitimize (or, indeed, delegitimize) "individual and collective actions," and identifying their tendency to combine "the description and evaluation of acting and befalling," as well as to communicate "the *normative stances* from which they [the acting and befalling] resulted" (Schuff and Seel 2016a, 33; my translation).

As Schuff and Seel write:

> The emergence and persistence of norms to which justifications can refer relies on the support of narrative development, appropriation, and *actualization* whereby concrete justifications are often placed in further narrative interrelationships. Justifications, whether of single actions, broader action contexts, or even comprehensive orders of a juridical, political, and ideological nature, are significantly supported by the forms

and structural elements of storytelling. (Schuff and Seel 2016a, 31; italics added; my translation)

Hence, the dependency of norms on a wide range of justifications, narratives, and actualizations, as well as on storytelling, reveals that the justification narrative of torture is also dependent on justifications and actualizations. In the debates on the legitimacy of torture following 9/11, the efforts to "legalize" torture during the Bush administration and the Obama administration's decision not to punish the perpetrators or architects of this torture were always accompanied by justifications expressed by a broad range of actors. Even if the two administrations' basic stances on torture might appear to have been very different, with Bush seeking to legitimize torture techniques, and Obama reversing the orders directly after taking office, their justifications were always embedded in the same web of storytelling.

Once a normative order has been established via manifold stories and broader narrative frames, however, the work of justification is still far from being done. The fact that normative orders are based on, and produce, justifications thus does not necessarily mean that these justifications have to be convincing. As a matter of fact, if we were to reconstruct the torture debate initiated in the aftermath of 9/11, we would notice that the justification efforts are rather brittle, and that the manifold stories told by US government employees frequently contradict each other, adding to the complexity of the storytelling web and making it difficult to establish a single order pertaining to torture. Nevertheless, the justification narrative appears to have been sufficiently powerful since the impunity of those involved in torturing POWs and detainees has persisted in spite of the many victim accounts testifying to the brutality of these practices.

Over the 21 years since 9/11, we have witnessed an ongoing chain of justifications which have been reiterated again and again by different governmental bodies and actors. Although the practice of torture and the impunity of the perpetrators and architects of the international torture network have become the normalized stance within the US, this stance and the actions it supports still have to be repeatedly justified via a broad range of stories. Normalizing and justifying the use of torture in the course of the US GWoT does not rely solely on the stories developed by US government employees which are then expressed at press conferences or in official documents. Significantly, the broader justification narrative of torture has considerably expanded beyond that which we would, strictly speaking, define as state-regulated storytelling, and has also found its expression in cinema. I will refer here to one specific filmic example, Kathryn Bigelow's film *Zero Dark Thirty* (2012), which dramatizes the CIA's assassination of Osama bin Laden, in other words, tells the story that, as I discussed in the previous subsection, constituted the final step in guaranteeing impunity for the perpetrators and architects of torture. Regarding the special status of film in the discursive web of justification stories, Martin Seel writes in "Narration und (De-)Legitimation: Der zweite Irak-Krieg im Kino" (Eng. "Narration and (De)Legitimization: The Second Iraq War in Cinema") that "[f]ilm can unfold situations through which it leads from the *inside to the outside* more than any other form of storytelling, because everything that becomes visible and audible in its course takes place in a horizon of spaces and times which *remain removed* from the events in the cinema or on another screen" (Seel 2013, 48; my translation).

Seel argues that "audiovisual *appearing*," and the strong feeling of "*presence*" in relation to the audience's perception of events shown on the screen, makes filmic storytelling particularly powerful because it can articulate a "perspective *through the storytelling* – and, with it, the potential *justification* of these perspectives and their normative evaluation" (Seel 2013, 49; my translation). The fact that film can tell a story in a way which justifies the actions and positions appearing within its frames makes it potentially a more powerful medium for structuring normative orders than still photographs. That is not to say that no photographs are capable of explaining or justifying what they depict in their own right. Nevertheless, as I argued in the first chapter of this book, photographs often depend much more heavily on the context of their publication to provide the viewer with the critique of, and justifications or explanations for, the actions visible in the photographic frames.

Although I am hesitant to formulate any arguments based on medium specificity, when considering the publication of the torture photographs in 2016, and their relationship to the policy of securing impunity for the perpetrators and architects of torture, it is helpful to briefly describe how films which refer to torture post-9/11 – especially fictional films – are liable to establish or support powerful, state-ordered justification narratives, while photographs often require further contextualization to justify what is visible, or indeed, remains hidden from the viewer, within their frames. As Judith Butler writes in relation to the distribution of the Abu Ghraib torture photographs:

> On the one hand, they are referential; on the other, they change their meaning depending on the context in which they are shown and the purpose for which they are invoked. The photos were published on the internet and in newspapers, but in both venues selections were made: some photos were shown, others were not; some were large, others small. (Butler 2009, 80)

What Butler terms the new contexts in which the photographs appeared are nothing less than the frames, or stories, which condition how they will be perceived by future viewers. She also states that the Abu Ghraib torture photographs "occupy no single time and no specific space" (Butler 2009, 78) because they are shown again and again, transposed from one context to another, and this history of their successive reframing and reception conditions, without determining, the range of public responses to torture. Here, Butler emphasizes that our perception of torture via a photograph is highly dependent on the context within which this photograph is discussed; or, in other words, on the discursive frame within which it is placed. In contrast to torture photographs which, according to Butler, cannot themselves fix the responses to torture made by the general public, films – especially fictional films about torture post-9/11 – are more than capable of providing their own discursive frame to justify their depiction of torture, which co-determines how this torture is perceived or understood by the audience. On the one hand, the way in which films narrate the depicted events establishes contexts as the story unfolds, for instance, by developing chains of events and placing them in a causal relationship. Therefore, I agree with Seel when he writes that the narrative techniques employed by films enable them to justify the actions and stances presented in their frames. On the other hand, the polysemy of photographs means that they not only need to be embedded in broader frames, but also that the circumstances and actions to which they refer usually need to be explained by further narrative forms – for example, by captions, statements, or news articles.

To return to Bigelow's controversial film, as Peter Maass argues in an article for *The Atlantic* magazine, *Zero Dark Thirty* "represents a troubling new frontier of government-embedded filmmaking" (Maass 2012). Released four years prior to the publication of the torture photographs I will discuss in detail later, this film uses a powerful storytelling device to support the idea that, under certain circumstances, torture is morally justifiable. The film, furthermore, echoes the ambiguity of the public debate on torture expressed during the Obama presidency – which, as I discussed in the previous subsection, saw the US government acknowledge the torture of detainees, but then fail to hold anyone to account for these war crimes. Although there are many films which actualize the broader justification narrative of torture, and many others which criticize the torture and maltreatment of detainees around the world, Bigelow's film enjoys a peculiar and special status within the web of storytelling. I am giving this film special prominence because of the involvement of CIA agents in the screenwriting and production process, and because its storytelling supports the view that torture is a justifiable means to an end. While other filmmakers have also engaged the expertise of soldiers and intelligence personnel to construct historically and factually accurate depictions of detainee interrogations in the post-9/11 world, in the case of *Zero Dark Thirty*, we can identify an extremely close collaboration between the CIA, Bigelow, and her screenwriter, Mark Boal. In 2013, as a result of a FOIA request submitted by *VICE*, the US government was ordered to publish documents pertaining to an internal investigation, which disclosed detailed information about this collaboration (CIA 2013). This report discloses that the CIA had access to the *Zero Dark Thirty* screenplay from its early stages and gave Boal significant input with regard to the portrayal of certain events and scenes, which led, for instance, to Boal cutting material from his screenplay (CIA 2013). As Jason Leopold and Ky Henderson write for *VICE*:

> The ethics report contains remarkable details about how Bigelow and Boal gave CIA officers gifts and bought them meals at hotels and restaurants in Los Angeles and Washington, DC – much of which initially went unreported by the CIA officers – how they won unprecedented access to secret details about the bin Laden operation, and how they got agency officers and officials to review and critique the *ZDT* [*Zero Dark Thirty*] script. (Leopold and Henderson 2015)

Furthermore, in the course of his research for the film, Boal was granted access to CIA facilities, and to details about the Agency's internal celebrations of the mission's success just one month after bin Laden's assassination (Leopold and Henderson 2015). According to the report, at least ten CIA officers directly involved in the mission to capture bin Laden supported Bigelow and Boal with firsthand intelligence, and closely collaborated with the filmmakers on the script. Importantly, the CIA's collaboration with the filmmakers occurred at the same time as the Agency was under public scrutiny due to the then-ongoing investigation by the US Senate Select Committee on Intelligence into the CIA's Detention and Interrogation Program (US Senate 2015).

In a letter addressed to Michael Lynton, then Chairman and CEO of Sony Pictures Entertainment, Intelligence Committee chairperson Dianne Feinstein and committee members Carl Levin and John McCain, who were investigating the CIA's conduct, write:

> We understand that the film is fiction, but it opens with the words 'based on first-hand accounts of actual events' and there has been significant media coverage of the CIA's cooperation with the screenwriters. As you know, the film graphically depicts CIA officers repeatedly torturing detainees and then credits these detainees with providing critical lead information on the courier that led to Usama Bin Laden. Regardless of what message the filmmakers intended to convey, the movie clearly implies that the CIA's coercive interrogation techniques were effective in eliciting important information related to a courier for Usama Bin Laden. We have reviewed CIA records and know that this is incorrect. (Feinstein, Levin, and McCain 2012, 1)

This letter emphasizes that *Zero Dark Thirty* powerfully presents the core arguments of the justification narrative of torture by suggesting to the audience that torture techniques are not only effective, but have also helped to prevent further terrorist attacks. Despite being a fictional film, the opening onscreen text – "[t]he following motion picture is based on firsthand accounts of actual events" (Bigelow 2012, 00:39) – gives the storytelling a strong documentary appeal. The film's aesthetic choices with regard to lightning and color also encourage the audience to see the film as if it were a documentary. As Christa Van Raalte writes, the "limited colour palette, naturalistic lighting and understated performances further serve to create what might be described as a reality affect" (Van Raalte 2007, 23).

After the opening onscreen text, Bigelow chose to proceed with a black screen accompanied by an atmospheric collage featuring actual recordings of the last phone calls made by victims of the 9/11 terror attacks.[4] These recordings of calls made by passengers on the hijacked planes to their family members and by airline staff, along with recordings of 911-calls made by people trapped in the Twin Towers, are edited and mixed in the film in a manner which reinforces their high emotional impact. This opening scene, which functions chiefly on the level of sound, and withholds the iconography of the falling Twin Towers already so familiar to viewers, evokes in a very intimate way not only the horrors of September 11, 2001, but also the real, factual deaths of the attack's victims. At the end of this opening scene, which lasts around 90 seconds, Bigelow cuts to a conversation between a woman – Melissa Doi – trapped in one of the towers and a 911-operator:

> Melissa Doi: Are you able to get somebody up here?
> 911 Operator: Of course, Ma'am. We will come up for you.
> Melissa Doi: Well, there is no one here yet and the floor is completely engulfed. We're on the floor and we can't breathe.
> 911 Operator: One second please.
> Melissa Doi: I'm gonna die, aren't I?
> 911 Operator: No, no, no, no, no!
> Melissa Doi: I'm gonna die.
> 911 operator: Ma'am... ma'am... now...
> Melissa Doi: I'm gonna die, I know it.
> 911 operator: Stay calm, stay calm, stay calm, stay calm.
> Melissa Doi: Please god.
> 911 operator: Ma'am you're doing a good job, you're doing a good job.
> Melissa Doi: It's so hot, I'm burning up.
> 911 operator: You're gonna be fine, we're gonna come get you. Can anyone hear me? Oh my god. (Bigelow 2012, 01:39–02:08)

---

4   Some family members of the 9/11 victims were deeply upset by how Bigelow used the recordings. Harry Ong, the brother of Betty, who was a flight attendant on one of the flights, asked Bigelow and her crew to "apologize and … recognize that they used Betty's voice and Brad's and others at liberty" (as cited in Doane 2013). Some family members requested that Bigelow acknowledged the identities of the victims by providing further context for the use of the recordings in her film.

The soundtrack leaves the audience with the impression that they have just heard the exact moment in which the woman making the distress call died. Furthermore, Bigelow and Paul N. T. Ottosson, the film's sound designer/re-recording mixer, cut out significant parts of this and other recordings, and reassembled only a few of their pieces to emphasize the emotional impact and gravity of the recordings – which already, in themselves, present an incredibly moving and shocking auditory experience. In the final recording used in the opening sequence, the techniques of editing and mixing give the excerpt from the distress call made on 9/11 by Doi – who was working on the 83rd floor of the South Tower when one of the airplanes hit the building – an even stronger narrative coherence by cutting down the actual conversation.[5]

By using these recordings for the film's opening scene, Bigelow sets the broader narrative frame for her storytelling, and establishes a striking justification narrative for her subsequent depictions of the brutal torture techniques and violence inflicted upon detainees. The scene directly following this atmospheric opening sound collage, which is also the first torture scene in the film, is introduced by the following onscreen text: "[t]wo years later" (Bigelow 2012, 02:11). The viewer is then immediately presented with the words "The Saudi Group," which dissolve into images of an interrogation room. An unmasked man enters the room – Dan, a CIA agent – and the viewer sees another person following him in, wearing a ski mask. As both people enter, the film cuts to reveal their backs and a man standing on a mattress in front of a tarpaulin-covered wall. The man on the mattress is being watched by three other masked guards. Based on the sound made by the ski-masked person's shoes entering the room, the audience can immediately deduce that she is a woman – in fact, the CIA analyst and film's protagonist, Maya – even before the film cuts to a close-up of her eyes. The visual iconography of this scene, with the darkened windows, the detainee, and masked interrogators – as well as the fact that the film cuts to this interrogation and torture scene directly after referring to 9/11 – makes it clear that the film depicts a CIA interrogation at a so-called "black site." In the course of the interrogation, Dan fails to ask the detained man – whose name is Ammar – any of the relevant questions

---

5   Listening to the actual recordings, it becomes immediately clear that Bigelow stripped down their context and content using the techniques of audio editing and mixing. Nevertheless, the recording I have transcribed above is well known to the US public since parts of it were widely distributed by the news media. With regard to the length of the original call, which lasted approximately 24 minutes, it can be argued that the film deceives the audience to some extent because it cuts off at a highly emotional passage, leaving us with the impression that these were Doi's final words, and the operator is reacting to her death. According to government records, the original recording does not end with the operator saying "[o]h my god." Instead, after Doi asked the operator to help her and the other people trapped on the 83rd floor, and after describing the situation, she requested to be connected to her mother. Although the operator could not forward her call, she passed on the message to Doi's mother on that same day.

which, we might assume, are the main purpose of an interrogation. Instead, he approaches the detainee and screams: "I own you Ammar, you belong to me," and "look at me!" (Bigelow 2012, 02:29–33 and 02:36–8).

When Dan and Maya leave the room, still without having asked Ammar any questions, or Dan succeeding in forcing the detainee to look into his eyes, the film cuts back to Ammar as the other guards force him into a stress position by tying his hands with ropes to the ceiling: one of the many clean torture techniques approved by Rumsfeld in 2002 (Haynes II 2002). Before cutting to the next torture scene, the viewers are shown a conversation between Dan and Maya – who takes off her mask outside the darkened interrogation room – which provides further information about the identities of the protagonist, the other agent, and the detainee. Maya then suggests that they reenter the room and asks Dan whether the detainee will ever get out, to which he replies, "never," implying that Ammar will remain detained indefinitely by the CIA.

Maya goes back into the interrogation room without her mask and reveals her face to Ammar. During the second interrogation, Dan tells the detainee that the CIA knows he paid 5,000 US dollars to one of the hijackers who caused the trauma of 9/11, and that they have also found 150 kilograms of explosives at his home. Dan continues to question Ammar about the so-called "Saudi Group," and holds a photograph of a man against his face. When Ammar refuses to reveal the Saudi e-mail address of the man pictured in the photograph, the viewers see how Dan, with the help of his masked colleagues and Maya, water-boards him using a bucket of water and a towel. While Ammar is subjected to waterboarding, a torture technique which creates the feeling of drowning to death, Maya is shown looking away and closing her eyes at the sight of the brutal treatment. However, although she appears to be shocked by what she is seeing, she not only remains present in the room, but also actively participates in the torture of Ammar by putting water into the bucket.

In just these ten opening minutes of her film, Bigelow both refers to, and supports, a powerful justification narrative for the use of torture in the aftermath of 9/11. By interlinking the horrifying recordings of the final calls made by the 9/11 victims with the torture of Ammar, who has supposedly provided financial support for the attacks of 9/11, which led to deaths of nearly 3,000 people, the film constructs a casual chain of events which justifies the brutal torture techniques used by CIA agents in the following scenes. This justification narrative of torture is not only emphasized by Bigelow's framing of the story with the 9/11-recordings, but also by the film's ending, which portrays Maya's successful assistance in the assassination of bin Laden. Although the film's causal chain of events clearly supports the justification narrative of torture, and suggests its efficacy to the audience, Jennifer L. Gauthier provides us with another, more positive interpretation of the use of montage in the opening sequence in her essay "Making it 'Real' / 'Reel': Truth, Trauma, and American Exceptionalism in *Zero Dark Thirty*," writing that:

> Although detractors of the film suggest that this editing choice functions to justify the use of torture, one might argue just the opposite. By following the audio recordings from 9/11 with graphic scenes of 'enhanced interrogation,' Bigelow asks us to confront our shared emotions and the lengths to which we were willing to go (allow the government to go) in order to find and kill the perpetrators of this national tragedy. (Gauthier 2018, 90)

This surprising reading of Bigelow's montage not only disregards its ideological implications; it also fails to acknowledge how the subsequent storytelling in the film further lends strength to the justification narrative of torture so thoroughly shaped by the US government. With regard to the aforementioned description of the film's ability to produce causal chains by employing various filmic techniques, and how it successfully justifies the actions appearing within its frames, it is not only the recordings of the calls made by 9/11 victims which legitimize the brutal torture of Ammar by the CIA. The film continues to justify the torture of detainees through its various representations of terrorist attacks and deaths of people close to Maya.

Other scholars have argued that the film's stance on torture is an ambiguous one, since Maya never makes her position on the torture of the detainees clear, so the viewer cannot deduce whether or not she approves of it. However, the entire film lends credence to the legitimacy of torture by the way in which it organizes its story. In his essay, "Genre-Hybridisierung als (parapraktische) Interferenz: Zero Dark Thirty" (Eng. "Genre Hybridization as (Para-Practical) Interference: Zero Dark Thirty"), Thomas Elsaesser places the critiques expressed towards the film's representation of "enhanced torture techniques" into three categories (Elsaesser 2016, 72f.). Firstly, some commentators criticized the way in which Bigelow portrays torture because none of the characters in the film condemns the techniques or contextualize them as an illegal practice. Secondly, the film suggests that there is a "causal relationship between the use of torture and the capture of bin Laden" (Elsaesser 2016, 73; my translation). Thirdly, the whole discussion about whether it was torture which led to bin Laden's assassination implicitly legitimizes its use as an "acceptable means of politics," and relativizes a practice "which not only represents a violation of international law, but is also morally unacceptable" (Elsaesser 2016, 73; my translation). By interlacing the recordings of the final words spoken by the 9/11 victims to their families or to 911-operators, and by stating in its second scene that the tortured detainee financially supported one of the hijackers, the film suggests that torture is a necessary means to an end, a means to prevent further terrorist attacks. The use of the recordings not only justifies, on an emotional level, the violence

and the unbearable, painful torture techniques with which the viewer is confronted in the film; it also reiterates within an ambiguously fictional framework the arguments formulated by the Bush and Obama administrations as to
why US government employees should not be accused of war crimes.

Furthermore, the film clearly depicts US citizens and even CIA employees as
victims within its story. Thus, although CIA agents also appear as perpetrators
who torture detainees, the way in which Bigelow characterizes them and the
detainees suggests that only the latter are the true perpetrators. As Susan L.
Carruthers rightly observes in her *Cinéaste* review of the film, *Zero Dark Thirty*
"directs disgust more toward the victim than the perpetrator" (Carruthers
2013, 51). A final important moment in the film which supports this distinction
and consolidates the broader narrative comes after the end credits, when
Bigelow fades up the following acknowledgment:

> The filmmakers wish to especially acknowledge the sacrifice of those men,
> women, and families who were most impacted by the events depicted
> in this film: the victims and the families of the 9/11 attacks; as well as the
> attacks in the United Kingdom; the Marriott Hotel in Islamabad, Pakistan;
> in Khobar, Saudi Arabia; and at the Camp Chapman forward operating
> base in Afghanistan. We also wish to acknowledge and honor many extra-
> ordinary military and intelligence professionals and first responders who
> have made the ultimate sacrifice. (Bigelow 2012, 02:35:56–36:09)

This acknowledgment summarizes the narrative which has been continuously
deployed by the US government to justify the violation of international
law and the use of torture. The film not only depicts the use of torture as a
necessary means to prevent further attacks; it also constructs a normative
distinction between the lives of US citizens and CIA employees, which are
shown as worth protecting, and the lives of detainees, which are shown as
non-grievable and justifiably injured. Hence, although the film renders torture
practices visible, its technique of embedding torture in the causal chain of
events which lead to bin Laden's assassination and justifying it via the revelation of violent terrorist attacks marks the representation of torture in the
film with a crucial ambiguity. Indeed, the viewer might get the impression that
it is not the detainees who are the victims of torture; instead, the true and
only victims are US government employees and the many people who have
died in terrorist attacks.

Bigelow's storytelling thus ascribes different values to the fictional lives it
depicts. The lives of US citizens and CIA agents are shown in a way which
makes them grievable, and they are indeed grieved for within the story.
The emotionally loaded beginning of the film suggests that horrors like 9/11
must be prevented, while the manner in which Maya grieves the death of
her colleague, killed by a suicide bomber, supports the idea that the lives

of US citizens should be protected at all costs. The detainees, in contrast, are continuously violated, injured, and depicted as mere sources of information. For example, even though, in the course of the film, the viewer learns that bin Laden is living at his secret location in the company of his wife and children, he is depicted in such an abstract manner – we never see his face, and he is not even shown in the aerial images of his hideaway – so that the viewer is prevented from developing any relationship with his character. This is exacerbated by the way the film suggests his involvement in the terrorist attacks. The justification narrative of torture, as I argued above, is also dependent on depictions like the one provided by Bigelow's film, which due to its broad audience, has co-shaped the US public's understanding of torture and its necessity. In light of the way the US government referred to detainees being transported to Guantánamo, namely as "the worst of the worst" (Seeyle 2002),[6] or of Bush's statement made only a few weeks after the arrival of the first detainees at the Guantánamo detention camp, "[r]emember, these are – the ones in Guantánamo Bay are killers [,] [t]hey don't share the same values we share" (Bush 2002b), it is important to acknowledge how these and other forms of storytelling continued to shape the public's understanding of torture during Obama's presidency, and were actualized in films like Bigelow's.

In this section, I analyzed the justification narrative of torture, examining how Bigelow's film actualizes this narrative and ascribes different values to the lives of the perpetrators and the victims of torture, while also supporting the ongoing impunity of the many actors involved in torture post-9/11. This analysis establishes a broader frame for the discussion of the torture photographs published by the Obama administration in 2016. These photographs, and the manner in which they were published, are also inscribed in the web of storytelling which justifies torture and which has protected the perpetrators and architects of the global torture network. Importantly, apart from the photographs published in the course of the Abu Ghraib torture scandal, there are very few available images of torture at CIA black sites and in other military prisons around the world. Furthermore, as I discussed in the previous chapter, the Obama administration devoted great effort to making it legally challenging, if not impossible, to access images documenting the torture of detainees in Iraq, Afghanistan, Guantánamo, and other undisclosed locations abroad.

---

6   This phrase is usually assigned to Rumsfeld, however, according to an article published in the *Washington Post*, it is unclear who actually coined it. Rumsfeld's spokesman said that "[i]t is wrongly attributed to him" (Stein 2011).

The Frame of Torture Photographs

Invisibilizing Torture, its Victims, and its Perpetrators

By investigating the legal loopholes which were carefully designed by both the Bush and Obama administrations, and the legal and political efforts pursued by both administrations to secure impunity for the perpetrators of torture, I have sought to establish the broader frame for my analysis of what we see in the 2016 PDF file, and also what remains invisible to us. The decision by the Obama administration and the DoD to publish 198 photographs in one simple PDF file, and the particular photographs they chose to include, are indicative of the efforts they took to ensure the impunity of a wide range of actors who were, or still are, involved in the torture of detainees and POWs suspected of terrorism. Building on Rejali's attempt to write "a *different* history of torture," rather than "an *absence* of [such a] history" (Rejali 2007, 405), I argue that, despite the fact that the published images appear to speak of a threefold absence – of torture, its victims, and its perpetrators – by investigating them and their original contexts more closely, we can render visible, at least to a certain extent, that which had been concealed.

When analyzing this collection of photographs and the public discourses they initiated, it is important to note that they are not immediately recognizable as images of torture. Often, it is only thanks to the fact that they are embedded in torture discourses that the viewer sees not just a bruised body, but a tortured one. However, to refute Iacopino's initial statement that these photographs do not show the abuse of detainees and POWs (PHR 2016), I will read them as being, or containing, traces of clean torture which was – and probably still is – perpetrated by US military and intelligence personnel or DoD contractors in various prisons, detention facilities, and black sites around the world.

So what can we see in the PDF file? Around 130 of its 198 photographs show close-ups of body parts of detainees and POWs, including hands, arms, legs, feet, eyes, redacted faces, tops of heads, foreheads, backs, and the inside of mouths. Many of these images are blurred and/or overexposed, and appear to have been taken with a basic digital camera. The PDF file does not reproduce the original digital files of the photographs. Instead, the people who created this file scanned printed-out photocopies of pages from medical or investigative reports – a process which has affected the quality of the photographs so badly that sometimes it is even difficult to recognize what, or, more precisely, which body part, the photograph is documenting. Nevertheless, in many of the close-ups it is still possible to recognize particular body parts, as well as additional objects which appear within their frames. In some of the less grainy images, we see a ruler or coin next to the person's skin, providing a scale for what can be seen on the bodily surfaces, and also indicating the forensic or medical context of the images' production. These rulers and coins raise the expectation that we are seeing something out-of-the-ordinary, invoking, as they do, the popular imaginations of photographs from medical and forensic reports. However, what we can actually see in most of the photographs could not be further from meeting this expectation. In a large number of them, it is impossible to identify any injuries on the skin – such as bruises, scars, or wounds. Even where such phenomena are visible, they appear to be only small bruises or non-life-threatening grazes and abrasions, and at times, the darker marks on the skin might even be mistaken for dirt.

Furthermore, not every photograph is given its own page, and some pages contain between two and four photographs. Thus, for 198 photographs there are only 162 pages in the file. It is often the case that the same person was photographed multiple times, with only minimal changes to the camera angle or lighting, which we can deduce from the exhibit numbers written in pencil on or next to the photographs, or from case numbers mechanically inscribed onto the pages. For example, page 160 contains two photographs of a person's back, taken on April 29, 2003[7] (DoD 2016, 160). The upper photograph shows the entire back, with the camera perspective revealing that the subject is sitting on the ground. The lower photograph provides a close up of part of the back, but the viewer is unable to see anything particular or out-of-the-ordinary in the image, because the page on which it was originally printed on has been photocopied in black and white and then scanned. It is only thanks to the upper photograph that we can assume the lower photograph depicts the skin on the back of the same person as in the first image. The few pages not depicting close-ups of body parts contain photographs which appear to have been taken at "crime scenes." The four photographs which appear on page 13, for instance, are divided in two categories: "Weapons Found in Car" and "Detainees" (DoD 2016, 13). The two photographs belonging to the former category show a staged scene in which we see weapons from a raided car neatly arranged on the ground. Behind these weapons are four kneeling men with redacted faces and, in the background, the car with an open door. The latter category contains two close-up photographs of the detained men, with black lines covering their eyes to hide their identities.

Some of the PDF pages disclose further information, such as the institutional setting in which a particular photograph was taken. For example, on page 108, we can see the name of the institution which was conducting the investigation – the US Naval Criminal Investigative Service: Southwest Field Office – and whose employees presumably took the photograph appearing on the page (DoD 2016, 108). In the center of the page is a photograph of a man in a tiled room that resembles a bathroom or a medical examination room

7   The quality of the scan is so bad that the year could also be 2005.

pulling up the sleeve of his grey t-shirt to show his left arm and elbow to the photographer. On the arm, we can make out what appear to be scratches or older scars; it does not appear to be a fresh or life-threatening wound. Beneath the picture are five sections containing additional information: a redacted title section, the criminal case number "25Jun04–SWND-0350-7HNA," the redacted name of the Special Agent who conducted the investigation, a blank field for the date when the photograph was taken, and the following description: "Photo #5: Photo provided by ▇▇▇▇▇ showing left elbow and upper arm of ▇▇▇▇▇" (DoD 2016, 108). Despite the criminal case number, which could potentially help the viewer to research the original context in which the photographs were taken, a search for it in the Naval Criminal Service database leads nowhere. Nevertheless, not all the numbers in the PDF file are unsearchable. For instance, some pages contain numbers – in particular, the case numbers of the US Army Criminal Investigation Command – which lead to detailed case files in the ACLU's *Torture Database* (ACLU 2022a). However, many of the pictures lack any points of reference, either because they bear no number, or because the case number has been cropped during the copying or scanning procedure. The photograph of a hand with a medical or forensic ruler on page 81, for instance, does not contain a case or file number, but instead the exhibit number "I-123-76C 2006" (DoD 2016, 81), which yields no results when put into various search engines. Although the frames or case numbers relating to some of the images allow us to speculate about their production context, in most of them, the viewer cannot see any reference to the person who took the photograph – and this is not just the case in the instances where the photographers or units to which they belong have been redacted.

Moreover, although many of the photographs contain a ruler, which indicates that someone was documenting these body parts, almost every image has the ruler placed directly on the skin, so it is impossible to see the hand of the person who placed it there. Likewise, the frames of the photographs usually cut out any reference to the person who took it (apart from the camera angle). On one page of the PDF file, however, we can see a series of four mugshots and a hand (which does not belong to the photographed subject) holding a piece of paper displaying the prisoner's or detainee's identification number (DoD 2016, 155). The viewer can make out this person's fingers, and even their full hand, but this is the only page in the PDF file where the "staging apparatus" (Butler 2009, 74) is so clearly visible. Hence, the photographic frames in the file clearly delineate what can be perceived by the viewer, and what is permitted to be shown. The images themselves produce a form of incomprehensible visibility in which the act and consequences of torture, the torturer, and the staging apparatus are all rendered imperceptible to the viewer, thus shielding US government employees from potential lawsuits.

Despite the increasing public pressure and the ongoing lawsuit, *ACLU v. DoD* ((2017), 04. Civ 4161 (AKH), 1), which forced the US government to publish these torture photographs from its *"shadow archive"* (Sekula 1986, 10), the released photographs make it clear that the Obama administration was working hard to keep the promises it made in 2009 and 2014 to protect past, current, and future US government employees. The way the DoD certified and distributed these photographs tacitly implies its compliance with the broader policies of impunity and the justification narrative that were so robustly established between 2001 and 2016. The certification of these and other photographs under the *Protected National Security Documents Act* of 2009 is one process amongst many others undertaken by federal departments to claim control over photographs documenting torture, and thus to secure their powers of secrecy, while also offering protection to the employees of military and intelligence agencies, amongst others (US Congress 2009). In direct contrast, to recall the statement made by Lyndon B. Johnson in 1966, at that time president of the US, upon signing the *Freedom of Information Act* (FOIA), the lawsuit initiated by the ACLU and other human rights organizations can be seen as embodying the idea that democracy can only function if the public is knowledgeable and has access to information about the conduct of its government. Johnson writes that "[n]o one should be able to pull curtains of secrecy around decisions which can be revealed without injury to the public interest" (Johnson 1966). He argues that in democracies the public requires a legal basis in order to be able to inquire about the conduct of its government; he then directly follows up by pointing to the restrictions of access to information and emphasizes the right to secrecy of that same government and its military. By returning to "threats to peace" and appealing for the necessity of "military secrets" (Johnson 1966), Johnson's statement provides an ambivalent message, drawing a line between the public's right know and the government's right secrecy in the context of democracies. Thus, "pulling curtains" on military secrets is exactly what occurred in the course of the ALCU lawsuit, both throughout the time when the DoD withheld many images (as it continues to do), but also in the very moment that it distributed the 198 photographs in this PDF file. The FOIA was thus supposed to ensure the availability of information of public interest, and to change the basic stance of the US government toward a doctrine of the public having a right to know.

In the case of the PDF file, it is not only the photographs which were subject to a legal debate about what was more important: the public's right to know, or the government's right to secrecy. The interpretation of the photographs which were actually published was also dynamic, non-stable, and "up for grabs" (Sekula 2003, 444). Hence, the publication of these photographs did not mean that the DoD was respecting the public's right to know, since, as I hope I have made clear, what the photographs actually depict is far from being known.

These images mirror the stealthy nature of clean torture techniques and extend the arguments formulated by Bybee and Yoo in their 2002 memorandum (Bybee 2002) about what was legally regarded as torture, and what was not. The visual absence of evidence of clean torture practices from the PDF file indicates a double form of institutional stealth: the obfuscation of the torture practices themselves, and of their visual representation. The way these photographs were published encourages viewers to see them as neither showing violence inflicted on people detained in Iraq, Afghanistan, Guantánamo, and CIA black sites, nor providing proof of torture which could hold the perpetrators to account in courts of law. From the viewpoint of contemporary surveillance infrastructures, as Toni Pape makes clear, the notion of "stealth" carries a positive connotation – it provides a way to escape the structures of power organized around the visibility of citizens for whom "an *aesthetic of stealth*, that is, the staging of acts of becoming-imperceptible ... [is] a condition for efficient political action" (Pape 2017, 630). However, in the case of the PDF file, the specific techniques of torture, the visual practices of photography, and the way in which the images were distributed were all used in a "stealthy" way to safeguard the *status quo*, and to make what can be seen in these photographs unknowable. Here, stealth is intended to prevent any effective political action against the perpetrators and the government and to disable the proper functioning of *"public monitoring"* (Rejali 2007, 8). Importantly, the incomprehensibility of who or what is visible in these photographs goes hand-in-hand with the ungraspable nature of, redaction from, and invisibility of the torture perpetrators in the images. Rejali is right to point out the political guile involved in clean torture, and how, in democratic societies, the lack of photographic evidence associated with this practice is intended to make victim allegations less credible (Rejali 2007, 8). In addition to the fact that clean torture usually cannot be proven by photographic means, as Rejali rightly observes, "[s]tealth torture breaks down the ability to communicate" (Rejali 2007, 8). His observations also apply to the photographs in the published document, and human rights lawyers have responded quite strongly to the fact that this file conceals the systemic dimension of torture and its painful consequences. The practices of clean torture render the pain and suffering experienced by victims invisible to the viewer; even worse, the PDF file conceals the mere fact that such practices have been carried out, and hides the identities of the victims and perpetrators.

This PDF file offers a counterargument to Hilbrand's view that clean torture is unrepresentable, given that clean torture techniques are designed to ensure that the general public and lawyers cannot see any evidence of them or use photographs and other indexical practices to prove that they have been deployed. Claiming clean torture to be unrepresentable fails to acknowledge the fact that photographs which do not show bruises or severe injuries might still testify to torture, if they are reframed by the appropriate discourses. As

Sebastian Köthe rightly argues, the unrepresentable nature of clean torture is a mere fantasy – a fantasy which is shared by the DoD and some scholarship alike. He states that "the excessive amount of technologically stored and managed information shows that … however minimal and insignificant they [the traces of clean torture] might appear … [they are] almost impossible to erase" (Köthe 2020, 397f; my translation). The PDF file is precisely such a result of "technologically stored and managed information" (Köthe 2020, 387f.; my translation), and, despite the fact that the photographs were published without any information on the context of their production, we can still learn to read traces of torture in these images, thereby unlearning what we think we know about the physical consequences and representations of torture.

Increasing the Polysemy of Torture Photographs

The status of the PDF file with regard to torture is an ambiguous one. On the one hand, the images themselves do not resemble the imagery of torture practices witnessed by the public following the publication of the photographs from the Abu Ghraib prison in 2004. In contrast to the Abu Ghraib torture photographs, in which we see soldiers committing acts of torture and the bodies of the detainees in moments of experiencing pain and suffering, the PDF file contains no such images. On the other hand, whereas the images in the PDF file cannot immediately be read as depicting the consequences of torture, if we investigate the origins and production context of these photographs, we can establish that they do in fact show the results of abuse and that, despite the presumed tracelessness of clean torture techniques, these images testify not only to torture itself, but also to the efforts made to erase or deny it. The initial response from the organizations who initiated the lawsuit and the FOIA request which led to the publication of the 198 photographs differed strongly from the approach I am proposing in this chapter. On the same day as the PDF file was published, "PHR noted that the released photos do not include images of abuse known to be part of the 2,000 photos, such as pictures of detainees being beaten, stepped on, sexually humiliated, placed in stress positions, threatened with dogs, and subjected to simulated sodomy" (PHR 2016). According to their statement, the photographs failed to show what was already known to be happening in extra-territorial prisons and detention facilities – abuses similar to the ones witnessed in 2004 following the leak of images from the Abu Ghraib prison in Iraq. The 198 photographs and the format in which they were published thus bestow a type of incomprehensible visibility on the bodies of tortured individuals. We could even say that the file creates a contorted visibility whose task is not only to make the situations to which these photographs refer incomprehensible, but also to shield the perpetrators from public scrutiny. It is a form of visibility which offers many possible readings to viewers, but not one which would allow us to come close to understanding what and whom these photographs actually depict.

By stripping these photographs of their original contexts, this PDF file increases their semantic availability, making them less specific and opening them to many interpretations. This polysemy helps the DoD to conceal the reality of torture and restrain the photographs' potential to disrupt the broader justification narrative of torture. The DoD's deliberate intensification of the polysemic nature of photographs is not only evident in the PDF file; it is also integral to Ashton Carter's certification process, which preceded its publication. This process appears to have been founded on a central premise: namely, that photographs can function in illustrative ways, and are defined by a generic appeal. As I discussed in Chapter 3, during the certification, an unidentified attorney initially categorized approximately 2,000 images in relation to what they depicted, and then re-categorized them according to criteria designed to assess the perceived likelihood that each photograph's publication would harm the US government. This still unknown and unnamed attorney then created a "true representative sample that contained the full spectrum of what the full group of photographs depicted" (*ACLU v. DoD* 2017, 04. Civ 4161 (AKH), 12), which was followed by a similar categorization process undertaken by commissioned officers from the DoD, who also selected representative samples to stand in for larger sets of photographs. Apparently, there was then a third level of certification in which new attorneys compared the results of the two previous reviews, however, we do not know if they reviewed all the photographs anew at this stage, or just compared the two samples. According to Judge Hellerstein's *Opinion and Order* on the *ACLU v. DoD* lawsuit, "[t]his process led to a recommendation to Secretary Carter: 198 photographs should be released, and the rest, an unspecified number, should be kept secret" (*ACLU v. DoD* 2017, 04. Civ 4161 (AKH), 13).

This brief reconstruction of the certification process supports my thesis that the creation of the PDF file, as well as the certification that preceded it, deliberately set out to strip the photographs of their context. More explicitly, when photographs come to be employed as "representative" of other photographs, the specificity of what they depict becomes less important than how they relate to the other images involved in the lawsuit. The certification process also shows that the DoD ascribed illustrative functions to photography, even with regard to photographs documenting specific torture practices and particular lives. To a certain extent, the way in which the DoD certified these photographs, focusing on their non-specificity or visual equivalence, and its decision to publish images without their context, established a normative frame that influenced how the general public responded to the file. It also set the basis for the initial misinterpretation of the forensic value of these images, and the widespread perception that they did not provide proof of torture. For example, directly after the images were published, PHR questioned the value of the information contained within them:

> PHR said that the vast majority of released photos *show indistinct images of bodies with no clinical or forensic value*. There are *a handful of images showing nonspecific injuries*, including likely contusions, abrasions, and lacerations, but it is not possible to draw conclusions about whether detainee abuse occurred without corresponding clinical information. (PHR 2016; italics added)

As this statement demonstrates, the US government's deliberate attempts to increase the polysemy and genericity of these torture photographs meant that their forensic value became unclear, rendering invisible the perspective of the victims and concealing, yet again, the identities of the perpetrators. Through this PDF file in particular, and the polysemy of photographs in general, the DoD sought to secure the impunity of the torturers by showing that, even if the photographs came to be read as documentation of (clean) torture, this torture concerned no one in particular, mirroring Obama's stance on the non-disclosure of the identities of the US government employees involved.

As I discussed in relation to McCoy's Guantánamo photographs in Chapter 1, polysemy is inherent to photographs. However, the polysemy of certain photographs may be increased due to the manner of their production and distribution. The way that the DoD distributed the 198 torture photographs intentionally diversified how they could be read, so they came to function simultaneously as historic, news, and stock images. The details of the certification process, in which some photographs were used to represent other photographs, and the assumptions about the generic and non-specific nature attributed to photography by the DoD, thus reveals that the issue of stock photography not only concerns companies which specialize in the sale of such images (including Getty Images, as well as other image banks), but also that the DoD had the power and means to turn these highly specific photographs – whose very nature should render them non-interchangeable – into generic "stock images."

In media studies scholarship, a crucial divide has arisen concerning how we should define stock images. Some scholars argue that the most distinctive feature of stock photography is its aesthetic features, whereas others focus on the distribution models introduced by the "'visual content industry'" (Frosh 2003, 6), and argue that it is primarily the infrastructure which makes an image a stock photograph. The former group defines stock photography by focusing on how some photographs are less specific than others. According to this definition, stock photographs are those which contain very little specific information about the reality to which they refer, increasing their polysemy and giving the impression of a more generic form of indexicality. As Matthias

Bruhn argues, the pictures archived and sold by image agencies must exhibit a "balance between freshness and storability, between anonymity and an appealing character, between recognizability and the location-neutrality of their subjects" (Bruhn 2003, 50; my translation). The universal appeal of such photographs – thanks to the anonymity of their subject matter, and the non-specificity of their locations – multiplies their potential uses. An important aspect of defining stock photographs via their capacity to illustrate a wide range of topics is to differentiate them from so-called "journalistic" or "news photography," which is usually based on the premise that the images refer to specific persons, objects, or events, and that they were taken at a specific point in time.

However, as Paul Frosh writes, image banks have contributed to the blurring of borders between the different "genres" of photography:

> Thus stock photography is being subsumed within a globalized and digitized 'visual content industry' ..., whose ramifications include, among many other things, the accelerated blurring of boundaries between pre-viously distinct institutional and discursive contexts of production and distribution: in particular, between fine art, news and advertising images, and in a culture glutted with authentic and fabricated 'vintage' images, between historical and contemporary photographs. (Frosh 2003, 6)

Frosh's stance can be seen to belong to the latter side of the scholarly divide which defines stock photography via the way that images are distributed. Nevertheless, despite focusing on the aesthetic features of stock photography, Bruhn also writes that "every archive which stores photographs for later use could in principle be defined as 'stock photography'" (Bruhn 2003, 57; my translation).

There are at least two larger points to support my argument that the manner in which the DoD distributed the torture photographs in the PDF file increased their polysemic nature to such an extent that it removed their historic dimension and connection to torture, pushing them to be seen more and more as generic stock images. Firstly, the distribution practice shifted their function from news to stock photography by giving viewers the impression that the images could have been taken anywhere, at any time, and could depict anyone. Secondly, the way news agencies added some of the photographs to their online databases confirms and emphasizes their apparent genericity, revealing that they came to function as both news and stock images at the same time.

For example, on the same day that the Pentagon released the PDF file, Associated Press (AP) Images added a few of the photographs provided by the US government to their online repositories. The corporate frame of AP Images, and the way they stocked and described these very different and specific photographs, had an equalizing effect on them. Thus, in addition to the US government's certification process and its presentation of the PDF file as an archive, the image banks also emphasized a certain "generic appeal" of the photographs. Looking at how AP Images stored some of the images from the PDF file thus supports Allan Sekula's thesis on the equalizing function of archives (Sekula 2003, 445), since, in the AP Images databank, each individual photograph from the PDF file is accompanied by the same caption:

> This image provided by the Department of Defense shows one of the 198 photos of detainees in Iraq and Afghanistan, involving 56 cases of alleged abuse by US forces, that were released Friday, Feb. 5, 2016, in response to a Freedom of Information request from the American Civil Liberties Union. *The often dark, blurry and grainy pictures are mainly of detainees' arms and legs, with faces redacted by the military, revealing bruises and cuts, and they appear far less dramatic than those released more than a decade ago.* (AP Images 2016; italics added)

AP Images devalues the information contained in the individual photographs by comparing each one to all the others, as well as by referring to the images taken at the Abu Ghraib prison as more "dramatic" (AP Images 2016). Another troubling aspect of the caption is that it fails to refer to the specificity of what each photograph depicts, making the five photographs which the AP added to its archive stand in for every type of photograph to be found in the PDF file. This generalized description not only fails to address the specificity of what can be seen in the file; it also fails to frame the images with reference to torture practices, or to include a critique of how the file conceals the perpetrators, hides the staging apparatus, and contributes to the ongoing impunity of those involved in the global torture network. The AP positions these photographs as news images – by providing information about how they were published – but by emphasizing their genericity, it also contributes to the reading of them as non-specific stock photographs.

We should not disregard the importance of the caption, and the image bank's infrastructure, when considering the news coverage of this image event. Whereas it might appear that such image banks merely provide a starting point for journalists, who will then undertake further research, the ways in which news agencies frame images, and the issues they emphasize in their captions, often co-determine the manner in which the news media report on the photographs. Significantly, many newspapers subscribe to news wire services like AP or Reuters, and these companies often act as the first source of information for the papers' daily business. As Zeynep Gürsel writes in her book *Image Brokers: Visualizing World News in the Age of Digital Circulation*, "[w]ire services (such as AP and Reuters) would transmit images of a significant event to their subscriber base of mostly daily publications over the wires" (Gürsel 2016, 56). Beyond this, their choice of images also contributes to what will come to be regarded in the future as an important event. Gürsel is primarily interested in the role of image brokers in shaping the daily news, and by describing them as figures who undertake "acts such as commissioning, evaluating, licensing, selling, editing, and negotiating" (Gürsel 2016, 2), she demonstrates that their roles go beyond that of mere intermediaries – they must also decide which news is worthy of forwarding to their clients, and frame how certain images will be read in the future. By being added to the AP's image bank, the pages from the PDF file, and their interpretation, become framed by the news wire infrastructure and its actors. Gürsel is right to point out that "[n]ews images are fundamentally shaped by the infrastructures of representation in which they are produced and circulated" (Gürsel 2016, 309).

Recalling the critical role played by the news media in reframing McCoy's photographs depicting the arrival of the detainees at Guantánamo, the ensuing discussions about them as revealing techniques of sensory deprivation, abuse, and brutality, and press speculation that the DoD had violated international law (see Chapter 1), it may be surprising that the media discourses which initially followed the publication of the PDF file failed to engage critically with what the 2016 photographs depict. The initial responses by the ACLU, PHR, and the news media were dominated by the observation that the DoD had sidestepped the order to publish photographs that would actually prove the abuse of detainees. Furthermore, the news media failed to research and describe the photographs in the file appropriately. The discussions initiated by their release thus appear to conform to the manner in which the DoD no doubt wished these photographs to be read: *as generic, non-specific images which are unrelated to torture*. Significantly, many articles covering the publication event largely focused on the legal or procedural aspects of the ACLU lawsuit, and often speculated about photographs still being withheld by the DoD. Hence, the media interest did not lie in the photographs themselves, or their relationship to torture. Instead, the articles expressed the desire to see something else.

For example, writing in *The New York Times*, Charlie Savage stated that "[t]he pictures, taken more than a decade ago during the Bush administration, consist largely of close-up views of scrapes and bruises on detainees' bodies" (Savage 2016). He went on to mention the number of photographs withheld from the public, and to reconstruct the course of the lawsuit as well as the certification process. His article frames the photographs in a way which made them seem irrelevant, with their publication just serving as a distraction from the "really serious" photographs which showed the "real" consequences of the abuse. To lend strength to his argument, Savage paraphrases Jaffer who stated that "the 'selective disclosure' of the presumably more innocuous photographs should not be a distraction from what was still being concealed" (Savage 2016). The article and statement it paraphrased suggest that the published photographs were only useful in pointing us towards other photographs; the images themselves do not contain information that is of forensic value, or which would contribute to the ongoing torture debate.

We find a similar argument in an article published by the PHR, which cited Iacopino's statement that "[t]hese photos fail to show a single act of abuse which the government's own records describe as having taken place," and who further commented on the release as follows:

> The failure to release virtually any image responsive to the ACLU's request is tantamount to obstruction of justice. There was widespread and systematic torture and ill-treatment of detainees in military custody, as our investigations have previously shown. The release of those photos could shed light on one of the darkest chapters in US history. The public has a right to see all the photos and to know what was done in its name. (Iacopino as cited in PHR 2016)

Here again, the reader's attention is directed towards areas of obscured knowledge, and the published images are discredited as not providing sufficient proof of what was actually going on in Iraq, Afghanistan, Guantánamo, and CIA black sites. *Newsweek* and other newspapers appear to have been caught up in similar rhetoric, where the value of the published photographs was belittled, clean torture was not raised once, and the focus lay on the lawsuit and on what the public could not access.

Nevertheless, Lauren Walker, in her article, "The Pentagon Released 200 Images of Detainee Abuse in Iraq and Afghanistan," went into slightly more detail about what the photographs actually reveal, stating that "[t]he images, some of which are partially redacted to conceal identities, show alleged injuries sustained by detainees through harsh treatment while in US military custody" (Walker 2016). However, once again the emphasis lay on the images being "benign" (Walker 2016), as she cited a DoD spokesman saying. In contrast to the news media coverage of the publication of the first photographs from the Guantánamo detention camp in 2002, none of the articles about the PDF file appeared to be interested in the particularities of these photographs, or in investigating whom they depict and where they were taken. This was despite the fact that the same anonymous DoD spokesman reportedly stated that these images pertained to 14 substantiated, and 42 unsubstantiated allegations. He added that "[f]rom those cases with substantiated allegations, 65 service members received some form of disciplinary action. The disciplinary actions ranged from letters of reprimand to life imprisonment, and of the 65 who received disciplinary action, 26 were convicted at courts-martial" (Walker 2016).

The small amount of research that initially went into contextualizing the images also resulted in the dissemination of misinformation. For instance, the

BBC stated that "[n]one of the photos released on Friday involved detainees held in Abu Ghraib or at the US detention facility at Guantánamo Bay, Cuba, the Pentagon said" (BBC News 2016). While it may be true that none of the photographs were taken at Guantánamo (although we cannot be sure, since not all the case numbers mentioned in the images are searchable), it is certainly wrong that none of the detainees whose pictures were published were imprisoned in Abu Ghraib. As my own research has uncovered, some of the photographs directly refer to investigations conducted at that notorious prison. For example, pages 34 and 35 of the PDF file show two black and white photographs depicting a male leg in close-up (DoD 2016, 34 and 35). In one, the man holds a pen against his leg, on which it is not possible to see any bruises. My search in the ACLU's *Torture Database* of the case number visible in the right upper corner of the page, and below the photograph itself – "0222-04-CID259-80256" – led me to a medical report from June 20, 2004, concerned with a leg injury suffered by a prisoner at the Abu Ghraib prison (US Department of Administration 2004b). The summary of this document in the ACLU database reveals that "[t]he detainee states that he was captured by American forces in Baghdad, Iraq and was hit on the head with a rifle butt and kicked in the legs by a soldier during capture and once in custody. The medical report did not find any signs of injury" (ACLU 2005). Another image, on page 60 of the PDF file, was also taken at the Abu Ghraib prison (DoD 2016, 60). It depicts a detainee lifting up his shirt to reveal his back. According to the investigation, there was "sufficient evidence to prove the offense of Aggravated Assault and Cruelty, and Mistreatment did not occur as alleged" (US Army Criminal Investigation Command 2005a, 1) while the detainee was being transported from Al Baghdadi via the Baghdad International Airport to the Abu Ghraib prison.

These initial responses thus appear to align themselves with how the DoD wanted these photographs to be perceived by the public. Rather than reading the images as depicting traces of abuse, or as documenting specific persons in specific locations with specific histories and stories, the initial responses interpreted the PDF file as an unreadable inventory of arbitrarily chosen photographs. Furthermore, the online media descriptions of the photographs appeared to emphasize their lack of significance. Rather than researching the origins of the images to discover the traces of abuse and torture they contain, the aforementioned news media articles focused on what they believed the images failed to reveal: another scandal like Abu Ghraib. Sekula is thus right to point out that archives introduce an "*abstract visual equivalence* between pictures" (Sekula 2003, 445). In the context of the PDF file, I would go even further and argue that the file establishes an abstract visual equivalence not only between the photographs, but also between the traces of abuse and the affected individual lives. The file contributes to the construction of what I have called the image of a "generalized body" of the detainees in Chapter 3, presenting these highly specific photographs in a way which led them to be read as generic, indistinct, polysemic stock images. Like the online repositories of image banks, the PDF is a digital infrastructure which increased the polysemy of the photographs, and set their varying contents in relation to each other – and thus yet again concealed the torture, its victims, and its perpetrators.

Negating the historical dimension of these images and their relationship to torture, as well as the particularity of the affected lives and the identities of the perpetrators, led a wide range of actors to an apparently contradictory reading of the photographs: on the one hand, the publication of the file was a news event worthy of reporting; on the other, it consisted of generic, non-specific, and indistinguishable images – belonging to an imaginary world without torture – that were not, in themselves, news.

Reframing Indistinct Photographs

Reification and the Alienated Perception of Torture Victims

The US government's response to the court order requiring it to reveal knowledge that it had initially sought to suppress serves to hinder rather than aid the public's understanding of the realities experienced by people detained in extra-territorial facilities in the post-9/11 era. Following the release of the 198 torture photographs, Jaffer remarked that, rather than being a valuable source which could inform the ongoing debate about torture, the PDF file "forces you to ask what might be in the other photos that are still being withheld" (as cited in Savage 2016). Whereas the photographs "show individuals with injuries of various severity," the actual question raised by the file is: "[w]hat's in the 1,800 photographs the government still hasn't released?" (Jaffer as cited in Savage 2016). Presenting a collection of apparently indistinguishable images of bruised body parts also had a significant impact on future readings of the photographs, and considering the remarks made by PHR, rather than revealing acts of abuse, the PDF file appears to gather "indistinct images of bodies" (PHR 2016), or reified body parts with minor contusions and abrasions. The notion of "reification," widely discussed within Marxist criticism of capitalist value production and its consequences for the relationship between people in a society, can help us reach an understanding of both of the review process undertaken by Secretary Carter to find "'representative sample[s]'" (*ACLU v. DoD* 2017, 04. Civ 4161 (AKH), 13), on the one hand, and the logic behind publishing forensic and medical images, on the other. As I argue in this subsection, the distribution of the 198 photographs contributed to the reification of the detainees via photographic and administrative procedures. With regard to the perception of the file, I will also introduce another, closely related term: "alienation." I will argue that the visual representation of the detainees' bodies and the format in which the DoD published these photographs hinder the viewer's ability to establish a meaningful relationship with the people these images depict, and hence encourage the viewer to adopt an alienated perception of them.

I have already discussed the issue of reification as denial of recognition in the final section of Chapter 1. Here, I will look at the phenomenon of reification as understood by Georg Lukács, on whose writings Axel Honneth based his interpretation of reification as the forgetfulness of recognition (Honneth 2008; Lukács 1972). In his chapter entitled "Reification and the Consciousness of the Proletariat," Lukács remarks that the birth of modern capitalism led the commodity become the dominant model which governs both the world of people, and the world of things (Lukács 1972, 86). He writes that

> [t]he commodity can only be understood in its undistorted essence when it becomes the universal category of society as a whole. Only in this context does the reification produced by commodity relations assume decisive importance both for the objective evolution of society and for instance for the stance adopted by men towards it. Only then does the commodity become crucial for the subjugation of men's consciousness to the forms in which this reification finds expression and for their attempts to comprehend the process or to rebel against the disastrous effects and to liberate themselves from the servitude to the 'second nature' so created. (Lukács 1972, 86)

According to Lukács, our relationship with commodities influences our relationship to society as a whole, as well as our relationship to ourselves, to others, and to labor – all of which have been subject to major changes since the rise of capitalism. This redefined relationship between people and things, people and people, and individuals and society, all being based on the logic of commodities, leads to the reification of areas of life which were previously excluded from, or were never intended to become embedded in, such market-oriented logic.

The idea of alienation, to which I will come later, and the "*contemplative* nature of man under capitalism" (Lukács 1972, 97), where people observe each other rather than engage with each other in a meaningful way, as Lukács puts it, might indeed help us to understand the kind of relationship which the PDF file establishes between the viewer and the photographs, as well as the nature of the exchange taking place between these two entities. Lukács remarks that "the subject of the exchange is just as abstract, formal and reified as its object" (Lukács 1972, 105), which might explain the difficulties I experienced when trying to locate and define the particular subjects and objects involved in the exchange processes in relation to the PDF file. However, to think about the PDF file in terms of exchange – in the most basic sense, an exchange of information – requires us to reflect on the identity of the subjects involved in this exchange, and, maybe even more importantly, to ask the question: what is the actual "thing" which is being exchanged?

In the framework of contemporary service economies, it is clear that not only inanimate, material things are subject to exchange. The search for new places to conquer or commodify led capitalist structures to rediscover or recontextualize the human body, and what it can do and provide, as potential capital. As Oliver Decker and Lea Schumacher argue in "Körperökonomien: Zur Kommodifizierung des menschlichen Körpers" (Eng. "Body Economies: About the Commodification of the Human Body"), the border between the human body and the world of things is being constantly relocated, meaning that the status of neither the object nor the subject is stable or secure (Decker and Schumacher 2014, 14). Thinking about photography and archival practices as processes which are closely related to the economy of information exchange also requires us to reflect on the relationship between photographs as exchangeable goods, and the archive as an economic frame which enables such an exchange. In "Reading an Archive: Photography Between Labor and Capitalism," Sekula observes that not only is photography embedded in economies – for instance, by selling photographs or photographic services, but that photography also "constructs an *imaginary economy*" (Sekula 2003, 444) in its own right. More specifically, his reflection on how archives can be seen to produce certain territories of images brings us closer to an understanding of the way in which archival practices might colonize and occupy photographic works in terms of land or territory:

> Archives, then, constitute a *territory of images*: the unity of an archive is first and foremost that imposed by ownership. Whether or not photographs in a particular archive are offered for sale, the general condition of archives involves the subordination of use to the logic of exchange. Thus not only are pictures *literally* for sale, but their meanings are up for grabs. (Sekula 2003, 444)

Building on Sekula's reflections, I argue that one of the central operations of the DoD's image archive is to increase the semantic availability, or polysemy, of photographs. In this reading, establishing the *"territory of images"* (Sekula 2003, 444) frees the 198 photographs from their contextual specificity: from the initial context of their production and distribution, as well as from their relationship to specific acts of abuse. This operation of de-contextualization or "liberation" is, according to Sekula, also "a loss, an *abstraction* from the complexity and richness of use, a loss of context" (Sekula 2003, 444). Although such liberation might be productive – for instance, for artists – in the case of the PDF file, it must be seen as a horrendous and violent loss because "[t]his *semantic availability* of pictures in archives exhibits the same abstract logic as that which characterizes goods in a market place" (Sekula 2003, 444). The loss of context and abstraction imposed on the 198 photographs is what strikes me the most – the sudden semantic availability of these images shifts their function from providing evidence of specific cases of abuse to illustrating an imaginary world without torture. Furthermore, creating the PDF file as an archive not only stripped the pictures of their specific contexts, it also violently relocated the border between the human body and the world of things, attributing object-like properties to the human lives captured by the photographic camera.

Beyond the difficulty of reconstructing the contextual specificity of the photographs, a close analysis of the PDF file through the prism of reification shows another problematic perceptual phenomenon. The reification processes initiated by the DoD's certification of the photographs and its publishing practices also encourage those who encounter these images to adopt an alienated perception of the people depicted in them. What I mean by this is that a feeling of involvement in, and a critical view on, what we are seeing may be overwritten by, or superimposed with, a more uninvolved or even detached perceptual attitude. Whereas commodity fetishism brings inanimate "things" to life, the PDF file's translation of intersubjective relations to relations between people and things does exactly the opposite: the images, and the format of their publishing, place the bodies of the detained men somewhere between the living and the dead; between the world of people and the world of things, without allocating them clearly to one side or the other.

Guy Debord's arguments about images, commodity fetishism, and the "Society of the Spectacle" (2006) are also productive for thinking about this torture archive. In "Separation Perfected," Debord observes that, in the so-called "Society of the Spectacle," "[i]mages detached from every aspect of life merge into a common stream, and the former unity of life is lost forever" (Debord 2006, 12). The glimpses or fragments of the bodies of the detainees and POWs in the PDF file conform to this thesis, not only insofar as fragmentation becomes the leading visual principle of the file; the single images also appear to follow the principle of fragmentation on the level of their composition. The close-up aesthetics, cropping of pages and photographs, redaction of individual features – all this creates the notion of a tortured body which is fragmented in itself, and which the viewer cannot even reassemble into a coherent whole, never mind attempt to recover the unity of the tortured lives. According to Debord, "[a]pprehended in a partial [or fragmented] way, reality unfolds in a new generality as a pseudo-world apart, solely as an object of contemplation" (Debord 2006, 12). It is telling that Debord, in his description of the role which images play in capitalist structures, then shifts his emphasis, arguing that "[t]he spectacle is not a collection of images," but, instead, "it is a social relationship between people that is mediated by images" (Debord 2006, 12). In line with Debord's thesis, the collection of torture images in the PDF file functions as a diversion from the possibility of establishing meaningful social relations – relations which would not take on "the fantastic form of a relation between things" (Marx 1990, 165), but which instead would lead to a meaningful relationship between two human subjectivities. For Debord, the whole purpose of the spectacle is to produce a sense of alienation – to ourselves, to our lives and work, as well to other people and society (Debord 2006, 14) – and the PDF file seems to enforce an alienated view of what and whom the photographs depict.

Rahel Jaeggi contributes an important qualification to the definition of "alienation" when she writes that alienation "is a concept with 'fuzzy edges'" (Jaeggi 2014, 3). Significantly, these fuzzy edges exist because we cannot entirely separate the phenomenon of alienation from such phenomena as reification, and "[t]hese 'impure' mixes make for a diverse field of phenomena that can be associated with the concept of alienation" (Jaeggi 2014, 4). Jaeggi also illustrates how difficult it has become to distinguish between "concepts such as reification, inauthenticity, and anomie [and that it] say[s] as much about the domain within which the concept operates as do the complicated relations among the various meanings it has taken on in both everyday and philosophical language" (Jaeggi 2014, 3). The idea of an alienated perception of the PDF file and its photographs, following Jaeggi's arguments, closely relates to the thesis that the DoD seeks to reify the bodies of the detained people via its use of photography, as well as by its archival and publishing practices. We should perceive this relationship as an "'impure' mix" (Jaeggi 2014, 4), and relate reification and alienation to each other, showing that not only are they characterized by fuzzy edges, but also that they reciprocally inform and influence each other. As Jaeggi writes:

> The depersonalization and reification of relations among humans, as well as of their relations to the world, counts as alienated insofar as these relations are no longer immediate but are instead (for example) mediated by money, insofar as they are not 'concrete' but 'abstract,' insofar as they are not inalienable but objects of exchange. (Jaeggi 2014, 4)

In contrast to Jaeggi's view, I have already argued in Chapter 1 that it is possible to think about media objects such as photographs in a non-alienating way since not every encounter with a person depicted in a photograph – that is, a person mediated to us via an image – necessarily implies a reified or alienated apprehension of this person. However, in the case of the PDF file, it appears to be more difficult to comprehend the relationship between myself, as the viewer, and the lives of the detained persons who were photographed as concrete rather than abstract.[8]

8   Even though some of the close-ups are very concrete, they have an alienating and abstracting effect by obscuring the referent. / What I have previously described as the commodification of areas which were previously excluded from the logic of capitalistic

The idea of fragmentation is present in Jaeggi's thoughts not just in the description of the alienated perception of other people, but also of oneself. Although she is actually describing the division of labor, and the fact that the worker cannot overview the entire process of which they are a part of – a situation which certainly applies to the position of the torturer, who stands at the very end of a large torture network they cannot oversee – Jaeggi's thesis also relates to the fragmentation of the whole human being, which can be understood to be the living selfhood of a person captured in these torture photographs. Following Debord, if the world created by media objects and fragmented views of reality is only a "pseudo-world," it appears that the world presented to us in the PDF file must also be an alienated one (Debord 2006, 12). If we acknowledge the fact that media objects like this file have the ability to create worlds – at least, imaginary worlds – then it becomes crucial to see the incomprehensible nature and the lack of context of the world this file creates as striving to alienate the potential viewer from the real circumstances depicted in its photographs: that is, to ensure that the torture, its victims, and its perpetrators are all rendered invisible. The fragmentation of the detainees' bodies, as well as the fragmentary view of the consequences of torture, thus create a world to which the outside viewer – someone who has not been directly affected, or who does not belong to the military or intelligence apparatus – can relate to only on a minimal level.

The PDF file thus functions as an inventory of reified, indistinct body parts which appear to have lost their connection to the individual lives to which they belong, and which have also been stripped of their individuality by means of comparison, and the equalizing function of archival practices. The political and legal consequences of the confusion over what these photographs reveal, the experiences they capture, and the particular lives they depict, is that this form of visibility conceals what the images are actually documenting and, once again, hides the identities of the perpetrators. By stripping these photographs of their initial contexts, and their connection to the experience of torture by the victims, the DoD not only hinders the epistemic capabilities of the viewer; it also seeks to remove the possibility of us relating to the affected lives in a meaningful way. Furthermore, considering the dominant justification narrative of torture, the way in which these images were published was intended to prevent a disturbance or irritation in the state-governed narrative, where torture is presented as a justifiable means to an end, and the lives of torturers are discussed as lives which must be protected from prosecution.

market exchange also finds expression in Jaeggi's analysis of the various phenomena of alienation when she writes that "[t]he commodification of goods or domains that were previously not objects of market exchange is an example of alienation" (Jaeggi 2014, 4f.). For Jaeggi, it is what she terms "[t]he claim that bourgeois society, dominated by relations of equivalence" that "destroys the uniqueness of things and of human beings, destroys their particularity and nonfungibility" (Jaeggi 2014, 5).

The reification of the bodies of the detainees and the alienated perception of them propagated by these torture photographs make it difficult for the viewer to recognize the depicted individual as "a life that will have been lived" (Butler 2009, 15). In other words, the way in which the DoD distributed the photographs in this single PDF file reduced, or even obliterated, the perception of what I will call in the next subsection the "narrative quality" of the depicted lives. In this particular case, Susan Sontag's argument that photographs are unable to "explain anything," and are, instead, "inexhaustible invitations to deduction, speculation, and fantasy" (Sontag 2008, 23), finds its perfect expression – reflected in the difficulty of understanding the contextual specificity of these photographs, and the particularity of the photographically captured lives.

Photographs Telling Stories of Grievable Lives

As I have argued so far, the reifying qualities of the PDF file result in a perceptual situation in which the relationship between the viewer and the depicted lives takes on an abstract form, while the manner in which the photographs were distributed makes it difficult for the viewer to relate to these lives in a meaningful way. I will explore this idea further by shifting the focus from the discussion of the reifying qualities of the PDF file to how these reification processes hinder the viewer's understanding of the depicted subjects as "'narrated life'" (Kristeva 2001, 6). Whereas the ACLU, as I will show, focused on the stories behind the photographs, in this section I will exemplify how we, the broader public, can come to comprehend these photographs as telling stories of grievable and tellable lives by recourse to the stories told by the victims themselves, if such stories are accessible to us. Thus, I will demonstrate how we can oppose the way in which the PDF file strips the detained men of their biographies, and can instead inscribe, at least discursively, a narrative quality back into the photographs. The act of telling or writing the stories behind these torture photographs or the people depicted in them is, nevertheless, inevitably embedded in the broad field of pre-existing storytelling connected to the use of torture post-9/11 which has been constructed during the 21 years. Such stories about state-regulated torture and its necessity (or unacceptability) have been told in a wide variety of formats, including news reporting, soldiers' testimonies, detainees' biographies, and interviews, as well as in fiction and documentary films. The effort to tell or narrate the violence to which the photographs of the PDF file refer, and to render visible what was deliberately withheld by the DoD at the moment of the PDF file's publication, always "answers … to other stories and other forms of storytelling" (Schuff and Seel 2016b, 7; my translation), and is, by necessity, related to the broad discursive formation of stories which have already been told. Thus, every effort to add another view on torture – for instance, by embedding these 198 photographs in their initial production contexts, and restoring the narratives, or the narrative quality, of the affected lives which have been hidden from the public – is always connected, in one way or another, to a "mesh of stories and counter-stories" which can be "so dense that it is often unclear to which other stories ... and in which ways a certain storytelling reacts" (Schuff and Seel 2016b, 7; my translation).

To return to the vocabulary I have used so far in this book, we might call these stories and narratives *frames*. Thus, what I will propose here is an *ethical reframing* of one of the photographs by introducing a counter-story. Significantly, as I have demonstrated in each of my chapters so far, counter-narratives or counter-stories – the respective reframings – relate to, and position themselves in response to, the more dominant, state-regulated narratives. Thus, the critiques expressed in the reframing inevitably position themselves in relation to these state-produced and regulated frames, too. This is important to acknowledge, since it reveals that reframing as a form of critique does not, and cannot, entirely escape the already existing web of storytelling; it always relates to this web, even when it is countering the dominant narrative.

Thinking again about the discursive distinction between the value of the lives of US citizens and government employees, on the one hand, and the lives of detainees, on the other, and how this discrepancy in value is part of the larger justification narrative of torture, it seems crucial to reiterate here that the PDF file not only stripped the photographs of their contextual specificity, leading them to become abstract, but that it has also hollowed out their narrative qualities. As Hannah Arendt incisively observed, human lives not only constitute events; these lives are "full of events" themselves, events "which ultimately can be told as a story, establish a biography" (Arendt 1998, 97). In view of Arendt's reflections on "tellable lives" – that is, on lives which constitute events that then can be, and are, told as stories – it is important to note how the DoD blurred the knowledge that these torture photographs relate to specific lives and to their events, stories, and biographies, and how this hindered the viewer's ability to perceive these lives as tellable lives; lives which have been injured and should be grieved. Regarding Butler's observation on the narrative quality of lives which presupposes such lives to be grievable, working to re-establish the connection of these photographs to the stories of the detainees and POWs depicted in them and then retelling their stories is essential to understanding the gravity of what the PDF file shows, and the violence which was inflicted on the depicted persons (Butler 2009, 15).

Thus, the manner in which the DoD increased the polysemy of these 198 torture photographs to conceal the perpetrators and hinder the viewer's ability to comprehend the experiences of the detainees and POWs has yet another consequence, one which was possibly unforeseen by the DoD.

Specifically, the many ways in which these images can be read, and also the fact that, in some cases, we can find information indicating the initial context pertaining to what they are documenting, means that we – the viewers of the PDF file – can render visible and critically engage with the violent torture practices conducted by the US forces abroad. That some of my colleagues and I have become emotionally engaged by these photographs, despite the fact that, in the beginning, we were not able to understand them, shows that the DoD's operations can, and actually have, failed to secure the way in which these images are perceived. In this subsection, I will expand on this idea of failed frames, and show how we, the viewers, can break with the normative logic in which these images were published, and instead choose our own frames to help us comprehend the gravity of what the PDF file is showing, and tell the stories to which these photographs refer. I believe that such minor media objects like this PDF file, if discussed in an appropriate way, have the ability to disrupt the normativity of the dominant torture narrative and, more specifically, the justification narrative of torture. One feature that can help us in this endeavor is the fact that the PDF file has not been framed by any particular narrative put forth by the DoD. This suggests that the file is located on the edges of what I have described as the web of government-driven storytelling about torture. It also means that, in contrast to Bigelow's film, the photographs are open to be re-read as images which tell stories of tellable lives by being embedded in further narrative forms.

The ACLU's reaction to these photographs provides an important case study in which an initially failed reading was followed by a more complex re-reading of these photographs. Initially, in line with the news coverage at the time, they failed to appropriately discuss what these photographs actually document. However, only one week later, the ACLU revised its stance and published the results of its research into the original contexts of the photographs. In the first ACLU article commenting on the photographs, entitled "Pentagon Releases 198 Abuse Photos in Long-Running Lawsuit: What They Don't Show Is a Bigger Story," the ACLU argued that the bigger and more important story was the photographs which continued to by withheld by the DoD (Relman 2016a). To lend strength to this argument, Eliza Relman referred to three photographs which the Pentagon was continuing to withhold, and described the abuse as follows:

> The photos still being withheld include those related to the case of a 73-year-old Iraqi woman detained and allegedly sexually abused and assaulted by US soldiers. According to the Army report detailing the incident, the soldiers forced her to 'crawl around on all-fours as a 'large man rode' on her,' striking her with a stick and calling her an animal. Other pictures depict an Iraqi teenager bound and standing in the headlights of a truck immediately after his mock execution staged by US soldiers.

Another shows the body of <u>Muhamad Husain Kadir</u>, an Iraqi farmer, shot
dead at point-blank range by an American soldier while handcuffed.
(Relman 2016a)

The names or descriptions of the subjects who were victims of abuse were
hyperlinked in the article to reports which further detailed their torture. A
69-page report on the abuse of the Iraqi woman, for example, is accessible by
clicking on the underlined blue passage in Relman's article (US Army Criminal Investigation Command 2004). The ACLU also made easily accessible
the charge sheet which meticulously describes how the US soldiers staged
a young man's mock execution on June 22, 2003 (US Department of Administration 2003). Therein, we can read the summaries of witness statements,
such as "[I] [h]eard a 'pop' like a shot, saw thru NVGs [night-vision devices]
██████████ holster his weapon, and saw detainee face down on the ground,
hands over his head, sounded like he was crying, at a distance of about 10 feet.
Did not hear or see anything like a dog" (US Department of Administration
2003, 4). The perpetrator admitted to scaring the young man and stated that
"██████████ told him to scare the detainees, and let all three go after they
cried. Admits discharging the round to scare the detainees" (US Department of
Administration 2003, 5).

The first ACLU article thus discusses at length the stories behind the
photographs we cannot see, describing them in much more detail than the
ones related to the photographs which had actually been published. In light
of the violence rendered visible by the hyperlinked documents, this is an
important acknowledgment of the scope of violence and torture committed
by the US troops abroad. However, at the same time, the narrative put forward by the article is problematic, because it disregards the value of the
published photographs. Furthermore, Relman writes that "[s]uppressing the
most powerful evidence of our government's abuses makes confronting those
abuses impossible" (Relman 2016a), a statement which – when considering the
photographs which were actually published, and the way in which I read them
as traces of clean torture – is not only problematic, but in need of revision.
Some of the published photographs are undeniably directly connected to
torture practices. However, it is not the PDF file which renders this connection
visible, instead, it was ACLU's re-reading of these photographs one week after
their initial response which made this connection explicit, and it is our task as
viewers to deepen this connection.

Approximately one week after their first article, the ACLU published the
results of their efforts to place some of the photographs in their original contexts, and revised their initial statement that these images failed to show the
abuse of detainees (Relman 2016b). This second article, published on February
11, 2016, with the title "The Stories Behind the Government's Newly Released
Army Abuse Photos," argues that, despite the fact that the photographs do

not show the grave physical consequences of abuse – such as open wounds or large scars – the PDF file and its photographs still present us with a way to critically engage with torture (Relman 2016b). In this article, Relman comments on the fact that "[t]he government didn't provide any information about the human beings depicted or the contexts in which they were photographed," and notes that "[t]he photos … mostly show close-ups of body parts – arms, legs, and heads, many with injuries. There are also wider shots of prisoners, most of them bound or blindfolded" (Relman 2016b). In spite of this, however, and mirroring the ACLU's previous efforts to render visible the knowledge about photographs withheld from the general public, this second article also discussed what the ACLU was able to learn from the seemingly unspecific photographs in the PDF file.

ACLU employees connected 42 of the 198 photographs to 14 cases of abuse and to investigative reports in their *Torture Database* (ACLU 2022a). Although the article does not specify which 42 photographs they were able to trace, it reproduces a single photograph for each of the 14 cases, describing whom it depicts and the abuse they suffered, and providing a link to the investigation report for further context. Hence, whereas the first ACLU article provided readers with links to reports which had originally contained photographs documenting the abuse, but which were not published in the 2016 PDF file – that is, abuses which should also be acknowledged by the public despite the withheld photographs – the later article shows how some of the published photographs can actually be read as traces of abuse and torture in themselves.

Now, I will look in more detail at how the ACLU re-contextualized one particular photograph which depicts the sole of Khalid Samir al-Ani's foot [fig. 17], and expand their perspective on what kind of stories this photograph can tell its viewers. In the ACLU article, the page of the PDF file on which the photograph initially appeared is cropped, showing us only the photograph without the scarce accompanying information from the released scan. The article text provides us with the following description:

> This photo relates to the case of a 'high value' Iraqi detainee, who, according to a report by The Constitution Project, was Ibrahim Khalid Samir al-Ani, a Baathist intelligence officer wrongly accused of having met with 9/11 hijacker Mohammed Atta before the attacks. Al-Ani was captured by Joint Special Operations Command troops in July 2003. He told investigators that during his capture, he was forced to lie on his stomach in the back of a vehicle with his hands bound and head covered in a plastic bag. According to a letter al-Ani wrote, his captor 'put his foot on my back and started screaming and cursing me in English, which I do understand. And after 15 minutes, I felt that one side of my belly and thigh started to burn due to the heated air that was coming out of the car. And the back of my

feet started to burn. I asked the responsible to be careful but he did not care.' Al-Ani was subsequently hospitalized for three months for extensive burn injuries, which required skin grafts and the amputation of one finger. While Army investigators determined there was 'sufficient evidence to believe [al-Ani] was the victim of Assault and Cruelty and Maltreatment,' the investigation was ultimately dropped. (Relman 2016b)

This description includes the name of the abused man, his profession, the unsubstantiated allegations which led to his capture, and the torture he experienced. Importantly, the article cites al-Ani's description of how he was maltreated by his captors, and how this abuse caused extensive burns to his foot. In light of al-Ani's letter [fig. 18], and the ACLU's description, the viewer of the photograph can recognize the darker surfaces on the foot as a painful wound caused by US forces, and not merely as a dirt stain [fig. 17]. Hence, the abuse which was rendered invisible by increasing the polysemy of the photograph and making the circumstances it was documenting incomprehensible to the viewer, here becomes re-inscribed in the image. The victim, the act, and the experience of torture, as well as information about the perpetrators, are all revealed. In the final part of the ACLU's description of the photograph, we read about the terrible failure of the investigation into the episode of abuse the image testifies to, and the fact that, despite being able to prove that al-Ani was tortured, the investigation was dropped. This closing statement frames the way in which the ACLU intends the photograph and al-Ani's story to be understood by readers, and reveals that the failures of the US government go far beyond the failure to publish photographs pertaining to torture.

Relman's description of the photograph makes evident an idea which I would like to elaborate on further: in order to ethically engage with what and whom such photographs show, we must, whenever possible, highlight the perspectives of the people who have experienced the torture. The article mentions that al-Ani "*told* investigators that during his capture, he was forced to lie on his stomach in the back of a vehicle with his hands bound and head covered in a plastic bag" (Relman 2016b; italics added), which immediately confronts us with a perspective that is usually rendered invisible in DoD discourses: namely, that of the detained and tortured man. Nevertheless, even after reading this description, the image associated with this case, and the abuse endured by al-Ani, remains an incomplete one. Although the article provides the reader with a summary of the story behind the photograph, and shows how it in fact contains traces of the abuse suffered by al-Ani – *an abuse which failed to conform to the parameters of clean torture, and, hence, left severe traces on the victim's body* – the reader must undertake additional research to get a more comprehensive idea of the complexity and particularity of the person this photograph depicts and the abuse they suffered. I believe that recontextualizing photographic material by referencing the perspective of those who have suffered torture allows us to see past a reified body to a life which has been told by the person who was, and often still is, living it.

Importantly, however, as Butler writes in *Frames of War: When is Life Grievable?*, even if we apprehend someone as living, this does not necessarily mean that we also recognize this as a life (Butler 2009, 7f.). A life, according to Butler, is not something which simply exists and is encountered each time in the same manner. Instead, "a life is produced according to the norms by which life is recognized" (Butler 2009, 7). She argues that the narrative of "'this will be a life that will have been lived'" presupposes a grievable life; if there is no grievability, then

> there is no life, or, rather, there is something living that is other than life. Instead, 'there is a life that will never have been lived,' sustained by no regard, no testimony, and ungrieved when lost. The apprehension of grievability precedes and makes possible the apprehension of precarious life. Grievability precedes and makes possible the apprehension of the living being as living, exposed to non-life from the start. (Butler 2009, 15)

Hence, we can perceive the photograph of the burnt foot as tracing a figure of someone who is living, but not necessarily as a depiction of a life. To recognize a life as a grievable life also means to recognize its narrative quality. In the PDF file, the DoD has strictly regulated this narrative quality by stripping these images of their initial contexts as well as separating them from the testimonies of the injured detainees. However, as Butler makes clear, to understand the photographs as representations of grievable lives requires us not only to restore the initial context of these images, but also to reconstruct the narrative quality of the particular lives which are captured in them.

In spite of the DoD's strategic deployment of a context-less PDF file, I will now demonstrate how we can extend the efforts taken by the ACLU to re-inscribe grievability into the photographs of these seemingly reified body parts. Returning to Relman's article, clicking on the underlined passage, "the case of a 'high value' Iraqi detainee" (Relman 2016b), redirects us to the report from November 11, 2005, in which the US Army Criminal Investigation Command (2005b) reproduced al-Ani's letter. By reading al-Ani's letter, we can not only go behind the story of the associated photograph; we can also re-inscribe perspectives which are usually censored by the DoD. Reframing the photograph of the foot through the tortured man's personal storytelling allows us to emphasize an ethical understanding of the lives which have been injured, and acknowledge their complex biographies as stories of grievable lives.

The heavily redacted report with the subject line, "CID Report of Investigation – Final/SSI-0176-2004-CID259–90265/5C2B/5Y2E," begins with a summary of the investigation, stating that "there was sufficient evidence to believe Mr. ▮▮▮▮▮▮▮ was the victim of Assault and Cruelty and Maltreatment," "however, all investigative efforts to identify the specific Special Operations group or personnel responsible for the capture of Mr. ███████ met with negative results" (US Army Criminal Investigation Command 2005b, 2). The summary also lists the attachments, mentioning that al-Ani's letter was initially handwritten in Arabic on March 11, 2004, and then translated into English on that same day. It furthermore lists all the documents not contained in the report, including the "Compact Disc (CD), containing photographic images of Mr. ███████," on which the image published in the 2016 PDF file was probably initially stored (US Army Criminal Investigation Command 2005b, 3). The original handwritten letter was withheld "due to: Foreign Language" (US Army Criminal Investigation Command 2005b, 8). Although it is impossible to verify whether the English translation does justice to the original, this translation does allow us to encounter the particularity of al-Ani's story, and the complexity of his life before and after torture.

Al-Ani begins his letter with a thorough review of his legal status as a "Prisoner of War," and argues that this status does not apply to him since, as a Secret Service Officer, he was part of a "civil institute [which has] … no relationship whatsoever with the military work" (al-Ani 2004, 1). Thanks to his college degree in Law and Politics he was, as he mentions, able to review his status in accordance with the *Geneva Convention III*. After stating that he was never a soldier and never worked for the military, he continues with a detailed description of the way in which he was captured, how the coalition forces broke into his house, how his family begged the soldiers to treat him more carefully due to his medical condition, and how he was hit and subjected to hot vehicle exhaust gases which caused extensive burns to his body:

> 3 – on 2003/7/2, after midnight, the American forces engirded my house in Baghdad. When I heard the noise of the coalition powers, I asked my nephew to open the main door of the house and let them in without any resistance. But they broke into my house through different doors and I was captured without any resistance or refusal. And if I knew I was wanted by the American powers, I would have surrendered myself willingly and as soon as possible. I did not know the reason for my capture at the moment. I thought it would be a simple and conventional investigation. I thought that someone who does not really know me denounced me. And me being home on 2003/4/9 is a proof about my ignorance about all what was going around me. Everyone knew that I was home.
> 4 – when I was captured I was suffering from a tear on my capillary vessel and a blood thickening in my left leg. I could not walk. And the American responsible whom I do not know his name or rank treated me in a harsh way. My hands were fettered behind my back in a painful way, and they put a plastic case on my face despite my family's begging because I have chronicle asthma. I was pushed roughly to the car that was in front of

the house and was on the floor on my belly and my hand cuffed behind my back, plus the plastic bag on my face. I was wearing very light Iraqi clothes. When we got to the car, the same person put his foot on my back and started screaming and cursing me in English, which I do understand. And after 15 minutes, I felt that one side of my belly and thigh started to burn due to the heated air that was coming out of the car. And the back of my feet started to burn. I asked the responsible to be careful but he did not care. He started slapping me on my face, three times. I begged him on the name of God, Jesus and the Holly [sic][9] Bible to be careful but he refused. Due to the burns that I had, I turned on my back with my cuffed hands. They got burned badly too. And after an hour of driving we got to an unknown place. They got me off the car and I was in a bad shape. I could not walk. I fainted and I was taken to a small hospital by a jeep. I knew afterward that it was camp cropper [sic]. I was taken to a hospital close by on 2003/7/8. A helicopter took me and I was taken care of. After more than one month I woke up after being under anesthesia. (al-Ani 2004, 2f.)

Al-Ani describes how he was extracted from his home, and how his capture was witnessed by his nephew, who opened the door. The letter recounts the events of July 2, 2003, in great detail, and refers to al-Ani's medical history and to how his family begged the troops to be careful with the plastic bag they placed over his head due to his asthma and the imminent danger of suffocation. Al-Ani continues his letter by listing all the injuries he sustained at the hands of the unit which captured him, the many surgeries he went through, and his experience of hospitalization, as well as revealing the fact that he has no recollection of one month of his life due to being placed under anesthesia:

5 – I stayed there [in the small hospital] from 2003/7/8 to 2003/8/18 and after that I was taken to Ibn-Sina hospital, that the American forces has taken and used as [a] military hospital, and this was [sic] my injuries:
1 – the upper part of my thumb on my right hand was broken. They operated on me and they cut the upper part of my thumb and my nail.
2 – my forefinger of my right hand was burned and broken. They operated on me in order to fix it. It is still broke up till now and I cannot move it.
3 – I have small burns in my right hand arm.
4 – my left hand was broke[n] and I can not move it.
5 – my left hand palm was burned brutally. They did operate on it.
6 – the back of my left hand was burned. They did operate on it.
7 – the front side of my right and left leg was burned. They did operate on them.

---

9   I am consciously marking the errors in the citations from al-Ani's documents as the translator's or interviewer's errors.

8 – the front side of my right and left thigh was burned. They did operate on them.

9 – brutal burns on my belly. They did operate on it.

10 – my right and left ankles were burned badly.

6 – Due to all these burns, they had to cut big parts of my leg for the prosthetic surgeries. All this has left big scares [*sic*] and I suffered through the whole surgeries. I had more than 10 surgeries according to the people working at the hospital, because most of the surgery I had were under anesthesia. I also suffered physically and emotionally due to the operation and the bad marks that are all over my body. Despite all that I asked the hospital direction to stop the whole rehabilitation process and to send me to the camp. I was hoping that they would finish the investigations and let me go back to my family and normal life in order to get over all the physical and emotional pains. I was taken to the camp on 2003/10/17. (al-Ani 2004, 3)

The letter renders visible the violence which is only very partially expressed in the photograph that was published on February 5, 2016, and which was also not extensively discussed in its description provided by the ACLU on their webpage. Reading al-Ani's list allows us to imagine the enormous pain and suffering he had endured. He describes how he suffered major injuries to his right and left hands, including burns and broken bones, and how his leg and stomach were burnt so gravely that he required surgery. Furthermore, reading that parts of his leg had to be removed leaves us wondering whether it concerned the right foot pictured in the photograph, evoking a sense of mourning, and making us reflect on all the things he will no longer be able to do due to the severity of his injuries. Not only was al-Ani abused and mistreated, his description also indicates how his perception of his body has changed due to all the surgeries he went through, and that the physical scars have also scarred him emotionally:

8 – the burns and the injuries that I have suffered from on top of my chronicle asthma slow me down and crippled me. I am not even able to do my private business by myself while I am in prison. I am relying all the time on my friends to help me do everything. Also, the burns and the multiple operations I have had made me depressed. The scars are extremely noticeable and will stay with me the rest of my life.

9 – besides all this suffering that I went through due to my capture and extreme injuries, I have lost my job. I have no way of making money, knowingly that I have a big family compounded of (two wives, 4 children, one of them is at the university, the others are in junior and high school, a sick and crippled mother, and two sisters) and I am their official and legal supporter and they have no one else to count on. (al-Ani 2004, 4)

The emphasis al-Ani places on his scars reveals that the photographs collected in the PDF file do indeed contain visible traces of torture practices. Here, the victim recalls in vivid detail how he will have to live in the future with the scars he has sustained as a constant reminder of the brutal maltreatment and disregard for his life and health which he experienced at the hands of the coalition forces. Furthermore, al-Ani's letter reveals that the foot which was so severely injured belongs to a man who is the sole provider of his large family, who is interested in law and politics, who was well aware of his legal situation, and of the unnecessary violence committed by the troops. It details the true extent of the bodily injuries he suffered, the psychological consequences of his maltreatment, and his desperation to get back to his family. Al-Ani's over-riding desire at the moment of writing the letter was to return to his "family and normal life in order to get over all the physical and emotional pains" (al-Ani 2004, 3). In his letter, he also expresses gratitude to the medical personnel who saved his life, and emphasizes their humanity, while also even going so far as to pardon the perpetrator:

> 10 – despite all these circumstances stated above, I have no problem about being captured. I think it is your right and you have to make sure about everything that has to do with your safety issues. But at the same time I would like you to know that I am innocent and I am very sure that I do not present any threat against you[r] coalition powers and the new situation in Iraq. In the two religions: Islam and Christianity, I believe that what happened was a destiny and God wants it to happen. Probably the person who captured me does know any better. Therefore, I do pardon and forgive him, especially after the outstanding job the people in the military hospital have done. They were very amazing and showed their beautiful human side. And I am proud of them for saving my life. Plus I am not asking for any physical or moral indemnity or compensation because I believe it is God's will and I am forgiving everyone for everything that happened to me.
>
> 11 – finally after this detailed letter about my legal rights, and about my health condition and familial situation, I am asking you kindly to help me and decide on my case. I want to go back to my family and be able to live with them and finish my rehabilitation program. I want to be able to take care of my family and spend the rest of my life helping at the [*sic*] building of the new Iraq. I will be a good citizen.
>
> And this is the ways on how you can help me,
>
> 1 – To speed up the legal procedures in order to take a final decision concerning my case, since I was captured since 2003/7/6, which makes it about eight months and a half.
>
> 2 – Or to grant me partial freedom and make sure that I would not leave the country. I will sign all the papers that you may think is necessary. And I will promise that I will abide by every word in it.

3 – I will promise you that I would not be the source of any form of trouble and I will be able to do my best to help building the new Iraq, and I will be very active in doing so.

I have already sent a similar letter to all the responsibles. You can check my medical record and the pictures that were taken of me one day after I was captured and also the pictures that were taken of me at the hospital. Or you can just come and see me and check my medical file at Ibn-Sina hospital.

Yours respectfully,

███████████

(Prisoner of War)

Number ███████████

2004/2/11. (al-Ani 2004, 4f.)

Here, despite the proof of torture, al-Ani is waiving his right to hold the perpetrators accountable. We can only speculate that this might be due to his knowledge that the coalition forces will try to protect "their own," and hence might continue to imprison him indefinitely. Importantly, during his initial questioning, al-Ani was asked to describe the soldier who put him in the vehicle:

Q. can you describe the soldier who placed you in the truck x help you down [sic]?

A. A person of a white skin, around 184 centimeters. Easy moving body and of sport like body, and after he arrested me and while riding in the car I saw him wearing a white prescription eye glasses, has a white metal frame. Of a long face... has no hair in his front upper head.

Q. do you know what military unit or branch of service the soldier who captured you were in?

A. No. but later I learned from a manager in the camp that he is from the navy [.]

Q. Who told you that and when?

A. Sergeant ███████████, he was responsible of camp Cropper [sic] management in the date of my detention, and he took pictures of all my injuries and store them in the camp's computer and he is a member of (MP 115) [.]

Q. have you been abused in any way since the night you were captured?

A. Absolutely no. (al-Ani 2005, 32f.)

In view of the immense legal and political efforts undertaken by the Bush administration to secure the impunity of the perpetrators of torture, al-Ani's letter appears to be an acknowledgment of the fact that, if he wants to return to his family, he will be forced one way or another – for example, by the threat of having his imprisonment extended – to drop his charges against the US soldier. In spite of the fairly detailed description of his abuser provided by al-Ani, and the fact that the US military meticulously tracks the movements of all its troops, the investigation was ultimately dropped. This demonstrates how military structures have protected their employees from being charged with crimes or having to face disciplinary measures, since it is hard to imagine that, in the course of this investigation, the investigators could not identify who was responsible for al-Ani's maltreatment, abuse, and torture.

The complex image drawn by al-Ani in his letter – about his life prior to his capture, about the pain and suffering caused by his torture, and the medical care he subsequently received – re-inscribes into the photograph the story which the DoD tried to obliterate at the time of the file's publication: namely, of a life that was gravely injured and must be grieved. It also reinforces the fact that we must hold both the US government and the perpetrators of torture to account for the violence inflicted upon the lives of the people detained in its GWoT. The perspective deemed by the DoD to be "impermissible to show" (Butler 2009, 73), which was invisibilized by stripping this image of al-Ani's foot of its initial context, can be rendered visible again and used as a frame to oppose the reading enforced upon us by the DoD and its publishing practices. Although photographs and written words are citable and can be reiterated, copied, and multiplied as many times as desired, it is our responsibility to describe and position the context-less photographs published in 2016 in a way that reflects on the injustice and various losses they represent, as well as on the precariousness and grievability of the lives they depict. By citing al-Ani's letter in such an extensive manner, I have shown that it is not just the type of frames we choose which is significant when we perceive images like the photograph of Al-Ani's burnt foot; *it is also the approach we take to citation itself*.

Journalists and scholars alike display a tendency to narrow down perspectives and omit passages they deem to be less relevant, and this can contribute to the fragmentary ways in which we come to comprehend particular stories of injustice and torture. I have argued above that the photographic practices of the DoD led the bodies of the detainees and POWs to become fragmented, and that this fragmentation can be seen as the major technique deployed by the Department to create a fragmented view of reality, concealing the victims and their experiences of torture, and hiding the perpetrators. Hence, it is very important to avoid reproducing this technique in our own approaches to the citation of stories like the one told by al-Ani in his letter. Every word in al-Ani's letter is relevant, as well as every part of his story. We should not only focus on the failure of the criminal investigation, but also indicate the future consequences of his maltreatment.

Reframing this initially context-less photograph of a burnt foot with the stories told by the person to whom this foot belongs to is a way of opposing the equalizing functions of the PDF file. By making the testimonies and letters of those who have been affected by torture a lens through which we perceive the stories told by the photographs, we begin to hear the stories as told by grievable lives, and can partially succeed in de-reifying the bodies captured in the photographs, as well as countering the alienated perception of them introduced by the PDF file. Moreover, by revealing the stories behind these images, we can position them as a response to what I have called the broader justification narrative of torture, and oppose the ways in which the DoD sought to level the historic dimension and neutralize the power of the images so that they would not disturb the narrative deployed to justify the use of torture. However, it is also important to acknowledge that, although a reframing with the victims' stories contributes to the plurality of perspectives, such readings are far from being the dominant ones. Despite the critical potential of such actions, it is still difficult to completely disrupt the broader justification narrative of torture which has been shaped by so many actors over the past 21 years.

To conclude, these 198 torture photographs depict lives full of events, and establishing their biographies depends upon our choice of frames. These frames should re-inscribe in the photographs the narrative quality of the affected lives that was stripped away from them. This does not mean that the frames should only emphasize the parts of the story that we, the images' viewers, can relate to; it also means revealing how these lives are told by those who lived them, with all their inherent complexities. For example, we should not censor the fact that al-Ani was an intelligence officer under Saddam Hussein, or that he worked for the Iraqi Secret Service, even though this information runs the danger of becoming weaponized in the framework of the justification narrative of torture. A "tellable life" means a complex life – a life which can be, and has been, told in many different ways. The question of how we can come closer to reaching an understanding of the experience of torture by following the victims' "testimonies along with their silence and stutter" (Köthe 2020, 69; my translation) should also be asked with regard to indistinct images. These photographs are not able to explain their contexts by means of their surfaces alone. Only when they are reframed through stutters, inconsistencies, and the desires expressed by the people they depict can they come to be understood not only as torture photographs, but also as images which tell stories of tellable and grievable lives.

Summary and Conclusion

In his *Philosophical Investigations*, Ludwig Wittgenstein asks whether "an indistinct photograph [is] a picture of a person at all?" and whether "it [is] even always an advantage to replace an indistinct picture by a sharp one? Isn't the indistinct one often exactly what we need?" (Wittgenstein 1986, 34). These questions (the third of which is simultaneously an affirmative statement) summarize what I have set out to demonstrate in this chapter. Following the publication of the PDF file, the public debates about the 198 photographs questioned their forensic value, emphasizing the fact that human rights organizations and news media were neither able to recognize the persons depicted in them, nor to detect the type of significant injuries which the public expects to see in torture images. Various organizations went on to repeatedly express the wish to see photographs similar to the ones leaked in 2004, which revealed the brutal maltreatment of prisoners at the Abu Ghraib prison in Iraq. This wish directly relates to Wittgenstein's second question. I believe the expressed desire to replace the 198 indistinct, blurred, overexposed photographs with something which was already known is not only troubling; in view of Wittgenstein's third question-statement; it also failed to acknowledge that these 198 photographs are actually as important as those of the torture committed at the Abu Ghraib prison. This is because, as I have sought to make clear, thinking about these photographs, their contexts, and their frames helps us to revise the popular imagery of torture images burnt into our memories. These photographs are so important precisely because they trace what usually remains untraceable. Through them, we can listen to stories about injured lives which have been told by those living them, by people who are (now) grieved, despite the fact that their stories have been continuously erased from public discourse.

In the first section, I reconstructed the legal and political discourses on the techniques of clean torture deployed by democratic regimes, looking at the impunity of perpetrators under the Bush and Obama administrations. This set the broader frame for my detailed analysis of why, and how, the DoD published these photographs in 2016. By showing how the impunity of perpetrators was already embedded in the legal disputes about the definition of torture in the *US Code*, I illustrated that the ways the PDF file invisibilized torture actually prolonged a much older policy put into place in the aftermath of 9/11 (*18 US Code §§2340* (April 30, 1994)). Already, so-called "clean torture" had been designed to undermine the "*public monitoring of human rights*" (Rejali 2007, 8) and to make it impossible to use forensic and medical images to prove torture had been perpetrated. The way Bybee interpreted the definition of torture from the *18 US Code §§2340* added another layer to the US government's efforts to render torture and its consequences invisible (*18 US Code §§2340* (April 30, 1994); Bybee 2002). This was chiefly undertaken by making the perpetrator's intent and their perspective on what they had done a crucial element in the determination of whether or not an act amounted to torture, once again making the tortured person's perspective on the pain and suffering they endured invisible at the level of administration of justice. I went on to argue that the effort to ensure the impunity of the perpetrators and other actors, and to make it difficult for human rights lawyers and torture victims to hold the perpetrators accountable, was not restricted to the Bush presidency alone. By referring to various instances when Obama admitted that US forces had tortured the people which were detained in the course of the US GWoT, I demonstrated that rather than holding the perpetrators, politicians, and contractors to account for torture, his administration instead helped to co-shape "a legal framework for impunity" (Jaffer as cited in McCoy 2012, 245 and *The New York Times* 2009). During Obama's presidency, the US government promised that, despite acknowledging "past" wrongdoings, it would not punish – or reveal the names of – past, current, or future employees of its military and the CIA who were or would become responsible for torturing detainees and POWs.

This context helps us to understand the operations of the PDF file. All of these efforts to render the experiences of torture invisible, and to shield US government employees from prosecution for their involvement in the torture of detainees, were largely supported by different forms of storytelling that justified the violence inflicted upon the lives of POWs and detainees all over the world. What I have described as the dominant justification narrative of torture, and the discursive web of storytelling, which has contributed to the ongoing impunity of its perpetrators, provided the broader frame for this discussion. By examining Bigelow's film, *Zero Dark Thirty* (2012), I sought to show how this justification narrative was actualized in a medium beyond press conferences and government-issued documents, as well as the way in which the film presented a distinction between the value of the lives of detainees, and those of government-employees and US citizens. This crucial distinction would be reiterated again and again in different forms of storytelling, and also appears to be the guiding principle for the manner in which the DoD published the torture photographs in 2016. It is this distinction which justifies the violence inflicted upon detainees, while establishing that the lives of CIA agents and other actors involved in the global post-9/11 torture network are grievable and worth protecting at all cost.

In the second section, I shifted the focus to how the DoD prolonged and expanded the violence of torture via its documentation and distribution practices. The visibility of bodies, and the desire to understand what the 198 photographs in the PDF file actually depict, inevitably distracted the public from another crucial aspect of the file. In addition to encountering difficulties in identifying who is depicted in the photographs and what they experienced, viewers of the images were also kept in the dark about the identities of the perpetrators and what they had done. By exposing fragments of bodies which sometimes appear only to be marked by minor bruises or minimal traces of violence, the file ensures that the tortured people and their experiences continued to be ungraspable to the general public, prolonging the difficulty of mediating the experience of torture. The file made the perpetrators ungraspable as well: the manner in which these photographs were created and presented ensured that no specific person could be identified or held accountable for their actions. I also argued that the frame enforced by the DoD on viewers by means of the PDF file is one which fails to distinguish among the particularities of the photographed lives, and the abuse which these lives were forced to endure.

Regulating our perception of the photographs by stripping them of their initial contexts, while also rendering them and the subjects they depict incomprehensible to the viewer, the PDF file reifies the bodies of these detained men, and encourages the viewers to adopt an alienated perception of them. Nevertheless, as I demonstrated in the third and last section, this process is not necessarily irreversible. I proposed what could be called an "ethical approach" towards these photographs, demonstrating how we can reinscribe the narrative quality inherit in the affected lives by reframing these images with reference to their initial contexts, as well as to the stories told by those depicted in them. With my discussion of the letter written by al-Ani [fig. 18], whose burnt foot is visible in one of the PDF file's photographs [fig. 17], and by citing extensively from this letter, I argued that it is crucial for us to acknowledge the perspectives of those who were tortured when we take an ethical approach to these images. Yet we must also be more attentive to our own citation styles because there is a risk that we may introduce fragmentation by means of omissions in our citations, which has the potential to prolong the violence of the fragmented views of torture in these photographs. A way to resist the perception of the bodies in these photographs as reified entities is to restore the particular contexts and biographies of the people depicted in them, ensuring that the images can again be read as what they actually are: representations of grievable and tellable lives.

Perceiving torture photographs through the narrative frames of the lives they depict in fragments means that the indistinct photographs produced by a violent torture regime have the ability to make us listen to stories of tellable lives, and to oppose the dominant justification narrative of torture. Ultimately, uncovering and rediscovering the narratives in these images can disrupt or rupture – if only to a small extent – this violent justification narrative.

Is it true that the grass grows again after rain?
Is it true that the flowers will rise up in the Spring?
It is true that birds will migrate home again?
Is it true that the salmon swim back up their stream?

It is true. This is true. These are all miracles.
But is it true that one day we'll leave Guantánamo Bay?
Is it true that one day we'll go back to our homes?
I sail in my dreams, I am dreaming of home.

To be with my children, each one part of me;
To be with my wife and the ones that I love;
To be with my parents, my world's tenderest hearts.
I dream to be home, to be free from this cage.

But do you hear me, oh Judge, do you hear me at all?
We are innocent, here, we've committed no crime.
Set me free, set us free, if anywhere still
Justice and compassion remain in this world!

– Osama Abu Kabir, *Is it True?* (Falkoff 2007, 50;
© 2007 by University of Iowa Press)

Responding to Guantánamo Frames

The recently released set of photographs showing the arrival of the first detainees at Guantánamo's Camp X-Ray, and the manner of their publication by *The New York Times* in June 2022, described on the first pages of this book, circumvent the ways the US Department of Defense (DoD) has been "managing the visual narrative" (Lieberman, Rosenberg, and Taylor 2022) related to this camp over the past 20 years. These photographs complicate the "image of" Guantánamo that has been so carefully designed by the US government and open up a novel perspective on a future that is yet to come, a future which may be comprised of comparable image events revealing bit by bit what can be perceived from the camp, but which remains hidden for now. Showing the known, but yet unseen, through the publication of these photographs – for instance, by revealing the blindfolded, earmuffed, and cuffed detainees as they were struggling with military personnel, or how they were picked up by their armpits and carried – lets this publication event fall outside the visual and institutional frames implemented and enforced by the DoD and the Joint Task Force-Guantánamo (JTF-Guantánamo) over nearly two decades. The four chapters in this book explored precisely how frames were put into place by the US government, as well as how they have co-shaped the idea that there is a certain "*self-evidence*" (Berlant 2007, 669) to the public perception of Guantánamo and its media objects.

However, as my analyses of prominent and marginal photographs, videos, and documents related to this detention camp have revealed, this perception is, in fact, *neither settled nor self-evident*. In spite of the heavily regulated and restricted manner in which the public perceives the "inside" of the detention camp, my analyses of how the DoD and the JTF-Guantánamo have framed media objects pertaining to it – and of the subsequent reframing of the objects' effects and operations by journalists, lawyers, and artists – have shown that even the initial frames and the ideological effects of these objects are far from being stable. The DoD's insistence on the idea that Guantánamo is a transparent detention facility, ostensibly demonstrated by the JTF-Guantánamo's publication of thousands of photographs from the camp, as well as of videos of guided tours through Camps 4, 5, 6, and Camp X-Ray, and by officially permitting journalists to visit the camp and participate in guided tours *in situ*, has contributed to this apparent self-evidence. My analyses of these media objects have revealed that, despite the public being able to see a great number of images, the institutional discourses framing them have made "'not-seeing' in the midst of seeing" (Butler 2009, 100) into the tacit rule guiding our perception of Guantánamo. Thus, although there is much that we can see of the camp, the released material does not reflect the real living conditions of the detainees, nor does it help us to understand the violent regime put in place by the US government or the invisible operations of the frames the DoD has imposed following the attacks of 9/11. As I have shown, seeing Guantánamo, the detainees' living conditions, and their injured lives, often means seeing through fragments or confronting – and circumventing – intentional areas of opacity.

As members of the general public, we may assume that we know what Guantánamo is, and that we understand the violent regime that governs how the detention camp operates. However, in the four chapters of this book, I have demonstrated how this "knowing of Guantánamo" is a form of knowing which has been carefully designed by the US government during the past 20 years. My analyses of objects published or leaked in 2002, 2003/2004, 2008, and 2016 reveal how the DoD has continuously co-shaped our knowing about the camp into a knowing that works even to obscure the fact that we know much less than we believe we do. Instead of accepting our presumptive knowledge of what Guantánamo is and the apparent self-evidence of photographs, videos, and documents, I have exposed and reconsidered the frames through which the DoD has restricted the perception of Guantánamo and continues to restrict it today. I have also analyzed how the US government has shaped our knowledge about the detention facility and what is happening to the men detained there via the strategic publication and withholding of media objects. This has led me to argue that the semblance of self-evidence that surrounds the public understanding of Guantánamo is not only the result of the critical engagement undertaken by scholars and human rights organizations into what is happening in the camp. Importantly, this self-evidence also results from the way in which the DoD has designed the "image of" Guantánamo over the past years.

Thomas Keenan's observation that we can "make claims for [documents] and with them, inscribe them in struggles, work with them to make things happen" (Keenan and Steyerl 2014, 62), which I referenced in the introduction to this book, applies equally well to the photographs, videos, and documents I have analyzed throughout the preceding chapters. Rendering them readable or understandable not only means describing their contents; it also means showing how our perception of these objects is conditioned and regulated by technological, institutional, visual, and normative frames. Moreover, it means revealing the flaws and ruptures in the frames which the DoD and the JTF-Guantánamo have introduced around such media objects, and how legal, journalistic, and artistic discourses have been capable of making them speak "against [their] … ideological grain" (Kellner 1995, 5). The fact that I and other scholars or members of the general public respond differently to these objects reveals that the way they are perceived is historically and ideologically malleable, and that the way they affect us and our thinking about Guantánamo depends on the frames through which we choose to perceive them, or which we employ to reframe them. Thus, the media objects through which we perceive the camp and the detainees are not simply given, and never have been. If we want to engage with these objects and their relationship to state power in a critical and ethical manner, we must continuously counteract their operations in order to widen the ruptures occurring within their frames, to render visible the operations of power and their manifold failures to enforce the US government's perspective on what the Guantánamo detention camp is. It is up to us, the viewers, to co-constitute the meanings of such objects, and to consistently resist the logic of power framing their production, distribution, and perception. Consequently, it is not only the interpretation of the media objects related to Guantánamo which is unstable; there is also an ongoing potential to transform the way we perceive Guantánamo itself.

Analyzing the media objects from the camp has led me to see Guantánamo, and the men detained therein, in a new light. By highlighting the frames and operations of power related to these objects, and the difficulties related to "deciphering" (Hussain 2007, 738) them, I have demonstrated that responding to these objects is not something which should be relegated to the past; instead, it is very much a matter for the present and the future. For a long time, I have been concerned with how *my response to these objects can take on the form of a critical and ethical responsiveness* which not only consists of reframing everything anew, but which also includes a discussion of how this has already been done, and how the objects themselves propose a way to read them against the state-governed operations. In each of my chapters, I have undertaken precisely this task, illustrating how, by analyzing minor media objects and the various frames and their reframing that influence how we perceive them, we can render visible the violent operations conducted by the DoD and the JTF-Guantánamo to shape our perception and understanding of the camp. By discussing these operations in terms of *stabilizing the inter-pretation of photographs*, *rendering the faces of the detainees invisible*, *obscuring knowledge about photographic practices*, as well as *the concealing visibility of a PDF file*, I have suggested strategies for how we might engage critically with the abstract ideological effects of these objects, and how we can counteract those effects.

In the first chapter, I explored how the DoD tried to stabilize the public's perception of the photographs depicting the arrival of the first detainees at the Guantánamo detention camp taken by Shane T. McCoy, as well as the way these images were intended to express and ensure the denial of social and legal recognition to the detained men. However, as I illustrated in my discussion of the institutional history of the US military's Combat Camera, as well as my analysis of the discourses following the release of the photographs, the DoD failed on both these counts: it was neither able to control the way viewers and the press responded to the photographs, nor to prevent these readings from reframing the images and raising concerns about how the US government was denying recognition to the detainees.

In the second chapter, I illustrated how the decision to render the faces of detainees invisible was not only carried out in relation to McCoy's images – in which we see the first detainees being forced to wear blackened goggles, facial masks, and ear protectors, hiding their individual features and identities from the viewer – but also how the practice of invisibilizing faces came to govern what we see in other photographs and videos from the camp. Specifically, I discussed how photographs taken at the camp by journalists participating in guided tours, as well as videos shot by the JTF-Guantánamo, often rendered the bodies and/or faces of the detainees invisible. Nevertheless, by considering the videos of virtual visits to the detention camp and Debi Cornwall's artistic practice, I argued that this absence or disappearance is never absolute or definite. If we understand the photographs of the detainees' backs as "scene[s] of agonized vocalization" (Butler 2004, 133), and listen to the stories told by images of empty camps and cells, we may once again perceive the bodies and faces of the detainees, along with their stories of pain and injustice.

In the third chapter, I turned to another form of invisibility – to the US government's continuous refusal to publish photographs used on the "inside" of the military apparatus to document the detainees' bodies and faces. By engaging with the counter-archival practices employed by the American Civil Liberties Union (ACLU), I illustrated how independent organizations transform the DoD's "antiepistemology" (Galison 2004, 236) – their attempts to conceal or obscure knowledge – into an epistemology that the public can engage with. Hence, whereas in the second chapter I was interested in the ways the DoD's claim that Guantánamo is a transparent detention facility does not hold true, and how the Department actually employs a strategic form of opacity to render the situation at the camp incomprehensible to the public, in the third chapter I described the DoD's antiepistemic operation of obscuring knowledge about the mere existence and content of certain photographs, and how it partially failed at this operation.

Finally, in the last chapter, I turned my attention to a case in which the DoD was actually forced by an ACLU lawsuit to publish and distribute torture photographs. However, rendering photographs visible does not necessarily mean that they are comprehensible to their viewers. In fact, the way that the DoD published the 198 torture photographs, in a context-less PDF file containing scans from medical and military reports or criminal investigations, has been deliberately designed to make what is depicted in the photographs impossible for the public to grasp. I then argued that we can oppose the reifying qualities of these distribution practices, and the ways they provoke an alienated perception of the people visible in the PDF file, by reframing these images through stories told by those who were tortured, and who are shown in the photographs. In this way, instead of perceiving an indistinct body part, we can come to perceive the photographs as telling stories of injured, tortured, grievable, and tellable lives.

The responses of journalists, lawyers, detainees, and artists to the media objects discussed in this book, as well my own responses to the frames and subsequent reframing of these objects, show that what we know about Guantánamo and the men who were, or still are, detained there is by no means settled. In each of my chapters, I have explored how the reframing of these objects illustrates that the initial frames are inherently flawed or ruptured, and have not been fully successful in imposing their intended, officially sanctioned readings of these objects on viewers. Importantly, the ruptures in these frames have provided – and will continue to provide – entry points for a critical engagement with the ensemble of techniques, practices, norms, and ways of seeing, or indeed, not-seeing related to the Guantánamo detention camp. My analyses of these media objects have made it clear that the camp and the objects pertaining to it are freed of the logic of "old" and "new," and that the "case of" Guantánamo is far from being closed. The various institutional efforts undertaken by the DoD and the JTF-Guantánamo to frame these objects, and hence frame what we know about the camp, *are unintentional invitations to respond, and to oppose their effects not only today, but also in the future.*

This book is also an invitation to respond to what I have defined as the operations of *stabilizing interpretation*, *invisibilizing faces*, *obscuring knowledge*, and *concealing visibility*, and to appropriate them as conceptual tools to think with when analyzing other media objects from (and beyond) the Guantánamo detention camp. It is an invitation to reframe these operations, to think about them via the frames of other images, and frames produced by other state powers and detention facilities, as well as to reconsider what I had to leave out of this book. It is an invitation to think about how the frames which regulate what we can perceive from Guantánamo – and from other camps or detention facilities – are always "shadowed by... [their] own failure[s]" (Butler 2009, 7). It is an invitation to re-appraise the state-regulated visual, institutional, and normative frames in order to recognize them as unsettled entities, and to assess their inherent ruptures, inconsistencies, stutters, and failures.

Closing the frame of this book is the poem *Is it True?*, cited in the epigraph to this conclusion, in which Osama Abu Kabir appeals to the readers, asking: "But is it true that one day we'll leave Guantánamo Bay? Is it true that one day we'll go back to our homes?" (Osama Abu Kabir in Falkoff, 2007, 50). He indeed left Guantánamo in 2007 to witness once more the growing grass, the blooming flowers, the migration of birds, and swimming salmons – "all miracles" (Osama Abu Kabir in Falkoff, 2007, 50) of this world. 744 detainees were released from

Guantánamo to their countries of origin or to third countries (Almukhtar, et al. 2022). But, is it true that Guantánamo will be soon closed, as the Biden administration promises? As of today, 36 men remain in detention at Guantánamo, showing that the answer to this question is far from self-evident. The violence inflicted on both the detainees who remain and those who have been released or died adds to the continuing urgency of Kabir's questions and the ones I have posed throughout this book, as well as the necessity of the ongoing debate on the "case of" Guantánamo. The Guantánamo detention camp, the violence experienced by the detainees, and the US government's violation of international human rights are and continue to be a burning issue. This book and my arguments are thus also a call not to relegate our responsibility of responding to Guantánamo and its frames to the past, but to continue to reveal that many of the histories and stories of this detention camp, and the men detained in it, still lie before us.

.

Acronyms

ACLU	American Civil Liberties Union
ALSA	Air Land Sea Application
AP	Associated Press
ASD (PA)	Assistant to the Secretary of Defense (Public Affairs)
AV	Audio-Visual
FBI	Federal Bureau of Investigations
CCTV	Closed-Circuit Television
CIA	Central Intelligence Agency
CID	Criminal Investigation Command
COMCAM	Combat Camera
CSRT	Combatant Status Review Tribunal
DoD	US Department of Defense
FOIA	*Freedom of Information Act*
GTMO, GITMO	Guantánamo
GWoT	Global War on Terror
ISN	Internment Serial Number
JIIF	Joint Interagency Interrogation Facility
JTF-Guantánamo	Joint Task Force-Guantánamo
MP	Military Police
NMR	News-Media Representatives
NVG	Night-Vision Device
OFT	Office of Transformation
PA	Physician Assistant
PHR	Physicians for Human Rights
POW	Prisoner of War
PNSDA	*Protected National Security Documents Act*
RDI	Rendition, Detention, and Interrogation
SCIF	Sensitive Compartmented Information Facility
SOP	Standard Operating Procedure
VI	Visual Information
UDHR	*Universal Declaration of Human Rights*
UN	United Nations

References

Online and Print References

Aamer, Shaker. 2014. "The Declaration of No Human Rights." *VICE*, November 10. Accessed July 9, 2022. https://www.vice.com/en_uk/article/exm87w/the-us-declaration-of-no-human-rights-guantanamo-bay-812.

Abu Kabir, Osama. 2007. "Is it True?" In *Poems from Guantánamo: The Detainees Speak*, edited by Marc D. Falkoff, 49–50. Iowa City: University of Iowa Press.

Alloa, Emmanuel, and Dieter Thomä. 2008. "Transparency: Thinking Through an Opaque Concept." In *Transparency, Society and Subjectivity*, edited by Emmanuel Alloa and Dieter Thomä, 1–13. Cham: Palgrave Macmillan.

Alloa, Emmanuel. 2008. "Transparency: A Magic Concept of Modernity." In *Transparency, Society and Subjectivity*, edited by Emmanuel Alloa and Dieter Thomä, 21–55. Cham: Palgrave Macmillan.

Almukhtar, Sarah, Jeremy Ashkenas, Andrew Chavez, Asmaa Elkeurti, Andrew Fischer, Jacob Harris, Alan McLean, Carol Rosenberg, Matt Ruby, Charlie Savage, Andrei Scheinkman, Rachel Shorey, Archie Tse, Margot Williams, and Derek Willis. 2022. "The Guantánamo Docket." *The New York Times*, June 28. Accessed July 9, 2022. https://www.nytimes.com/interactive/2021/us/guantanamo-bay-detainees.html.

Althusser, Louis. 1971. "Ideology and Ideological State Apparatuses (Notes Towards an Investigation)." In *Lenin and Philosophy and Other Essays*, 127–86. Translated by Ben Brewster. New York: Monthly Review Press.

Aly, Götz, and Karl Heinz Roth. 2004. *The Nazi Census: Identification and Control in the Third Reich*. Translated by Edwin Black. Philadelphia: Temple University Press.

American Civil Liberties Union. 2022a. *The Torture Database*. Accessed July 9, 2022. https://www.thetorturedatabase.org/search/apachesolr_search.

———. 2022b (2015). *TorturePhotos.xlsx*. Microsoft Excel Open XML Spreadsheet. *ACLU*. Accessed July 9, 2022. https://www.aclu.org/files/TorturePhotos.xlsx.

———. 2005. "Medical Report: 24-Year-Old Iraqi Male, Abu Ghraib, Iraq re: Leg Injury (0222-04-CID259-80256)." June 20. *The Torture Database*. Accessed July 9, 2022. https://www.thetorturedatabase.org/document/medical-report-24-year-old-iraqi-male-abu-ghraib-iraq-re-leg-injury-0222-04-cid259-80256?search_url=search/apachesolr_search/0222-04-CID259-80256.

Arden, Roy, and Jeff Wall. 1999. "The Dignity of the Photograph." *art press* (251): 16–25.

Arendt, Hannah. 1988. *The Human Condition*. Chicago: University of Chicago Press.

Ash, Juliet. 2010. *Dress Behind Bars: Prison Clothing as Criminality*. London: I. B. Tauris.

Associated Press Images. 2016. "Pentagon Detainee Abuse Photographs." *AP Images*, February 5. Accessed July 9, 2022. http://www.apimages.com/metadata/Index/Pentagon-Detainee-Abuse-Photos/2afdd5e107914b00a6f09828f37fa0ea/3/0.

Associated Press. 2002. "US Fears Iran is Trying to Subvert Afghan Regime." *Chicago Tribune*, January 19.

———. 2000. *Stylebook and Briefing on Media Law*. New York: The Associated Press.

Baetens, Jan. 2007. "Conceptual Limitations of our Reflection on Photography: The Question of 'Interdisciplinarity'." In *Photography Theory*, edited by James Elkins, 53–73. New York: Routledge.

Baker, Peter. 2010. "Winning, Losing and War." *The New York Times*, August 28. Accessed July 9, 2022. https://www.nytimes.com/2010/08/29/weekinreview/29baker.html.

Banchik, Anna Veronica. 2018. "Too Dangerous to Disclose? FOIA, Courtroom 'Visual Theory,' and the Legal Battle Over Detainee Abuse Photographs." *Law & Social Inquiry* 43 (4): 1164–87.

Barthes, Roland. 1982. *Camera Lucida: Reflections on Photography*. Translated by Richard Howard. New York: Hill and Wang.

Baudrillard, Jean. 2003 (2002). *The Spirit of Terrorism*. Translated by Chris Turner. London: Verso.

Baudry, Jean-Louis. 1974–5. "Ideological Effects of the Basic Cinematographic Apparatus." Translated by Alan Williams. *Film Quarterly* 28 (2): 39–47.

BBC News. 2016. "US Military Abuse Scandal: Pentagon Releases 198 Prisoner Photos." *BBC News*, February 6. Accessed July 9, 2022. https://www.bbc.com/news/world-us-canada-35511425.

Bennett, Bruce. 2012. "X-Ray Visions: Photography, Propaganda and Guantánamo Bay." In *Controversial Images: Media Representations on the Edge*, edited by Feona Attwood, Vincent Campbell, I.Q. Hunter, and Sharon Lockyer, 67–82. New York: Palgrave Macmillan.

Berlant, Lauren. 2007. "On the Case." *Critical Inquiry* 33 (4): 663–72.

Blaschke, Estelle. 2016. *Banking on Images: From the Bettmann Archive to Corbis*. Leipzig: Spector Books.

Bloom, Paul. 2017. "The Root of all Cruelty? Perpetrators of Violence, We're Told, Dehumanize their Victims – The Truth is Worse." *The New Yorker*, November 20. Accessed July 9, 2022. https://www.newyorker.com/magazine/2017/11/27/the-root-of-all-cruelty.

Bock, Mary Angela. 2008. "Together in the Scrum: Practice News Photography for Television, Print, and Broadband." *Visual Communication Quarterly* 15 (3): 169–79.

Boehm, Gottfried. 1999. "Iconic Turn: Ein Brief." In *Bilderfragen: Die Bildwissenschaften im Aufbruch*, edited by Hans Belting, 27–36. Munich: Wilhelm Fink Verlag.

Boorstin, Daniel J. 1992. *The Image: A Guide to Pseudo-Events in America*. New York: Vintage Books.

Bruhn, Matthias. 2003. *Bildwirtschaft: Verwaltung und Verwertung von Sichtbarkeit*. Weimar: Verlag und Datenbank für Geisteswissenschaften.

Burkeman, Oliver, Richard Norton-Taylor, and Nicholas Watt. 2002. "Camp X-Ray Row Threatens First British Split with US." *The Guardian*, January 21.

Butler, Judith. 2009. *Frames of War: When Is Life Grievable?* London: Verso.

———. 2008. "Taking Another's View: Ambivalent Implications." In Axel Honneth, *Reification: A New Look at an Old Idea*, edited by Martin Jay, 97–119. Oxford: The Regents of the University of California.

———. 2004. *Precarious Life: The Powers of Mourning and Violence*. London: Verso.

Cagnolatti, Lance T. 2022. "Bio." *The Broadcast Report: Home of all Things Mr. Broadcast*. Accessed July 9, 2022. https://www.thebroadcastreport.com/bio.

Caldwell, John Thornton. 2008. *Production Culture: Industrial Reflexivity and Critical Practice in Film and Television*. Durham: Duke University Press.

Cambridge Dictionary. 2022a. "template." *Cambridge Dictionary*. Accessed July 9, 2022. https://dictionary.cambridge.org/de/worterbuch/englisch/template.

———. 2022b. "snapshot." *Cambridge Dictionary*. Accessed July 9, 2022. https://dictionary.cambridge.org/de/worterbuch/englisch/snapshot.

Campt, Tina M. 2017. *Listening to Images*. Durham: Duke University Press.

Carruthers, Susan L. 2013. "Review of *Zero Dark Thirty* by Megan Ellison, Colin Wilson, Ted Schipper, Greg Shapiro, Kathryn Bigelow and Mark Boal." *Cinéaste* 38 (2): 50–2.

Cavell, Stanley. 1976. *Must We Mean What We Say?* Cambridge, UK: Cambridge University Press.

Chalfen, Richard. 1987. *Snapshot Versions of Life*. Bowling Green, OH: Bowling Green State University Popular Press.

Clarke, Victoria "Torie." 2006. *Lipstick on a Pig: Winning in the No-Spin Era by Someone Who Knows the Game*. New York: Free Press.

Constitution Project's Task Force on the Detainee Treatment. 2013. *Report of the Constitution Project's Task Force on the Detainee Treatment. Open Society Foundations*. Accessed July 9, 2022. https://www.opensocietyfoundations.org/uploads/dfocff14-09b4-46e3-9f61-e38b89f3a4c9/constitution-project-report-on-detainee-treatment_0.pdf.

Cornwall, Debi. 2022a. "Gitmo on Sale." *Artist Homepage: Debi Cornwall*. Accessed July 9, 2022. https://www.debicornwall.com/Welcome-to-Camp-America/2--Gitmo-on-Sale/1/thumbs-caption.

———. 2022b. "Welcome to Camp America: Beyond Gitmo | غوانتانامو خليج وراء ما." *Artist Homepage: Debi Cornwall*. Accessed July 9, 2022. https://www.debicornwall.com/Welcome-to-Camp-America/3--Beyond-Gitmo/1/caption.

———. 2017a. "Acknowledgments." In Debi Cornwall, *Welcome to Camp America: Inside Guantá-namo Bay*. Santa Fe: Radius Books.

———. 2017b. "Djamel." In Debi Cornwall, *Welcome to Camp America: Inside Guantánamo Bay*. Santa Fe: Radius Books.

———. 2017c. "Hamza." In Debi Cornwall, *Welcome to Camp America: Inside Guantánamo Bay*. Santa Fe: Radius Books.

———. 2017d. "Murat." In Debi Cornwall, *Welcome to Camp America: Inside Guantánamo Bay*. Santa Fe: Radius Books.

———. 2017e. "Safe, Humane, Legal and Transparent." In Debi Cornwall, *Welcome to Camp America: Inside Guantánamo Bay*. Santa Fe: Radius Books.

———. 2017f. "Sami." In Debi Cornwall, *Welcome to Camp America: Inside Guantánamo Bay*. Santa Fe: Radius Books.

———. 2017g. *Welcome to Camp America: Inside Guantánamo Bay*. Santa Fe: Radius Books.

Cubitt, Sean. 2014. *The Practice of Light: A Genealogy of Visual Technologies from Prints to Pixels*. Cambridge, MA: The MIT Press.

Daase, Christopher. 2008. "Den Krieg gewonnen, den Frieden verloren: Revolution und Konterrevolution in Military Affairs." In *Die Transformation der Streitkräfte im 21. Jahrhundert: Militärische und politische Dimensionen der aktuellen 'Revolution in Military Affairs'*, edited by Jan Helming and Niklas Schörnig, 249–69. Frankfurt am Main: Campus Verlag.

Das, Veena. 1997. "Language and Body: Transactions in the Construction of Pain." In *Social Suffering*, edited by Veena Das, Arthur Kleinman, and Margaret Lock, 67–92. Berkeley: University of California Press.

Dauenhauer, Katrin. 2013. "Between Ethics and Aesthetics: Photographs of War during the Bush and Obama Administrations." *Amerikastudien / American Studies: Iconographies of the Calamitous in American Visual Culture* 58 (4): 625–46.

Davis, Morris D. 2008. "The Influence of Ex Parte Quirin and Court-Martial on Military Commisions." *Northwestern University Law Review Colloquy* 103: 121–31.

Därmann, Iris. 2017. "Zur Nummerntätowierung im Konzentrations- und Vernichtungslager Auschwitz-Birkenau." In *Unter die Haut: Tätowierungen als Logo- und Piktogramme*, edited by Iris Därmann and Thomas Macho in collaboration with Nina Franz, 231–53. Munich: Wilhelm Fink Verlag.

Debord, Guy. 2006 (1994). *The Society of the Spectacle*. Translated by Donald Nicholson-Smith. New York: Zone Books.

Decker, Oliver, and Lea Schumacher. 2014. "Körperökonomien: Zur Kommodifizierung des menschlichen Körpers." In *Körperökonomien: Der Körper im Zeitalter seiner Handbarkeit*, edited by Oliver Decker and Lea Schumacher, 7–23. Giessen: Psychosozial-Verlag.

Denbeaux, Mark, and Jonathan Hafetz, eds. 2009. *The Guantánamo Lawyers: Inside a Prison Outside of Law*. New York: New York University Press.

Denbeaux, Mark, Joshua Denbeaux, Matthew Darby, Adam Deutsch, Jennifer Ellick, R. David Gratz, and Michael Ricciardelli. 2011. "Captured on Tape: Interrogation and Videotaping of Detainees in Guantánamo." *Seton Hall Law Review* 41 (4): 1307–17.

Denbeaux, Mark. 2009. "A Fate Worse than Guantánamo." In *The Guantánamo Lawyers: Inside a Prison Outside of Law*, edited by Mark Denbeaux and Jonathan Hafetz, 320–9. New York: New York University Press.

Derrida, Jacques. 1995. "Archive Fever: A Freudian Impression." Translated by Eric Prenowitz. *Diacritics* 25 (2): 9–63.

Dewey, John. 1981a. "Affective Thought." In *The Later Works (1925–1953) – Vol. 2*, edited by Jo Ann Boydston, 104–10. Carbondale, IL: Southern Illinois University Press.

———. 1981b. "Qualitative Thought," in *The Later Works (1925–1953) – Vol. 5*, edited by Jo Ann Boydston, 243–62. Carbondale, IL: Southern Illinois University Press.

———. 1958. *Experience and Nature*. New York: Dover.

Dickens, Charles. 1942. *American Notes for General Circulation*. London: Chapman & Hall.

Didi-Huberman, Georges. 1999. *Ähnlichkeit und Berührung: Archäologie, Anachronismus und Modernität des Abdrucks*. Translated by Christoph Hollender. Cologne: DuMont Verlag.

Doane, Seth. 2013. "9/11 Families Upset Over 'Zero Dark Thirty' Recordings." *CBS News*, February 26. Accessed July 9, 2022. https://www.cbsnews.com/news/9-11-families-upset-over-zero-dark-thirty-recordings/.

Downie, Richard Duncan. 1998. *Learning from Conflict: The US Military in Vietnam, El Salvador, and the Drug War.* Westport: Praeger Publishers.

Elsaesser, Thomas. 2016. "Genre-Hybridisierung als (parapraktische) Interferenz: Zero Dark Thirty." In *Erzählungen und Gegenerzählungen: Terror und Krieg im Kino des 21. Jahrhunderts*, edited by Jochen Schuff and Martin Seel, 71-100. Frankfurt am Main: Campus Verlag.

Fallis, Don. 2015. "What is Disinformation?" *Library Trends* 63 (3): 401–26.

Finkelstein, Claire, and Michael Lewis. 2010. "Should Bush Administration Lawyers Be Prosecuted for Authorizing Torture?" *158 U. Pa. L. Rev. Pennumbra* 195: 195–224.

Forst, Rainer. 2013. "Zum Begriff eines Rechtfertigungsnarrativs." In *Rechtfertigungsnarrative: Zur Begründung normativer Ordnung durch Erzählung*, edited by Andreas Fahrmeir, 11–28. Frankfurt am Main: Campus Verlag.

Foucault, Michel. 2009. *Security, Territory, Population: Lectures at the Collège de France 1977–8.* Basingstoke: Palgrave Macmillan.

———. 1978. *The History of Sexuality – Vol. 1, An Introduction.* New York: Pantheon Books.

Frosh, Paul. 2003. *The Image Factory: Consumer Culture, Photography and the Visual Content Industry.* Oxford: Berg Publishers.

Galison, Peter, Victor S. Navasky, Naomi Oreskes, Anthony Romero, and Aryeh Neier. 2010. "What We Have Learned About Limiting Knowledge in a Democracy." *Social Research: An International Quarterly* 77 (3): 1013–49.

Galison, Peter. 2004. "Removing Knowledge." *Critical Inquiry* 31 (1): 229–43.

Gardiner, Beth. 2002. "Prisoner Photos Trouble British." *Boston Globe*, January 21.

Gates, Kelly A. 2011. *Our Biometric Future: Facial Recognition Technology and the Culture of Surveillance.* New York: New York University Press.

Gauthier, Jennifer L. 2018. "Making it 'Real' / 'Reel': Truth, Trauma, and American Exceptionalism in Zero Dark Thirty." In *True Event Adaptation: Scripting Real Lives*, edited by Davinia Thornley, 87–109. Cham: Palgrave Macmillan.

Geimer, Peter. 2007. "Image as Trace: Speculations About an Undead Paradigm." Translated by Kata Gellen. *Differences* 18 (1): 7–28.

Gervais, Thierry. 2017. *The Making of Visual News: A History of Photography in the Press.* London: Bloomsbury Academic.

Glissant, Édouard. 1997. *Poetics of Relation.* Translated by Betsy Wing. Ann Arbor: The University of Michigan Press.

Goffman, Erving. 1974. *Frame Analysis: An Essay on the Organization of Experience.* London: Harper and Row.

Golden, Tim. 2006. "US Toughens its Stance Against Hunger-Strikers." *The New York Times*, February 6. Accessed July 9, 2022. https://www.nytimes.com/2006/02/09/world/americas/09iht-gitmo.html.

Goldman, Jan, ed. 2014. *The War on Terror Encyclopedia: From the Rise of Al-Qaeda to 9/11 and Beyond.* Santa Barbara: ABC-CLIO.

Gordon, Avery F. 2008. *Ghostly Matters: Haunting and the Sociological Imagination.* Minneapolis: University of Minnesota Press.

Greenberg, Karen J., and Joshua L. Dratel, eds. 2005. *The Torture Papers: The Road to Abu Ghraib.* Cambridge, UK: Cambridge University Press.

Greenberg, Karen J. 2009. *The Least Worst Place: Guantánamo's First 100 Days.* New York: Oxford University Press.

Grieveson, Lee, and Haidee Wasson, eds. 2018. *Cinema's Military Industrial Complex.* Oakland: University of California Press.

Griffiths, Zachary. 2018. "In Defense of the Military Bureaucrat." *Modern War Institute at West Point*, April 4. Accessed July 9, 2022. https://mwi.usma.edu/defense-military-bureaucrat/.

Grigg, Richard. 2009. "A Human Face." In *The Guantánamo Lawyers: Inside a Prison Outside of Law*, edited by Mark Denbeaux and Jonathan Hafetz, 19–20. New York: New York University Press.

Grinberg, Daniel. 2019. "Some Restrictions Apply: The Exhibition Spaces of Guantánamo Bay." *JCMS: Journal of Cinema and Media Studies* 58 (4): 45–72.

Grossman, Vasily. 2017 (2006). *Life and Fate*. Translated by Robert Chandler. London: Vintage Classics.

Gürsel, Zeynep Devrim. 2016. *Image Brokers: Visualizing World News in the Age of Digital Circulation*. Oakland: University of California Press.

Hariman, Robert, and John Louis Lucaites. 2017. *No Caption Needed: Iconic Photographs, Public Culture, and Liberal Democracy*. Chicago: The University of Chicago Press.

Hatfield, Zack. 2018. "Debi Cornwall's Welcome to Camp America." *The Guardian*. February 25. Accessed July 9, 2022. https://www.theguardian.com/culture/2018/feb/25/observer-anthony-burgess-prize-runner-up-zack-hatfield-welcome-to-camp-america.

Hediger, Vinzenz. 2015. "Begehen und Verstehen: Wie der filmische Raum zum Ort wird." In *Wissensraum Film: Trierer Beiträge zu den Historischen Kulturwissenschaften*, edited by Irina Gradinari, Dorit Müller, and Johannes Pause, 61–86. Wiesbaden: Reichert Verlag.

———. 2016. "Der unfassbare Feind: Gilo Pontecorvos *Battaglia di Algeri* und die Doktrin der asymmetrischen Kriegsführung." In *Erzählungen und Gegenerzählungen: Terror und Krieg im Kino des 21. Jahrhunderts*, edited by Martin Seel and Jochen Schuff, 241–74. Frankfurt am Main: Campus Verlag.

Heidegger, Martin. 1993. *Sein und Zeit*. Tübingen: Niemeyer.

Hickman, Joseph. 2015. *Murder at Camp Delta: A Staff Sergeant's Pursuit of the Truth about Guantánamo Bay*. London: Simon and Schuster.

Hilbrand, Carola. 2015. *Saubere Folter: Auf den Spuren unsichtbarer Gewalt*. Bielefeld: Transcript Verlag.

Honneth, Axel. 2008. *Reification: A New Look at an Old Idea*. Edited by Martin Jay. Oxford: Oxford University Press.

———. 2001. "Invisibility: On the Epistemology of 'Recognition'." *Aristotelian Society Supplementary Volume* 75 (1): 111–26.

———. 1996. *The Struggle for Recognition: The Moral Grammar of Social Conflicts*. Translated by Joel Anderson. Cambridge, MA: The MIT Press.

Hrusovsky, Michael, and Konstantin Noeres. 2011. "Military Tourism." In *The Long Tail of Tourism: Holiday Niches and their Impact on Mainstream Tourism*, edited by Alexis Papathanassis, 87–94. Wiesbaden: Gabler Verlag.

Human Rights Watch. 2022. "IV. Impunity for the Architects of Illegal Policy." *Human Rights Watch*. Accessed July 9, 2022. https://www.hrw.org/reports/2005/us0405/6.htm#_ftn135.

Hussain, Nasser. 2007. "Beyond Norm and Exception: Guantánamo." *Critical Inquiry* 33 (4): 734–53.

Ito, Suzanne. 2008. "At Guantánamo, Iguanas Have Rights: Detainees, Not So Much." *ACLU*, May 28. Accessed July 9, 2022. https://www.aclu.org/blog/national-security/guantanamo-iguanas-have-rights-detainees-not-so-much.

Jaeggi, Rahel. 2014. *Alienation*. Translated by Frederick Neuhouser and Alan E. Smith. New York: Columbia University Press.

Jirsa, Tomáš. 2016. "Portrait of Absence: The Aisthetic Mediality of Empty Chairs." *Zeitschrift für Medien- und Kulturforschung: Medien der Natur* 7 (2): 12–28.

Kaplan, Amy. 2005. "Where is Guantánamo?" *American Quarterly* 57 (3): 831–58.

Keenan, Thomas, and Hito Steyerl. 2014. "What Is a Document?: An Exchange Between Thomas Keenan and Hito Steyerl." *Aperture* (214): 58–64.

Kellner, Douglas. 1995. *Media Culture: Cultural Studies, Identities and Politics Between the Modern and the Postmodern*. London: Routledge.

Khalili, Laleh. 2013. *Time in the Shadows: Confinement in Counterinsurgencies*. Stanford, CA: Stanford University Press.

Kittler, Friedrich. 1986. *Grammophon – Film – Typewriter*. Berlin: Brinkmann und Bose.

Köthe, Sebastian. 2021. "Guantánamo bezeugen: Aisthetiken von Widerstand und Folter." PhD diss., University of the Arts Berlin.

———. 2020. "Guantánamo bezeugen: Aisthetiken von Widerstand und Folter." PhD diss., University of the Arts Berlin. Unpublished manuscript, PDF file.

Krämer, Sybille. 2015. *Medium, Messenger, Transmission: An Approach to Media Philosophy*. Amsterdam: Amsterdam University Press.

Kristeva, Julia. 2001. *Hannah Arendt: Life Is a Narrative*. Toronto: University of Toronto Press.

Kurnaz, Murat. 2007. *Fünf Jahre meines Lebens: Ein Bericht aus Guantánamo*. Berlin: Rowohlt Verlag.

Le Feuvre, Lisa. 2010. "Introduction: Strive to Fail." In *Failure*, edited by Lisa Le Feuvre, 12-21. London: The MIT Press and Whitechapel Gallery.

Lennard, Natasha. 2014. "The True Barbarism of Guantánamo Force-Feeding." *VICE*, May 16. Accessed July 9, 2022. https://www.vice.com/en_us/article/a38yxk/the-true-barbarism-of-guantanamo-force-feeding.

Leopold, Jason, and Ky Henderson. 2015. "Tequila, Painted Pearls, and Prada – How the CIA Helped Produce 'Zero Dark Thirty'." *VICE*, September 9. Accessed July 9, 2022. https://www.vice.com/en_us/article/xw3ypa/tequila-painted-pearls-and-prada-how-the-cia-helped-produce-zero-dark-thirty.

Leopold, Jason. 2015. "Guantánamo Prisoners Get to Play Video Games in a Recliner – While Being Force-Fed." *VICE*, January 1. Accessed July 9, 2022. https://www.vice.com/en_us/article/8x7eax/guantanamo-prisoners-get-to-play-video-games-in-a-recliner-while-being-force-fed.

Leung, Rebecca. 2004. "Abuse at Abu Ghraib." *CBS News*, May 6. Accessed July 9, 2022. https://www.cbsnews.com/news/abuse-at-abu-ghraib/.

Levinas, Emmanuel. 1999. "Peace and Proximity." In *Alterity and Transcendence*, 131–44. Translated by Michael B. Smith. London: The Athlone Press.

Lieberman, Rebecca, Carol Rosenberg, and Marisa Schwartz Taylor. 2022. "The Secret Pentagon Photos of the First Prisoners at Guantánamo Bay." *The New York Times*, June 12. Accessed July 9, 2022. https://www.nytimes.com/interactive/2022/06/12/us/guantanamo-bay-pentagon-photos.html.

Lippit, Akira Mizuta. 2005. *Atomic Light (Shadow Optics)*. Minneapolis, MN: University of Minnesota Press.

Lowther, William, and Carol Rosenberg. 2002. "Horror of Camp X-Ray: First Pictures Show Use of Sensory Deprivation to Soften up Suspects for Interrogation." *Mail on Sunday*, January 20.

Lukács, Georg. 1972 (1971). *History and Class Consciousness: Studies in Marxist Dialectics*. Translated by Rodney Livingstone. Cambridge, MA: The MIT Press.

Maass, Peter. 2012. "Don't Trust 'Zero Dark Thirty'." *The Atlantic*, December 13. Accessed July 9, 2022. https://www.theatlantic.com/entertainment/archive/2012/12/dont-trust-zero-dark-thirty/266253/.

Mail on Sunday. 2002. "Tortured." *Mail on Sunday*, January 20.

Marcus, Josh. 2018. "Trump Finally Gave Himself Permission to Fill Up Gitmo with 'Bad Dudes'." *VICE*, January 31. Accessed July 9, 2022. https://www.vice.com/en_us/article/3k5xwn/trump-finally-gave-himself-permission-to-fill-up-gitmo-with-bad-dudes.

Marx, Karl. 1990 (1976). *Capital: A Critique of Political Economy – Vol. 1, The Process of Production of Capital*. Translated by Ben Fowkes. London: Penguin Classics.

McCoy, Alfred W. 2012. *Torture and Impunity: The US Doctrine of Coercive Interrogation*. Madison: University of Wisconsin Press.

McCoy, Shane T. 2022. "Shane T. McCoy." *LinkedIn*. Accessed July 9, 2022. https://www.linkedin.com/in/shanemccoy/.

Melamed, Laliv. 2018. "Simulated Scenarios: Flight Simulation and the Politics of the Phantasmatic." Paper presented at *Visible Evidence XX*, Indiana University Bloomington.

Menke, Christoph, and Arnd Pollmann. 2007. *Philosophie der Menschenrechte zur Einführung*. Hamburg: Junius Verlag.

Menke, Christoph. 2020. *Critique of Rights*. Translated by Christopher Turner. Cambridge, UK: Polity Press.

Merriam-Webster Dictionary. 2022. "snapshot." *Merriam-Webster*. Accessed July 9, 2022. https://www.merriam-webster.com/dictionary/snapshot.

Mitchell, William John Thomas. 1994. *Picture Theory: Essays on Verbal and Visual Representation*. Chicago: The University of Chicago Press.

Nagl, John A. 2002. *Counterinsurgency Lessons from Malaya and Vietnam: Learning to Eat Soup with a Knife*. Westport, CT: Praeger Publishers.

Oleson, James C. 2020. "Dark Tours: Prison Museums and Hotels." In *The Palgrave Handbook of Incarceration in Popular Culture*, edited by Marcus Harmes, Meredith Harmes, and Barbara Harmes, 541–54. Cham: Palgrave Macmillan.

Open Society Foundations. 2022. *The Report of The Constitution Project's Task Force on the Detainee Treatment. Open Society Foundations*. Accessed July 9, 2022. https://www.opensocietyfoundations.org/publications/report-constitution-project-s-task-force-detainee-treatment.

Paddock, Stanton M. 2017. "The Institutionalization of Photojournalism Education: Bringing the Blue-Apron Ghetto to American Schools of Journalism." PhD diss., University of Maryland.

Pape, Toni. 2017. "The Aesthetics of Stealth: Towards an Activist Philosophy of Becoming-Imperceptible in Contemporary Media." *Feminist Media Studies* 17 (4): 630–45.

Physicians for Human Rights. 2016. "US Government Releases Photos of Detainee Abuse at US Military Facilities Obama Administration Continues to Hide Most Torture Evidence." *Physicians for Human Rights*, February 5. Accessed July 9, 2022. http://physiciansforhuman-rights.org/press/press-releases/us-government-releases-photos-of-detainee-abuse-at-us-military-facilities.html.

Piché, Just, and Kevin Walby. 2010. "Problematizing Carceral Tours." *British Journal of Criminology* 50 (3): 570–81.

Pious, Richard M. 2011. "Prerogative Power in the Obama Administration: Continuity and Change in the War on Terror." *Presidential Studies Quarterly* 41 (2): 263–90.

Priest, Dana, and R. Jeffrey Smith. 2004. "Memo Offered Justification for Use of Torture." *The Washington Post*, June 8. Accessed July 9, 2022. https://www.washingtonpost.com/archive/politics/2004/06/08/memo-offered-justification-for-use-of-torture/17910584-e7c3-4c8c-b2d1-c986959ebc6a/.

Pugliese, Joseph. 2013. *State Violence and the Execution of Law: Biopolitical Caesurae of Torture, Black Sites, Drones*. Abington, Oxon: Routledge.

Quadflieg, Dirk. 2019. *Vom Geist der Sache: Zur Kritik der Verdinglichung*. Frankfurt am Main: Campus Verlag.

Rejali, Darius. 2007. *Torture and Democracy*. Princeton, NJ: Princeton University Press.

Relman, Eliza. 2016a. "Pentagon Releases 198 Abuse Photos in Long-Running Lawsuit: What They Don't Show Is a Bigger Story." *ACLU*, February 5. Accessed July 9, 2022. https://www.aclu.org/blog/national-security/torture/pentagon-releases-198-abuse-photos-long-running-lawsuit-what-they.

———. 2016b. "The Stories Behind the Government's Newly Released Army Abuse Photos." *ACLU*, February 11. Accessed July 9, 2022. https://www.aclu.org/blog/national-security/torture/stories-behind-governments-newly-released-army-abuse-photos/.

———. 2015. "A Picture of Torture Is Worth a Thousand Reports." *ACLU*, April 28. Accessed July 9, 2022. https://www.aclu.org/blog/national-security/torture/picture-torture-worth-thousand-reports.

Rochelle, Safiyah. 2020. "Capturing the Void(ed): Muslim Detainees, Practices of Violence, and the Politics of Seeing in Guantánamo Bay." PhD diss., Carleton University. Accessed July 9, 2022. https://curve.carleton.ca/bfc26f34-08cd-4fab-a4a4-cbd6ced74567.

Rosenberg, Carol. 2018. "Pentagon Plans to Raze Camp X-Ray, Guantánamo's Eyesore and Enduring Symbol of Torture." *Miami Herald*, March 6. Curve: Carleton University Research Virtual Environment. Accessed July 9, 2022. https://www.miamiherald.com/news/nation-world/world/americas/guantanamo/article203645719.html.

———. 2014. "Guantánamo Commander: 70 Percent of Captives no Longer Locked Down." *Miami Herald*, March 19. Accessed July 9, 2022. https://www.miamiherald.com/news/nation-world/world/americas/article1961684.html.

———. 2011. "Inside the Convicts Cellblock Where War Criminals Stay at Guantánamo." *Miami Herald*, February 27. Accessed July 9, 2022. https://www.miamiherald.com/news/nation-world/world/americas/guantanamo/article1937810.html#storylink=cpy.

———. 2008. "Sailor's Photos Became Icons of Guantánamo." *Center for the Study of Human Rights in the Americas*, January 13. Accessed July 9, 2022. http://humanrights.ucdavis.edu/projects/the-guantanamo-testimonials-project/testimonies/prisoner-testimonies/sailors-photos-became-icons-of-guantanamo.

Savage, Charlie. 2016. "Pentagon Releases Small Portion of Photos from Detainee Abuse Cases." *The New York Times*, February 5. Accessed July 9, 2022. https://www.nytimes.com/2016/02/06/us/politics/pentagon-photos-detainee-abuse.html.

Schneider, Rebecca. 2018. "That the Past May Yet Have Another Future: Gesture in the Times of Hands Up." *Theatre Journal* 70 (3): 285–306.

Schuff, Jochen, and Martin Seel. 2016a. "Einleitung: Erzählung, Rechtfertigung, Terror und Krieg im Kino." In *Erzählungen und Gegenerzählungen: Terror und Krieg im Kino des 21. Jahrhunderts*, edited by Jochen Schuff and Martin Seel, 17–47. Frankfurt am Main: Campus Verlag.

———. 2016b. "Vorwort." In *Erzählungen und Gegenerzählungen: Terror und Krieg im Kino des 21. Jahrhunderts*, edited by Jochen Schuff and Martin Seel, 7–16. Frankfurt am Main: Campus Verlag, 2016.

SCIF Global Technologies. 2022. "What is a SCIF?" *SCIF Global Technologies*. Accessed July 9, 2022. https://scifglobal.com/scif-definition-what-is-a-scif/.

Scott, Clive. 1999. *The Spoken Image: Photography and Language*. London: Reaktion Books.

Scott, James C. 1998. *Seeing Like a State: How Certain Schemes to Improve the Human Condition Have Failed*. New Haven, CT: Yale University Press.

Seel, Martin. 2013. "Narration und (De-)Legitimation: Der zweite Irak-Krieg im Kino." In *Rechtfertigungsnarrative: Zur Begründung normativer Ordnung durch Erzählung*, edited by Andreas Fahrmeir, 45–57. Frankfurt am Main: Campus Verlag.

Seeyle, Katharine Q. 2002. "Threats and Responses: The Detainees; Some Guantánamo Prisoners Will Be Freed, Rumsfeld Says." *The New York Times*, October 10. Accessed July 9, 2022. https://www.nytimes.com/2002/10/23/world/threats-responses-detainees-some-guantanamo-prisoners-will-be-freed-rumsfeld.html.

Sekula, Allan. 2014. "Photography and the Limits of National Identity." *Grey Room* 55 (55): 28–33.

———. 2003. "Reading An Archive: Photography Between Labour and Capitalism." In *The Photography Reader*, edited by Liz Wells, 443–52. New York: Routledge.

———. 1986. "The Body and the Archive." *October* 39: 3–64.

Smith, David. 2016. "A Tour of Guantánamo Bay: Ghostlike Figures Wait as a Promise Goes Unfulfilled." *The Guardian*, February 15. Accessed July 9, 2022. https://www.theguardian.com/us-news/2016/feb/15/guantanamo-bay-tour-detainees-obama-administration.

Sobin, Bernard. 2002. "Treatment of Detainees is Justified." *Los Angeles Times*, January 26.

Sontag, Susan. 2008. *On Photography*. London: Penguin Modern Classics.

———. 2004. *Regarding the Pain of Others*. New York: Picador.

Stein, Jeff. 2011. "Rumsfeld Complained of 'Low Level' GTMO Prisoners, Memo Reveals." *The Washington Post*, March 3. Accessed July 9, 2022. http://voices.washingtonpost.com/spy-talk/2011/03/rumsfeld_complained_of_low_lev.html.

Stein, Rebecca L. 2016. "#StolenHomes: Israeli Tourism and/as Military Occupation in Historical Perspective." *American Quarterly* 3 (68): 545–55.

———. 2008. "Souvenirs of Conquest: Israeli Occupations as Tourist Events." *International Journal of Middle East Studies* 40 (4): 647–69.

Steyn, Johan. 2004. "The Legal Black Hole." *The International and Comparative Law Quarterly* 53 (1): 1–15.

Szörényi, Anna. 2018. "Facing Vulnerability: Reading Refugee Child Photographs Through an Ethics of Proximity." In *Ethical Responsiveness and the Politics of Difference*, edited by Tanja Dreher and Anshuman A. Mondal, 151–68. Cham: Palgrave MacMillan.

The New York Times. 2009. "Impunity or Accountability?" *The New York Times*, December 14. Accessed July 9, 2022. https://www.nytimes.com/2009/12/15/opinion/15tue2.html.

Trial International. 2020. "Geoffrey D. Miller." *Trial International*, July 14. Accessed July 9, 2022. https://trialinternational.org/latest-post/geoffrey-d-miller/.

Turkle, Sherry. 2007. "Introduction." In *Evocative Objects: Things We Think With*, edited by Sherry Turkle, 3–10. Cambridge, MA: The MIT Press.

Urry, John, and Jonas Larsen. 2011. *The Tourist Gaze 3.0*. London: Sage Publications.

Urry, John. 2002. *The Tourist Gaze: Leisure and Travel in Contemporary Societies*. London: Sage Publications.

———. 1990. *The Tourist Gaze: Leisure and Travel in Contemporary Societies*. London: Sage Publications.

Van Raalte, Christa. 2007. "Intimacy, 'Truth' and the Gaze: The Double Opening of Zero Dark Thirty." *Movie: A Journal of Film Criticism* (7): 23–30.

Van Veeren, Elspeth S. 2016a. "Orange Prison Jumpsuit." (Pre-publication draft.) *ResearchGate*. Accessed July 9, 2022. https://www.researchgate.net/publication/301897961_Orange_Prison_Jumpsuit.

———. 2016b. "Orange Prison Jumpsuit." In *Making Things International 2: Catalysts and Reactions*, edited by Mark B. Salter, 122–36. Minneapolis, MN: Minnesota University Press.

———. 2011a. "Captured by the Camera's Eye: Guantánamo and the Shifting Frame of the Global War on Terror." *Review of International Studies* 37 (4): 1721–49.

———. 2011b. "Guantánamo Does not Exist: Simulation and the Production of 'the Real' Global war on Terror." *Journal of War and Culture Studies* 4 (2): 193–206.

Vismann, Cornelia. 2008. *Files: Law and Media Technology*. Translated by Geoffrey Winthrop-Young. Stanford, CA: Stanford University Press.

Von Schlieffen, Alfred. 2003. "War Today, 1909." In *Alfred von Schlieffen's Military Writings*, 198–9. Translated by Robert T. Foley. London: Frank Cass.

Walker, Lauren. 2016. "The Pentagon Released 200 Images of Detainee Abuse in Iraq and Afghanistan." *Newsweek*, May 2. Accessed July 9, 2022. https://www.newsweek.com/pentagon-defense-department-200-images-detainee-abuse-iraq-afghanistan-423625.

Weber, Max. 1978 (1968). *Economy and Society: An Outline of Interpretive Sociology*. Translated by Ephraim Fischoff, Hans Gerth, A. M. Henderson, Ferdinand Kolegar, C. Wright Mills, Talcott Parsons, Max Rheinstein, Guenther Roth, Edward Shils, and Claus Wittich. London: University of California Press.

WikiLeaks. 2011. "The Guantánamo Files." *WikiLeaks*. Accessed July 9, 2022. https://wikileaks.org/gitmo/name.html.

Wilson, James Q. 1992. *Bureaucracy: What Government Agencies Do and Why They Do It*. New York: Basic Books.

Wittgenstein, Ludwig. 1986 (1958). *Philosophical Investigations*. Translated by G. E. M. Anscombe. Oxford: Basil Blackwell Ltd.

Young, Liam Cole. 2017. *List Cultures: Knowledge and Poetics from Mesopotamia to Buzzfeed*. Amsterdam: Amsterdam University Press.

Government-Issued Documents and Legal References

18 United States Code §§2340 (added Pub. L. 103–236, title V, § 506(a), Apr. 30, 1994, 108 Stat. 463; amended Pub. L. 103–415, § 1(k), Oct. 25, 1994, 108 Stat. 4301; Pub. L. 103–429, § 2(2), Oct. 31, 1994, 108 Stat. 4377; Pub. L. 108–375, div. A, title X, § 1089, Oct. 28, 2004, 118 Stat. 2067). *Cornell Law School: Legal Information Institute*. Accessed July 9, 2022. https://www.law.cornell.edu/uscode/text/18/2340.

Air Force Public Affairs. 2022. "1st Combat Camera Squadron." *Air Force Public Affairs*. Accessed July 9, 2022. https://www.publicaffairs.af.mil/Units/1st-Combat-Camera-Squadron/.

Air Land Sea Application (ALSA) Center. 2003. *COMCAM: Multi-Service Tactics, Techniques, and Procedures for Joint Combat Camera Operations*, FM 3-55.12. March.

al-Ani, Khalid Samir. 2005. "Sworn Statement." October 21. In United States Army Criminal Investigation Command, "CID Report of Investigation – Final/SSI-0176-2004-CID259–80265/5C2B/5Y2E." November 11, 2005. 32–3. *The Torture Database*. Accessed July 9, 2022. https://www.thetorturedatabase.org/files/foia_subsite/pdfs/DOD054697.pdf.

———. 2004. "Letter to Headquarters Combined Joint Task, Force Seven, Baghdad, Iraq, APO AE 09303, Office of the Staff Judge Advocate." March 11. In United States Army Criminal Investigation Command, "CID Report of Investigation – Final/SSI-0176-2004-CID259–80265/5C2B/5Y2E." November 11, 2005. 11–5. *The Torture Database*. Accessed July 9, 2022. https://www.thetorturedatabase.org/files/foia_subsite/pdfs/DOD054697.pdf.

American Civil Liberties Union v. US Department of Defense. 2018. Docket No. 17-779. *Justia*. Accessed July 9, 2022. https://law.justia.com/cases/federal/appellate-courts/ca2/17-779/17-779-2018-08-21.html.

American Civil Liberties Union v. US Department of Defense. 2017. 04. Civ 4161 (AKH). *ACLU*. Accessed July 9, 2022. https://www.aclu.org/legal-document/aclu-v-dod-order-and-opinion-granting-summary-judgment-plaintiff.

American Civil Liberties Union. 2003. *Request Submitted Under the Freedom of Information Act*. October 7. *ACLU*. Accessed July 9, 2022. https://www.aclu.org/sites/default/files/torturefoia/legaldocuments/nnACLUFOIArequest.pdf.

Ashcroft, John. 2002. "On the Status of Taliban Detainees Under the Geneva Convention." Letter to President George W. Bush. February 1. *Astrid*. Accessed July 9, 2022. http://www.astrid-online.it/static/upload/protected/0201/020102.pdf.

Assistant Secretary of Defense (Manpower and Reserve Affairs). 1975. *Audio-Visual Management Task Force Report*.

Associated Press v. United States Department of Defense. 2006. 06 Civ. 1939 (JSR). *Casetext*. Accessed July 9, 2022. https://casetext.com/case/associated-press-v-us-dept-of-defense.

Bush, George W. 2007. *Interpretation of the Geneva Conventions Common Article 3 as Applied to a Program of Detention and Interrogation Operated by the Central Intelligence Agency*. Executive Order 13440. Federal Register 72, no. 141. July 20. *Govinfo*. Accessed July 9, 2022. https://www.govinfo.gov/content/pkg/FR-2007-07-24/pdf/07-3656.pdf.

———. 2002a. *Humane Treatment of Taliban and al Qaeda Detainees*. Official memorandum. February 7. *University of Minnesota: Human Rights Library*. Accessed July 9, 2022. http://hrlibrary.umn.edu/OathBetrayed/Bush%202-7-02.pdf.

———. 2002b. "Remarks by the President to the Travel Pool." March 20. *The White House: President George W. Bush*. Accessed July 9, 2022. https://georgewbush-whitehouse.archives.gov/news/releases/2002/03/20020320-17.html.

———. 2001a. "Address to Citadel Cadets at the Citadel, Charleston, SC." December 11. *American Rhetoric: Online Speech Bank*. Accessed July 9, 2022. https://www.americanrhetoric.com/speeches/gwbushcitadelcadets.htm.

Bybee, Jay S., and John Yoo. 2002. "RE: Standard of Conduct for Interrogations under 18 U.S.C. §§2340–2340A." Official memorandum. *The United States Department of Justice*. August 1. Accessed February 27, 2022. https://www.justice.gov/olc/file/886061/download.

Central Intelligence Agency. 2013. *CIA Memorandum on Rewriting Zero Dark Thirty Script*. Official memorandum. April 22. *Gawker*. Accessed July 9, 2022. https://s3.documentcloud.org/documents/696468/boal-cia-memo.pdf.

Cheney, Richard B. 2002. "Interview of the Vice President on Fox News Sunday." *The American Presidency Project*, January 27. Accessed July 9, 2022. http://www.presidency.ucsb.edu/ws/index.php?pid=85610.

Criminal Investigative Task Force. 2002. "Interview of Guantánamo Bay Detainee re: Detainee's Treatment While at Guantánamo Bay." November 8. *The Torture Database*. Accessed July 9, 2022. https://www.thetorturedatabase.org/files/foia_subsite/pdfs/DOD045043.pdf.

Crocker, Sean. 2013. "Defense Visual Information History." November 1. Unpublished manuscript, PDF file. Fort Meade: Defense Media Activity.

Declaration of Megan M. Weis (December 19, 2014), *American Civil Liberties Union v. Department of Defense*, (2017), 04. Civ 4161 (AKH). *ACLU*. Accessed July 9, 2022. https://www.aclu.org/sites/default/files/field_document/2014.12.19_dkt_530_declaration_of_megan_weis_and_recommendations_of_generals_allen_mattis_and_dempsey.pdf.

Defense Information School. 2022. "About." *Defense Information School*. Accessed July 9, 2022. https://www.dinfos.dma.mil/About.

Defense Visual Information Joint Combat Camera Program. 2015. *Joint Combat Camera (COMCAM) / Visual Information (VI): Smart Book (2015)*. *America's Navy*. Accessed September 1, 2020. https://imagery.navy.mil/training/Joint%20COMCAM%20Smartbook2015.pdf.

DuBois, Raymond F. 2003. *Mandatory Review of DoD Directives*. Official memorandum. December 16. *Donald Rumsfeld*. Accessed July 9, 2022. http://library.rumsfeld.com/doclib/sp/2834/2003-12-16%20from%20Ray%20DuBois%20re%20Mandatory%20Review%20of%20DoD%20Directives.pdf.

Ex Parte Quirin. 1942. 317 US 1. *Justia*. Accessed July 9, 2022. https://supreme.justia.com/cases/federal/us/317/1/.

Federal Bureau of Investigation. 2004a. *Response to Canvass Email Concerning Treatment of Detainees at Guantánamo Bay*. Official memorandum. December 7. *The Torture Database*. Accessed July 9, 2022. https://www.thetorturedatabase.org/files/foia_subsite/pdfs/DOJFBI003732.pdf.

———. 2004b. *FBI Memo re: Reports on Fingerprint Processing of Military Detainees in Afghanistan and Guantánamo*. Official memorandum. July 16. *The Torture Database*. Accessed July 9, 2022. https://www.thetorturedatabase.org/files/foia_subsite/pdfs/doddoacid006859.pdf.

Feinstein, Dianne, Carl Levin, and John McCain. 2012. "Letter to Michael Lynton." December 19. *United States Senator of California: Dianne Feinstein*. Accessed July 9, 2022. https://www.feinstein.senate.gov/public/_cache/files/a/b/abcf714a-38fa-4c49-8abe-e06eed51e364/28CCB6CC961DB37AF0D927C8F1BA6EF7.12-12-19-sony-letter.pdf.

Feinstein, Dianne. 2015. "Foreword." In US Senate, *The Official Senate Report on CIA Torture: Committee Study of the Central Intelligence Agency's Detention and Interrogation Program*, 1–6. New York: Skyhorse Publishing.

Force Transformation, Office of the Secretary of Defense. 2003a. *Military Transformation: A Strategic Approach*, Arthur K. Cebrowski. *Homeland Security Digital Library*. Accessed July 9, 2022. https://www.hsdl.org/?view&did=446223.

———. 2003b. *Network-Centric Warfare: Creating a Decisive Warfighting Advantage*, Arthur K. Cebrowski. *Homeland Security Digital Library*. Accessed July 9, 2022. https://www.hsdl.org/?view&did=446193.

Geneva Convention III. 1949. August 12. *International Committee of Red Cross*. Accessed July 9, 2022. https://www.icrc.org/en/doc/assets/files/publications/icrc-002-0173.pdf.

Goldwater-Nichols US Department of Defense Reorganization Act. 1986. October 1. Public Law 99-433. *Historical Office: Office of the Secretary of Defense*. Accessed July 9, 2022. https://history.defense.gov/Portals/70/Documents/dod_reforms/Goldwater-NicholsDoDReordAct1986.pdf.

Hamdi v. Rumsfeld. 2004. 542 US 507. *Justia*. Accessed July 9, 2022. https://supreme.justia.com/cases/federal/us/542/507/.

Haynes II, William J. 2002. *Counter-Resistance Techniques*. Official memorandum. November 27, approved by Donald Rumsfeld December 2, 2002. *The National Security Archive: Washington University*. Accessed July 9, 2022. https://nsarchive2.gwu.edu/NSAEBB/NSAEBB127/02.12.02.pdf.

Headquarters, Department of the Army. 2011. *Army Tactical Standard Operating Procedures*, ATP 3-90.90. November 2011. *US Army*. Accessed February 27, 2022. https://armypubs.army.mil/epubs/DR_pubs/DR_a/pdf/web/atp3_90x90.pdf.

Johnson, Lyndon B. 1966. "Statement by the President Upon Signing S. 116." July 4. *The National Security Archive: Washington University*. Accessed July 9, 2022. https://nsarchive2.gwu.edu/nsa/foia/FOIARelease66.pdf.

Joint Task Force-Guantánamo. 2004. *Camp Delta Standard Operating Procedures (SOP)*. March 1, 2004. *WikiLeaks*. Accessed July 9, 2022. https://file.wikileaks.org/file/gitmo-sop-2004.pdf.

———. 2003. *Camp Delta Standard Operating Procedures (SOP)*. March 28. *WikiLeaks*. Accessed July 9, 2022. https://file.wikileaks.org/file/gitmo-sop.pdf.

Margolis, David. 2010. *Memorandum of Decision Regarding the Objections to the Findings of Professional Misconduct in the Office of Professional Responsibility's Report of Investigation into the Office of Legal Counsel's Memoranda Concerning Issues Relating to the Central Intelligence Agency's Use of 'Enhanced Interrogation Techniques' on Suspected Terrorists*. Official memorandum. January 5. *The New York Times*. Accessed July 9, 2022. http://graphics8.nytimes.com/packages/pdf/politics/20100220JUSTICE/20100220JUSTICE-DAGMargolisMemo.pdf.

Memorandum of Understanding. 1988. *Visual Information Combat Camera Assistance to the Office of the Joint Chiefs of Staff*. April 14.

Miller, Geoffrey D. 2003. *Approval of Camp Delta's Standard Operating Procedure*. March 27. In Joint Task Force Guantánamo, *Camp Delta Standard Operating Procedures (SOP)*, 3. Official memorandum. March 28. *WikiLeaks*. Accessed July 9, 2022. https://file.wikileaks.org/file/gitmo-sop.pdf.

Obama, Barack. 2009. *Ensuring Lawful Interrogations*. Executive Order 13491. Federal Register 74, no. 16. January 22. *Govinfo*. Accessed July 9, 2022. https://www.govinfo.gov/content/pkg/CFR-2010-title3-vol1/pdf/CFR-2010-title3-vol1-eo13491.pdf.

Phifer, Jerald. 2002. *Request for Approval of Counter-Resistance Strategies*. Official memorandum. October 11. *Wikimedia Commons*. Accessed July 9, 2022. https://commons.wikimedia.org/wiki/File:Request_for_Approval_of_Counter-Resistance_Strategies_2002-10-11.pdf.

Rasul v. Bush. 2004. 542 US 466. *Justia*. Accessed July 9, 2022. https://supreme.justia.com/cases/federal/us/542/466/.

Reader, William A. 1990. *Minutes of Special Issues Visual Information Working Group (SIVIWG) Meeting, March 6, 1990*. Official memorandum. March 26.

The Defense Information School. 2020. "Public Affairs Qualification Course: The Role of Combat Camera."

The White House, Office of the Press Secretary. 2014. "Press Conference by the President." August 1. *The White House: President Barack Obama*. Accessed July 9, 2022. https://obama-whitehouse.archives.gov/the-press-office/2014/08/01/press-conference-president.

———. 2009. "Statement of President Barack Obama on Release of OLC Memos." April 16. *The White House: President Barack Obama*. Accessed July 9, 2022. https://obamawhitehouse.archives.gov/the-press-office/statement-president-barack-obama-release-olc-memos.

UK Parliament. 2002. "British Nationals Detained at Guantánamo Bay." Vol. 630 cc1361-7. January 21. *UK Parliament*. Accessed July 9, 2022. https://api.parliament.uk/historic-hansard/lords/2002/jan/21/british-nationals-detained-at-guantanamo.

United Nations General Assembly. 1987. *Convention Against Torture and Other Cruel, Inhuman or Degrading Treatment or Punishment*. June 26. *United Nations Human Rights: Office of the High Commissioner*. Accessed July 9, 2022. https://www.ohchr.org/en/professionalinterest/pages/cat.aspx.

———. 1948 (2015). *Universal Declaration of Human Rights (UDHR)*. December 10. *United Nations*. Accessed July 9, 2022. https://www.un.org/en/udhrbook/pdf/udhr_booklet_en_web.pdf.

United States Army Criminal Investigation Command. 2005a. "CID Report 190-04-CID259-80234." February 5. *The Torture Database*. Accessed July 9, 2022. https://www.thetorturedatabase.org/files/foia_subsite/pdfs/DOD054697.pdf.

———. 2005b. "CID Report of Investigation – Final/SSI-0176-2004-CID259–80265/5C2B/5Y2E." November 11. *The Torture Database*. Accessed July 9, 2022. https://www.thetorturedatabase.org/files/foia_subsite/pdfs/DOD054697.pdf.

———. 2004. "CID Report of Investigation – Final "C"/SSI-0094-04-CID259-80177/6F8A/6C1/5C1█/7G1A1/5Y2." June 10. *The Torture Database*. Accessed July 9, 2022. https://www.thetorturedatabase.org/files/foia_subsite/pdfs/DODDOACID000335.pdf.

US Congress. 2009. *Protected National Security Documents Act*. Public Law 111–83, Title V, Sec. 565. October 28.

———. 2006. *Military Commission Act*. 109th Cong. October 17.

US Department of Administration. 2004a. "DOD Hospital Patient Record re: Incident at Guantánamo Hospital." October 7. *The Torture Database*. Accessed July 9, 2022. https://www.thetorturedatabase.org/files/foia_subsite/pdfs/DOD056357.pdf.

———. 2004b. "Medical Report: 24-Year-Old Iraqi Male, Abu Ghraib, Iraq re: Leg Injury (0222-04-CID259-80256)." June 20. *The Torture Database*. Accessed July 9, 2022. https://www.thetorture-database.org/files/foia_subsite/pdfs/DOD003881.pdf.

———. 2003. "Army Criminal Charge Sheet." August 28. *The Torture Database*. Accessed July 9, 2022. https://www.thetorturedatabase.org/files/foia_subsite/pdfs/DOD003109.pdf.

US Department of Defense. 2021. *Media Policy at Guantánamo Bay, Cuba: Agree to Abide*.

———. 2016. *Pod86O-photos_previously_certified_under_the_protected_national_security_doc-uments_act_of_2009_redacted-opt.pdf*. *ACLU*. Accessed July 9, 2022. https://www.aclu.org/other/aclu-v-dod-198-photos-previously-certified-under-protected-national-security-doc-uments-act.

———. 2010. *Media Policy at Guantánamo Bay, Cuba: Agree to Abide*. September 10. *McClatchy DC*. Accessed July 9, 2022. http://media.mcclatchydc.com/static/pdf/guantanamo-rules.pdf.

———. 2006a. *Joint Combat Camera (COMCAM) Program*. Instruction 5040.04. June 6. *Homeland Security Digital Library*. Accessed July 9, 2022. https://www.hsdl.org/?view&did=785775.

———. 2006b. "List of Detainees Who Went Through Complete CSRT Process." April 20. *Washing-ton Headquarters Services*. Accessed July 9, 2022. https://www.esd.whs.mil/Portals/54/Doc-uments/FOID/Reading%20Room/Detainne_Related/detainee_CSRT_list.pdf.

———. 2006c. "List of Individuals Detained by the Department of Defense at Guantánamo Bay, Cuba from January 2002 Through May 15, 2006." May 15. *US Department of Defense*. Accessed September 1, 2020. https://archive.defense.gov/news/May2006/d20060515%20List.pdf.

———. 2005a. *Army Regulation 15–6: Final Report: Investigation into FBI Allegations of Detainee Abuse at Guantánamo Bay, Cuba Detention Facility*. April 1. *The Torture Database*. Accessed July 9, 2022. https://www.thetorturedatabase.org/files/foia_subsite/pdfs/schmidt_furlow_report.pdf.

———. 2005b. *Visual Information*. Directive 5040.2. August 30. *United States Army Intelligence and Security Command*. Accessed July 9, 2022. https://www.inscom.army.mil/Contracting/VIMES/504002p[1].pdf.

———. 2004. "Statements of Guantánamo Hospital Personnel and Military Police re:, Oct 7, 2004 Incident at Guantánamo Hospital." October 7. *The Torture Database*. Accessed July 9, 2022. https://www.thetorturedatabase.org/files/foia_subsite/pdfs/DOD056340.pdf.

———. 2003. *Transformation Planning Guidance*, Donald Rumsfeld. *IWS*. Accessed September 1, 2020. http://www.iwar.org.uk/rma/resources/dod-transformation/2003-transformation-planning-guidance.pdf.

———. 2002a. *Joint Combat Camera (COMCAM) Program*. Directive 5040.4. August 13. *The Climate Change and Public Health Law Site: Professor Edward P. Richards J. D., M. P. H.* Accessed July 9, 2022. https://biotech.law.lsu.edu/blaw/dodd/corres/pdf/d50404_081302/d50404p.pdf.

———. 2002b. "DoD News Briefing," Donald Rumsfeld and Peter Pace. January 22. *Scoop*. Accessed July 9, 2022. https://www.scoop.co.nz/stories/WO0201/S00055/news-briefing-sec-retary-rumsfeld-and-gen-pace.htm.

———. 2002c. "DoD News Briefing," Donald Rumsfeld and Richard B. Meyers. February 12. *US Department of Defense*. Accessed July 9, 2022. https://archive.ph/20180320091111/http://archive.defense.gov/Transcripts/Transcript.aspx?TranscriptID=2636.

———. 1999. *Handbook for Writing Security Classification Guidance*. DoD 5200.1-H. November. *Defense Technical Information Center*. Accessed July 9, 2022. https://apps.dtic.mil/dtic/tr/fullt-ext/u2/a440897.pdf.

———. 1996. *Joint Combat Camera (COMCAM) Program*. Directive 5040.4. September 30. *Defense Technical Information Center*. Accessed July 9, 2022. https://apps.dtic.mil/dtic/tr/fulltext/u2/a320465.pdf.

———. 1990. *Joint Combat Camera (COMCAM) Operations*. Instruction 5040.4. March 5.

———. 1987. *Visual Information*. Directive 5040.2. December 7. *The Climate Change and Public Health Law Site: Professor Edward P. Richards J. D., M. P. H.* Accessed July 9, 2022. https://biotech.law.lsu.edu/blaw/dodd/corres/pdf2/d50402p.pdf.

———. 1985a. *DoD Joint Visual Information Services*. Directive 5040.3. December 12. *Internet Archive.* Accessed July 9, 2022. https://archive.org/details/DTIC_ADA272009.

———. 1985b. *Visual Information*. Directive 5040.2. October 11.

———. 1979a. *Defense Audiovisual Agency*. Directive 5040.1. June 12. *National Archives Catalog.* Accessed July 9, 2022. https://catalog.archives.gov/id/10447008.

———. 1979b. *Management and Operation of DoD Audiovisual Activities*. Instruction 5040.2-R. November 1.

US Department of Justice, Office of Legal Counsel. 2002. *Re: Application of Treaties and Laws to al Qaeda and Taliban*. Official memorandum. January 22. *Homeland Security Digital Library.* Accessed July 9, 2022. https://www.hsdl.org/?view&did=741728.

US Department of the Army, Office of the Surgeon General. 2005. *Final Report Assessment of Detainee Medical Operations for OEF, Guantánamo, and OIF*. 13 April. *University of Minnesota: Human Rights Library.* Accessed July 9, 2022. http://www1.umn.edu/humanrts/OathBetrayed/Army%20Surgeon%20General%20Report.pdf.

US Department of the Army. 2004. "CID Report: 0260-2004-CID023-67287." July 16. *The Torture Database.* Accessed July 9, 2022. https://www.thetorturedatabase.org/files/foia_subsite/pdfs/doddoacid006859.pdf.

———. 2002. *Visual Information Operations*, FM 6-02.40. January 24.

———. 2001. *Field Manual No. 3-0: Operations*, FM 3-0. June 14. *The Torture Database.* Accessed July 9, 2022. https://www.thetorturedatabase.org/files/foia_subsite/pdfs/DODDOA007871.pdf.

US Joint Chief of Staff. 2020. *DOD Dictionary of Military and Associated Terms. Homeland Security Digital Library.* Accessed July 9, 2022. https://www.hsdl.org/?view&did=813130.

US National Security Agency. 2022. *Redaction of PDF Files Using Adobe Acrobat Professional X. Columbia University: Computer Science.* Accessed July 9, 2022. https://www.cs.columbia.edu/~smb/doc/Redaction-of-PDF-Files-Using-Adobe-Acrobat-Professional-X.pdf.

US Senate. 2015. *The Official Senate Report on CIA Torture: Committee Study of the Central Intelligence Agency's Detention and Interrogation Program*. New York: Skyhorse Publishing.

Weinberger, Caspar. 1985. *Disestablishment of the Defense Audiovisual Agency (DAVA)*. Official memorandum. April 19.

(Audio)Visual Material

al-Ani, Khalid Samir. 2004. *Scan of the First Page of Ibrahim Khalid Samir al-Ani's Letter*. PDF converted into JPEG. "Letter to Headquarters Combined Joint Task, Force Seven, Baghdad, Iraq, APO AE 09303, Office of the Staff Judge Advocate." March 11. In United States Army Criminal Investigation Command, "CID Report of Investigation – Final/SSI-0176-2004-CID259–80265/5C2B/5Y2E." November 11, 2005. 1. *The Torture Database.* Accessed July 9, 2022. https://www.thetorturedatabase.org/files/foia_subsite/pdfs/DOD054697.pdf. The appearance of US Department of Defense (DoD) visual information does not imply or constitute DoD endorsement. © American Civil Liberties Union, Inc. 2006.

American Civil Liberties Union. 2022b (2015). *TorturePhotos.xlsx*. Screenshot. *ACLU.* Accessed July 9, 2022. https://www.aclu.org/files/TorturePhotos.xlsx. © American Civil Liberties Union, Inc. 2006.

Bigelow, Kathryn. 2012. *Zero Dark Thirty*. US. 157 min.

Burns, Scott Z. 2019. *The Report*. US. 119 min.

Cornwall, Debi. 2017. *Welcome to Camp America: Inside Guantánamo Bay – Book Cover*. Digital Image. © Debi Cornwall.

———. 2015. *Feeding Chair, Camp 5*. Digital Photograph (originally a pigment print from scanned medium-format negative hand). © Debi Cornwall.

———. 2015. *Loose Sheet with the Portrait of Murat Kurnaz – Back Side*. PDF converted into JPEG. © Debi Cornwall and Radius Books.

———. 2015. *Portrait of Murat Kurnaz*. Digital Photograph. © Debi Cornwall.

———. 2014. *Compliant Detainee Media Room, Camp 5*. Digital Photograph. © Debi Cornwall.

Defense Visual Information Joint Combat Camera Program. 2015. *VI Planning/Operations Snap-shot Template*. PDF converted into JPEG. In *Joint Combat Camera (COMCAM) / Visual Information (VI): Smart Book (2015)*. 13. *America's Navy*. Accessed September 1, 2020. https://imagery.navy. mil/training/Joint%20COMCAM%20Smartbook2015.pdf. The appearance of US Department of Defense (DoD) visual information does not imply or constitute DoD endorsement.

———. 2015. *Imagery Flow/Release Authority*. PDF converted into JPEG. In *Joint Combat Camera (COMCAM) / Visual Information (VI): Smart Book (2015)*. 54. *America's Navy*. Accessed September 1, 2020. https://imagery.navy.mil/training/Joint%20COMCAM%20Smartbook2015.pdf. The appearance of US Department of Defense (DoD) visual information does not imply or con-stitute DoD endorsement.

Getty Images, and Tim Chapman. 2002. *Joint Task Force Spokesman, US Marine Major Steve*. Digital Photograph. January 11. *Getty Images*. Accessed July 9, 2022. https://www.gettyimages.com/detail/news-photo/ joint-task-force-spokesman-us-marine-major-steve-cox-holds-news-photo/1211939043.

Joint Task Force-Guantánamo. 2003. *Map of Camp Delta*. PDF converted into JPEG. *Camp Delta Standard Operating Procedures (SOP)*. March 28. 225. *WikiLeaks*. Accessed July 9, 2022. https:// file.wikileaks.org/file/gitmo-sop.pdf. The appearance of US Department of Defense (DoD) visual information does not imply or constitute DoD endorsement.

———. 2003. *Detainee Behavioral Tracking*. PDF converted into JPEG. *Camp Delta Standard Operating Procedures (SOP)*. March 28. 174. *WikiLeaks*. Accessed July 9, 2022. https://file. wikileaks.org/file/gitmo-sop.pdf. The appearance of US Department of Defense (DoD) visual information does not imply or constitute DoD endorsement.

MAHARBAL5022. 2015. *US Army Combat Camera (Documentary)*. Video. August 10. 21 min., 51 sec. *YouTube*. Accessed July 9, 2022. https://www.youtube.com/watch?v=TEE3GCWtpMc. The appearance of US Department of Defense (DoD) visual information does not imply or con-stitute DoD endorsement.

McCain, John. 2014. *Senate Floor Statement by Senator John McCain*. Video. December 9. 32 min., 34 sec. *C-Span*. Accessed July 9, 2022. https://www.c-span.org/video/?323106-7/ senators-mccain-rockefeller-cia-interrogations.

McCoy, Shane T., and US Department of Defense. 2002. *The Arrival of the First Detainees at Camp X-Ray – View from Above the Barbwire*. Digital Photograph. January 11. The appearance of US Department of Defense (DoD) visual information does not imply or constitute DoD endorsement.

———. 2002. *The Arrival of the First Detainees at Camp X-Ray – View Through the Grid*. Digital Pho-tograph. January 11. The appearance of US Department of Defense (DoD) visual information does not imply or constitute DoD endorsement.

Reuters. 2013. *Activists Wearing Orange Jumpsuits Mark the 100th Day of Prisoners' Hunger Strike at Guantánamo Bay During a Protest in Front of the White House in Washington*. Digital Photograph. May 17. *Alamy*. Accessed July 9, 2022. https://www.alamy.com/activists-wearing-orange-jumpsuits-mark-the-100th-day-of-prisoners-hunger-strike-at-guantanamo-bay-during-a-pro-test-in-front-of-the-white-house-in-washington-may-17-2013-reutersjoshua-roberts-united-states-tags-politics-civil-unrest-image399318190.html.

Schaller, Stefan. 2013. *5 Jahre Leben*. DE/FR. 95 min.

Soldier Media Center Videos. 2010. *What is Combat Camera?* Video. April 13. 3 min., 46 sec. *YouTube*. Accessed July 9, 2022. https://www.youtube.com/watch?v=7zszEEWtmfo. The appearance of US Department of Defense (DoD) visual information does not imply or con-stitute DoD endorsement.

The Broadcast Report. 2008a. *Guantánamo Bay Detention Facility – Virtual Visit Camp 4*. Video. June 6. 3 min., 26 sec. *YouTube*. Accessed July 9, 2022. https://www.youtube.com/watch?v=-RmbBS8qkKB0. The appearance of US Department of Defense (DoD) visual information does not imply or constitute DoD endorsement.

———. 2008b. *Guantánamo Bay Detention Facility – Virtual Visit Camp 5*. Video. June 6. 3 min., 48 sec. *YouTube*. Accessed July 9, 2022. https://www.youtube.com/watch?v=p2Nd-5U3eD0. The

appearance of US Department of Defense (DoD) visual information does not imply or constitute DoD endorsement.

———. 2008c. *Guantánamo Bay Detention Facility – Virtual Visit Camp 6*. Video. June 6. 2 min., 9
sec. *YouTube*. Accessed July 9, 2022. https://www.youtube.com/watch?v=zp76AlOgHPg. The
appearance of US Department of Defense (DoD) visual information does not imply or constitute DoD endorsement.

———. 2008d. *Guantánamo Bay Detention Facility – Virtual Visit Camp X-Ray*. Video. June 6. 3 min.,
25 sec. *YouTube*. Accessed July 9, 2022. https://www.youtube.com/watch?v=Hf229F_vKoc. The
appearance of US Department of Defense (DoD) visual information does not imply or constitute DoD endorsement.

US Department of Administration. 2004a. *Page Two of the "DOD Hospital Patient Record re:
Incident at Guantánamo Hospital" Document*. PDF converted into JPEG. October 7. *The Torture
Database*. Accessed July 9, 2022. https://www.thetorturedatabase.org/files/foia_subsite/
pdfs/DOD056357.pdf. The appearance of US Department of Defense (DoD) visual infor-
mation does not imply or constitute DoD endorsement. © American Civil Liberties Union,
Inc. 2006.

US Department of Defense. 2016. *Scan of a Photograph Showing Ibrahim Khalid Samir al-Ani's
Burnt Foot*. PDF converted into JPEG. *Pod860-photos_previously_certified_under_the_protected_
national_security_documents_act_of_2009_redacted-opt.pdf*. 71. *ACLU*. Accessed July 9, 2022.
https://www.aclu.org/other/aclu-v-dod-198-photos-previously-certified-under-protected-
national-security-documents-act.

———. 2010. *Page 4 of the Media Policy at Guantánamo Bay, Cuba: Agree to Abide*. PDF converted
into JPEG. September 10. 4. *McClatchy DC*. Accessed July 9, 2022. http://media.mcclatchydc.
com/static/pdf/guantanamo-rules.pdf. he appearance of US Department of Defense (DoD)
visual information does not imply or constitute DoD endorsement.

Wolff, Richard. 2009a. *Media Tour of Guantánamo Bay's Camp X-Ray*. Video. February 2. 7 min.,
15 sec. *Dvids: Defense Visual Information Distribution Service*. Accessed July 9, 2022. https://
www.dvidshub.net/video/71160/media-tour-guantanamo-bays-camp-x-ray. The appearance
of US Department of Defense (DoD) visual information does not imply or constitute DoD
endorsement.

———. 2009b. *Media Tour of Joint Task Force Guantánamo*. Video. February 9. 10 min., 24 sec.
Dvids: Defense Visual Information Distribution Service. Accessed July 9, 2022. https://www.
dvidshub.net/video/70450/media-tour-joint-task-force-guantanamo. The appearance of
US Department of Defense (DoD) visual information does not imply or constitute DoD
endorsement.

Acknowledgments

I want to express my sincere gratitude to all the people who have contributed to the completion of this book and the dissertation on which it is based, and who have supported me during the past years. First and foremost, I am greatly indebted to Vinzenz Hediger and Juliane Rebentisch for their supervision, mentorship, and critical input on the dissertation. Their questions about my theoretical framework and observations about the media objects discussed throughout this book helped me to establish why I wanted to write about the Guantánamo detention camp, how I wrote about it, and why it is still vital to think about the camp 20 years after the arrival of the first detainees. I would also like to express my sincere gratitude to Martin Seel, who supported the writing process with his extensive feedback and close readings of the chapters.

I am deeply grateful to my fellow PhD students and Postdocs in the Graduate Research Training Program "Configurations of Film" at the Goethe University Frankfurt – Marie Sophie Beckmann, Nicole Braida, Karin Fleck, Philipp Dominik Keidl, Andrea Polywka, Antoine Prévost-Balga, Rebecca Puchta, Marin Reljic, Philipp Roeding, Guilherme da Silva Machado, Laliv Melamed, Kalani Michell, and Alexander Stark – for reading my drafts and sharing their crucial input in the dissertation seminars. I also want to thank the Principal Investigators – Sonia Campanini, Malte Hagener, Bernd Herzogenrath, Rembert Hüser, Angela Keppler, Marion Saxer, Alexandra Schneider, Nikolaus Müller-Schöll, Marc Siegel, Florian Sprenger, Wanda Strauven, and Yvonne Zimmermann – for supporting our cohort with their helpful advice, as well as the Mercator Fellows for our reading sessions. This book also benefited greatly from critical discussions with the diploma and doctoral students participating in Juliane Rebentisch's philosophy colloquium at the University of Art and Design in Offenbach, and I would like to extend my thanks to them. I am also very grateful to my colleagues at the Institute for Film, Theater, Media and Cultural Studies at Johannes Gutenberg University Mainz for their comments on the late drafts of my chapters in the colloquia led by Alexandra Schneider, Marc Siegel, and Gabriele Schabacher.

Although the active part of writing the dissertation began in 2017, I began to conceptualize it in 2016 when I drafted the first proposal for job applications and I would like to thank Markus Klammer for his intellectual support during this period, and for his friendship ever since. I am also grateful to Ute Holl and the media studies colloquium at the University of Basel for providing me with the first opportunity to discuss my ideas and test them in an intellectually stimulating environment. In addition, I would like to thank Fabienne Liptay for giving me my first glimpses into academic life as her student assistant and for encouraging me to think critically about images of war.

My special thanks go to Sebastian Köthe, for his invaluable comments, questions, and criticism with regard to the manuscript. What started as a discussion about our shared fear of writing the same dissertation developed into a sincere intellectual friendship for which I am deeply grateful.

And finally, I am most obliged to my family for their continuous, loving support.